Assembled in Japan

Assembled in Japan

ELECTRICAL GOODS AND THE
MAKING OF THE JAPANESE CONSUMER

Simon Partner

UNIVERSITY OF CALIFORNIA PRESS

Berkeley / Los Angeles / London

Studies of the East Asian Institute,
Columbia University

The East Asian Institute is Columbia University's
center for research, publication, and teaching on
the modern Asia Pacific region. The Studies of
the East Asian Institute were inaugurated in 1962
to bring to a wider public the results of significant
new research on modern and contemporary
Asia Pacific affairs.

A Study of the East Asian Institute

University of California Press
Berkeley and Los Angeles, California

University of California Press, Ltd.
London, England

© 1999 by the
Regents of the University of California

Library of Congress Cataloging-in-Publication Data

Partner, Simon.
    Assembled in Japan : electrical goods and the
making of the Japanese consumer / Simon Partner.

        p.   cm.
    Includes bibliographical references and index.
    ISBN 0-520-21792-6 (alk. paper).—
    ISBN 0-520-21939-2 (pbk. : alk paper)
        1. Electronic industries—Japan.
2. Consumers—Japan.   I. Title.
HD9696.A3 J39317   1999
338.49762138190952—dc21   98-37375
                                CIP

Manufactured in the United States of America

08   07   06   05   04   03   02   01   00   99
10 9 8 7 6 5 4 3 2 1

The paper used in this publication meets the
minimum requirements of ANSI/NISO Z 39.48-
1992 (R 1997) (*Permanence of Paper*). ∞

To Big Peter

Contents

Illustrations

Tables

Acknowledgments

I would like to express my sincere gratitude to the many people and institutions who have assisted me with this book. The book started its life as a doctoral dissertation, and first and foremost I thank my advisors at Columbia University: Henry Smith, Carol Gluck, and Hugh Patrick. It would be impossible to find a more helpful and involved group of teachers. Also at (or attached to) Columbia, I would like to thank Barbara Brooks, David Weiman, Scott O'Bryan, Suzanne O'Brian, and Franziska Seraphim. I am also immensely beholden to Andrew Gordon, who read the entire book twice and provided invaluable comments and advice. My colleagues at Duke University also provided helpful feedback, in some cases based on painstaking reading of manuscript drafts. I thank particularly Kären Wigen, Alex Roland, Kris Troost, and Anne Allison.

In Tokyo, I found the ideal home from home in the Institute of Social Science, University of Tokyo. My one-year stay at ISS eventually turned into three. I thank in particular Professor Kudō Akira, who was extraordinarily helpful and hospitable at every stage of my research. I am happy to be one of the long list of foreign scholars who have received outstanding support from Professor Kudō. I would also like to acknowledge Professors Hashimoto Jurō and Banno Junji, both of whom were extremely helpful at various points in my stay. Also part of the ISS "family" were Sebastian Conrad, Stephen Johnson, Eric Jolivet, and Harald Fuess, from all of whom I received invaluable input. I am particularly grateful to Harald Fuess for allowing me to present a part of the thesis at the first Deutsches Institut für Japanstudien (German Institute for Japanese Studies) workshop in Tokyo.

My thanks also to Mr. Nishi Mitsuo for invaluable help in arranging introductions to well-known figures in the electrical goods industry; and to Egawa Toshio, Hanada Mitsue, Morimoto Keiko, Masushima Shō, Sakagami Hiroshi, Kataoka Katsutarō, and Kanoi Nobuo for sharing their reminiscences. Also to Mr. Yoshitani and his colleagues at the Matsushita archives for their hospitality.

At the University of California Press, Laura Driussi offered encouragement, enthusiasm, and helpful advice, for all of which I am grateful. I also thank an anonymous academic advisory board committee member, and another anonymous reader, for detailed and helpful comments. Thanks also to Jean McAneny, who oversaw editing and production.

Finally, I am grateful to the Japan Foundation for financial support during my research in Japan.

Introduction

In the sunny living room of his home near Osaka, 26-year-old
Seiji Hayakawa last week contemplated his existence and
found it good. Mornings, Seiji and his young wife Kumiko
wake to the bubbling of their automatic rice cooker, turned
on minutes before by an electric timing device. Evenings they
watch Laramie or the *samurai* dramas on their television set
and fight off the winter chill by toasting their feet on an electric footwarmer. So well paid are their jobs at the nearby
Matsushita Electric Company radio plant—as a foreman,
Seiji makes $61.12 a month, plus a bonus of 6 1/2 months
pay last year—that they also own a refrigerator, transistor
radio, vacuum cleaner, electric iron and washer. If the expec-
tant Kumiko presents him with a son next month, Seiji even
talks confidently of sending the boy to a university. "What
more could I want?" Seiji ruminates contentedly—and answers himself, "I can't think of anything."[1]

This was how *Time* magazine opened its February 23, 1962, cover story
on Japan's extraordinary postwar recovery. On the magazine's cover
was a portrait of Matsushita Kōnosuke,* founder and chairman of the
Matsushita Electric Company. The story paid glowing tribute to the
achievements of Japanese industry, calling it "the biggest and most
hopeful economic news out of Asia since the end of World War II." But
the article did not focus on statistics of steel or ship manufacturing.
Rather, it emphasized the consumer and the "daring" companies that
were bringing a better standard of living to ordinary Japanese people.
Around 1960, Japanese consumers began to believe that high economic

*Throughout this book Japanese names are given in Japanese order (family name first).

growth was there to stay, and analysts began charting the "lifestyle revolution" that was sweeping Japanese society.

This book examines the arrival of a mass consumer society. Its locus is Japan, but the phenomenon it describes is common to all the advanced industrial societies and has, for better or worse, profoundly affected our lives. At the same time, this is the story of one of the great successes of Japanese economic history: the rise of the consumer electrical goods industry.

It was the latter story that first attracted me. I grew up with names like Hitachi, Sony, Panasonic (a Matsushita brand), and Toshiba stamped on my mind by way of the hardware of my school days: transistor radios, cassette players, and stereo systems. At the time, I never stopped to think about where these objects of desire originated. Later, as a management consultant during the boom days of Japanese acquisitions in the United States, I frequently came across these companies in a different context: as wielders of awesome financial might. By that time, the laments over the decline of the American consumer electronics industry (excluding computers) had almost faded away: there was little left to lament. The Japanese giants of the electronic age had appeared on the world scene with dramatic suddenness, and now they were known—and their products owned—by virtually every household in the industrialized world. Where on earth had these corporations come from?

My initial agenda was simply to understand the origins of these Japanese electronics giants and to explain how they rose to such dominance in the global market. But I had not gone far in my research before I realized there was another question of equal or greater importance. Japanese consumer electronics exports began at the end of the 1950s with the transistor radio, followed soon after by black and white televisions. By that time, Japanese companies had already enjoyed almost a decade of extraordinary growth in the domestic market, which analysts agree was an essential prerequisite for the takeoff of exports. Indeed, the unprecedented boom in Japanese consumption of durable consumer goods left contemporary analysts gasping for superlatives. This growth was all the more remarkable given that, by any objective measure, Japanese incomes were still close to the poverty level. Per capita income was $97 per year in 1950 and had grown only to $318 by 1960. A television in 1955 cost ¥110,000 ($305) in Japan. How could Japanese people buy televisions and washing machines when they apparently lacked many of life's bare essentials?

As I pondered these questions, a third, much broader group of questions kept reemerging. The story of Japanese electrical goods intersects some of the biggest issues in the modern (particularly the late modern) history of Japan—indeed, of all advanced industrial societies. One such issue is the relationship of technology to the startling changes that have swept over all of our lives during the course of the past century. As the Electronics Samurai—my term for the engineers and entrepreneurs who led the industry's growth in Japan—tell it, technological prowess lay at the heart of their stunning success. What role did technology play in the great changes that took place during the 1950s, both in the electrical goods industry and in Japanese society as a whole?

A second broad issue is that of consumption and the role of the consumer in the construction of the late modern political economy. I argue in this book that one of the keys to the prosperity of the electrical goods industry was the creation of a middle-class consuming public. Electrical goods companies consciously engaged in market-creating activities even though incomes in Japan were apparently too low to support a consumption-oriented lifestyle. By the end of the 1950s, an elite consensus had emerged around the idea that consumption was a key ingredient in the political economy of high growth. This consensus subsequently drew both praise and criticism: praise as a model of rapid economic development, criticism as an allegedly cynical ploy to hide real and growing inequalities in wealth and power under the mantle of a "middle mass" ideology.

A third issue is the construction of gendered roles during the postwar era. Constructed gender enters my story in two important ways. At the turn of the 1950s, despite a history of increasing emphasis on the role of women as household managers, housewives still constituted a minority in Japan. Early sales campaigns by electrical goods companies focused less on housewives than on household heads—usually the patriarchal family head. But during the course of the 1950s, companies increasingly came to see the importance of the housewife as a decision maker and manager of household consumption. In this they were guided by the model of the idealized American middle-class family with a housewife at its center. The images of idealized homes created by electrical goods companies surely helped consolidate gender roles in postwar Japan. Yet, paradoxically, electrical goods companies at the same time depended on the availability of nimble-fingered, relatively powerless young women willing to work for extremely low wages—women who bore almost no similarity to the housewife stereotype.

These major issues are crucial to any coherent interpretation of the trajectory of modernity in the late twentieth century, and all are closely related. Technology, particularly with respect to marketing and the mass communications media, was a tool in the creation of markets and demand. Women in the home and the workplace also played their part in the story of corporate success: the idealized middle-class household with a housewife-manager was as important to corporate efforts as the availability of cheap female labor. I will be happy if this book succeeds in throwing even a small ray of light on these large and difficult issues.

Behind the growth of the postwar Japanese electrical goods industry lay a profound continuity. Everything that happened in the boom years of the 1950s and 1960s—including the development of leading-edge technologies, the birth of a consumer culture, the promotion of electronics through government policy, and the phenomenon of high growth itself—had its antecedent in the prewar and wartime eras. Those antecedents are the subject of Chapter 1.

But my interpretation focuses on important new developments after the war—developments that were the product of a catastrophic defeat attributable in part to the failure of Japanese technology. My story revolves around the visions that established business leaders, bureaucrats, and entrepreneurs, as well as ordinary Japanese people, developed during the formative years of the Allied Occupation of Japan (1945–52). This is the topic of Chapter 2. During these early postwar years, Japanese businessmen and others began quite consciously to search for the keys to the immense prosperity of the United States—a prosperity that was all the more tantalizing given its contrast with life in a Japan prostrate from defeat. Although these visions were diverse and often contested, key protagonists in this story focused on a few common themes that were to unlock, for them, the gates to prosperity.

The first of these "keys to prosperity" was the power and influence of the media, particularly the new medium of television. In Chapter 3, I argue that despite the gloomy economic conditions of the early postwar years, some entrepreneurs saw immense business opportunities in the emerging new technologies of mass communication. One man in particular—Shōriki Matsutarō, a newspaper magnate who well understood the power and profitability of the media—forged alliances with politicians, bureaucrats, and investors to bring television to Japan much sooner than conventional economic logic would have suggested. In doing so, he both created a new industry and contributed to the transformation of Japanese society.

The second key was the importation of technology on a massive scale. Although this importation took place across the board, the electrical goods industry was a particularly large buyer of foreign technology. In spite of the fact that imported electronics technologies made a negligible short-term contribution to the national mission of industrial recovery and export growth, electrical goods companies joined in an orgy of product and process technology acquisitions in order to bring the latest communications products to Japan. However, as I argue in Chapter 4, this feast of technology represents only part of the story. Japanese companies had to develop not only new products but also markets for those products. Toward that end Japanese companies imported a wide range of production, management, and marketing techniques, a process at least as important as the importation of product technologies.

I turn to the domestic market in Chapter 5. As early as the turn of the 1950s, some visionary Japanese business leaders saw the production of an American-style middle-class society as crucial to Japanese prosperity. In such a society, the consumer was vitally important. In spite of the poverty that continued to haunt Japan, these businessmen set out to emulate their American counterparts and pioneer new markets—particularly a market for expensive electrical products.

A final key to prosperity increasingly has been forgotten in the recent celebration of Japanese technological prowess: the cheap labor of the underprivileged classes, particularly young women. This is the focus of Chapter 6. Cheap labor was Japan's traditional advantage in the international marketplace, and it was surprisingly appropriate to the manufacture of "high-tech" goods such as radios and televisions. Indeed, it lay behind Japan's first great export success in the electrical goods industry: the portable transistor radio.

I use the term "electrical goods industry" to describe the focus of this book. For the most part, my study is limited to consumer products. The exception is the transistor, an industrial component that was a key ingredient in the transistor radio. "Electrical goods" is an umbrella term that includes both electronic products (radios and televisions) and household appliances such as washing machines and refrigerators. Before and during World War II, the market for electrical household appliances was virtually nonexistent, so Chapter 1 focuses more specifically on the electrical communications industry, forebear of the modern electronics industry.

1

Electrifying Japan

TECHNO-NATIONALISM AND THE
RISE OF THE MASS SOCIETY

The postwar Japanese electrical goods industry did not spring from out
of nowhere. On the contrary, the takeoff of Japanese electrical goods in
the 1950s marked the culmination of a century of ardent endeavor,
proud achievement, and rapid—and apparently accelerating—growth.
Increasingly, students of Japanese technology have come to recognize
the importance of the long period of development preceding the
"miraculous" flowering of the postwar era.[1]

This technological background, which included great triumphs as
well as some disasters, is crucial to understanding the ready absorption
and rapid adaptation of sophisticated electrical technologies in the
1950s. Equally important is the background of prewar and wartime social change, which foreshadowed the sudden emergence at the end of
the 1950s of a mass consumer market for electrical goods.

IN THE SERVICE OF THE NATION

The eight decades from the Meiji Restoration to Japan's defeat in World
War II witnessed extraordinary growth and development, both industrial and technological. Although this period ended in a dreadful catas-
trophe—total defeat in an all-out war—the prewar and wartime development of the electrical goods industry left vitally important legacies of
technological development, government support, institutional infrastructure, and high growth.

Unwelcome Gifts

On March 22, 1853, four black-hulled ships pulled quietly into the Uraga Channel at the mouth of Edo Bay, twenty miles from present-day Tokyo. For all their insignificance against the limitless backdrop of the Pacific Ocean, the ships presented a sinister profile to the Japanese officials sent hastily to intercept them. Their paddle-wheeled silhouettes reflected the latest maritime technologies. Stacks on their decks belched out black smoke. Gunports winked at the undefended shoreline. The flag they flew, the Stars and Stripes, had not previously been thought a major threat by the Japanese—their main concern was Russia—but with this visit it became a symbol of menace.

The arrival of Commodore Matthew Perry and his "black ships" turned out to be one of the most traumatic events in Japanese history. The shock appears vividly in the drawings and illustrations of Japanese observers, who portrayed Perry as a fearsome man with stark eyes staring from under bushy brows. The U.S. delegation made political demands, certainly: its mission was to end Japan's centuries-long policy of isolation. But the shock of the Perry mission was more potent than any immediate military threat it posed. The powerful warships, the displays of discipline, the well-oiled guns, the authoritative body of law and precedent, and the many accoutrements of a rapidly advancing technological prowess bespoke the yawning gap that had opened between Japan's civilization and the virulent forces of modernity. To Japanese observers, this was something akin to a visit by extraterrestrials.

The Americans were fully conscious of this powerful psychological impact. When Perry returned the following year to sign a treaty between the United States and Japan, he made an ostentatious presentation of gifts from home. The largest items put on display for the assembled Japanese officials were a miniature steam engine with a circular track and a late-model electric telegraph machine inscribed "To the Emperor of Japan," the latter accompanied by a mile of connecting wire. The expedition's official narrative recounts:

> [A] piece of level ground was assigned for laying down the circular track of the little locomotive, and posts were brought and erected for the extension of the telegraph wires, the Japanese taking a very ready part in all the labors, and watching the result of arranging and putting together of the machinery with an innocent and childlike delight. The telegraphic apparatus, under the direction of Messrs. Draper and Williams, was soon in working order, the wires extending for nearly a mile, in a direct line, one end being at the treaty house and another at a building expressly allotted for the purpose. When

communication was opened up between the operators at either extremity, the Japanese watched with intense curiosity the *modus operandi*, and were greatly amazed to find that in an instant messages were conveyed in the English, Dutch, and Japanese languages from building to building. Day after day the dignitaries and many of the people would gather, and, eagerly beseeching the operators to work the telegraph, would watch with unabated interest the sending and receiving of messages.

Nor did the railway with its Lilliputian locomotive, car, and tender excite less interest. All the parts of the mechanism were perfect, and the car was a most tasteful specimen of workmanship, but so small that it could hardly carry a child of six years of age. The Japanese, however, were not to be cheated out of a ride, and, as they were unable to reduce themselves to the capacity of the inside of the carriage, they sat themselves on the roof. It was a spectacle not a little ludicrous to behold a dignified mandarin whirling around the circular road at the rate of twenty miles an hour, with his loose robes flying in the wind. As he clung with a desperate hold to the edge of the roof, grinning with intense interest, and his huddled-up body shook convulsively with a kind of laughing timidity, the car spun rapidly around the circle.[2]

These gifts, the latest miracles of Western technology, contained both a promise and a threat. They embodied the key theme of the modern era: rapid communications. The same rapidity had enabled Perry's ships to cross the vast expanse of the Pacific in just three weeks, bringing both toys and guns to Japan. The Americans were offering a Faustian bargain to the Japanese: simply adopt our system, they implied, and you can have all these marvelous goods with the same ease with which we came here and set up the telegraph lines in that field.

The Americans were frankly contemptuous of their reluctant hosts, whom they ridiculed with a condescending distaste, making little distinction between the Japanese and a tribe of island savages. The official narrative described a "disgusting exhibition" of barely clad sumo wrestlers, adding: "It was a happy contrast, which a higher civilization presented . . . In place of a show of brute animal force, there was a triumphant revelation of the success of science and enterprise, to a partially enlightened people." Michael Adas refers to the "ideologies of dominance," based on the perceived superiority of Western science and technology, that were used to justify the exploitation, enslavement, and even extermination of non-Western races during the nineteenth and early twentieth centuries. It was precisely in terms of such an "irresistible certitude" of scientific and technological superiority that Perry's chronicle structured the relationship between the Americans and their unwilling hosts.[3]

Although Perry's visit in many ways emphasized the extraordinary gap that had opened up between the advanced West and a closed-off

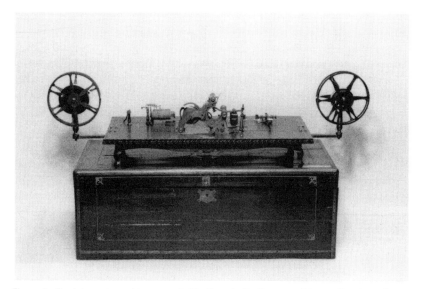

Figure 1　The telegraph machine presented by Perry to the Emperor of Japan. (Courtesy of Communications Ministry, Tokyo)

Japan, it also obscured the extent to which some Japanese were staying abreast of events in the rest of the world. At the time of Perry's visit there was already at least one working telegraph in Japan. It was not an import but had been built by a Japanese engineer.

Sakuma Shōzan was a samurai intellectual who, through painful study of Dutch texts, became a leading exponent of "Dutch learning." Sakuma realized early that the tendency of Confucian scholars to dismiss out of hand anything related to foreign "barbarians" was dangerous and shortsighted. "The foreigner," he concluded, "has clarified and explained things which the classics have not yet illuminated." Indeed, although Sakuma argued for the preservation of traditional Japanese thinking in a fusion of "Western technology with Eastern ethics," he concluded that the foreign threat was "an unprecedented event for which Japan's historical experience was insufficient preparation." This challenge could only be met by an extraordinary effort to understand and reproduce Western technology.[4]

Sakuma was unusual among Japanese intellectuals in that he not only studied Western knowledge but also put his studies into action. By the end of the 1840s he had opened a laboratory in which he made glass, chemicals, batteries, and guns. He came across a book on the electric telegraph in 1848—just five years after its invention in Baltimore by Samuel F. Morse. Intrigued by the technology as well as by its practical implications, Sakuma set about constructing a telegraph system on the grounds of his lord's castle in Shinano province. By 1851, Sakuma had a working telegraph system between the inner and outer grounds of the castle. He had built his own Volta batteries and used locally made porcelain insulators and copper wire.[5]

Sakuma's story illustrates the extent and availability of knowledge to those Japanese who sought it. He recognized the need to master the breakthroughs of the West and proved that new technologies could be reproduced in a short space of time. Certainly the Japanese officials who ignored his pleas to take Western culture seriously were guilty of shortsightedness, but the arrogant American visitors may have been even more blind: they failed to see how narrow was the gap separating them from the "unenlightened" Japanese. That failure of perception was equally apparent a century later, in the aftermath of World War II.

Bridging the Gap

In 1868 the Shogunal regime that had governed Japan for almost three hundred years ended after a brief civil war. One of the chief causes of the regime's demise was its failure to come up with a credible response to the foreign threat. The new government revolutionized Japan's political and social institutions, abolishing the centuries-old caste system and freeing restive samurai to pursue careers in business. The 1868 revolution served as a starting gun for Japan's modernization. Within a remarkably short space of time, the new Japanese government had established the basic infrastructure and policies that provided the foundation for more than a century of rapid development.

At first much of the infrastructure of modernization came by way of the United States and Europe. In 1869, a year after the Restoration, the new government contracted with a British engineer, George Miles Gilbert, to build a telegraph line between Tokyo and Yokohama. Gilbert completed this task in January 1870. The network then rapidly expanded to encompass the nation's main communications routes, with a Tokyo-Nagasaki line opening in 1872 and a Tokyo-Aomori-Sapporo line in service the following year. Private overseas cables were also laid in 1871 by the Great Northern Telegraph company between Nagasaki and Shanghai and Vladivostock. Thus, within a very short time of the creation of a national government, Japan possessed a national and international telegraph system.

In a country notorious for its difficult communications, the telegraph conferred obvious benefits. Within a short time, its importance for the management and control of a modern state became compellingly clear. On February 7, 1877, the government received a message relayed from its Nagasaki telegraph bureau: "Samurai of Kagoshima, Saigō and Kirino as leaders, plan shortly to launch offensive."

The national government's victory against the Satsuma rebellion proved decisively the superiority of modern weapons and Western technology over traditional samurai martial values. The government set up mobile telegraph stations to transmit to and from the front, and its ability to send information rapidly on troop movements, needed reinforcements, and enemy positions kept it ahead of Saigō and his forces. The telegraph was also a medium for transmitting orders and encouragement, both of which were needed for the desperate defense of Kumamoto against overwhelming rebel forces. One surviving cable contains the grim admonishment: "Acknowledge shortage of troops. Depending on enemy's position, will send reinforcements. Your troops must defend their posts to the death."[6]

The policy of using communications networks for national defense was thus established at an early stage. It was one of four planks that would provide a vital foundation for the postwar growth of Japan's electrical goods industry. Defense infrastructure, domestic manufacturing, technical education, and the creation of government research institutions all would help Japanese electrical technology catch up to that of the West in both the prewar and postwar eras.

Rapid introduction of new technologies with defense implications remained a major goal of Japan's electrical communications policy. Indeed, the government adopted the telephone much more quickly than it had the telegraph. The first telephone was brought to Japan in 1877, just one year after Alexander Graham Bell's patent application, by Izawa Shūji, a pioneer educator of deaf mutes who had worked with Bell. The following year an experimental line was installed between the Department of Works and the Imperial Household Ministry, which sat two kilometers from one another. Once again, the emphasis was on official communications and national defense. The government did not launch private telephone service until the end of the 1880s.[7]

A second long-term policy, the emphasis on domestic manufacturing, also dates to the early days of the Meiji government. The government, undoubtedly to promote economic development, used local resources whenever possible. For example, although virtually all the parts were imported for the Tokyo-Yokohama telegraph connection, the government insisted on commissioning the vital porcelain insulators from a Saga pottery house.[8] In 1873 the Department of Works set up a manufacturing section within its telegraph office. This agency immediately set about commissioning domestically produced telegraph equipment, choosing a traditional Japanese craftsman to manufacture transmitters and receivers. Tanaka Hisashige was until the Restoration employed by Kurume domain in his native Kyushu, helping the domainal government develop a modern navy. By the time he moved to Tokyo to work for the national government, he was already in his mid-seventies. Although in recent years he had turned his attention to shipbuilding and gunnery, his widespread fame in Japan came from his consummate skill as a maker of *karakuri*, or mechanical gadgets. Tanaka's company had by his death in 1882 become one of Japan's foremost electrical engineering concerns; now called Toshiba, it remains an industry leader.[9]

Technical training constituted the third plank of the government's technology development program. The Department of Works opened a telegraphy school in 1871 (in 1877 it was absorbed into the College of Engineering). Within two years the school had hired ten British teachers and enrolled sixty Japanese students. Instruction was conducted entirely in English. The school produced its first twenty-three graduates in 1879, and the government selected eleven of them to go to England for further study. If the government appeared to be lavishing undue resources and care on the education of a new technological elite, it had a very clear and specific motive. In 1879 the Department of Works was employing some 150 foreigners for a wide range of technical and educational projects at a total cost of ¥350,000 a year, or 70 percent of the total departmental budget. The works minister stated that the purpose of educating Japanese engineers was to replace the foreign technicians and thus to save money. The group sent to England constituted the first cohort of Japanese teachers and practitioners of electrical engineering.

By 1883, when the College of Engineering merged with the physics department of Tokyo Imperial University, it had graduated close to 1,300 students and had an enrollment of 275. The combined institution, which became the engineering faculty of the Imperial University, remains one of the nation's premier training grounds for top-flight electrical engineers.[10]

The fourth plank of the government's infrastructural strategy was the creation of research institutions. The government reorganization of

1885 included the formation of a Ministry of Communications, which inherited most of Japan's public communications infrastructure. In August 1891 the ministry launched the Denki Shikenjo (electrical testing laboratory, commonly referred to by Japanese as the Electro-Technical Laboratory) absorbing the insulator testing center and other testing bureaus of the old Department of Works.

The Denki Shikenjo from its inception took part in every aspect of electrical and communications research. Within its first decade, the Denki Shikenjo spearheaded two pioneering projects. The first was the laying of an undersea cable from Kyushu to Taiwan, completed in 1897. Although not based on original research, the project marked the first time that a developing country had laid a long-distance cable, and it utilized all the research capabilities and expertise of the Denki Shikenjo. The agency headed the effort despite strenuous objections from some members of the government: Katō Kōmei, at the time ambassador to London, wanted the project to be given to British engineers, believing that Japanese technology was not up to the task.[11]

The next revolution in communications, the wireless radio, came to Japan with relative ease. The first Japanese radio transmission took place in 1897, just one year after Marconi's pioneering experiments from the British coast. By the turn of the twentieth century, Japanese radio technology was on a par with any in the world. Indeed, Japan's stunning military defeat of Russia in 1905 resulted in no small part from the advanced radio equipment carried by Japanese warships. In a now legendary encounter, the Japanese patrol ship Shinano-maru sighted the Russian Baltic fleet in May 1905 and sent the signal *tekikan miyu* ("enemy ships sighted"), enabling Admiral Tōgō Heihachirō to secure a decisive victory in the Battle of Tsushima Strait. This was the first time that the military applications of wireless had been tested in action, and there can be no doubt that the eyes of the world were on Japan. The army also applied the wireless in field combat, using elaborate portable installations to gain a significant communications advantage.[12]

Miraculous Advance

By the turn of the twentieth century, Japanese electrical technology rivaled that of the world leaders. Japan had come a long way in the space of thirty years, narrowing a deficit of what had seemed decades, if not centuries, to a year or two. Basil Hall Chamberlain, a Briton who lived in Japan for many years, aptly described the remarkable transformation of Japan into a modern, technologically advanced nation when he remarked: "To have lived through the transition stage of modern Japan makes a man feel preternaturally old; for here he is in modern times, . . . and yet he can himself distinctly remember the middle ages."[13]

Japan's prewar technological advances played a vital role in the dramatic rise of the postwar electrical goods industry. Just as Japan was not as backward as it appeared to the first American visitors in 1853, so the postwar recovery rested on a solid foundation of past achievement. The prewar successes of Japanese electrical technology resulted from government policies that dated back to the start of Japan's modern era and were pursued consistently for eight decades or more. These policies—the pursuit of advanced technology for purposes of national defense, the domestication of manufacturing, and the early establishment of educational and research institutions—were clearly vital prerequisites for the establishment of a viable domestic industry. Richard Samuels has rightly stressed the importance of the government's defense policy to technological development throughout Japan's modern era.[14] Remarkably, these trends bridged the divide of World War II, continuing through the Occupation and postwar governments despite radically divergent political circumstances.

Moreover, Japan's rapid prewar development illustrates the ease with which a newcomer could assimilate advanced technologies. Some scholars have emphasized the existence of requisite capabilities—the tradition of fine crafts, for example—in the premodern period.[15] But it is clear that given the right infrastructural and educational resources, Japanese researchers were able to gain access to, and replicate, the latest technological advances within a very short space of time.

Several characteristics of the electrical industry help explain this ease of assimilation. One is the relative ineffectiveness of patent protection. When technology is being pursued for national policy ends, the threat of commercial patent infringement action carries little weight. For example, although the research team duplicating Marconi's experiments argued that he had filed his Japanese patent application too late to protect the technology, the patent issue was probably never a major factor in their calculations. Similarly, when Takayanagi Kenjirō copied RCA's iconoscope television camera tube in the late 1930s, the question of patents apparently never arose.

Additionally, leading Western companies were willing to transfer their technologies in exchange for a presence in the growing markets of

Japan and Asia. General Electric and Westinghouse provided their Japanese affiliates—Tokyo Denki and Nippon Denki, respectively—with free access to their leading technologies, even dispatching engineers to Japan to smooth the process. Similarly, when Alexander Graham Bell began commercial exploitation of the telephone, he pursued a global strategy from the start. Telephone technologies were introduced into Japan with Bell's full knowledge and approval.

Sophisticated as they were, the breakthrough technologies of the nineteenth century were not unduly difficult to replicate. Many of the inventors were lone researchers with modest financial backing, working in home laboratories without the assistance of a big organization. The Japanese research establishment, by contrast, was well organized and purposeful. It is not surprising that, given the government's major infrastructural support, Japanese researchers were able to keep up with technological advances in the West. The circulation of technical and professional journals also helped immeasurably. For example, the Denki Shikenjo began research on wireless transmission after Ishibashi Akihiko, a government employee in charge of marking shipping channels, read an article in the *London Electrician* magazine reporting on Marconi's experiments. Ishibashi conceived the idea of transmitting wireless signals to ships from lighthouses and approached the Denki Shikenjo about undertaking the research.[16]

But whether Japan caught up to the West in electrical communications because of effective government policy, pre-Restoration skills, or the nature of the technologies themselves, the continuity of technological development from the Meiji period onward played a key role in helping Japanese companies assimilate complex technologies after World War II. As we will see, these trends actually gained intensity and momentum as Japan entered the fateful years of isolation and all-out war.

A TIME FOR DREAMS

Continuities of growth and government policy are not enough in themselves to explain the dynamic of Japan's electrical technology development. First, they do not explain the catastrophic failure of Japanese technology to meet the needs of Japan's war effort. More important, they cast little light on one of the key features of Japan's electrical goods industry in the twentieth century: its role in the creation and growth of a mass consumer market. Mass consumption of electrical goods arrived in Japan with explosive suddenness in the mid-1950s, and the industrial growth engendered by this consumption helped Japanese electrical goods companies achieve international competitiveness. However, just as postwar industrial and technological growth reflected a century of development, so, too, did the mass consumer market in Japan have a long prelude. This continuity receives much less attention than the more conventional themes of industrial growth and technology development.

The "Mass Society"

The arrival of telegraph lines, postal services, and railway lines indelibly affected the rhythms of everyday life in Japan. Stories abound of the suspicion and misunderstandings these modern tools engendered. Country people allegedly believed, for example, that the telegraph lines were used to transport the blood of peasants to feed the appetites of Westerners. Provincials who politely took their shoes off before boarding a train were surprised, it was said, that the shoes were not waiting for them at their destination. But despite their wariness, the Japanese absorbed and used these new amenities. In one notable area, government and business took action that had marked consequences for ordinary people: electricity came to rural Japan with great rapidity. By 1920 Japan was one of the world's leaders in per capita electrification, with 7 million of the nation's 11 million households connected—although "electrification" meant little more than providing electric light, with usually no more than one outlet per family.[17]

Of course, the modern industrial system asserted itself most powerfully in the cities. Here, during the first two decades of the twentieth century, the outlines of a mass consumer society slowly emerged.

By the turn of the 1920s, the United States was already experiencing the first full manifestation of mass consumer culture. The developments of the previous fifty years—the unification of the country by railroads, the development of mass production systems, the pioneering of mass merchandising by department stores and mail-order firms—combined to create the potential for an industrial and commercial system such as the world had never before seen. But American industrialists perceived that they could not fully realize this potential unless they also created buyers for their products. Henry Ford ensured that all workers on his assembly lines had a minimum wage of $5 per day because he saw that the continued sales growth of his automobiles depended in no small part upon purchases by factory workers.[18] An advertising trade journal commented:

"Modern machinery made it not only possible but imperative that the masses should live lives of comfort and leisure; that the future of business lay in its ability to *manufacture customers* as well as products."[19]

In order to create mass consumption for the products of mass assembly, American companies drew heavily on the new techniques of advertising and marketing. These techniques, based in part on the developing behavioral sciences, were abetted by the rapid growth of mass-circulation newspapers and magazines—and, after the turn of the 1920s, commercial radio. Stuart Ewen argues that producers consciously set out to create a new social structure and ideology that would promote consumption even of goods that were not necessary for survival or basic well-being: "Consumerism, the mass participation in the values of the mass-industrial market, thus emerged in the 1920s not as a smooth progression from earlier and less 'developed' patterns of consumption, but rather as an aggressive device of corporate survival."[20]

Whether through free choice, chance, or coercion, mass production—and the high wages offered by factories—put the prerogatives of a wealthy elite within reach of ordinary working people. Automobiles were snapped up as soon as they moved off the assembly line. Food packaging and processing techniques allowed working families to enjoy an abundance and variety unavailable to princes of an earlier age. Visiting Europeans commented (with distaste) on the fashionable clothes worn even by housemaids. The American home began gradually to fill up with conveniences—hot and cold running water, bathrooms, central heating, gas stoves, and, increasingly, electrical products such as washing machines and refrigerators.

The Roaring Twenties were not only an American phenomenon. Throughout the world, newly emerging urban middle classes threw off the gloom of World War I by listening to jazz, studying Marx, cutting their hair short, agitating for female suffrage, and reveling in the spirit of modernism. In Tokyo this new spirit took hold against a background of violent destruction: the great Kanto earthquake of 1923, which leveled large parts of the capital. Maruyama Masao suggests that the efflorescence of "mass society," albeit in a tiny portion of Japan's population, grew directly out of this destruction. He cites the following contemporary comment:

> To an unbelievable extent the great city was reduced to burnt ruins that stretched as far as one could see. In this burnt-out field the incarnation of speed, i.e., automobiles, appeared to wander about the streets, soon followed by the monster of sound called radio; then the model of birds, the air-

plane, began to fly in the sky for practical use. All of these are embodiments of modern science, coming forth in Japan one by one immediately after the earthquake disaster.[21]

The 1920s tend to conjure images of bob-haired, short-skirted "modern girls" walking the streets of Tokyo arm in arm. Tanizaki Junichirō's novel *Chijin no Ai* (A Fool's Love, 1924) is a classic portrait of the modern girl, a sexually provocative Mary Pickford look-alike who lived in a Western-style "cultural home," danced with foreigners, and upturned social conventions by reducing her master to the position of a groveling slave.[22] To a surprising extent, the trends of the 1920s prefigured the mass consumer society that burgeoned in the late 1950s and 1960s. It is important to note that these developments applied only to a very small proportion of the overall population: one estimate places the proportion of adults with secondary education and white-collar jobs at 5 to 8 percent of the population in 1920 (suggesting that there were about half a million middle-class households).[23] Nevertheless, this statistic in itself reflects extraordinary growth over the course of the two preceding decades.

The emergence of a literate mass market in Japan was reflected in the burgeoning of popular magazines and the spread of newspaper readership. *King*, for example, sold 740,000 copies of its first issue in 1925. Radio, too, attracted large numbers of urban listeners when broadcasting began in 1925. Japan's national radio network anticipated 10,000 listeners in the first year but instead received 35,000 license requests within three months.

Middle-class culture also took firmer root in Japan during the 1920s. The ideal of the Western-style family home (*hōmu*) based on a love-marriage and without the appendages of parents-in-law, concubines, or extended relatives already had a long tradition in Japan. As early as the 1890s, Christian reformers were promoting such a living arrangement, and although the thought of banishing ancestors seemed radical to many, the government and members of the upper class happily agreed on the new custom of regular family meals around a dining table.[24] But with the establishment of large numbers of white-collar households having only loose ties to the traditional patriarchal household structure, the *hōmu*, or "cultural dwelling" (*bunka jūtaku*), became a cherished symbol of the new middle class. A popular song from the 1920s refers to "my small but happy home" (*semai nagara tanoshii wagaya*), prefiguring the much-discussed postwar ideal of "my home" (*mai hōmu*).[25]

The 1920s also witnessed the consolidation of a new archetype: the "rational" housewife-consumer at the center of the middle-class home. Jordan Sand describes the gradual reconceptualization of the housewife from an upper-class manager and supervisor of servants to a hands-on cook and housecleaner who performs many of the functions of a servant. As one indicator of this shift, upper-level education for girls increased enormously during the decade. At the turn of the century, only a small cadre of upper-crust girls received high school (*jogakkō*) education. The 1911 Ministry of Education examination for instructors at these schools included questions such as: "You are to prepare a banquet for friends whom your husband has invited, and will prepare the game that they have caught while sport-hunting as the main dish. Detail the menu and method of preparation."[26] By 1926 the number of students in women's high schools had risen to 370,000, an increase of at least ten times since the beginning of the century, and the education was aimed at the management of a modest, middle-class home.

Magazines for this new market of housewives developed accordingly. Although publications such as *Jogaku Zasshi* ("Women's Studies Magazine") and *Katei no Tomo* ("Family's Friend") had catered to household managers since the 1890s, the first two decades of the twentieth century brought an enormous increase in both the number and circulation of such periodicals and a concomitant shift in content toward a more middle-class audience. By the 1920s the leading women's magazine, *Shufu no Tomo* ("Housewife's Friend"), was printing a quarter-million copies of each issue. *Shufu no Tomo* published articles on the minutiae of running a household, including the very important issue of money management for families that, although functionally middle-class, still struggled financially.[27] The rise of women's magazines brought with it a new culture of advertising, focusing in particular on the kitchen. The assumption was that middle-class wives had enough influence over family finances to initiate purchases. Gas companies were major advertisers, as by the 1920s more than 30 percent of Tokyo households were connected to gas mains.

However, the concept of the middle-class housewife remained subject to ideological dispute in the 1920s, coexisting as it did with alternative models of the modern girl and the activist for women's rights. Sheldon Garon argues that a coalition of government bureaucrats and realistic women's leaders collaborated to create a new domain for women in the home of the 1920s, the "separate sphere of reforming daily life." In exchange for accepting a subordinate status in the political process, women's leaders claimed a separate-but-equal status in the home as "domestic managers." In this new role they looked to the model of the Western housewife, who was "portrayed as the equal of her husband because she managed the domestic sphere." As Garon puts it, "These champions of 'daily life improvement' did not oppose the prevailing gender construction of the 'good wife and wise mother,' but they emphatically rejected the subordination of wives to their husbands. Rather, middle-class women's groups called on women to draw on their domestic talents as teachers and rational homemakers and take the lead in transforming society."[28]

The transformation they aimed for hinged on "rationalization" and "lifestyle improvement," two slogans that carried over into the postwar era with increasing resonance. Indeed, in 1920 the government launched its own "lifestyle improvement" campaigns, whose primary goals included "rationalization" of lifestyles through the reduction of waste. Garon points to the contradictory attitudes encompassed in this movement, which "recalled shogunal injunctions of the Tokugawa era" in preaching the evils of extravagance but simultaneously "employed the language of modernization," lecturing housewives on "scientific diligence and thrift," "rational consumption," and "rational, budgeted living and savings."[29]

Even the vast majority of Japanese who did not belong to the middle class were influenced by the idealization of middle-class lifestyles portrayed in the burgeoning mass media. Factory workers and craftsmen read magazines and newspapers that exalted Westernized middle-class families and their "rational" lives, and they had discretionary income available for the purchase of consumer items such as cigarettes and magazines. Popular leisure activities aimed at the working classes, such as spectator sports, saw enormous increases in popularity, a trend reinforced by heavy newspaper coverage.

The Tap of Plenty

The promise of the new era of mass culture and mass communications brought forth a new kind of entrepreneur in Japan. In the Meiji period, great entrepreneurs such as Iwasaki Yatarō (founder of the Mitsubishi group) received state support and worked on grand mandates closely connected to the ideal of the "rich nation, strong military." But the 1920s was an era for a different kind of dreamer, one who could envision a mass market for the everyday accoutrements of modern life—

clothes, cosmetics, prepared foods, and electrical goods. Such a vision was not easy to believe in, because Japan in 1920 lacked most of the prerequisites for a mass consumer society; it had essentially no mass production, no national retail chains, and no disposable income. Businessmen who recognized the potential of the consumer market and had the ability to nurture it realized their visions and reaped immense rewards. One such man was Matsushita Kōnosuke, the founder of the Matsushita company and one of the great entrepreneurial legends of Japan.

Born in 1894 into a family of well-off farmers and rice merchants, Matsushita saw his fortunes change completely during the first years of his life. His father lost everything in the crash of 1896 and had to sell his house and land and take a clerical job in Osaka. Unable to take care of his own family, he sent Kōnosuke at the age of eight to be apprentice to a *hibachi* maker. His salary was ¥0.05 a month. A year later, in 1905, Matsushita was transferred to work as errand boy for Osaka's first importer of bicycles. Compounding his misfortunes, Matsushita's father and two elder brothers died in 1906, leaving him the nominal head of a sadly reduced family. Determined to restore the fortunes of his family after the traumas of his father's failure, Matsushita decided to become a businessman. He enrolled in night school, but financial difficulties and the death of his mother forced him to give up his education. Later he would say of these experiences: "If I had been educated, I might have gone into a white-collar office job, and would not be where I am." He added: "Any person who becomes great has undergone hardship."[30]

Matsushita worked for eight years in the bicycle shop, receiving only pocket money for wages. He later recalled:

> We received only three days off a year. There was no thought of even one day off a week. We looked forward all the more to New Year's Day, the Emperor's birthday, and o-Bon [the summer festival of the dead]. We worked from early morning until late at night. [My starting pay was] between ¥0.30 and ¥0.40, though by the time I was fifteen it increased to ¥2 per month. Unlike other shop boys, though, I did not receive any clothes from my master.

Matsushita remembered the spartan living conditions of his apprenticeship: "For breakfast and supper, we had rice with only a side dish of some pickled vegetable. For lunch there was a cooked vegetable with the rice. Our shop used to provide a fish dish on the first and fifteenth of every month. That was really a feast!"[31]

At sixteen Matsushita got a break, using family contacts to wangle a job as a trainee electrician with the local utility. After six years in this position, Matsushita had risen to a comfortable position as wiring inspector. His salary was now ¥60 a month, enough to support a wife and family. At twenty-two, he still had his whole life ahead of him. Matsushita could well have given thanks for his good luck and stuck with what promised to be a comfortable and secure career. Instead, he decided to roll the dice one more time. In 1916 he quit the utility and launched his own business selling electrical accessories.

Matsushita's first product was a primitive socket made of a composite paste he mixed in a pan on the wood-burning stove in his tiny shared room, using ingredients from the local pharmacy. In his first four months Matsushita sold only a hundred of the plugs at ¥0.10 each. His future looked dire. But before the end of his first year he had a breakthrough. A local contractor ordered a thousand electric fan regulator bases made from Matsushita's paste instead of the traditional porcelain. In 1918 Matsushita cleared profits of more than ¥100. He founded the Matsushita Electrical Company in March of that year.

This gave Matsushita enough money to develop his next product: a bicycle lamp. At the time the bicycle was just coming into general use in Japan. Although bicycle lamps were available, most were primitive affairs using candles or stored gas. The few electric bicycle lamps on the market had very short battery lives. Matsushita concentrated on the battery, working with local manufacturers to make one that ran for more than thirty hours—at least ten times as long as competing lamps. Matsushita was sure he had a winning product, but conservative wholesalers—and bicycle companies—would not take a chance on this untried supplier. Matsushita had contracted for enough regular parts deliveries to make 2,000 lamps a month; within a few weeks, he had a bulging inventory of unsold lamps.

Matsushita described his next strategy as "the single most important ever adopted by the Matsushita company."[32] Rather than admit defeat, he decided to give the lamps away directly to retailers. Matsushita hired a pair of door-to-door salesmen and sent them around to electrical shops throughout the Osaka area. They delivered three or four lamps to each shop, telling the shopkeepers: "Please try our lamp out. If you are convinced it's a good product, then sell it to your customers. And if they buy it from you, then please send us the money." Within three months orders were flooding in for the lamp, and Matsushita's sales began a steep climb that, with just one or two interruptions, would continue for the following fifty years.

Matsushita was by no means an intellectual. His vision of the future for the Japanese electrical goods market was based not on extensive study or structured analysis but rather on something approaching a mystical inspiration or revelation. One day, legend has it, he was standing in the street watching a vagrant helping himself to water from an outdoor outlet. It occurred to him that the water was private property, but it was highly unlikely that anyone would upbraid the vagrant for the theft.

> Processed tap water has value. Normally, anyone stealing something of value will be punished. However, if someone turns on a roadside tap to drink, he may be reproached for bad manners but he will not be punished for drinking the water, although it costs money. Why? This is because water is available in such abundance. Does this not point to the real mission of the manufacturer? That mission is to supply the people with essential goods as cheaply and abundantly as tap water, thus enriching their lives and contributing to happiness.[33]

Matsushita would see his dreams fulfilled beyond even his own imagining. But his story is by no means uncomplicated. For in addition to cultivating the consumer market, Matsushita was in turn cultivated by the mandarins of Japan's quest for Asian hegemony in the 1930s and 1940s. There was a nightmare quality to the dreams of Japan's great popular leaders, as we shall see in the next section.

THE NIGHTMARE

The conventional wisdom holds that demand for radios, electric appliances, and other consumer products was snuffed out by the exigencies of military escalation and, finally, all-out war. However, both the military and civilian components of the Japanese government recognized the importance of certain mass consumer products as means of channeling the energy of the people and of exerting psychological control. Indeed, sales of radios and newspapers saw rapid expansion right up until the period of absolute shortage at the end of the war. Far from being "peaceful" goods, these media both reflected and spurred support for the war effort. The tendency of the leaders of society to promote— and simultaneously to exert a measure of control over—the mass media continued unabated after the war, and it has continued to provoke a stubborn critique of the role of the media in modern society.

However, the government's policy of technological isolationism—or, to borrow Richard Samuels's phrase, "techno-nationalism"—clearly helped bring about Japan's catastrophic defeat in World War II.[34] The failure of this policy led to a fundamental break with the past: never again would the Japanese government pursue a "go it alone" policy on industrial technology.

Harnessing the Masses

In 1920 the world's first commercial radio broadcaster went on the air in Pittsburgh. By 1922 there were more than four hundred radio stations throughout the United States, and radio sets were already becoming a household staple. The radio brought music, advertising, news, sports, entertainment, and celebrities into the lives of Americans. Japanese politicians and bureaucrats recognized electrical technologies' potential to effect change, and they were torn between the desire to promote them as tools of influence and control, on the one hand, and the desire to restrict them in subordination to defense-oriented development, on the other. This conflict was particularly visible in the events surrounding the launch of Japanese radio in 1925.

An explosion of literature reflected great popular interest in radio, at least among urbanites, even before broadcasting began. The magazine *Wireless* was founded in January 1918, followed in 1924–26 by *Wireless and Experimentation, Home and Wireless, Wireless Telephone, Radio Fan, Japan Radio, Wireless Research*, and *Daily Radio News*. Book publications included *The Wireless Telephone* (1922) and *Wireless Telephone (Anyone Can Understand It)* (1923). There was also a Wireless Telephone Exhibition in Ueno in 1924.[35]

But all of these promotional publications had to accept one unpleasant fact: radio research and transmission, even of the amateur variety, were banned by Japanese law, as was the manufacture of radio sets, even by large companies. This ban reflected the government's perception of electrical communications as essentially military technologies—vital for national defense and expansion but dangerous in the wrong hands. According to Amishima Tsuyoshi, the basic premise of the then-operative Wireless Communications Law was that "the people did not have the right to use the airwaves."[36]

The move to authorize radio broadcasting came in response to a flood of requests for broadcasting licenses beginning as early as 1921. Ministry of Communications bureaucrats began planning the launch of

Figure 2   An early poster advertising radio. (From *Nihon Hōsō Shi* [The History of Japanese Broadcasting], Japan Broadcasting Corporation Publishing)

radio in the following year, visiting the United States to observe its broadcasting practices firsthand. Obviously impressed by what they saw, the committee based its plan on the U.S. model. Radio stations would be privately owned, but they would derive their income from license fees rather than, as in the United States, from advertising.

However, as the implications of this plan sank in, politicians and bureaucrats reconsidered the question of private radio. Government planners recognized that radio offered unparalleled potential to influence opinion and behavior, and they became increasingly concerned at losing control over this powerful instrument. Minister of Communications

Adachi Kenzō commented that radio should be treated not as a private amenity but as "an affair of state."[37] Eventually, the government about-faced and restricted radio broadcasting to a government-owned network, Nihon Hōsō Kyōkai (NHK, or the Japan Broadcasting Company). Moreover, when radio broadcasting began in 1925, the Ministry of Communications opted to charge listeners a license fee of ¥1 per month—immediately putting radio out of reach of much of the population—rather than allow broadcasting to support itself through advertising.

Thus far, the arguments for restriction and control seemed to have the upper hand among government planners. The decision to create a state-owned network was by no means unprecedented. In spite of its venerable democratic tradition, for example, the British government had also opted for a government monopoly based on license fees out of concern that unleashing commercial radio would be "akin to introducing dog racing, smallpox, or the bubonic plague." But in Japan, Gregory Kasza argues, the decision for state ownership "helped smooth the way for military rule a decade later."[38] The fact that these decisions were made at the height of the period of "Taishō democracy" merely adds irony to the outcome. Indeed, party politicians actively intervened in opposition to private radio broadcasting.

However, the Ministry of Communications and NHK did take extraordinary measures to promote state-run radio. NHK created a radio network reaching most of the country, villages included. This was a vast undertaking. From 1926 to 1934 NHK spent some ¥10 million on developing the first stage of this network. The decision to adapt the network for reception by cheap crystal radio sets increased the cost, requiring NHK to build relay stations at closer intervals than would have been necessary for vacuum tube sets. Eventually, NHK built no fewer than fifty relay stations, ranging in power from 500 to 10,000 watts.[39]

Following the 1931 invasion of Manchuria, Japan's abrupt withdrawal from the League of Nations rallied the nation around an ideology of autonomy. Japan had no friends in the world, as the newspapers never stopped reminding their readers, and therefore must defend its own vital interests. Among these interests was the development of technology, particularly technologies of aggression and control. As it happened, another nation harbored similar feelings of isolation, and Japan increasingly came to look upon it as a model in its quest for autonomy: Nazi Germany. Even before their political takeover of the country, the Nazis had developed a sophisticated ideology that emphasized the use of technology to control and manipulate the population. Joseph

Goebbels, Hitler's minister for national enlightenment and propaganda, sought to exploit mass media of communication, particularly the newest and most alluring medium: radio. "What the press has been for the nineteenth century, radio will be for the twentieth," Goebbels claimed at the turn of the 1930s, adding: "I hold radio to be the most important instrument of mass influence that exists anywhere." Goebbels's use of the radio was based on the philosophy that "the mobilization of the mind is as necessary as, possibly even more important than, the material mobilization of the nation."[40]

The Nazi propaganda campaigns chillingly demonstrated the cynical uses to which the techniques of persuasion could be put. Adolf Hitler wrote in *Mein Kampf*: "Propaganda must be entirely for the masses. It should aim to be understood by the lowest intellectual level. The greater the number of the masses, the lower must the intellectual level become. The receptivity of the people is extremely limited, and their understanding is low; on the other hand, their forgetfulness is great."[41] As contemporary critics such as Theodor Adorno recognized, the same cynicism and techniques were also at work in the "free" nations of the world. Indeed, Edward Berneys, described as "a founder and a leader of modern commercial public relations," foreshadowed Hitler when, in 1928, he wrote of the future of public relations:

> If we understand the mechanism and motives of the group mind, it is now possible to control and regiment the masses according to our will without their knowing it.
>
> Mass psychology is as yet far from being an exact science and the mysteries of human motivation are by no means all revealed. But at least theory and practice have combined with sufficient success to permit us to know that in certain cases we can effect some change in public opinion by operating a certain mechanism.[42]

An advertising industry insider echoed this concept when he described advertising as the "science of unlocking the human mind."[43]

In 1934 the Nazi regime launched its highly effective "one household, one radio" campaign, providing incentives and promotion to ensure that every German family owned the hardware of the new medium of indoctrination. The government persuaded manufacturers to design and mass produce a "people's receiver" (*Volksempfänger*) priced at thirty-five Reichsmarks, making it the cheapest set available in Europe. Although the "people's receiver" had only a limited listening range, this was considered a benefit by the Nazis, who wanted to prevent Germans from tuning in to foreign broadcasts. The government subsidized both

Figure 3 A poster sponsored by the army, navy, home, and communications ministries. The caption reads: "All together for the defense of the nation: radio." (From *Nihon Hōsō Shi* [The History of Japanese Broadcasting], Japan Broadcasting Corporation Publishing)

the manufacture and purchase of receivers and encouraged communal radio listening as a way of converting "the anarchic intellectualism of the individual to the organically developed spirituality of the community." The government created a corps of "radio wardens" to marshal audiences for important speeches and rallies, putting up loudspeakers in public places and presiding over broadcast "national moments."[44]

By the end of the 1930s the Nazis had achieved 70 percent penetration of radio ownership and were turning their attention to television, aiming to launch an empirewide broadcasting service and put a television inside every German home. Unlike the U.S. and Japanese television development programs, the German effort was maintained throughout the war: regular broadcasts in French and German began in occupied Paris in June 1943 and continued until a week before the liberation.[45]

The Japanese government responded to the German initiative with enthusiasm. As Japan's involvement in overseas conflicts grew during the course of the 1930s, military and civilian planners increasingly recognized the mass media's importance in creating national support for the war effort through "the total mobilization of the people's spirit, as well as the arousal of domestic opinion and of correct thinking."[46] By the mid-1930s, the general economic prosperity had caused a substantial increase in urban radio ownership, which reached 35 percent in 1935. But in the countryside, which remained crucial to the government's ideological campaign, radio penetration remained at only 6 percent. After 1937 Japanese government ministries worked actively to increase radio ownership, culminating in the "one household, one radio" campaign of 1938, which was modeled specifically on the German initiative. Posters advertising the importance of radio to national defense appeared under the joint sponsorship of the army, navy, and communications and home ministries. Large numbers of lectures and public demonstrations were also held. License fees were reduced or, for the families of servicemen and other targeted groups, eliminated altogether.

Spreading radio ownership among rural households remained a challenge, mainly because of lack of disposable income. In 1933 the Agriculture Ministry estimated annual entertainment expenses of farm-owning families at ¥3.82. Thus, even after radio license fees were reduced to ¥0.5 per month in 1935, this remained a substantial burden for rural families—quite apart from the purchase of radio sets.[47] Another problem was the relative unavailability of electricity. Many villages only had power during the evening and were therefore unable to listen to radio during the daytime. Moreover, payment was based not on consumption of electricity but on the number of light bulbs in the home. Honest farmers therefore felt it was cheating to plug an additional appliance into the light socket. The government, together with radio manufacturers, attempted to circumvent these problems by rebating fees, promoting communal radio listening, and encouraging electrical utilities to promote radio listening.

Olympian Hopes

The government's supportive media policy—and the conflicts that constantly tugged at it—reached a new level of intensity with the decision to launch television broadcasting in Japan in time for the 1940 Tokyo Olympics. This extraordinary project illustrates just how deeply involved Japan's administrative leaders had become in the promotion of mass communications. It also helps explain the speed with which Japan's electronics industry recovered and advanced after the war.

Once again, Nazi Germany was the model. The 1936 Berlin Olympics were a public relations triumph for Hitler and a showcase for German communications technology. The events were broadcast on a closed-circuit television network to the Olympic village and the hotels where visiting VIPs were staying. When Japanese diplomats and athletes reported this to Tokyo, it became an important component in Japan's successful strategy to secure the 1940 Olympics.[48]

The Japanese Olympic committee felt confident in promising televised Games because the decade-long television research effort in Japan had recently borne fruit. Indeed, the Japanese government planned to launch a general television broadcasting service soon after the Tokyo Olympics. These plans were based in large part on the endeavors of one man. Takayanagi Kenjirō, today revered in Japan as the "father of television," was one of the nation's great electronics pioneers. By the time of his death in 1990 at the age of ninety-three, he had received Japan's highest civilian honor from the Emperor, and a permanent display of his exploits sat on view at the NHK Museum in Tokyo.

Takayanagi was a humble boy from the provinces. His father, a failed businessman who became the manager of a commercial fish pond, could not send him beyond elementary school, so Takayanagi resigned himself to a life of simple toil. Then he was taken up by a childless aunt and a school principal who happened to have seen his calligraphy (used for patching the shoji windows of the family's home). Thanks to these fortunate turns, Takayanagi managed to progress to middle school and technical college, finally landing a job as an instructor at Hamamatsu Technical High School. Even with this success, though, Takayanagi's status remained extremely modest. The school catered to teenagers, most of whom would go on to be electricians and technical operatives. Research was not a part of Takayanagi's job description.

Takayanagi had been obsessed with radio from an early age—ever since, he reminisced, a team from the Japanese navy had come to his elementary school classroom to demonstrate the medium's great success against the Russians. In his student days in Yokohama he accosted foreigners in the doorways of hotels, asking them questions about the latest developments in radio. One summer Takayanagi used a contact in the shipping industry to get himself hired as radio operator on a merchant ship crossing the Pacific to San Francisco. Once in California, he visited as many radio installations as he could, then went straight back to Japan.[49]

By 1924, the year Takayanagi started working as a teacher, radio technology was already well established. But Takayanagi already had his sights set on a more distant goal: adding the dimension of sight to the miracle of broadcasting. In a 1924 article he described this dream:

> My family gathers in front of a single machine. I adjust a knob, and we can suddenly hear celestial-sounding music. On the screen in front of our eyes, a gorgeous dance appears from the Imperial Theater. This beautiful drama has just begun. Oh! the actors' faces look absolutely real! I can even hear the rustle of the audience. The very drama that's unfolding in the Imperial Theater is playing here in our home in the mountains a hundred miles away, at the same time!
>
> I've been daydreaming without stopping. Oh, if we could only make a wireless with vision, by how much would our happiness increase! Once, we dreamed, "If only we could fly like birds." People worked towards that end, and today it's possible to fly all over the world. The dream of hearing people's voices from far away led to the telephone; and now we've progressed to the glory of modern culture, the wireless age. All of you on the sea! Now you can forget the loneliness of the ocean. When you're yearning for the far-off rising sun, or when you can't sleep for the sound of the waves, and find yourselves thinking about your far-away families, then the silent radio waves that travel through the air for ten thousand miles will tell you of the goings-on at home.
>
> All of you deep in the mountains, you light-house keepers on remote islands, you humble folk living in the countryside: there's no need for you to make the long trek to the city. The pleasures of the city will travel over the ether to visit you in your homes. Ah, radio waves, what a strange substance you are! ... [50]

Takayanagi succeeded in wringing a small research allowance from his school principal. When that money ran out, he claims, he spent his wife's dowry of ¥500. Working in almost total isolation, Takayanagi finally succeed in 1927, transmitting a single Japanese character from a camera in one room to a screen in another.

In order to follow developments in the West, Takayanagi had trained himself to read English, French, and German. But much of the research going on in Europe and the United States was not being reported in magazines; the stakes were too high. So Takayanagi remained cut off from the work of the two great American pioneers of television: Philo T. Farnsworth, the Utah farm boy, and Vladimir D. Zworykin, the sophisticated Russian who with the backing of the mighty RCA would eventually dominate the world television industry. Both of these men had developed not only electronic television screens—the breakthrough for which Takayanagi is remembered in Japan—but also electronic cameras, which Takayanagi was never able to develop on his own.

Still, Takayanagi's success attracted widespread attention and made him a hero in Japan. In 1928 his humble provincial school received a visit from a living god—the Emperor Hirohito. Takayanagi, who was using primitive cathode-ray tubes made especially for him by Tokyo Electric, had two oversized tubes made for the Emperor's visit. But one of them exploded, dramatically and out of the blue, while sitting on a shelf in Takayanagi's lab. He was terrified that the other tube would explode during the Emperor's visit, leading to extreme embarrassment at best and accusations of lèse majesté or attempted regicide at worst. In the end the tube behaved itself. The Emperor watched in complete silence as Takayanagi transmitted images of calligraphy reading, "Your reign will last for eight thousand generations" (the first line of the Japanese national anthem).

By 1936 Takayanagi Kenjirō was a respected researcher with a well-known program. So far he had worked largely in isolation from the government and other researchers. But the time had come for the individual pioneer to be pulled in for the benefit of the nation: Takayanagi was put in charge of the Olympic television project.

He faced a huge challenge. Where once he had struggled alone with only his intellect to guide him, he suddenly found himself in charge of a staff of two hundred engineers and a budget of millions of yen. Takayanagi the dreamer suddenly became Takayanagi the manager, with heavy responsibilities on his shoulders. At the outset of the project he developed working television receivers and cameras (the latter modeled on RCA's iconoscope camera). But his experimental systems had always been closed-circuit; he had never produced a wireless broadcast system. He also had to establish standards for suppliers, enlarge the receiver screens, select the site for and manage construction of a broadcast station, and design moving cameras to record live sports events.

The massive organization and dedication involved suggest the depth of the government's commitment to developing television. Indeed, it is one of the many paradoxes of the time that this quintessentially populist medium should have been the product of an ideology and organizational structure based on centralized authoritarianism. The paradox created deep tensions that ultimately destroyed the project. In July 1937, one year after Tokyo was selected as the next Olympic site, Japanese troops invaded China. What began as a rampage turned into a bitter war of attrition, absorbing more and more of Japan's resources and increasingly drawing the opprobrium of the West. By 1938, as Europe itself teetered on the brink of all-out war, it had become clear that the Tokyo Olympics would never take place. Even within Japan, the increasingly powerful military had little interest in diverting resources to sporting events. The army, which controlled steel supplies, refused to allocate the material for construction of the Olympic stadium. In July 1938, the Olympics were cancelled.

The Failure of "Techno-Nationalism": Japan's Development of Radar

The television project illustrated the government's conflicting efforts to promote and simultaneously to control the technologies of mass culture. It also points to another crucial trend of the prewar and wartime years: increasing technological nationalism. Rather than rely on foreign technology that might be cheaper and more reliable, bureaucrats during the 1930s advocated the development of domestic technologies and industries. Toward the end of the decade, the government actively closed off the avenues of foreign technological cooperation.

The "domestication of production" movement (*kokusanka undō*) encompassed political doctrines of autarchy (implying preparation for an all-out war), nationalistic assertions of native Japanese capabilities, a call for a unique Japanese industrial culture, and economic arguments about the hypocrisies and outright failures of the Western economic system. From the beginning of the 1930s, bureaucrats launched a series of assertive legislative and propaganda campaigns to promote domestic production. The Ministry of Commerce and Industry, for example, in 1932 designated sixty-five product categories for priority purchase from Japanese makers—even if quality was inferior. The *kokusanka* campaign also included songs, slogans ("By All Means *Kokusan!*"), poster campaigns, even a *kokusan* postage stamp series bearing the slogan: "Imports in Meiji, *Kokusan* in Shōwa."[51]

The *kokusanka* movement caused deep anxiety among members of the scientific community in the 1930s, indicating the soul-searching that accompanied Japan's departure into the unknown realm of great-power imperialism. Virtually all of the nation's greatest electrical scientists agreed that Japan was unready to pursue a path of technological independence. In particular, they pointed to Japan's very poor record in developing original inventions. A 1936 committee on domestication issues came to some deeply pessimistic conclusions about Japan's ability to go it alone. A committee member, Tōhoku University professor Watanabe Yasushi, commented:

> What is the condition of technology, which is the most important consideration for an independent manufacturing industry? As you all know, with one or two exceptions our technology still is far from the level of the leading Western countries. I don't think it's an exaggeration to say that hitherto almost all our major industries have been built through copying foreign technologies. Communications technology is by no means an exception. All the companies are using foreign patents, introducing foreign manufacturing technologies, and buying high quality materials from abroad.

The committee's report concluded:

> Japan's communications equipment industry is heavily dependent on foreign intellectual capital, even more than we had imagined. . . . For example, transmitting equipment and vacuum tubes have in the past ten years undergone rapid development, but in Japan there has been almost no progress, and we are now being sorely pressed by Europe and America. If we look at the condition of our country in this area from the point of view of patents, we are completely overwhelmed.[52]

The *kokusanka* policy was, however, irreversible, especially as Japan became entangled in military adventures that increasingly isolated it from the world's technological leaders.

The *kokusanka* movement must take its place among the many complex factors that contributed to Japan's catastrophic defeat in World War II. In the previous seventy years of economic development, Japan had benefited from open access to foreign technologies, which were for the most part readily reproducible. When government planners shut off this path, Japanese technology was cut off from an element as necessary as air. In retrospect, it is hard not to ask: Why did the government do this, when the status quo was so clearly beneficial? The expansionist bureaucrats' failure to recognize and accept the dependence of Japanese technology was surely one of the most harmful miscalculations on the road to war and, finally, defeat.

All-out war erupted in December 1941. The conflict provided a massive stimulus for the electrical goods industry. Later assertions by Japanese scientists that the war was a "blank space" in technology developments are ludicrous: Matsushita, Toshiba, Hitachi, and other manufacturers made unprecedented advances, and Japanese engineers gained experience that would prove invaluable in subsequent decades. Ultimately, though, Japan could not match the fearsome research prowess of the world's technological leaders, and this shortcoming was one of the prime causes of Japan's destruction. It was a bitter lesson for government leaders, but they learned it well. Despite their nationalistic tendencies, Japanese bureaucrats would never again force a policy of technological isolationism on Japanese industry.

Vacuum tubes represented the Achilles' heel of Japanese electronics technology. The country had been about even with world technological leaders at the turn of the century, but it failed to keep up with the rapid advances made by Western nations in vacuum tube-based applications. In 1939, when it merged with Shibaura Seisakujo to form Toshiba, Tokyo Denki was one of only two Japanese manufacturers of vacuum tubes (the other was Nippon Denki), and it depended heavily on General Electric. Worse, its exclusive ties had prevented other Japanese manufacturers from entering the field,[53] and the government's near-monopoly of applications further dampened competition. Consumer demand was limited to the simple vacuum tubes required for radios (and even this demand was minimal because most Japanese still used non-tube radios). As a result, by 1936 some 55 percent of total communications equipment demand came from the military.[54] New and more sophisticated products such as transmitting tubes and radar tubes remained the exclusive preserve of the government, primarily the military. Government control surely played a major part in Japan's failure to keep up with overseas advances in tube technologies, which often were stimulated by the prospect of large consumer markets. The case of television tubes exemplified the disadvantages of Japan's protective strategy: Takayanagi Kenjirō had to rely for his experimental television tubes on Tokyo Denki, which took six months to produce a part that RCA could make for Vladimir Zworykin in a week.[55]

This same weakness served as the greatest stumbling block in Japan's efforts to develop sophisticated radar applications. World War II included a crucial battle over radar, albeit one that took place in the musty silence of research laboratories. Japan's failure to match Allied advances in radar technology contributed directly to its defeat and revealed the fundamental weakness of Japan's prewar policy toward technology development: the chaining of research and innovation to the cause of national defense.

The Japanese military first heard of the existence of radar from a Nisei spy, who in 1935 reported that the United States had developed a device that could detect aircraft tens of miles away. The report added that the U.S. military planned to try to sell this technology to Japan—a detail that destroyed the credibility of the whole document. But reports of the existence of radar continued to filter in to army and navy researchers. In 1938, Nippon Denki's Kobayashi Kōji visited England to review progress in television. While watching a demonstration, Kobayashi was surprised to see the screen flicker and go blank when an airplane flew overhead. Later in the year, while testing mobile television receivers in a truck near Tokyo (as part of the Olympics project), he again noticed strong interference from planes. Kobayashi had close ties with the army's Scientific Research Center and passed on his findings to it; Nippon Denki and the army eventually collaborated to produce an aircraft detector using this interference principle. Because of the noise that it generated when it encountered aircraft interference, it was known as the "barking" (*wan-wan*) detector. The device was immediately put into service on Chinese battlefields.[56]

The Japanese army and navy were well known for their secrecy and mutual suspicion. Because of this, and because the military leadership at first did not appreciate the importance of radar, development occurred in piecemeal fashion. It is probably impossible to inventory all of the separate radar-related efforts scattered throughout the research facilities of the army, navy, and private corporations. But by the latter half of the Pacific War, virtually the entire electronics community was working flat-out on radar.

With the declaration of war and the breaking of Tokyo Denki's ties with General Electric, the military forced the company (now called Toshiba) to share its vacuum tube technologies with rival companies, including Hitachi, Nippon Denki, Nihon Musen, Matsushita, and Kōbe Kōgyō. Intensive research on vacuum tube technologies also took place in the main military research institutes, particularly the navy's Gijutsu Kenkyūjo (Technical Laboratory, Giken). The proliferation of research led to rapid new developments. In 1939, Giken enlisted the help of Nihon Musen, an independent manufacturer, to help develop magnetrons (the vacuum tube used in advanced microwave radar). Giken transferred its own technology to Nihon Musen, which formed a large team that by the end of the year had developed a 500-watt magnetron tube. Similar top-secret work in Britain, the most advanced country in radar research at the time, produced a 20,000-watt magnetron.

In retrospect, it is easy to see that the Giken/Nihon Musen effort was on the right track. Although too weak and fragile for any practical applications, the magnetron developed by Nihon Musen could have led to the early introduction of microwave radar. But naval leaders suspended Giken's research in 1940. One reason was their failure to see the significance of radar as a weapon of modern warfare—naval leaders have been much criticized for their unshakable faith in battleship size and firepower—but another was Japan's increasing military ties with Germany, from whom national authorities expected to receive a transfer of radar technology.

The Japanese military leadership had good reason to respect German radar technology. In 1940, Germany's newly developed Würtzburg radar was probably the world's most advanced practical application. Based on the pioneering work of Dresden University's professor Heinrich Barkhausen, it was used effectively in the European theater of operations. The Würtzburg, which used a long-wave signal, ultimately proved ineffective compared to the microwave versions introduced by the Allies, but as of 1940 it was the best available. Although this technology was shrouded in secrecy, the Japanese knew of it through their contacts with Barkhausen and the German military.

In mid-1941, a large group of Japanese naval officers under Admiral Nomura Kichisaburō visited Germany to study military technology and the progress of the war. The observers included Itō Yōji, Giken's leading electronics expert. The journey to Europe at the height of Germany's European offensive was the stuff of B-grade war films. The group traveled to Europe on a Japanese warship. They were prepared to pass all the way around Cape Horn, as the United States reportedly had closed the Panama Canal to armed vessels, but at the entrance to the channel Admiral Nomura presented himself in full military pomp to U.S. authorities and invited them to a lavish dinner on board. This proved an effective strategy. The Japanese received a full tour of the U.S. base and an airplane ride over the isthmus before being sent on their way through the canal. They proceeded across the Atlantic to Lisbon, whence they flew to Berlin.[57]

In Germany, the team spent two months attending lectures and demonstrations of German technology, then toured the battlefields of northern France, scenes of dramatic German victories. It was while at the German naval base in the Bay of Biscay that Itō first observed the top-secret Würtzburg radar. Although official requests for the precious technology were politely declined—Goering himself explained that not even Italy would receive it—the Japanese group returned home laden with plans and designs for other radar technologies, as well as battleships, submarines, aircraft, torpedoes, explosives, machine tools, and synthetic rubber.[58]

This promising beginning was followed by further concrete results. In early 1942, in a bizarre parallel with Perry's first gesture to the Japanese government, Adolf Hitler himself offered a Würtzburg radar system with accompanying documentation as a "personal gift" to the Emperor. The Japanese sent a brand-new submarine to Europe to pick up the highly prized cargo. The vessel arrived in the Bay of Biscay in early August 1942, after a journey of more than two months. The Germans equipped it with their latest soundproofing technologies and sent it on its long and hazardous journey home. The sub negotiated the North Atlantic, Indian Ocean, and South China Sea and proceeded safely to Singapore, but as it departed on the final leg of its journey, disaster struck: just outside the harbor area, the submarine ran directly into a British mine and sank within minutes. All but thirteen of the crew managed to escape, but the Würtzburg radar went to the bottom.[59]

A German U-boat delivered a working Würtzburg radar to Japanese shores in December 1943, but by this time Allied microwave equipment had surpassed the Nazi system. It was too late to help Japan's war effort.

By the end of 1942 all of the combatant nations recognized that the future of radar lay in the microwave. Although long-wave radars such as the Würtzburg were adequate for anti-aircraft detection, microwaves expanded the capabilities of radar to include bomb sighting, fire guidance, zero-visibility aircraft guidance, landing guidance, anti-submarine detection, ship-to-ship detection, and air-to-surface detection. The decisive lead in this area lay with the Allies; German and Japanese leaders reached the same conclusion by different routes. The Germans shot down a British bomber in February 1943 and confirmed that the plane had microwave radar installed for bomb sighting. The Japanese, meanwhile, suffered heavy losses at the Battle of the Solomon Islands (in August 1942) and in subsequent engagements largely because of the Allies' superior detection and fire-guidance techniques.

Germany had little to teach Japan in this field. Both countries began intensive work on microwave radar from the beginning of 1943. The Germans succeeded in developing a microwave radar in 1944, too late to affect the outcome of the war. For its part, Japan rapidly developed a new microwave radar, the "trumpet" radar, using a bulbous magnetron tube. However, a combination of design and production problems prevented it from playing a major part in the war effort.

The trumpet went into mass production as soon as its design was approved in mid-1943. A consortium of companies including Hitachi, Nihon Victor, and Toshiba divided up the manufacturing process and succeeded in making 150 sets a month. However, their quality was uneven at best. By mid-1943 the Allies had tightened their stranglehold on the Pacific, reducing Japan's access to raw materials, particularly for tubes, which required relatively exotic ingredients including nickel. Makers increasingly resorted to substitutes (such as iron instead of nickel), with obvious consequences for quality. At one time, word got out that Hong Kong coins contained high-quality nickel. A run on the Hong Kong currency market immediately ensued.[60]

Even major manufacturers experienced terrible parts shortages. In extreme cases, only one or two out of a hundred tubes would pass rigorous testing, and lifetimes were often no longer than one hundred hours. According to Takayanagi, Japan's weakening industrial infrastructure severely limited production: "No matter what ideas the researchers came up with, the abilities of the factories we depended on to make actual machines were declining. . . . By the last stage of the war, even if there was a budget, there were no factories to make the machines, and even if there were factories, their level of technology and skills was low and they weren't able to make usable products."[61]

Nor were parts shortages and plant inadequacies the only problems. The design of the navy's microwave radar failed to account for combat conditions. In particular, the jutting trumpet tubes were difficult to align and sensitive to jarring—something that could hardly be avoided in the heat of a naval battle.

In the end, Japanese radar proved inadequate to the demands of high-technology warfare. The trumpet radar was the last generation to be put into widespread operation; although work continued on more advanced designs, they remained on the drawing board at the end of the war. In the meantime, American B-29 bombers equipped with the latest rotating parabolic equipment launched devastatingly destructive attacks on the Japanese mainland, culminating in the atomic destruction of Hiroshima and Nagasaki.

Takayanagi's television research program, which grew steadily during the 1920s and 1930s, became smaller and smaller during the war years and eventually was disbanded altogether. Nevertheless, Taka-yanagi enjoyed special status as the senior television researcher in Japan. The war did afford sufficient research opportunities, some of them closely related to television, and his military research budgets continued to increase exponentially. His was a typical experience among Japan's prewar idealists: their dreams were often realized, and indeed they enjoyed opportunities beyond their imagining; but the circumstances left a bitter aftertaste, particularly in the dark shadow of defeat.

The Paradoxes of War

The war experience in many ways reversed the 1920s trend toward the emergence of a mass consumer society. Resource shortages severely curtailed consumption and progressively choked off the manufacture of goods. By 1944, with almost nothing left to consume, savings represented 44 percent of household income.[62] The Westernized mass culture seemed to have been forced back into its chrysalis by the exigencies of total war. But some of the trends toward massification continued unabated or even were intensified by the government's campaign for total mobilization. Newspaper circulation, for example, continued to rocket upward, and radio ownership continued to rise until by the end of the war 62 percent of urban and 39 percent of rural households owned radio sets. While popular sports such as baseball were discouraged as too Western, sumo continued to flourish, and the populace was, of course, treated to the great (though heavily controlled) spectacle of modern warfare. The white-collar segment of the population also grew substantially during this period, despite the conscription of large parts of the male population.[63]

Nor did the ideal of the Western housewife retreat significantly during the war; on the contrary, it gained strength. In both Nazi Germany and Japan, ideologies of racial purity and expansion prompted the passage of eugenics laws that placed mothering and nurturing ahead of laboring. The Japanese Welfare Ministry in 1940 announced a goal of increasing Japan's population from 73 million to 100 million within twenty years, and accordingly it adopted measures to keep women out of the workplace (although these measures eventually fell victim to the wartime labor shortage). The widespread departure of men into the military left women as effective family heads, further increasing female domestic autonomy and influence. In spite of official ideology promoting the traditional Japanese family structure, the everyday lives of women in Japan continued to converge with those of Western women.[64]

For Matsushita Kōnosuke, the growing international confrontation paradoxically helped him realize his prewar dreams. Beginning in the mid-1930s, Matsushita increasingly moved in the military's orbit. The army and navy had insatiable appetites for electrical equipment, sweeping up radios, lamps, batteries, and vacuum tubes until there was nothing left for ordinary people. As Japan became embroiled in conflict with China and then all-out war with the West, Matsushita Electric fell under the direct control of the armed forces. The military had Matsushita building new factories as fast as he could. His product line expanded continually, from electrical equipment into munitions, ships, and, finally, aircraft. His shipping company aimed to manufacture one wooden ship per day using assembly-line techniques learned in electrical goods manufacturing. Matsushita personally invested a huge fortune in these new ventures, and although he would lose almost every penny, his wartime activities had given his company a massive boost in scale, to the point where it was virtually guaranteed a share in the immense spoils to come—the spoils of defeat.

CONCLUSION

Japan's postwar electrical goods makers take great pride in pointing to their industry's dramatic growth since the turn of the 1950s—a rise made all the more stark by its apparent origin in the ashes of Japan's catastrophic defeat in World War II. Engineers and researchers universally refer to the years of war as a "blank space" (*kūhaku*)—an image that further adds to the impressiveness of the recovery. But a closer look shows that the Japanese electrical goods industry hardly stood still before and during the war. Indeed, important continuities extend throughout Japan's modern history.

Through the nineteenth and early twentieth centuries, the single most powerful motive propelling Japan's technology development was the nation's urge to achieve military parity with the West. In the second half of the nineteenth century, Japan was one of only a handful of nations in Asia that evaded colonial subjugation; as the nation's leaders saw it, Japan's very survival was at stake. Thus, the purpose of industrial development was neither economic growth per se nor the enrichment of the Japanese people. Rather, the driver of change in nineteenth-century Japan was national defense and national expansion. It is no coincidence that the most quoted slogan of the era—"rich nation, strong military"—explicitly linked economic development with martial prowess.

This defense-oriented imperative led to government policies designed to facilitate the development of electrical technologies. Government support enabled Japanese engineers to replicate the latest international breakthroughs quickly. In addition, many of the basic infrastructural requirements for postwar development—including an advanced educational system and top-rank research institutions—were established as a result of the emphasis on defense. The result of these policies was a history of extremely rapid industrial growth that rivaled even the peak years of postwar growth (see Table 1, p. 243).

But the nationalistic underpinnings of Japanese technology coexisted with another enduring and vitally important trend, that of increasing popular consumption. Japanese society during the early twentieth century took on some of the basic contours of a mass society. These developments were exploited during the war years by nationalistic bureaucrats emulating the Nazi faith in technology-based mass control. But they were also to provide the basic outline for the efflorescence of mass culture in democratic postwar Japan.

A final theme, though, is one of discontinuity. From the 1930s until the end of World War II, the Japanese government chained technological development to defense policy, ensuring that electrical technologies remained weapons of national defense above all. This strategy proved to be disastrous, both industrially and militarily. Bound to the service of national expansion, Japanese technology in the first half of the twentieth century failed to keep pace with that of the West, a fact that helped decide the outcome of the war. After Japan's defeat, the government never again cut Japanese firms off from the inflow of foreign technological advance.

2

Reenvisioning Japan

Mark Gayn, a veteran U.S. journalist, arrived in Tokyo in December 1945. In his diary, he described his initial impressions of the devastated city:

> At night, driving past General MacArthur's headquarters, I saw a huge Merry Christmas sign go ablaze with a thousand lights. The sign cast light over the outer wall of the Imperial Palace, and was reflected in the rippling water of the wide moat. I thought of the symbolism inherent in this American light thrown on the darkest Japanese institution; on the debris piled up like monuments in lots which once contained the heart of the Japanese financial empire; on the steady procession of US army jeeps and trucks; and on the shivering Japanese girls soliciting GI custom at the entrance to Hibiya Park, "Very good, Joe, very cheap."[1]

The firebombings of March to July 1945 had changed the landscape of Tokyo almost beyond recognition. Again, Mark Gayn describes his impressions:

> I thought of this great city, which today contains little but rubble and an obstinate will to live, of a city which I can travel for ten and twenty and thirty blocks at a time and see nothing but shattered brick, a few chimneys, and a score or two of abandoned safes that had crashed down through the floors of burning buildings. The men and women who had once made Tokyo the world's third largest city have now gone into the country side, or moved into the few surviving buildings, three and four families to a room. And countless thousands have built shacks from rusty sheets of iron, or moved into the railway and subway stations. In the morning, one can see smoke rising from

what looks like a pile of junk and iron, but in reality is a home. Men still go to work in unbelievably crowded offices, and huddle close to the small warmth given out by a charcoal brazier.[2]

It is perhaps ironic to talk of a new energy and vitality being born amid the misery of abject defeat. Yet that was the case in Japan. The vanquished nation confronted grim realities in the late 1940s but also brought forth powerful aspirations. For some, indeed, it was a time of magnificent opportunity, a time in which anything came to seem possible.

Everyone had a different agenda for reshaping the environment. For the Allied (mainly American) victors, the Occupation offered an unprecedented opportunity for social reengineering: Japan was to be remolded into something more closely resembling the United States. For entrepreneurs Japan's defeat presented boundless possibilities, as long-entrenched interests crumbled or were pulled down. Those established business leaders who survived began strategizing about how to succeed in the new era, whereas government administrators engaged in a process of reflection: what had gone wrong with the management of Japan? How could some lessons be salvaged from the wreckage? For ordinary people, the postwar period was a time of longing: the magnificent prosperity of the victors was a mirage to feed their imaginations.

Indeed, the quest for American material wealth lay at the heart of the aspirations of Japanese businessmen, politicians, and ordinary people. The United States represented both a dream and a vision: a dream because it lay so far from Japan's reality, but a vision of what, with hard work and a basic reordering of lifestyles, Japan might someday become. What keys would open the door to this prosperity? Jazz music and Hollywood movies? Efficiency and rationality? Science and technology? Democracy? All of these themes were floating in the dust-filled atmosphere of postwar society, amid the hunger, power outages, penny-pinching, and crowding.

By the turn of the 1950s, many diverse groups had embraced a common vision of their, and Japan's, future. This vision would guide them through the coming decade. It had as its point of reference the unprecedented success and prosperity of the United States. It was a vision of how to bring that prosperity to Japan.

BEARING THE UNBEARABLE: DAILY LIFE IN OCCUPIED JAPAN

The early days following Japan's defeat were marked by infinite grimness. The harsh toll of war was compounded by the chaos of repatriation and the vindictive policies of the victorious Allied command. Chaos and suffering reigned. In his surrender speech, the Emperor commented that Japan must "endure the unendurable and suffer the insufferable."[3] The typical urban Japanese family was now finding out just what he meant.

The indiscriminate bombings of Tokyo, including a devastating attack on March 10, 1945, had destroyed between 30 and 40 percent of the city's housing stock. Despite the evacuation of more than half the population (as well as the deaths of more than 100,000 people in the bombings), the return of Tokyoites after the war caused a severe housing shortage. In 1946 an estimated 310,000 people occupied makeshift dwellings, often made from a few boards rescued from the rubble of the bombings.[4] Thousands of people lived in underground passages and subway stations. In the cold snap over the New Year's holidays at the beginning of 1947, eleven people died of exposure in Ueno station alone.[5] A February 1948 article in the *Asahi* newspaper reported on the large numbers of civil servants living full-time in their government offices. The Communications Ministry, for example, had 170 permanent residents, earning it the sobriquet "Communications Apartments."[6] Though the government made efforts to provide emergency housing, the situation grew worse, not better. The population of Tokyo doubled between 1945 and 1949, and no amount of troubleshooting could create sufficient housing for the returnees and newcomers.

Food, clothing, blankets, matches, and small luxuries such as tobacco were in desperately short supply. Most serious of all was the shortage of rice. Poor weather and lack of fertilizer limited the 1945 rice harvest to a disastrous 39 million *koku* (200 million bushels), a 35 percent decline from the previous year. In the winter of 1945–46, official rations provided 1,233 calories per day—only 54 percent of an adult's estimated requirements. In an interview on October 15 with United Press International, Minister of Finance Shibusawa Keizō predicted that if conditions remained the same, 10 million people would die of starvation and related diseases.[7] Perhaps he was merely trying to attract sympathy overseas, but his terrifying prediction seemed credible as it circulated in Japan. Two weeks later a professor at Tokyo High School (later amalgamated with Tokyo University) died of malnutrition. His death received widespread publicity.

Even with the provision of American food aid, the sense of crisis did not go away. In a celebrated incident, Tokyo district court judge Yamaguchi Ryōchū died in October 1947 of starvation after refusing to buy black-market food. The thirty-four-year-old judge's court dealt with economic crimes, most of them black market–related.[8] A year later, the government's first economic white paper spoke of the "three deficits": government, business, and families were all in the red.

Nakamura Takafusa has commented that amid this enormous economic dislocation there was remarkably little unemployment. His explanation is simple: to be unemployed was to starve.[9] In part for this reason, a curious vitality pervaded the early postwar period. Street markets immediately appeared all over Japan. In Tokyo they sprang up like mushrooms after a rainstorm, giving a curiously carnival-like atmosphere to the stricken city. A cluster of stalls might appear anywhere—a major street, the arches of an elevated railway line, a bombed-out plaza—offering a mind-stretching variety of goods. In Ikebukuro, peddlers sold footwear made from an eclectic range of materials. Those in search of durability could find traditional-style *geta* clogs made from recycled duraluminum—the material used for making aircraft bodies. At the other end of the spectrum, unscrupulous cobblers compensated for a shortage of leather by using dried squid to mend worn soles; the result was indistinguishable from the real thing until the owner went walking in the rain. Similar warnings were in order for those in search of caps: smart black hats that wilted in the rain turned out to be made of seaweed.[10]

In the stately Ginza, home to Japan's best-established merchants, vendors squatting by straw mats were now selling cheap toys as souvenirs for U.S. servicemen: views of Mount Fuji, windup dolls, postcards, silk handkerchiefs, decorated fountain pens. The prices were high and the quality atrocious, but, as Mark Gayn comments, the servicemen bought them anyway: "What the hell, it ain't money: it's only yen!"[11] Military personnel were probably more interested in the trade that flourished a few blocks away in the Yūrakuchō district, where for a few dollars women offered a service that with dismal appropriateness was known as *pan-pan*. The Sūkiya Bridge connecting the Ginza to Yūrakuchō was crowded with young women, earning it the nickname "*Pan-pan* Bridge." Under the railway tracks in Yūrakuchō, women drank their earnings in the form of a home-brewed liquor known as *kasutori*. When an NHK journalist went to interview the women in April 1947, he was besieged with propositions. An August 1946 article in the *Tokyo Nichinichi* on the hopeless life of a prostitute inspired the hit song "Wish Upon a Falling Star" (*Hoshi No Nagare Ni*).[12]

Alongside the street life of the markets there appeared another manifestation of postwar vitality: protest marches, demonstrations, and

May Day confrontations. The end of the war brought an immediate up-surge in left-wing activities, initially with the encouragement of the Occupation authorities. One of the Occupation's first orders, in October 1945, freed the three thousand political prisoners in Japanese jails (tragically, the order came too late to save the life of philosopher Miki Kiyoshi, who died in prison on September 26, 1945).[13] Shortly thereafter, Communist leader Nosaka Sanzō returned to Japan from exile in Moscow and immediately set about organizing political activities. Additionally, much labor activity came directly at the suggestion of the Occupation, which enthusiastically helped organize unions in newspapers, public organizations, and the movie industry. So readily did the Japanese people get the message that 150 fourth-year students at Ueno Women's High School went on strike in October 1945, protesting that the teachers were keeping all the produce of the school's garden.[14]

By coincidence, one remnant of this *après-guerre* vitality is the electronics market in Akihabara, which the Occupation moved to its current location from the streets of nearby Kanda. At the end of the war a relatively high percentage of Japanese owned radios, almost none of which worked. Their quality had not been good in the first place, and as the war dragged on all essential supplies were diverted to military use. Vacuum tubes, which required nickel (a scarce commodity), were especially hard to find. Despite official U.S. support for the revival of the radio industry, it was virtually impossible to make new radios because of shortages of parts and money. The Japanese radio industry literally disintegrated, its fragments on display in the street-market stalls.

These stalls were manned by returning radio operators from the military, graduates of Japan's elite electrical engineering schools, fired workers from big companies such as Toshiba and Hitachi, and anyone else who had access to precious radio parts. Most of those supplies came from military stockpiles. Within a year or two after the war ended, huge warehouses full of military supplies quietly evaporated into the underground economy.

The ultimate merchandise, American radio equipment, began to appear soon after the Occupation forces arrived in Tokyo. Most of the parts came from dismantled military equipment supplied by U.S. soldiers and the quartermasters responsible for managing military supplies. There was, of course, a strict ban on the sale of U.S. military equipment—even obsolete or surplus equipment, which had to be melted down or sliced up and sold as scrap. But it was possible to slice appliances up in such a way that their parts were still usable. In some cases, the officers enforcing the ban themselves made nocturnal visits to Kanda to unload trucks full of equipment. The authorities occasionally conducted investigations of these illicit activities, but there was something desultory about their efforts—amid the enormous corruption of the early postwar years, stolen radios constituted a minor issue.[15]

The street market catered to every radio need. Even major electronics companies scoured the stalls for the essential supplies they needed to revive their businesses. The crowded stalls were vibrant, alive against the backdrop of a ruined city. It is still possible to conjure up an echo of the restless energy of that time. In one of the many contradictions accompanying Japan's meteoric economic rise, the Akihabara market survives even when other market areas have been plowed up and replaced by giant department stores and office complexes. This small district at the intersection of two elevated railway lines remains today a chaotic jumble of small shops and stalls selling the very latest electronic gadgetry.

In spite of their many hardships, the late 1940s were in some ways years of inspiring optimism. The one thing that seemed certain was that Japan would change, and many Japanese looked forward to reforms that would bring about a more just, equitable, and prosperous society. During the course of the Occupation, U.S. administrators, aspiring entrepreneurs, chastened bureaucrats, established business leaders, and ordinary people formed new visions of Japan's postwar future. Most of these constituents were concerned first and foremost with their own self interest, but the actions they took in pursuit of their diverse goals would have profound consequences for Japan's social and industrial development.

THE "ELECTRICAL OK WORLD":
ORDINARY PEOPLE AND THEIR ELECTRIC DREAMS

The postwar aspirations of ordinary Japanese people are the hardest to pin down, both because of their diversity and because of the selective traces they have left. But clearly, for urban Japanese in particular, the affluence of American popular culture provided a striking contrast to the gloom of the postwar years. It is not surprising that the Japanese adopted many of its trappings as rapidly as possible.

This readiness to embrace American customs resulted in part from the long-running dialogue between Japanese people and foreign popular cultures. This exchange extended back to the Taishō period, with its jazz and "modern girls," and before. During the war, foreign amusements were increasingly controlled or—as in the case of jazz—suppressed outright. The flood of Americanization that followed defeat may be attributed to a combination of pent-up desires, new aspirations, and the wish to accommodate the new rulers—who actively encouraged the trend. The first out-and-out bestseller after the end of the war was *Nichibei Kaiwa Techō* (Japanese-American Conversation Handbook), released on October 3, 1945, and running within a year to 3.6 million copies.[16] When *Spring Overture,* the first American movie to appear in Japan since before the war, debuted on February 28, 1946, the lines stretched around the block—despite an entry fee three times that of Japanese films. During the next year John Wayne's *Gun Town,* Humphrey Bogart's *Casablanca,* and Bing Crosby's *Going My Way* all captured fervent audiences.

Jazz music and dancing were adopted with amazing rapidity and sophistication, thanks in part to seedy clubs catering to U.S. servicemen, bar girls, and prostitutes. Jazz also filled the airwaves on FEN, the U.S. military's radio station, which began broadcasting in September 1945. NHK launched its first jazz program, *Nyū Pashifuikku Awaa* (New Pacific Hour), in December. Its lead player was Matsumoto Nobu, a tenor saxophonist who had performed during the war in propaganda programs aimed at the Americans.[17] Dance halls and clubs soon proliferated in the cities, swinging in the fall of 1947 to the vibrant rhythm of the season's hit, "Tokyo Boogie-Woogie."[18]

Radio programming played its own part in altering the vision of the Japanese people. The popular "News from America" show tended to focus on the extraordinary affluence of Americans, one of the most visible symbols of which was electrical technology. An episode called "The Electrical OK World," for example, reported on the lifestyle of a typical middle-class family:

> The husband wakes up to the electric alarm clock, and shaves with an electric safety razor. There are sockets for these in steam trains and in college dorms. For breakfast he starts with orange juice, then vegetable juice such as celery and carrots, which are easily squeezed using an electric mixer. He spreads butter on his toast, which is done to a turn: the electric toaster automatically flips it up when it's done just right. He listens to the news and weather forecast on the radio while he drinks coffee, and then he goes to work. His wife then does the dishes, washing, and cleaning all at once. She puts sheets, towels, shirts, children's clothes, handkerchiefs etc. into the washing machine in a corner of the kitchen, adds soap, and flicks the switch.

.... Meantime she does the cleaning in a trice with an electric vacuum cleaner. When you beat the furniture with a stick and then sweep fine dust up into the air with a broom, your body suffers; but a vacuum cleaner cleanly sucks the dust and dirt inside, picking it up perfectly from thin curtains and thick carpets.[19]

American affluence was a revelation to the Japanese, and the press constantly played up its significance. Of course, anyone with eyes could see it in the shape of well-fed servicemen handing out chewing gum and money to clamoring Japanese children. It also lurked in the background of any reflections on the miserable state of Japan, which had dared to strike at this Goliath. The United States seemed to be a paragon of efficiency, productivity, good living, and happiness, a place where even the unemployed had flush toilets; where used cars still gleamed like new; where humble factory workers earned as much as a Japanese company president. The pilots who had flown bombing raids over Japan were said to have slept under electric blankets even as the bombs fell. Where did this magical prosperity come from?

SUPPORT FOR A NEW LIFE: AMERICAN PLANS FOR A NEW JAPAN

More Like Us

American leaders' vision for the future of Japan is most commonly associated with the program of democratization. U.S. policy at the highest level—that of statecraft and cold war politics—has been analyzed as a liberal democratization initiative that underwent substantial revision with the notorious "reverse course" of 1947.[20] To create a more democratic society, the Occupation wrote a new constitution and introduced a massive land reform that virtually eliminated the landlord class. The authorization and encouragement of trade unions also prompted sweeping changes in the structure of the workplace. After the "reverse course," the Occupation backpedaled on some of these reforms. Critics have argued that the U.S. government's vision for Japan at the end of the 1940s was ominously similar to that of the Japanese government in the mid-1930s, near the height of Japan's period of isolation.[21] The U.S. government clearly regretted the famous "peace clause" of the constitution, and support for militant unionism was abruptly withdrawn. At the highest levels, then, the United States compromised its vision of Japanese democracy out of political pragmatism.

However, for every great reform undertaken at the top, there were a dozen lower-level initiatives, many of which remained unaffected by the shifting policies of high statecraft. Many of these initiatives could be related as least somewhat to democratic principles. But they can better be understood as efforts to improve the daily lives of Japanese people and to make the Japanese "more like us." Some of these initiatives directly affected the electrical goods industry.

In the name of democratization, the Civil Information and Education (CIE) section issued directives banning movies that featured sword fights, revenge themes (the famed story of the forty-seven *ronin* was temporarily banished from the kabuki stage), arranged marriages, or images of Mount Fuji—all of which were seen as promoting feudal values. By contrast, kissing, which wartime authorities had banned from films, was now rehabilitated as a healthy democratic activity.[22]

The Occupation also unleashed on the Japanese public a varied array of "movements" designed to promote democratization. These produced varied and often unexpected effects. For example, the 4-H Club movement spread rapidly and, apparently, spontaneously throughout rural Japan, as former members of the now-banned Youth Associations sought new and officially sanctioned methods of association. The Occupation's Natural Resource Services bureau (NRS) put out pamphlets on the principles of 4-H, an American rural movement that today is associated more with horseback riding and country clubs than with an earnest peasantry. The NRS translated the movement's manuals into Japanese and brought American volunteers to travel around Japan to lecture on the philosophy of 4-H.

Another NRS-inspired initiative was the agricultural extension movement, a government-financed program whose "lifestyle improvement officers" traveled from hamlet to hamlet on distinctive green bicycles and lectured rural wives on nutrition, kitchen remodeling, "rationalization" of work clothes, and the benefits of goat husbandry. The NRS also acted to spread American-style "community recreation," including folk dances complete with clapping hands and banjos.[23]

Less directly concerned with democratization but perhaps more effective in spreading American values were a wide range of public health initiatives sponsored by the Occupation. These included the introduction, promotion, and mass production of penicillin; the fumigation of Tokyo with DDT; and the introduction of school lunches, which beginning in January 1947 offered milk, jam, macaroni, and unlabelled American ration tins (which guaranteed each child a surprise with every meal). These and other measures caused a dramatic improvement in the health of the Japanese people, resulting in a sudden and unprecedented decline in sickness and concomitant increase in life expectancy. Whether these measures made any contribution at all to the democratization of the country is highly debatable. But they did help prepare Japan for the arrival of an American-style mass consumption economy—although often not in the way the occupiers intended.

Until near the end of the Occupation, U.S. policies were not specifically concerned with bringing prosperity to Japan or with reproducing U.S. economic successes in Japan. Of much more concern to Occupation officials were how to control Japan and how to deliver on the Potsdam promise to democratize the nation. But as the contours of the new world order began to harden at the end of the 1940s, the issue of restoring Japan to prosperity gradually took its place among official U.S. policy objectives.

Supporting Technology

U.S. leaders early on recognized the importance of technology to Japan's potential for industrial recovery, and they initially took vindictive steps to cripple Japanese technology. According to the policy released by Occupation authorities on September 22, 1945, Japanese scientists were required to make monthly reports to relevant Occupation sections. On November 18 aircraft research was formally banned. On December 24 the ban was extended to television, radar, pulse communications, electronics-related appliances, and secret audio devices. In one of the most vindictive acts of the Occupation, U.S. soldiers seized and dismantled all five experimental cyclotron reactors in Japan, eventually sinking them in the Pacific Ocean.[24]

This retributive policy soon reached into the heart of the electrical goods industry. Many of the industry's leading figures were purged from office. Matsushita Electric was designated a *zaibatsu* (family-owned conglomerate), its activities virtually suspended, and its founder's assets frozen. Others were less fortunate still: Ōkōchi Minoru, founder of the high-tech Riken group, was arrested as a suspected war criminal.

But the realities of the Occupation worked against this vindictive stance. Almost from the beginning, Occupation administrators showed steadfast support for the development of Japanese technology, in part out of practical considerations: they needed a certain level of technological capability in order to implement their programs and control the nation. The good will of influential individuals also played a role. Over time, support for technology became an increasingly integral part of official U.S. policy in Japan.

The Occupation almost immediately showed interest in reviving the domestic radio industry. Commenting on the importance of radio, a Civil Communications Section memo stated:

> The fact is that broadcasting is being relied on for a major part of SCAP's [Supreme Commander, Allied Powers] information program. Enormous importance is attached to the present election broadcasts, popularization of the constitution and local government reforms, information on the purge, civil liberties, changes in the family system, civil service reforms, political parties, court reorganization, government reorganization—to mention only a few of the current and projected series of broadcasts. In many instances radio is being called upon for services no other information medium is equipped to perform. The elections have provided a good example of this.[25]

One of the Occupation's earliest initiatives was a plan to increase radio production, with the goal of placing radios in at least 50 percent of Japanese households.[26] The Occupation required the Japanese government to "assist each company in every way possible on matters of material, labor, fuel, food, transportation and machinery."[27] The Occupation also took direct steps to increase and improve vacuum tube and radio production. For example, the Economic and Scientific Section (ESS) arranged for the direct air shipment from the United States of parts needed for Toshiba's production machinery.[28] Moreover, beginning in early 1948 the Americans provided technology needed to upgrade Japanese radio sets from "in-line" to "superheterodyne" models, although the government officially denied that it was doing so.[29]

The Occupation also helped launch the quality control movement that was to be an important part of Japan's postwar industrial success. The concept of scientific management was by no means new to Japan: Japanese managers had from the 1920s shown a strong interest in the work of Frederick Taylor and other teachers of mass production technique. The Dai Nippon Gijutsu Kai (Greater Japan Technical Association) had been responsible for propagating quality management as a part of the war effort. When this organization was disbanded by the Occupation, its members regrouped to form the Nihon Kagaku Gijutsu Renmei (Japan Union of Scientists and Engineers, or JUSE). This rebirth symbolized the strong desire of the Japanese to learn the techniques that had fueled the U.S. war machine, techniques that were now seen as a key to the rationalization and modernization of Japan's industries.

JUSE, only one of a number of new organizations dedicated to spreading American management expertise, acted as a private consulting organization to Japanese businesses. Much of its early activity centered on a series of lectures by American experts, both military specialists from within GHQ and visiting engineers. The speakers included the now legendary W. Edwards Deming, whom JUSE asked in 1950 to speak in Tokyo, Osaka, Fukuoka, and Nagoya. From 1949 JUSE also offered courses on quality control taught by Japanese specialists. The courses lasted five days per month over six months and included both classroom instruction and factory inspections. In addition, in 1950 JUSE launched a monthly journal, *Hinshitsu Kanri* (Quality Management), and in 1951 it established the annual Deming Prize, funded by the royalties from Deming's own book on quality control.[30]

JUSE's activities received direct support from the Occupation, which saw nothing but benefits in helping improve the notoriously poor quality of Japanese products. CCS ran its own course on statistical quality control (the "CCS course"),[31] and Occupation specialists, generally military engineers, provided direct assistance to Nippon Denki, Toshiba, Fuji Denki, Hitachi, and other electrical companies. Statistical sampling techniques were taught to help these companies mass produce vacuum tubes and telephone equipment.

In addition to promoting quality control techniques, U.S. Occupation officials introduced basic marketing principles. At this early stage, the most common topic was the use of statistics for market surveys, which logically complemented the subject of statistical quality control. Indeed, on one of Deming's early visits to Japan he taught market survey techniques.[32]

If support for basic production technologies in strategic industries was overt and fairly uncontroversial, there were also more informal and unplanned benefits to Japanese technology. An example is the introduction into Japan of the transistor. The transistor was invented in December 1947 by a research team at Bell Laboratories and unveiled at a press conference on June 30, 1948. The invention took place at the very height of the United States's technological dominance—the same period that marked the depths of Japan's suffering and humiliation. Faced with a daily struggle for survival, barred by GHQ fiat from active electronics research, hard-pressed to gain access even to basic sources of information, the Japanese scientific community was about as far from the cutting edge as it was possible to be. Although some experimentation with semiconducting materials had taken place during the war, the majority of Japanese electronics researchers had little understanding of these materials and even less of their potential applications. It is thus all the more extraordinary that within a decade Japan would become a leading global player in the burgeoning semiconductor industry.

In 1948 the majority of advanced electronics research was still proscribed in Japan by the Occupation—at least, officially. But Nippon Denki researcher Nagafune Hiroe recalls that his introduction to transistors actually came from a U.S. official. Nagafune was assigned to show a visiting U.S. military officer around Nippon Denki's central research center: "As I was showing [the officer] round, he asked me, 'How might the army use transistors in a land battle?' Of course I didn't even know the word 'transistor.' So rather than answer the officer, I had to ask him, 'What is that?'. . . Once I understood that this was something totally new to me, I was really surprised."[33]

Other senior researchers learned about the invention of the transistor through their contacts with GHQ. The heads of major research organizations had to report regularly to GHQ officers to ensure compliance with the restrictions on their activities. Understandably, though, the scientists on each side were more interested in new discoveries than in rules and restrictions, so the meetings were often valuable sources of information for Japanese scientists. For example, Watanabe Hisashi, the head of Tōhoku University's Electrical Communications Laboratory, traveled regularly to Tokyo to report to Frank Polkinghorn of the CCS. Polkinghorn, himself on temporary transfer from Bell Laboratories, is remembered by Japanese researchers as a friend of Japanese science. Polkinghorn and Watanabe had similar scientific interests. On one occasion they had a discussion about transistors, during which Polkinghorn referred to a pile of materials on his desk. Watanabe, eyeing the stack greedily, asked if he could study them. Perhaps because such overt assistance would have violated Occupation policy, Polkinghorn declined the request. But a few minutes later he left the office, saying pointedly that he would be gone a while. Needless to say, Watanabe took advantage of the opportunity to scan the material and note the major points.[34]

Similarly, Komagata Sakuji, head of the Denki Shikenjo, reported to Harry Kelly of the ESS. Kelly, a young and idealistic scientist who found himself in a position of unexpected influence, is also acknowledged as a friend of Japanese science.[35] Soon after Bell Laboratories announced its invention of the transistor, Kelly handed Komagata a fifteen-page document containing a detailed summary of the military briefing Bell Labo-

REENVISIONING JAPAN / 57

ratories had held a week before its press conference. The summary had been prepared by a U.S. Air Force attendee. According to one of the Japanese teams that studied it, the officer had completely misunderstood the principle of the transistor. Nevertheless, the exchange of information testifies to the cooperation between Japanese scientists and their U.S. supervisors.[36]

Few Japanese enjoyed such direct access to the latest information in American electronics. But even junior researchers became aware of the invention of the transistor through published sources—at first through mass-circulation weeklies such as *Time* and *Newsweek,* which were available in the CIE's information centers. These centers, virtually the only official source of foreign technical information for Japanese researchers in the late 1940s, carried U.S. scientific journals such as *Physical Review* (which carried an article by the Bell team in July 1948), *Bell System Technical Journal,* and others. As a result, despite language barriers, government restrictions, scanty funding, and limited information, Japanese scientists began active research on transistor technology within months of Bell Laboratories' announcement.

All of these forms of assistance were essentially ad hoc rather than part of a formal policy of support for Japanese technology. But with the hardening of the lines of the cold war, the U.S. government finally did formulate such a policy—one that would remain a keystone of the U.S.-Japan relationship for at least three decades.

The year 1947 was a pivotal one in the Occupation. Beginning with Gen. Douglas MacArthur's last-minute prohibition of the general strike called for March 1, the United States gradually withdrew support for the more radical elements of reform and aligned itself with conservative Japanese leaders. For U.S. politicians and Japanese business leaders, senior bureaucrats, and entrepreneurs, this "reverse course" marked a new phase in the process of reenvisioning Japan. Although the principle of democratization was not, in theory, abandoned, the cold war lent new urgency to the task of getting Japan back on its feet. As the world's postwar political contours emerged, Japan stood alone as a bastion of the "free world" in Asia, and U.S. policy shifted toward support for Japan's industrial and economic regeneration.

The reverse course was part of a larger reformulation of global political relations. U.S. leaders recognized technology as a reward they could provide to their allies at a relatively low cost. In his 1949 inaugural address, President Harry Truman specifically named technology as a key to upholding the nation's self-appointed role as the guardian of the free world. The United States, he said, could no longer hoard the prosperity it was now enjoying. It must share its technical, managerial, and financial resources to keep the forces of communism at bay and to reward countries that accepted the doctrine of *pax americana*.

> [W]e must embark on a bold new program for making the benefits of our scientific advances and industrial progress available for the improvement and growth of underdeveloped areas.
>
> More than half the people of the world are living in conditions approaching misery. Their food is inadequate. They are victims of disease. Their economic life is primitive and stagnant. Their poverty is a handicap and a threat both to them and to more prosperous areas.
>
> For the first time in history, humanity possesses the knowledge and the skill to relieve the suffering of these people.
>
> United States is preeminent among the nations in the development of industrial and scientific techniques. The material resources which we can afford to use for the assistance of other people are limited. But our imponderable resources in technical knowledge are constantly growing and are inexhaustible.
>
> I believe that we should make available to peace-loving nations the benefits of our store of technical knowledge in order to help them realize their aspirations for a better life.[37]

The program launched as a direct result of this speech, known as the Point Four program (it was "point four" of the inaugural address), offered direct transfers of American technology to underdeveloped countries.

Japan was not a direct beneficiary of Point Four aid. Such assistance was directed toward the world's most backward economies, particularly in Southeast Asia and the Middle East. (It was described at times as a poor man's Marshall Plan.) Indeed, Americans were impressed and pleased that Japan was soon able to manage without direct financial aid or other giveaways. But the Point Four program established an important principle: the United States would not keep its unparalleled technological riches to itself.

THE NEW GOVERNMENT VISION

The nation's chief economic planners at the Ministry of International Trade and Industry (MITI) also saw technology as a key to Japan's future prosperity. Constituted in May 1949, MITI was concerned primarily with the dismally low competitiveness of Japanese industry. Although the economy had throughout the early postwar years been hampered by the effects of rampant inflation, demilitarization, and a

near-total trade embargo, those economic problems had eased by early
1949. But the Dodge Line, an austerity program implemented in mid-
1949, flung the country into its deepest depression since the end of the
war. Thousands of companies went under at the turn of the decade, and
labor disputes, despite Occupation support for restrictive measures, es-
calated to epidemic proportions.

Joseph Dodge arrived in Japan in February 1949 after leading a
highly praised initiative to control inflation in Germany. Dodge sub-
scribed to a conservative doctrine of economic management: he believed Japan could only achieve economic independence through fiscal
restraint and balanced budgets. The Dodge Line had four basic points:
a balanced budget (including all subsidiary accounts of the government,
which had previously hidden large-scale subsidies to ailing industries);
the suspension of Reconstruction Bank loans; the abolition of subsidies;
and the establishment of a single exchange rate. The plan also called for
the abolition of U.S. aid to Japan.[38]

The Dodge Line has been subject to widely divergent interpretations.
The *Oriental Economist* took a dim view of the much-contested exchange rate of ¥360 to $1, claiming that "under existing circumstances,
Japan's export trade is apparently doomed."[39] But as well as imposing
austerity, the Dodge Line promised independence: the basic philosophy
was that by rationalizing and modernizing, Japanese companies would
ultimately be able to stand on their own feet. The return to limited yen
convertibility made it possible to import foreign capital for the upgrading of Japanese plant and equipment. The Dodge Line was therefore a
blueprint for Americanization as much as it was a strict application of
neoclassical economic doctrine.

MITI seems to have agreed with the Dodge Line's basic principles.
Japanese companies needed to rationalize and modernize along American lines in order both to hold their own against imports and, ultimately, to regain competitiveness in world markets. MITI's planning
philosophy emphasized the concept of "industrial rationalization." By
the end of the 1940s, this concept entailed some brutal realities, including mass firings and factory closings. As such, "rationalization" became
(and remained) a term hated by the left wing.

But "rationalization" went through a significant shift in meaning as
the depression of the Dodge Line gave way to the euphoria of the Korean War boom. With the sudden recovery brought about by the outbreak of war, rationalization became MITI's key policy, justifying the
introduction of foreign technologies on an unprecedented scale. The

1950 MITI yearbook (published in mid-1951) commented: "In the area of production, labor and management, a great deal of rationalization has already taken place, and one could say that in these areas rationalization has reached its limits; so from now on, the most effective measures for rationalization will be in the renewal of industrial equipment, and modernization."[40] From this point forward, MITI focused on nurturing a few critical industries and upgrading Japan's industrial technology. "Technology promotion is one of MITI's basic policies," the Machinery Bureau commented in the 1950 yearbook. The bureau described its goals as "absorbing leading foreign technologies, improving our domestic technology, and domesticating production of imported machinery."[41] By 1950, with the support of the Occupation, MITI implemented mechanisms to allow the purchase and importation of technologies from abroad. The 1949 Foreign Exchange and Foreign Trade Control Law and the 1950 Foreign Investment Law enabled MITI to control the approval of applications for technology importation and to guarantee the allocation of foreign currency to pay for the imports.

In Chapter 1 I described the prewar government's obsession with the domestication of production (*kokusanka*). As Samuels and others have correctly observed, the *kokusanka* ideology by no means went away in the postwar era.[42] Indeed, it is remarkable how little this nationalistic ideology was subject to questioning, either in the immediate postwar years or later. MITI continued to stress *kokusanka* as a goal. But the emphasis, at least in the 1950s, lay within a framework of acknowledged technological dependence. For this reason the *kokusanka* policy was less binding on the electrical goods industry in the postwar period than in the prewar.

Notably absent from MITI's vision of Japan's economic future was the consumer. Although some discussion about the consumer did occur in the years just after the war, a consensus that personal consumption should play an important role in Japan's economic and social recovery did not emerge until several years later (see Chapter 5). Nevertheless, there are hints that MITI officials perceived the benefits that improved technology in a nonmilitarized Japan might provide for the consumer. The 1949 *Technology White Paper*, prepared by an agency of MITI, commented:

> Technology aims at the improvement and progress of human culture, and in [the] future it will help in the raising of the people's living standards. However in the past Japan's technology was used directly for the increasing of military might, and the living environment was forgotten. In [the] future, in

Japan too the mission of technology will be to act as the servant of all the people to raise living standards, and to improve the conditions of labor through the improvement of factories and mines. The essential role of technology is to directly increase the living standards of the people, and, conversely, the people's wish to increase their consumption levels acts as a perpetual stimulus on technology.[43]

Laura Hein has elaborated on the connection between the importation of leading-edge technologies and the well-being of the consumer, commenting that MITI and other elite planners at this time "took comfort from the widespread assumption that technology could enhance economic justice while avoiding redistribution of wealth. This dream of a technological fix for social problems was shared by Americans in Japan and Americans at home."[44]

THE PILGRIMAGE TO AMERICA: TOP MANAGEMENT VISIONS

With the restoration of trade relations and a convertible currency, Japanese businessmen were once again able to travel abroad. From the beginning of 1950, the presidents of leading companies journeyed to the United States and Europe to observe the conditions and opportunities firsthand and to study the mystery of the United States's fabulous prosperity.

The comments and impressions of these influential pilgrims appeared prominently in newspapers and magazines. A foreign trip was still a great rarity in those days of severe currency shortage. Visits were generally limited to men of influence, and their views carried weight. Almost in unison, those business leaders who spoke to the press expressed shock at the abundance and scale of American wealth and productivity. The difference with Japan seemed at times too great even to comprehend, let alone overcome. One after another, important men described the humility they felt, the sleepless nights during which they contemplated the immense gap that had opened between their country and this behemoth. When Nippon Denki's radio division head, Kobayashi Kōji, visited the United States at the beginning of 1951, he commented:

In the US, the manufacturing concept is totally different [from Japan]. The process of moving a product from the R&D center which says "let's make a new television or telephone," to its mass production in the factory, is something which completely exceeds our imagination. The ten-year blank space which opened up during the war is just too big: seeing what goes on in American factories was a major shock to me. After visiting a factory I would go back and lie in bed thinking about it, unable to sleep.[45]

But their reflections were also tinged with hope. If they could just grasp the principles of U.S. economic success, it might be possible to reproduce that success in Japan. Slowly, Japanese business leaders formulated an interpretation of the keys to American prosperity, an interpretation that would guide them in their leadership strategies for the next two decades.

The United States experienced a massive surge in demand for televisions in 1951, the fourth year in which they were commercially sold. By the end of the year, 12 million Americans owned television sets. Radio, too, was vastly more advanced in the United States than in Japan. The typical American model at the turn of the 1950s was a large, luxurious console-style model, but portable sets using miniature vacuum tubes were already booming in sales. The new products constantly released in the United States were a source of endless fascination to Japanese visitors, as was the system of production that allowed American manufacturers to produce televisions and radios in ever greater numbers and at ever lower cost. The combination of assembly lines, machinery, systematized work flows, and quality control left Japanese managers gasping.

Even this wide definition of product technology does not do justice to the magnetism of American technological might as perceived by Japanese businessmen at the turn of the 1950s. The observers also marveled at American businesses' extraordinary ability to create products for which there always seemed to be surging demand. What was the secret of this alchemy? Japanese analysts increasingly looked to management as the magic ingredient. For example, the Industrial Bank of Japan's Masayama Kiyotarō, after a stay at the Harvard Business School in 1951–52, concluded, "It is of course desirable for Japan to import all sorts of industrial technologies. But even more than that, I think the most important thing is to study the basics of American-style management."[46]

These analysts saw not just an affluent populace but also an attitude. American companies possessed an outstanding ability to pioneer new markets for existing products and to create markets for new goods. This "frontier" marketing mentality was particularly attractive for Japanese businessmen, who were painfully aware of the small size and limited capacities of their country. Before and during the war, the pressure of

Japan's growing population was constantly cited as one imperative for overseas expansion. Defeat in World War II had closed off the imperialist frontier. Now a new frontier was needed, a new outlet for Japan's creative energies. Many Japanese businessmen saw it in the buying potential of the Japanese people. Time and again, business leaders commented that the Japanese market, although small, was not being sufficiently exploited. If businesses could unleash the innate buying power of Japanese society, the potential for growth was unlimited. Toshiba president Ishizaka Taizō commented after a visit to the United States:

> The Japanese people are poor . . . but even based on current purchasing power, there are opportunities. Rural purchasing power is under-exploited, and there is still a great deal of waste in the people's lifestyles. Even now, there are opportunities to convert this waste to more rational uses. In short, although nothing can be done about the size of the land, there still remain many opportunities for developing the Japanese market. To this end, we need to learn the bold market-opening spirit of American businessmen.[47]

There was an enormous contrast between this vision of unlocked potential and the harsh realities of daily life for most Japanese. Poverty had been an unchanging feature of Japan's landscape, particularly in the countryside (where half the Japanese people still lived), since time immemorial. Was it really possible for an Asian country, with its supposed legacies of tyranny and overcrowding, to transform itself into a modern consumer society?

By the end of 1950, Matsushita Kōnosuke had at last surmounted a host of personal and business problems that came with Japan's defeat. Matsushita had been one of the leading industrialists supporting the war effort, and his company had grown into a huge conglomerate. In March 1946 the Occupation authorities declared Matsushita Denki a *zaibatsu* holding company and designated it for dissolution. All officers from managing director on up were supposed to resign. However, Matsushita fought this last provision with all the resources at his disposal, even mobilizing the support of the company's new labor union. The purge order was rescinded in May 1947.[48]

Still, as head of a designated *zaibatsu*, Matsushita saw his personal assets frozen. Unable to pay even his personal bills, he became the country's leading deadbeat taxpayer. In the depths of his despair, Matsushita founded a research institute, PHP (Peace, Happiness, and Prosperity), to unravel the secrets of postwar recovery. Matsushita subsequently described his motives in founding the institute as follows:

I asked myself: Why is it that humankind is in such a sorry state? Even though we are seeking prosperity and peace, we destroy our own prosperity and wreak havoc with peace. Is it true human nature to do this? Why do people engage in such wars, bringing down tragedy upon themselves and literally inviting misfortune? Even the flitting sparrows know how to enjoy themselves after eating a full meal. But human beings get themselves embroiled in wars and bring starvation upon themselves. Is this truly humanity as it was intended to be? Isn't it possible for us to live in a better way?[49]

However, conditions continued to worsen for Matsushita. In 1949, a severe recession in the radio industry accompanying the Dodge Line depression forced Matsushita Denki to impose its first layoffs ever, reducing its work force from a peak of roughly 15,000 to a mere 3,500.[50] The situation finally improved after 1950 as a result of the Korean War boom, enabling Matsushita Kōnosuke to resume his quest for Japanese prosperity and happiness. His first stop was the United States. In January 1951 Matsushita flew via Hawaii and Los Angeles to New York. Subsequently, he described his first impressions.

The material abundance in the United States was a constant source of amazement.... New York City at the time was extremely prosperous; in the eyes of us Japanese, it seemed extravagant to the point of wastefulness. The floor of Grand Central Station was solid marble, polished to such a sheen that I could see myself as if in a mirror. The lights in Times Square were not turned off even during the day.... When I asked a New Yorker why the lights were left on all day, he replied offhandedly that they might not be necessary, but it was "just nicer to have them on."[51]

The 1950s were truly a golden age for New York, as for much of the rest of the United States. Matsushita was deeply impressed with the city's cleanliness, efficiency, and civic pride. "I still have not once seen anyone spitting," he commented. "People really have an advanced sense of public duty."

Unlike many business leaders who had traveled abroad frequently and even studied overseas, Matsushita was provincial and had little formal education. This very lack of training, however, may have made him more willing to consider every possible explanation for U.S. success. He was not only open-minded but also clear-headed. By the end of his visit, he had formed a vision of Japan's future: a middle-class, consuming society structured along American lines.

Matsushita, who extended his stay for a month because "it is not possible to understand America in a single glance," explicitly stated that his mission in the United States was "to grasp the truth of American prosperity."[52] He considered a great many factors in trying to understand this "truth." At the beginning, he was inclined to credit American-style democracy as a key factor. Matsushita felt the U.S. political system possessed a near-mystical power and viewed it as the fount of prosperity. "One may understand democracy as a word," he said, "but still not understand what it really is, it is that deep a thing." Of the relationship between bureaucrats and people, he noted: "People are involved in politics for their own sake, so they make the bureaucrats do what the people themselves think is good. That's why even administrative controls are democratic. They are not the orders of bureaucrats, they are the orders of the people. I think that American prosperity may also lie in this fact."

Matsushita lauded the influence of religion in the United States, speaking in terms reminiscent of discussions among Meiji intellectuals about the adoption of Christianity as a prerequisite for modernization:[53]

> Although America has only a brief history, religion is very deeply established. To take an example, every university is equipped with a church. Just seeing that, one well understands how popular religion is, and one can infer the depth of American culture. As for Japan, which boasts of its 2,600 year history, we are completely beaten by America, which has only 200 years. The reason why that should be is something we must study deeply.

Gradually, Matsushita started to develop a more selective analysis of U.S. prosperity, zeroing in on the rational, scientific approach that he perceived as guiding American life. He found this rational approach both in the factory, where managers divided vast production systems into minute tasks, and in the home, where wives used technology to complete domestic work efficiently, freeing up time for entertaining and other important social responsibilities. As he dwelled on the differences between Japan and America, Matsushita gradually evolved a mission to create such a society in Japan, making some strikingly prescient comments:

> This morning I visited a vacuum tube factory. It was as well appointed as I imagined, and what impressed me even more was that it runs day and night, on three shifts. There's no need to dwell on the good points of the factory's equipment, but how good the wages are is very typical of America. Newly hired female factory workers are paid $55 for a five-day week, or $230 a month. If you calculate that in yen, it comes to ¥82,800, equivalent to the salary of a company president. Right now in America, about 80 percent of the people belong to the middle class. I feel now that I understand well what this means, and I feel painfully that I would like Japan to get to that point as

soon as possible. I am constantly thinking that there must be a way of achieving that.

In time Matsushita came to believe that such a goal could indeed be achieved in Japan. Toward the end of his stay, he commented:

> Since I have been here, I've come to believe firmly that Japan will develop marvelously from now, and become prosperous both materially and spiritually. I am not saying this from a nationalistic viewpoint, but from a deeper racial viewpoint. The Japanese people are luckily a blessed people. I think one can definitely say that.

Matsushita's American trip had a wide variety of consequences for his company. He studied specific technologies and negotiated for sales and patent rights with the U.S. subsidiary of Philips, the Dutch electronics giant. He also took his lessons on "rationality" and efficient management very much to heart, implementing a series of initiatives such as organizational reform, management accounting, and enhanced marketing. Perhaps most important, he constructed a vision and sense of mission from which the entire Japanese business community could draw inspiration.

THE SPOILS OF DEFEAT:
ENTREPRENEURS AND THE NEW LAND OF OPPORTUNITY

The visions of a new Japan did not belong solely to established business leaders and bureaucrats. The upheaval of defeat and Occupation reforms also spelled opportunity for entrepreneurs with a clear vision of where Japan, and they, might go.

The Occupation period was a cruel time for small businesses. The high hopes of the early postwar years were crushed by the rigors of the Dodge Line deflation and the Allies' support for the reconstruction of major prewar industrial concerns. The radio industry was particularly hard hit: after the artificial stimulation of production caused by Occupation-mandated programs, the Dodge Line austerity regime led to a collapse in demand. The industry's official history estimates that 90 percent of the two hundred radio manufacturers in Japan went out of business as a result of this recession.[54]

The survivors generally needed more than just vision. They also benefited from links with Japan's prewar and wartime establishment. For those with the right ideas, contacts, financing, and luck, the postwar environment offered unparalleled opportunity. Those who had the strongest commitment to the mass consumer market encountered the most success. For these men, the new postwar society offered spoils beyond imagining: the spoils of defeat.

In October 1948 two wartime comrades, Morita Akio and Ibuka Masaru, joined forces to found a new company. They named it Tokyo Communications Manufacturing (Tokyo Tsūshin Kōgyō, or Tōtsūkō). At thirty-eight, Ibuka was fourteen years older than Morita and an experienced businessman. During the war he built up a substantial business manufacturing measuring and testing devices for the military. With Japan's defeat, Ibuka's business evaporated. Like many others, he gravitated to the radio parts and repair business that centered on the Kanda/Akihabara market.

Morita's business experience differed markedly from that of Ibuka. He was the heir to a commercial empire that included a saké brewery, a soy sauce and miso enterprise, and one of Japan's largest flour and bread companies. He grew up in luxury with chauffeur-driven cars, servants, and every Western convenience at his disposal. Only twenty-four years old in 1948, Morita had been attending business meetings with his father for more than a decade.

But Morita's great passion in life was not saké but electronics. Since childhood he had been fascinated with radio and sound recording. He tried to build his first recording device at the age of twelve, and his study in the family mansion in Nagoya was always cluttered with radio components, vacuum tubes, and gramophone pickups. A gifted electrical engineering student at Osaka Imperial University, he was recruited in the middle of the war into the navy, which was an important training ground for Japan's postwar generation of electrical engineers. Here Morita worked on heat-seeking guidance systems. It was during this research that he met Ibuka.[55]

Morita could have opted for a plush life as head of an established business. Instead, he joined Ibuka to start a small company with an uncertain future. In this sense, he showed the kind of entrepreneurship and opportunism that was a hallmark of the new postwar order. One photo of Ibuka, Morita, and two of their colleagues captures the spirit of this hopeful era. The four young men are standing outside their shabby, tumbledown headquarters. (After visiting this decrepit wooden building, one of Morita's relatives wrote home in alarm: "Akio's become an anarchist.") They are wearing lopsided hats, white shirts, and baggy shorts, exaggerating their string-bean physiques. Through round tortoise-shell glasses, they are grinning at the camera as if they are a comedy team.[56]

Figure 4 Sony founders (left to right) Higuchi, Iwama, Ibuka, and Morita. (Courtesy of Sony Corporation)

It must be added, though, that Ibuka and Morita had circumstances in their favor. Both were well connected. Ibuka's father-in-law was Maeda Tamon, a former minister of education, who along with Morita's wealthy father joined the Tōtsūkō board. These heavy hitters brought in the legendary Bandai Junichirō, former head of the great Mitsui Bank—a vital contact when it came to arranging all-important financing. Like so many successful postwar enterprises, Tōtsūkō mixed deep links to the prewar and wartime establishment with a measure of fresh blood.

In addition to enjoying access to capital and influence in the business community, Ibuka and Morita surrounded themselves with very bright scientific people. Morita saw that the breakup of the great military research labs after the war left gifted electrical engineers drifting about with no way to make a living. Most of the big electrical companies were shrinking with alarming speed, failing to meet the payroll even for their existing staffs. Some engineers went to Akihabara and did their best to survive. Others got out of the electrical business altogether.

The majority of Tōtsūkō's initial contracts were with the Japanese government. In particular, the company focused on converting military radio equipment for civilian uses. Using their military contacts, Tō-tsūkō's founders were able to secure, apparently without charge, much of the army's communications equipment stockpile, stored in an air-raid shelter in the Nirasaki Mountains in Yamanashi.[57]

But even as they worked their army contacts to create a healthy cash flow, the leaders of Tōtsūkō were reaching for larger prizes. Ibuka and Morita had an amazing confidence in their own technological prowess. Unlike many other Japanese businessmen of the time, they refused to be cowed by Japan's defeat or overawed by the United States's technological superiority. As Ibuka put it on one trip abroad: "We are not defeated Japanese. We are technologists, just like you." And they were right: the technological gap between Japan and the United States was much slimmer than postwar conditions made it appear.[58]

Their first new product was a magnetic tape recorder. Tape recorders had appeared in the United States at the end of the war but had yet to gain widespread use. After carrying out initial research, the Tōtsūkō team discovered that one of the core technologies for tape recording—the AC bias recording head—had been patented in Japan *before* its development in the United States. Tōtsūkō bought the Japanese patent. As a result, the company had a right to royalties on all American-made tape recorders sold in Japan. Tōtsūkō caused a sensation when it successfully sued an American importer on this issue in 1951. Who had ever heard of a Japanese company suing Americans for patent infringement? Tōtsūkō built on this publicity—and on the undoubted quality of its products—to achieve its early consumer success.[59]

At the turn of the 1950s, Tōtsūkō remained an obscure and highly specialized company. But Morita and Ibuka were to lead it to unprecedented success and fame under the name it adopted at the end of the 1950s: Sony.

CONCLUSION

The Occupation years represent a fascinating, complex period in twentieth-century Japanese history. Scholars have tended to view it as an era of one-directional change, with the victorious United States bestowing democracy and economic benefits upon a defeated Japan. In fact, however, there were many forces at work, many constituencies pursuing varying agendas. What united them was the vision of America, with its magnificent prosperity. During the course of the Occupation a broad range of agents, both American and Japanese, tried to isolate the essentials of American prosperity and to develop plans to introduce those essentials into Japan. Some were motivated by an unselfish desire to lift the nation out of its postwar malaise. But in most cases, the primary motive was personal gain.

Between them, these diverse interests developed something approaching a common vision for the future of Japan. The introduction of foreign technology emerged as one key factor. Another was the creation of an American-style middle-class social structure, with its accompanying mass demand for consumer goods. A third factor was an emphasis on technologies of mass communication, particularly the new medium of television. In pursuit of these high-technology visions, Japan possessed one comparative advantage over its competitors: cheap labor. This represented the final ingredient in the recipe for prosperity.

3

The Vision of America

BRINGING TELEVISION TO JAPAN

THE GLITTERING NEW MEDIA

In 1948, after two decades of research and a bitter battle over standards, RCA and Westinghouse began broadcasting television programming and selling television sets in the United States. The newspapers of the time expressed great doubts about the viability and usefulness of this expensive medium. But television was an instant success in the United States. By 1951, 12 million sets had already been sold, and sociologists were charting the worrisome changes in lifestyle apparently caused by the new medium.

Like everything else about American life, the wildfire success of television received great attention in Japan. Newspapers carried stories on the sales boom, on the broadcasting companies springing up all over the United States, on the new forms of entertainment television offered, on the changes in family life it brought, and on the near-mythical deeds of television's great entrepreneurs, particularly RCA chairman David Sarnoff.

But there seemed little chance that television would come to Japan any time soon. In 1953—the year that, against all odds, television broadcasting began in Japan—per capita annual income was still only $97 (at the prevailing exchange rate of ¥360×$1), whereas television sets were predicted to cost at least ¥170,000 ($470). Japan's level of income, though higher than those of the destitute nations of Southeast

Asia and Africa, nevertheless placed the nation firmly among the world's have-nots. At the time the crucial decisions to launch television service in Japan were made, the standard of living still ranked well below the level prevailing before the war: the index of real wages, based on a 1937 level of 100, sank to 20 in March 1947 and had recovered only to 37 by September 1949.[1]

These numbers translated into great hardship for ordinary Japanese. People in the country's poorest regions sold their daughters into prostitution and servitude, as they had done for centuries during times of trouble. In 1950 a total of 377 people were arrested for trafficking in children; one allegedly arranged the sale of at least sixty-two young girls. The majority of these traffickers operated out of Tōhoku, which for generations had supplied the cities with prostitutes and indentured laborers. The prices they received averaged from ¥10,000 to ¥15,000 (about $30 to $40) per person. The youngest girl known to have been traded was only nine years old.[2]

Families of the urban working class, though not so desperate that they had to sell their daughters, had precious little margin for luxuries. A typical male factory worker in the textile industry earned about ¥7,000 ($19) a month in 1949. A day's supply of rice for a family of four cost $1 on the black market. Chicken cost $1 per 700 grams. Cooking oil cost $2.50 per half-gallon. A pair of shoes cost $7.50. Obviously, it was out of the question for people at this level of income to buy televisions. Even the wealthier salaried class averaged only ¥18,500 ($51) a month.[3]

The attitude of established companies was that television would inevitably come to Japan—but not for some time. Toshiba, Japan Victor, and other established firms continued to work with NHK on television development. Japan Victor had hired Takayanagi Kenjirō and many others who had worked on television for the aborted Tokyo Olympics project, and this team sat at the forefront of Japanese research. Takayanagi and others pushed the government to speed up the introduction of television in Japan, but none of them believed regular television broadcasting would arrive before the mid-1950s, and most thought widespread television ownership remained more than a decade away. Indeed, their own technology would take at least five years to develop to a commercial level.

Neither the Occupation nor the Japanese government had an official stance on the introduction of television into Japan, but Gen. Douglas MacArthur, head of the Occupation forces, was known to regard tele-

vision as a luxury item, inappropriate for a defeated and destitute nation. MacArthur adamantly opposed the use of precious dollars for
what he considered an unnecessary program.[4] This would seem a
deeply discouraging environment for the early launch of television in
Japan. But many ambitious people saw the opportunities in television—
and they were not willing to wait five or ten years for the chance to exploit them.

In mid-1948 a wealthy Japanese businessman traveled to the United
States to investigate opportunities for new business ventures in Japan.
Minagawa Yoshizo had made his fortune in an earlier era of dreams, introducing the technology for talking movies into Japan. During his visit
Minagawa met with an old associate, Lee de Forest, one of the great figures of the American electronics industry. Among his many accomplish-
ments, de Forest had invented the triode vacuum tube in 1907 and was
a key figure in the development of "talkie" technology. De Forest had
also been involved in the development of American television but had
been unable to convert his achievements into a significant business concern. Now, seeing the huge initial success of television, de Forest sought
to achieve a dominant role in television in another country. He and Minagawa discussed the possibilities for the launch of television in Japan,
and they concluded that it represented a viable business opportunity.

There was a problem, however. Bringing television to Japan was a
vast project. It would require not only substantial financing but also a
massive effort to ensure political acceptance, find adequate broadcasting content, make television sets widely available, and create a nationwide network. For all his business skills, Minagawa recognized that he
was not up to the task. What he needed was someone with excellent political contacts, access to enormous capital resources, the ability to manage vast projects, and, preferably, experience in the media. This was a
tall order by any standards. Minagawa's first move was to approach
Ayukawa Gisuke, the founder of the Nissan group of companies, to so-
licit his participation.[5]

Ayukawa was one of the extraordinary success stories of Imperial
Japan. A well-connected product of the Chōshū elite, he was a great-
nephew of the Meiji leader Inoue Kaoru. On graduating from Tokyo
Imperial University, Ayukawa joined Shibaura Seisakujo (later
Toshiba), leaving in 1909 to launch his own company. Ayukawa turned
out to be one of Japan's great entrepreneurs, becoming heavily involved
in the high-technology industries of the time: chemicals and transportation equipment. By 1938 Ayukawa controlled as many as seventy-seven

companies, with the massive Hitachi engineering group at the center of his empire.[6] He also controlled two of Japan's oldest electrical companies, Japan Victor and Nihon Columbia, which he had acquired with the specific intention of branching into television. In the end Ayukawa opted for the even more dazzling opportunity of expansion into Manchuria and sold his stakes in Victor and Columbia to Toshiba.

Given Ayukawa's ambition, it is not surprising that Minagawa should have approached him about the launch of television in Japan, nor that Ayukawa should have expressed interest. But in spite of his status in business circles and his undoubted entrepreneurial acumen, Ayukawa had one serious drawback: he was seventy-eight years old. Television was clearly an industry of the future and would take years to reach maturity. Whether in recognition of this limitation or for other reasons, Ayukawa decided to approach another of the business legends of prewar Japan.

Ayukawa had a unique relationship with the formidable Shōriki Matsutarō; the two had occupied facing cells in Sugamo, the Allied prison for Japanese war criminals. Born in 1885, Shōriki was the son of a prosperous building contractor in Tōyama prefecture. He attended the Fourth Higher School, entered the law department of Tokyo Imperial University, and then moved to the metropolitan police force, where he was put on the fast track for a top position.

Whether by chance or by inclination, Shōriki was involved in virtually every major incident of police repression up to 1923. He was the local bureau chief at the Waseda sit-in of 1917. In 1918 he was seriously injured while trying to parley with leaders of the Tokyo rice riots in Hibiya Park. In 1921 he was responsible for a severe crackdown on the Korean community after the assassination of a pro-Japanese Korean leader in the Marunouchi Station hotel. The following year Shōriki led a major roundup of communists and socialists, which earned him the lifelong hatred of the communist movement. Indeed, anti-communism was to become one of the defining characteristics of Shōriki's career, as well as one of his major credentials. In 1923, after the great Kanto earthquake, Shōriki was widely—although probably unjustly—implicated in the murder in jail of the anarchist Ōsugi Sakai and his companion, Itō Noe.[7]

In 1921 Shōriki became director of the Cabinet Secretariat, enabling him to form extraordinary political ties. During his short spell in this office, Shōriki befriended many of the reigning and future lords of the Japanese political establishment, including Gotō Shimpei (future home minister) and Konoe Fumimaro (future prime minister). In this position, too, Shōriki courted controversy: it is widely believed that he pleased his superiors by spying on the activities of the Peers.

Shōriki's official career came to an abrupt end in late 1923 when an assassin got within inches of a car carrying the regent crown prince and fired a pistol at point-blank range through the window, miraculously leaving the future emperor unscathed. The so-called Toranomon incident resulted in a flurry of resignations, starting with the entire cabinet and including the governor of Yamaguchi prefecture, which had schooled the assassin; the mayor of Kyoto, where the gunman had stayed on his way to commit the dastardly crime; and three top police officials, including Shōriki.

Shōriki probably could, after a suitable period of penance, have returned to the police force had he so desired. Instead he abandoned his official career and purchased a controlling interest in the *Yomiuri,* a Tokyo newspaper. This decision was closely connected to his interest in politics; Shōriki clearly had in mind an entry into the regional and then the national political scene. With the introduction in 1925 of universal male suffrage, the importance of newspapers was becoming ever more apparent to politicians. There is clear evidence that Shōriki's newspaper purchase was backed by political interests eager to buy a voice. The *Yomiuri,* an ailing third in the Tokyo market, had been up for grabs for some time. Indeed, in the wake of the 1914 Siemens scandal (a military procurements scandal that resulted in the fall of the government), the collapsing Yamamoto cabinet attempted to buy it for public relations purposes.[8]

The price for a controlling stake in the *Yomiuri* was set at ¥100,000—a sum far beyond Shōriki's means. He reportedly received money from Gotō Shimpei, who was home minister in the second Yamamoto cabinet following the Toranomon incident. Gotō, a flamboyant character with a distinguished career behind him as governor of Taiwan and mayor of Tokyo, evidently had Shōriki in mind as a protégé for future political office.[9] Where Gotō himself obtained funds on this scale prompts some unpleasant speculation. Moreover, Shōriki would later demonstrate a pronounced taste for illicit fund-raising. He was deeply implicated in two major political scandals: the 1928 Keisei Railway affair, in which the railway bribed Tokyo assembly members to permit it to extend its line within the city; and the 1934 Teijin scandal, which brought down several members of the political establishment. In the case of the Keisei scandal, Shōriki, who was a contender for mayor of Tokyo at the time, admitted to receiving ¥100,000. In the Teijin scandal, a complicated affair in which underpriced shares were handed out to political figures, he escaped without charges. Nevertheless, he was intensively questioned by the police and has since been implicated by a number of key participants. Shōriki's involvement in these notorious incidents led to a nearly successful attempt on his life by an ultranationalist group in 1935.[10]

Although these scandals set back his political career, Shōriki did enjoy a highly successful tenure at the *Yomiuri*. Readership increased substantially during the 1930s, and the paper improved its position against its main competitors, the *Asahi* and the *Mainichi*. Shōriki's genius lay in his ability to foresee accurately the emerging tastes of a mass readership. He showed an immense flair for advertising and promotion, happily losing money on ambitious publicity stunts in the knowledge that he was buying exposure and recognition. He also correctly read his audience's thirst for popular sports events. In 1934, Shōriki arranged for Babe Ruth and the New York Yankees to visit Japan; the following year he founded his own baseball team, the Yomiuri Giants. Aided by the general increase in literacy and newspaper readership that accompanied popular involvement in politics and military expansion, the *Yomiuri*'s circulation skyrocketed from a money-losing 130,000 in 1924 to almost 2 million in 1944.

Shōriki recognized the potential for mass appeal and influence in radio. He was one of the applicants for a radio license prior to the decision to grant a monopoly to NHK, and the *Yomiuri* was the first newspaper to publish a radio programming guide. If government policy had allowed him to, Shōriki would undoubtedly have gotten involved in broadcasting prior to World War II. But his reputation and influence were not yet strong enough to let him mold policy in his favor.

During World War II, Shōriki played an integral role in the government's media policy. Although the *Yomiuri* remained independent, it was known as the most avid supporter of Japan's imperial ambitions throughout the 1930s and into the war. As a reward for this loyalty, and in recognition of his formidable leadership skills, Shōriki was appointed to several key government propaganda organizations, including the New Political Order Preparation Committee, the Cabinet Information Bureau, and the Greater Japan Political Association, of which he was a national director.[11] Because of his heavy involvement in the war effort, Shōriki was arrested by the Allies in December 1945 and incarcerated for two years in Sugamo.

By the time of Ayukawa's approach Shōriki had been released from prison but, like Ayukawa, was still under official purge and thus banned from any public office or media position. When Shōriki heard about the plan to launch a television network in Japan, he considered it just the project for him; as a purgee, however, he was unable to play an active role. At Shōriki's suggestion, de Forest in early 1949 wrote a letter to Gen. W. F. Marquat, an Occupation official, outlining his vision for the future of television in Japan and mentioning Shōriki's importance to it. De Forest's letter was prophetic in places:

> While relatively few Japanese today can afford to purchase American television receivers, I am convinced from my intimate knowledge of such manufacture that Japanese radio manufacturers will have little difficulty in duplicating our cheaper sets, using native labor and materials, and importing very little except the kinescope tubes, at a price less than one half of our lowest American price. And Japanese manufacturers of radio tubes will have little difficulty in learning how to make kinescope tubes comparable to our best. And, barring U.S. tariffs, I can visualize Japanese-made television chassis successfully competing with those made here.[12]

De Forest's letter added a request to permit Shōriki's involvement in the enterprise, calling him "a man whose past record as organizer and manager stands unrivalled" and adding: "I am informed also that he has never known failure in his undertakings. Financial circles place great trust in him."

The Occupation authorities gave de Forest's letter a respectful but cool reception. Officials were concerned that television was a luxury in a country that still could not afford necessities. Moreover, they did not like Shōriki Matsutarō. One department commented that

> the purgee Shōriki is famed less as a popularizer of baseball than as a former police official who built up by strong-arm methods a chauvinistic newspaper which played no small part in misleading the Japanese people into the attitudes which brought on the war. Subterfuge would be necessary to qualify him for a role in any medium capable of influencing public opinion.[13]

Shōriki, it appeared, would be stymied as long as the Americans were in charge in Japan. But the Allied Occupation was already beginning to wind to a close. Negotiations were underway for a peace treaty that would restore Japan's independence, and the close ties between conservative Japanese politicians and the Allied authorities indicated that wartime activities would no longer be held against people. Shōriki had to bide his time just a little longer.

THE SEE BOMB

The first major salvo in Shōriki's battle to launch television broadcasting came from the heart of the U.S. political establishment: the United States Senate.

The U.S. government had been watching with mounting alarm as Communist forces in China scored one victory after another over the U.S.-supported Nationalists under Chiang Kai Shek. With each Communist success, U.S. political strategies in Asia had to be redrawn along with the maps. On June 25, 1950, the situation in East Asia plunged suddenly into crisis. From its stronghold in the north, an army under Kim Il Song invaded the U.S.-supported southern half of Korea. Two days later the United Nations, under strong U.S. leadership, announced its intention to restore "international peace and security" to the area. The Korean War had begun.

The outbreak of war on the Korean Peninsula created a deep sense of insecurity in Japan, which was the powerless host to one of the active belligerents. There were also grave concerns about the war's social and economic consequences. Commentators worried that refugees would flood into Japan, perhaps bringing "many cases of dreadful pestilence with them."[14] The war did nothing to make the timing of television's launch in Japan any more propitious. If anything, the pessimism that had opened the decade deepened as the year progressed. In the United States, however, a new philosophy was emerging about the potential uses to which this powerful new medium might be put in Japan. U.S. Sen. Karl Mundt of South Dakota expressed that philosophy on June 5, 1950, three weeks before the outbreak of hostilities in Korea, in a speech from the Senate floor entitled, "The Vision of America."

The fifty-year-old Mundt was a former high school teacher who possessed a love of rhetoric and, together with former House colleague Joseph McCarthy, a deep hatred of communism. He had been a House member since 1939 and had reached the Senate in the 1948 election. He had been a fervent member of the House Un-American Activities Committee (HUAC) and had co-sponsored a tough anti-communist bill with Richard Nixon. Perhaps because of his teaching background, Mundt saw education as a key weapon in the battle against communism. He authored the bill mandating the creation of UNESCO as well as legislation establishing the Voice of America, the U.S. radio propaganda network beamed by short wave from New York.

In his June 1950 speech, Mundt proposed to extend the concept of the Voice of America to television. "We are engaged in a weaponless struggle between two diametrically opposed ideologies for the minds and loyalties of people all around the world," he stated in his introduction. "It is my conviction that at this juncture of our national affairs, the ideological and informational factor is the most important element of our overall global strategy."

According to Mundt, the radio Voice of America had limited effectiveness. He explained: "Without radio receivers, even where our Voice of America broadcasts are adequate, people cannot hear our message." In order to combat the "revolutionary doctrines of dialectic materialism . . . conceived in the murky minds of Marx, Engel [sic], Lenin, Stalin, and their evil-minded ilk in every era and area of the world," Mundt proposed a "show-how, see-how, hear-how, know-how" television program: "Most of us are just coming dimly to realize that the world is today entering a new era of 'show-how.' When the history of the twentieth century is written, it may well be divided into two halves: the first, the period of mass hearing; the second, the period of mass seeing." Mundt went on:

> We must not leave Japan or Germany until we effect some conversion to basic democratic concepts.
>
> Why not let these people see for themselves? Why not show them our American system of living and being? Why not let them see our Bill of Rights as it operates in practice in America? Why not let them see how private enterprise, political independence, and individual initiative pay off for the American farmer, the American laboring man, and our little-business man? Why not let them see democracy and decency in action on the American scene? Why not let them see, by comparison, what communism would bring to them, with its Asiatic forms of tyranny and godless doctrines of materialism?

Mundt outlined a highly specific plan to introduce television into four countries that he considered crucial to the ideological battle: Japan, Turkey, the Philippines, and Indonesia. He had already commissioned a detailed study of Japan's geographical conditions; now he proposed to install by decree a central broadcast center and twenty-two mountaintop relay stations connected by microwave—enough to cover the whole country. Mundt estimated the total cost of this network at $4.6 million—only a little more, he pointed out, than the cost of a single B-36 bomber. He was vague about who would actually bear the cost of the network but suggested that in Japan, "General MacArthur has sufficient control—and I believe sufficient finances—to put this program into operation as rapidly as engineers can install the equipment and technicians can prepare the studios and plans for operation." To emphasize the theme that television was a potential weapon of the cold war, Mundt ended his speech by characterizing the medium as a "see-bomb." Television, he claimed, "can put in motion chain reactions for constructive good which will rival in their magnitude the destructive consequences of the chain reactions of the A-bomb."[15]

At the time it was delivered in June 1950, Mundt's speech reached Japan only as a faint echo. But its reverberations gradually increased over the coming months, erupting in a sudden crescendo in September 1951. Shortly after its delivery, the Mundt speech was picked up by a popular newscaster with NHK, Shibata Hidetoshi. Shibata, an ex-*Yomiuri* reporter, had been personally selected by the radio department of the Occupation's CIE to launch an American-style news show on NHK. A handsome man who had an easy rapport with Americans, Shibata was popular not only with the Occupation but also with the Japanese public: his audience was estimated at some 10 million listeners. He was also markedly conservative and at times a vocal critic of the left-wing politics of many Japanese journalists. His views undoubtedly helped him gain popularity among the occupiers; they also formed a bridge with Shōriki, who had been his boss at the *Yomiuri*.

Shibata stumbled on Mundt's speech during his daily scan of wire service reports and evidently was deeply struck by its possible implications for Japan. He did more than pass the story on to his listeners; he also telephoned Shōriki to discuss its practical application. The two met for lunch at the Marunouchi Club, where Shibata outlined the gist of Mundt's speech and urged Shōriki to become involved with the project. Shōriki replied that Shibata was preaching to the converted and explained his attempts over the past two years to win the lifting of his purge status so he could launch a television company. From that point on, Shōriki seems to have quietly dropped his old allies—Ayukawa, Minakawa, and de Forest—and moved to attach himself to the rising tide of American anti-communism.[16]

That tide already was sweeping the shores of Japan. On May 3, 1950, MacArthur had denounced the Japan Communist Party, and on June 6–7 all twenty-four members of its central committee, as well as seventeen members of the editorial board of *Akahata* (the party newspaper), were removed from their posts. Communist Party members were banned from the broadcasting, newspaper, communications, and motion picture industries on July 28 and from the coal and steel indus-

tries in September. Altogether, 1,177 teachers and government employees lost their jobs, as did 10,972 workers in other industries. At NHK,
119 employees were fired between June and August 1950, most in one
fell swoop on July 28. U.S. military police took up positions in NHK
offices, and purged employees were expelled forcibly from the premises.

As it happened, Shibata had been selected for a project that would
affect any decision to launch television in Japan. A delegation from the
newly created Radio Regulatory Commission (RRC) had been invited
to the United States, at U.S. government expense, to study the workings
of the Federal Communications Commission (FCC). The group was to
include one journalist, and Shibata had been selected for this role. Shibata acted as a representative of conservative, pro-U.S. Japanese opinion. At the conclusion of the tour, the Americans debriefed the members
of the study group and solicited their opinions. The report of this de-
briefing is frankly admiring of Shibata, who commented expansively
not only on his visit but also on the general political relationship between Japan and the United States. Shibata advocated rearmament of
Japan, which he saw as necessary to deter a communist invasion. He
concluded his remarks as follows:

> During this period, as well as in the immediate future, our informational
> media must play a vital role. Democratic journalism and radio, the media of
> mass communications, have a great responsibility. But most important, if it
> can be achieved—and I have realized this from my visit—is television for
> Japan. To strengthen and improve the role and influence of informational
> media in Japan in the years of great responsibility ahead, television must be
> introduced and developed in Japan. The educational significance and impact
> of television, used conscientiously, cannot be equaled by other media. Amer-
> icans take television for granted, but I am not looking at it American style.
> Economically, television in Japan might be hard to accomplish, but it must
> come. It is the greatest informational media to date, and Japan needs it for
> the difficult years ahead.[17]

Shibata did not mention that he had met with Senator Mundt and
proposed that Shōriki should implement Mundt's plan to establish a
television network in Japan. Mundt had responded enthusiastically and
provided Shibata with introductions to the men who had developed the
plan's specifics. Shibata extracted from them a promise to visit Japan in
person for the purpose of evaluating the potential for an early start to
television broadcasting.

Although Shōriki was the most powerful force at work promoting
television, he was by no means the only one. In February 1951, NHK

began experimental broadcasting using domestic technology. That same month a convoy from NHK braved a sixty-centimeter snowfall to bring a demonstration of television directly to the Diet. Perhaps as a result, television began to gain support. Japanese politicians rapidly learned to emphasize television's popular appeal instead of the political and economic considerations attached to it. On May 26, 1951, the Upper House passed a "resolution regarding the promotion of the start of television broadcasting." The resolution stated:

> The world has already entered into the television age. Now, all the people enthusiastically want the establishment of television, from which we can anticipate the development of Japan's broadcasting culture.
>
> Thus, we would like the government speedily to execute a specific plan containing effective and appropriate measures for the development of needed transmitting and receiving technologies, and for the spread of receivers. It is necessary to plan for the fullness of the people's cultural lifestyle.[18]

But there remained grave doubts about the viability and appropriateness of introducing television in a poor, economically dependent, debt-ridden nation. The comments of Shibata and others make it clear that they had abandoned the economic argument in favor of television and begun promoting it as an educational tool for the benefit of the political system and the "betterment of culture." This position strongly resembled the one taken before the war with regard to the spread of radio in Japan.

THE CAMPAIGN

The year 1951 opened with Asia engulfed in war. In the first days of January, which traditionally are celebrated as holidays in Korea, advancing Communist forces poured into a burning Seoul as millions of refugees streamed south. The following day United Nations forces abandoned Inchon. The world's attention was riveted on the dramatic events in the blighted Korean Peninsula. The implications were unfathomable: to many, it appeared that World War III had already started. The United States began evacuating its citizens from Hong Kong, despite the fact that this remained a British territory.

Japan's status in the conflict was uncertain and alarming. Because it remained under U.S. occupation, it was indistinguishable from the U.S. camp. And although China was not technically at war with the United States, Japan was nevertheless threatened with hostile action. A January 6 report in the *Nippon Times* cited warnings coming out of Taiwan that Japan was in danger of invasion by "reds." This external threat was augmented by a perceived internal threat: the same article commented that an invasion force would have an estimated 1.5 million supporters in Japan, comprising 1.2 million party members and 300,000 "fellow travelers."

It is hard to overstate the power with which the perceived communist threat hung over both Japan and the United States in early 1951. That April HUAC leveled charges of communist affiliation at various famous Americans, including Linus Pauling, Leonard Bernstein, Marlon Brando, Aaron Copland, and Albert Einstein. E. H. Norman, a Canadian diplomat and noted scholar on Japan, was accused of having communist ties, while Harvard professor John King Fairbank was banned from Japan by the U.S. Army for allegedly having helped a communist spy ring. Men like Karl Mundt were taking center stage in American politics.

On August 6, 1951, the Occupation, recognizing the inevitability of a mass pardon once its tenure ended, revoked the purges on a large list of former army officers, corporate leaders, and media figures, including Shōriki Matsutarō. Shōriki was now free to hold public office, run in political campaigns, and preside over any business activity he wished, including television. In 1945, Shōriki's hard-line anti-communist tactics had been cited in denunciations made against him by a newly powerful Japanese left wing enjoying U.S. protection. By 1951 the political climate had changed so much that Shōriki's anti-communist past was now his brightest credential.

The day after his pardon Shōriki held the first formal strategy session for his television license campaign. He planned to launch a network within a year. This was a tall order, as the RRC had not even begun deliberating whether Japan was ready for television. The official government position was that Japan was still too poor. Japanese leaders were pleading poverty because, among other reasons, they sought to avoid paying massive reparations to the Philippines, Korea, and other countries Japan had occupied during and before World War II. But on August 15 the *Nippon Times* contained two small news items that hinted at changes astir in the broadcasting world. One item announced the opening of Japan's first commercial radio station. Radio New Japan, in Osaka, was one of sixteen privately owned stations licensed by the Radio Regulatory Committee at the beginning of 1951. After a quarter-century of government monopoly, a new era in Japanese broadcasting had begun. The other item was a tiny report, via the wire service Agence France Presse, of a press conference held the previous day in Washington, D.C.: Senator Mundt had briefed the media on his vision for a television service to fight the communist threat in Japan.

The Mundt press conference was the first salvo in Shōriki's battle to bring television to Japan. Although held in Washington, the press conference had taken place at Shōriki's instigation. Japanese parliamentarian Okazaki Shinichi, a member of Japan's Upper House, accompanied Mundt. Though he gave the appearance of having collegial equality with Mundt, Okazaki was in fact a bought man: he was in Washington at Shōriki's express request. At the conference Mundt announced that a team of three American experts would leave for Japan the following week to study in detail the plan for a Japanese broadcast network. All three had assisted Mundt in preparing his initial projections on Japanese television. They included conservative New York lawyer Henry Holthusen; electrical engineer William Halstead; and Walter Duschinsky, a Czech exile credited with setting up the United Nations communications infrastructure.

When Shōriki received confirmation of the visit by Holthusen and his team, he set out to maximize publicity for the visit. His strategy was to ally himself to the fullest with the Mundt plan. Doing this enabled him in one stroke to borrow the credibility of a U.S. senator at the height of his power, the prestige and effectiveness of U.S. technology, and the impetus of the U.S. anti-communist campaign. Shōriki's own credentials as a confirmed enemy of the communists gave him added credibility within the propagandist context of Mundt's plan.

Shōriki essentially adopted this plan in full, differing from Mundt only with respect to ownership of the system. Rather than a U.S.-owned Vision of America, Shōriki proposed a Japanese-owned and -operated network that would carry Voice of America broadcasts as a method of financing. Having otherwise adopted the entire Mundt plan, he could allow the visiting Americans to speak for him as well as for Mundt.

Shōriki's first act, which may have taken place even before his depurging, was to forge an alliance between his newspaper, the *Yomiuri* (although no longer involved in management, Shōriki remained the largest shareholder), and the *Asahi* and *Mainichi* newspapers. The heads of the three publications agreed to put up capital jointly for a television venture. This kind of interrival cooperation was not unprecedented: one of the commercial radio stations about to go on the air in Tokyo was also the product of an alliance between the three papers.

Shōriki then went about lining up additional political and financial support for his venture. He started at the top. Within two weeks of his depurging he had persuaded Minister of Finance Ikeda Hayato to back him publicly—a move that was surely not in the spirit of the Occupation's "democratic" reforms. On August 20, Ikeda personally invited thirty bank, insurance, and securities company executives to a "television business promotion conference," to be held at the Finance Ministry on August 22. Ikeda, furiously busy with preparations for the upcoming San Francisco peace conference, attended only to make a brief speech, but the point was clear enough: Shōriki had the right people on his side.

That same day the American experts arrived at Haneda Airport, where they were met by the presidents of the *Yomiuri* and *Mainichi*, as well as by Shibata Hidetoshi. The Americans were immediately sent on a hectic tour of lectures and meetings. As Shibata reports in his memoirs, there were some tricky moments in this schedule; the Americans were under the impression that Shōriki had already raised the ¥2 billion he needed, when in fact one of the main purposes of the U.S. team's visit was to help Shōriki convince the Japanese business world to invest in his venture.[19]

A meeting at the Industrial Club on August 24 is representative. The Americans and Shōriki presented their plans to a large group of influential businessmen and financiers. The participants were given program sheets headed in English, "Meeting with the promoters of THE JAPAN NATIONAL NETWORK COMPANY at the Industrial Club." The Americans presented Mundt's plan in detail, showing a large map of Japan that illustrated the areas to be covered by each of the twenty-two relay stations. Their presentation emphasized the variety of uses to which this "multicast network" could be put, including air-to-surface communications, police and public safety communications, and phone and facsimile transmission.

The Americans assumed the role of impressively credentialed experts lecturing to a nonspecialized audience in a somewhat backward country. An important part of the purpose, from Shōriki's point of view, was to discredit Japanese technology as inadequate for the rapid introduction of television. In a special forum-style series in the *Yomiuri*, Yasuda Shōji, a *Yomiuri* director, asked Holthusen his opinion of Japanese television technology. The New York lawyer sardonically remarked: "Japan's television technology level is just about equivalent to that of 1932 French wine." This was a double-barbed comment, referring not only to the outdatedness of Japanese technology but also to what was reputedly an appalling vintage. It must have particularly hurt Taka-yanagi Kenjirō, who was present at the round table and whose most important work in television had been precisely at the turn of the 1930s.[20]

The Americans' attitude understandably upset some Japanese. Shibata reports that at one technical meeting a young engineer suddenly began shouting at them, "Don't mistake us Japanese engineers for uninformed babies. The things you're saying even a baby would know. Stop your boastful talk and go home." The amazed Americans asked for a translation of the outburst, but Shibata found himself unable to repeat these comments, so he simply requested that the young man leave the room.[21]

The Americans also met with Acting Prime Minister Masutani Hideji (Yoshida Shigeru had left for the San Francisco peace conference on September 1). In another big event, a dinner for prominent financiers, former munitions minister Fujiwara Ginjirō, a backer of Shōriki from his *Yomiuri* days, made a tearful speech in which he described his involvement with television as "exactly like an old man in the country planting an oak tree for the benefit of his grandchildren."

The Americans also visited Osaka as the guests of Matsushita Kōno-suke, who had expressed interest in investing in Shōriki's company. While they were there, Shibata reports, they listened to some of the early broadcasts from Japan's first commercial radio station. Matsushita, in fact, had a dual motive in hosting the Americans: he had learned that Holthusen represented the U.S. interests of Philips, with which Matsushita was on the point of concluding a large-scale joint-venture agreement. Matsushita reportedly plied the Americans with women to secure his support.[22]

Shōriki, meanwhile, began publicizing a very specific plan for his broadcasting network. He would start television broadcasting within six months, using technology imported from the United States. (In one speech he even claimed he would be ready to start broadcasting in January 1952, just four months away.) He estimated viewership of 300,000 in the first year and 3 million within five years. He proposed to deal with the vexing problem of foreign currency by carrying paid advertising and programming for the Voice of America. The United States was planning to build a television network covering Taiwan, South Korea, and the Philippines as well as Japan, so Shōriki's network could be a basic component in this system. Shōriki also challenged established institutions by stating that his microwave network would be able to handle telephone lines and wireless fax, thus contributing to the modernization of Japan's communications infrastructure.

Shōriki made introducing television sound as easy as saying "yes." The key point of his plan was the wholesale import of technology and equipment from the United States. There was undoubtedly an element of bravado in his statements. The user projections, for example, were extraordinarily ambitious—most other sources were projecting only about 25,000 viewers in the first year. (Shōriki's five-year projection, incidentally, turned out to be almost exactly on target.) Moreover, the plan to carry phone lines over his network clearly ran counter to Japanese law, which granted a monopoly to the government-run telephone system. When Shōriki formally applied for a broadcast license on October 2, it only covered television broadcasting, and only in Tokyo. But his main goal was to create momentum among politicians, regulators, financiers, and the general public that would establish him as the primary contender in the Japanese television industry. In this he succeeded admirably.

In response to Shōriki's onslaught, the Japanese press suddenly woke up to television. Whereas in the previous months articles on television had been few and far between, suddenly the papers were vying to offer analyses of the issues involved in bringing television to Japan and of the prospects for the industry. Some of this coverage was undoubtedly related to the newspaper sponsorship of Shōriki's company. But for whatever reason, television was suddenly news.

On August 23, 1951, the *Nippon Times* ran an editorial on the Mundt press conference of a few days earlier:

> The hopeful forecast is particularly welcome when, on the eve of Japan regaining her full autonomy with the signing of a peace treaty, the Japanese people face a tremendous task to strengthen democracy on the basis of lessons learned during the past six years. . . .
> The financing of the nationwide television network and of supplying low-cost receivers creates a tremendous problem. In terms of Japanese currency, the estimated cost of a nationwide network is an astronomical ¥1,801,200,000. At least an equal amount would be required for financing the purchase of a minimum number of receiving sets throughout the country.
> But the costs actually can be considered low [considering] the long term value and the overall advantages and purpose of the entire program.

On October 2, Shōriki's Nihon Terebi Hōsōmō (Nihon Television Network, or NTV) formally submitted its license application to the

RRC. In a rather surprising move, Shōriki enlisted the support of a consortium of Buddhist leaders, representatives of forty-five different organizations, who announced financial as well as spiritual support for Shōriki's project in the interest of promoting Buddhist education via television.

THE AMBIGUOUS ROLE OF MITI

On September 8, 1951, Yoshida Shigeru, accompanied by a large delegation of Japanese politicians, signed a treaty of peace in San Francisco, restoring normal relations with thirty-two other signatories. Japan was once again an independent nation. Soviet foreign minister Andrei Gromyko, in San Francisco for the negotiations, denounced the peace treaty as a "draft for a new war." Indeed, the following day Japan entered into a comprehensive security alliance with the United States. As though to underline the Faustian nature of the pact, all nineteen members of the Japan Communist Party's Central Provisional Directorate were arrested on September 4. Those who were Diet members lost their seats.

The peace treaty yielded a harvest of popularity for "one man" Yoshida, and it produced an optimistic mood in the nation as a whole. But for most Japanese, the economic situation in late 1951 could scarcely be called promising. An editorial in the *Nippon Times* commented gloomily on the 2 percent decline in real incomes over the preceding year: "Unfortunately, all too many of the people are under the illusion that their living standards would rise to new postwar heights after the peace treaty is ratified. But nothing could be further from the truth. There is absolutely no indication of our living level looking up."[23]

The timing of television broadcasting's launch in Japan involved important political questions, but it was also a very real economic issue. Inevitably, an early start would involve a heavy expenditure of foreign currency. Although the Korean War had alleviated Japan's acute foreign exchange crisis, it could hardly afford significant outflows of capital. The newly established Ministry of International Trade and Industry (MITI), which effectively controlled uses of foreign exchange, played a key role in resolving the issue. During the middle months of 1951 MITI discreetly made the decision to support an accelerated timetable for the introduction of television in Japan. On June 27, 1951, the Gaishi Iinkai (Foreign Investment Committee, or FIC), a MITI-controlled board overseeing long-term transactions involving foreign currency, released its fourth list of "desired" technologies. For the first time, the list included television. This was the first clear indication of MITI's support for the rapid introduction of television—and, by extension, for the creation of a domestic television industry based on imported technology.

At any given time, the FIC list named about forty key items targeted for import. Some were very specific, with several relating to a single industry. Inclusion on this list therefore implied a highly privileged status. The FIC's stated general principle was to "limit the introduction of foreign investment to that which will contribute to the self-support and sound development of the Japanese economy and to the improvement of the international balance of payments."[24] It is hard to see how television, which would inevitably cause a drain in foreign currency and which offered no obvious economic benefits, fit this description.

Indeed, by approving the import of foreign (mainly American) television technology, MITI risked dealing a heavy blow to Japan's established electrical goods companies. Toshiba, Japan Victor, Nippon Denki, NHK, and others had been working on television technology for close to two decades. They had a strong vested interest in developing Japanese television using Japanese technology and minimal imports. By opening the way for the wholesale import of U.S. technology, MITI essentially abandoned that long research effort. The (perhaps unintended) consequence of this policy was to enable smaller, less established companies to enter the Japanese television market and supplant the traditional leaders.

Why did MITI adopt this apparently counterproductive policy? One reason was no doubt the growing pressure from Shōriki and his associates, who had enormous political clout (including by this time the tacit support of Prime Minister Yoshida). All the same, MITI's bureaucrats would not have committed substantial foreign exchange resources to television unless they truly believed an early introduction of television was desirable. From the tone of public statements at the time, there is no doubt that MITI staffers and others believed television broadcasting would bolster national pride, raise morale, and enrich the culture. Japan's rulers had consistently supported new communications technologies for the past century—at no time more so than in the years of war and occupation.

Moreover, MITI had concluded that domestic technology was fundamentally inadequate to the task of bringing television to Japan in the near future. Japanese scientists had readily acknowledged the gap between Japan and the United States in this regard. Whereas NHK was still using versions of the prewar iconoscope camera, RCA had been using the far more sensitive image orthicon camera for years. The iconoscope required enormous amounts of light to record a picture. Satō Hidehisa, an NHK employee at the time, commented on the experimental broadcasts of early 1951 as follows:

> Rather than having illumination, it was more like building a huge fire, the lights were so powerful. At first there were no professional announcers, so we technicians filled that role. When we stood on the stage under those fierce lights, our pomaded hair would start giving off smoke, and would soon melt into a flat, wet mess. Musical instruments like accordions and violins would instantly go out of tune. At that time there were no make up or special effects professionals, and all sorts of strange phenomena appeared on the screen. People with gold teeth would look as though they had no teeth at all, while violins would catch the light and look as though they were on fire.[25]

Nevertheless, many of the scientists and companies working on television, as well as the technicians at NHK, felt that eventually domestic broadcasting could begin using only minimal imported technology. However, it would take time before Japanese technology improved to that point. By prioritizing U.S. technology, MITI placed Japan on a timetable that fit with Shōriki's ambitious plans.

But MITI also recognized the need to protect the domestic television industry. Japanese companies would use foreign technology freely and at considerable expense, but they would still manufacture domestically, and MITI would prevent an import free-for-all. Import restrictions were almost a foregone conclusion, given the cost of television sets and the very real constraints on foreign exchange at the time. Japan's total import budget in 1951 was some $1.6 billion. Although this was double the 1950 level, reflecting the foreign exchange inflow from the Korean War, the currency had to be used for essential imports such as petroleum, food, and raw materials such as iron ore. There simply was not enough money available for large-scale importation of a luxury item such as television. MITI itself pointed out in a 1953 publication that if NHK's projected diffusion level of 830,000 television sets by 1958 were to be met by imports, the cost would be $166 million.[26] Using Shōriki's much more aggressive (and ultimately correct) assumptions, the foreign exchange outflow would be at least $300 million.

However, restricting imports would artificially raise the price of televisions. An analysis in the *Nikkei* on January 9, 1952, concluded that a U.S.-made RCA 14-inch set could be brought to Yokohama for ¥79,000 and, after addition of import tax, goods tax, and luxury tax, be sold for

¥138,000. By contrast, a domestically produced set was projected to cost ¥150,000. Clearly a compromise was needed: MITI would protect and promote the domestic industry on the condition that Japanese manufacturers increased production to create economies of scale and reduce prices. MITI's pricing guideline was ¥150,000 per set in the first year, ¥100,000 in the second, and ¥70,000 by the third year—implying substantial economies of scale.[27]

THE RRC DECISION

If the decisions on Japanese television manufacturing and imports rested with MITI, the final word on television broadcasting came from the Radio Regulatory Commission (Denpa Kanri Iinkai, RRC). This independent agency played a highly controversial role in the inception of Japanese television. Indeed, the contentiousness that roiled around the RRC in many ways symbolized the larger conflicts that affected both television and the creation of a new political economy in Japan in the early 1950s.

The U.S. Occupation created the RRC and clearly saw it as a crucial element in the establishment of democratic institutions in Japan. Modeled on the U.S. Federal Communications Commission, it was to be independent of both politicians and bureaucrats and "uninfluenced by politics, power or pressure."[28] The Occupation authorities, particularly the Civil Communications Section, emphasized the function broadcasting might serve in furthering the goal of democratization. The vice chief of the CCS described the RRC as "a part of the Occupation objective to assist in the democratization of Japan and to permit a free and uncontrolled medium of information."[29]

The RRC incorporated several features that were quite new to Japanese politics. These included not only the independence of the commission itself but also its obligation to base its decisions on public hearings, which would in theory promote democracy in decision making. One of the commissioners commented just prior to the commission's inception: "The hearing procedure . . . [is] an epoch making system which has never been seen in other existing Japanese laws in this field."[30]

Perhaps because of its revolutionary features, the Radio Regulatory Commission was created over the objections of the Japanese government. The Yoshida cabinet wanted to place a cabinet minister in charge of the commission, ostensibly to ensure that the agency had proper representation in decisions relating to budgetary and other policy issues.

But CCS strongly resisted this move, claiming that the whole point of the commission was to ensure broadcasting's independence from the government. It took a letter from General MacArthur to Prime Minister Yoshida to resolve this issue. MacArthur firmly upheld the CCS line, stating that it was "mandatory" that the RRC remain free from "direct control or influence by any partisan group or other agency." The letter continued: "The requirements that a state minister be chairman of the commission and that the Cabinet have authority to reverse decisions of the commission completely negate the principle of independence and render the commission a mere advisory committee of the Cabinet."[31]

As a result of MacArthur's intervention, the commission was established under the terms proposed by CCS. But the government continued to object, and politicians and bureaucrats allied with the conservative administration immediately began to maneuver for the commission's abolition. As early as December 1950 (six months after creation of the RRC) the Administrative Management Agency, a government-appointed bureau charged with downsizing the government, proposed disbanding the RRC and moving its function back into the Communications Ministry.

The members of the RRC appear to have caught some of their U.S. advisers' spirit of independence. They collaborated enthusiastically in American-style public relations initiatives to bolster their image as representatives of the people. But their backgrounds hardly marked them as revolutionaries. Two of the members—Tomiyasu Kenji and Amishima Tsuyoshi—were career Communications Ministry bureaucrats. Tomiyasu, the RRC chairman, had been vice minister of the Communications Ministry before his retirement, and Amishima had been a senior officer in the communications bureaucracy right up to his appointment to the commission. Three other members were also veteran bureaucrats: Kamimura Shin'ichi had capped a distinguished Foreign Ministry career with an appointment as Japanese minister to Manchukuo; Sakamoto Naomichi had been the Paris representative of the South Manchurian Railway Company; and Okazaki Jōichi had been a judge. The two remaining commissioners, Segawa Masakuni and Nukiyama Heiichi, were professionals within the communications research establishment—the former a one-time head of Tokyo's Electrical Research Institute, the latter a professor at Tōhoku University. Moreover, the administrative staff of the commission had been transferred en masse from the interim Electrical Communications Ministry. There was little in these men's backgrounds to suggest they would behave in a way contrary to the interests or views of the bureaucracy.

Amishima's view of his role as a RRC commissioner seemed much more in sync with the government's point of view than with that of the Americans. In his memoirs, Amishima comments:

> The American plan was that radio administration including broadcasting should be totally separated from the cabinet and the prime minister—in other words that it must be a totally independent agency. But thinking about it from the Japanese side, the new Japanese constitution clearly stated that administrative powers belong to the cabinet. Hence it was quite impossible to think of radio regulatory powers lying outside the cabinet and its head, the prime minister.[32]

At the outset, the RRC was concerned primarily with radio. One of the three U.S.-inspired broadcast laws passed in 1949 specifically called for the opening of commercial radio stations, so upon opening its doors the RRC received a flood of license applications. After sifting through them, the RRC in early 1951 licensed sixteen commercial radio stations around the country. These license awards garnered a great deal of attention from the press and public, indicating a strong interest in the creation of commercial broadcasting.

With respect to television, the RRC played an essentially passive role, responding to license requests rather than initiating them. Nevertheless, the members of the RRC had made it clear by mid-1951 that they were interested in promoting television broadcasting. When the Upper House of the Diet passed its resolution requesting an early launch of broadcasting, RRC chairman Tomiyasu Kenji responded: "I have received your resolution to promote television broadcasting. . . . The government too believes that television will have a very big impact on improving the national culture and developing industry etc. Therefore, I would like to introduce measures to actualize it rapidly."[33]

Before this actualization could take place, the RRC had to address two vitally important issues. Both were highly controversial, with powerful political interests supporting them on either side. The first issue was the selection of a technical standard for Japanese television. The second was the award of broadcast licenses.

The leading lights of the television research establishment—with Takayanagi Kenjirō at their head—were proceeding on the assumption of a seven-megacycle standard. This would render Japanese television incompatible with American television, which operated on six megacycles. Abstruse as it may seem, this issue was of crucial significance for the launch of television in Japan, as it would strongly affect the competitiveness of Japanese television set manufacturers in the domestic market. If Japan selected the six-megacycle standard used in the American industry, then it would be possible to import receivers directly from the United States, as Shōriki was planning to do. Established companies that were developing an independent technology naturally opposed this strategy. These companies, together with NHK, maintained that a seven-megacycle bandwidth would provide better quality and make it possible to convert easily to color television, which was already on the point of introduction in the United States.

Such technical issues were overshadowed by the political and economic implications of the decision. The camp supporting the seven-megacycle standard included the major television research companies—Toshiba, Nippon Denki, and others—as well as the national broadcast company, NHK. By comparison, the Shōriki camp stood more or less alone. But by the final quarter of 1951—after Shōriki's dramatic debut as a license contender—it was clear that the RRC was leaning toward the American standard. Although NHK and the established companies seemed to represent the establishment view, apparently both the Diet and MITI—not to mention Shōriki himself—wanted the RRC to opt for the six-megacycle standard. MITI hinted at its view in its 1951 yearbook, which listed among the measures taken to promote the television industry: "Provision of opinion to RRC with regard to standards for black and white TV."[34] It seems unlikely that MITI would publicize this fact unless its opinion had been heeded.

On November 8, 1951, the RRC informally announced its intention to adopt the American format and officially confirmed the decision with the publication on December 4 of the "Standard Transmission Format for Black and White Television Broadcasting." The RRC charter required it to hold public hearings before finalizing such decisions; however, its hearings on the television standard did not occur until January 17, 1952, *after* the standard had been announced. This three-day hearing brought vociferous arguments against the six-megacycle standard; indeed, Shōriki and his associates appeared to be the only ones arguing in its favor. But this hearing was likely no more than a formality. The decision had already been made. Matsushita's television business plan, compiled in December, assumed a six-megacycle format and dismissed the public hearing with the comment: "[T]he formal decision for six-megacycles will be made after this hearing."[35] Although Amishima affirmed the importance of public hearings in correspondence to the Occupation authorities, there is little in the commission's record to indicate a real desire to consider the wishes of the general public.

In fact, the general public was not present at the January hearing—the audience consisted entirely of industry representatives and technical specialists. When the announcement was made confirming the RRC's decision, these parties created enough uproar to force the RRC to hold another public hearing in April. This final hearing, although also futile, was a highly charged event. Takayanagi Kenjirō, the "father of Japanese television," broke down and wept, unable to finish his remarks. He was watching his child sacrificed to the interests of an outsider.

Years after the event, Amishima commented on the committee's reasons for selecting the six-megacycle format:

> We heard the voices of the Diet and ordinary people saying we should start television as soon as possible. Even if we waited several years, it wasn't clear that Japanese technology would be up to the task. Also, if we used native technology, we wouldn't be able to swap programs or relay foreign programs. In the end, none of the committee members thought we should stick to Japanese technology. As for industry's argument that U.S. companies would be able to sell cheaply in Japan and undercut the Japanese, the general tendency of the RRC's opinion was that . . . if Japanese products were of high quality and low price, then quite the contrary, Japanese makers would also be able to export to the US. . . . Also I think some members felt that an early introduction of television would help support the culture of our people who were exhausted from defeat, and that it would give industry a boost of energy.[36]

By late 1951 the Japanese political establishment—including MITI and the Cabinet—had apparently decided that it was socially desirable to introduce television as rapidly as possible. That Shōriki was also pushing this view with his formidable political clout probably tipped the balance in favor of the six-megacycle format.

By the beginning of 1952, then, the key decisions for the future of the Japanese television industry had been made. Japan would adopt the six-megacycle format, permitting immediate use of American equipment and technology; and MITI would nurture and protect the domestic television industry. Many other issues, of course, remained unresolved. One was the scope of and prospects for the market; another was which companies would compete in the television set market; yet another was which commercial station or stations, if any, would be licensed; and a final question was when television broadcasting would actually begin. The most controversial of these issues in 1952 was the licensing question. By the end of 1951, both NHK and Shōriki's NTV had applied for licenses, and the RRC was already deeply embroiled in the inevitable political pressures accompanying this decision.

The implications were far-reaching. Although NHK had lost the battle over bandwidth, it maintained a vigorous fight to win the war over public versus private broadcasting. However, as Matsushita's planning document of late 1951 makes clear, the joint licensing of NHK and one or more commercial stations seemed highly likely and may even have been a foregone conclusion. Nevertheless, with both NHK and Shōriki mustering powerful support, the RRC could expect to take heat for whatever formal decision it made. It was a no-win situation.

In February 1952 the RRC's peace-loving chairman, Tomiyasu Kenji, resigned for reasons of ill health (he returned to his true love, composing haiku, and died in 1979 at the age of ninety-three). He was replaced by Amishima Tsuyoshi, who in mid-July was summoned to meet with Prime Minister Yoshida. Amishima went to the meeting with some trepidation and was surprised that, after asking some general questions about television, Yoshida talked mainly about his efforts to have the French government return the Matsukata collection of paintings to Japan. On his way out, though, Amishima was taken aside by chief cabinet secretary Hori Shigeru, who told him: "The Prime Minister wants you to give Shōriki a television permit." Amishima claims he felt no obligation to follow this advice because Yoshida did not broach the subject personally.[37] Another reminiscence, however, has Amishima admitting that Yoshida said: "Old man Shōriki is making such a fuss, we have to do something" (*Shōriki no oyaji ga urusakute shō ga nai*).[38]

Publicly, at least, Yoshida maintained a relatively neutral stance with regard to television. According to a March 26, 1952, report in the *Asahi*, Yoshida stated in response to a parliamentary question: "We are in no hurry to introduce television in Japan. The government has no money for it, and because of the high price it will be hard for all families to have it." But Satō Eisaku, minister of posts and telecommunications and an avowed opponent of the Shōriki plan, commented later: "In those days, Prime Minister Yoshida was relatively openly saying, 'Let's do it the American way.'"[39]

By the second quarter of 1952, the end was in sight for the commission itself. As the Occupation entered its final weeks, the Japanese government began drawing up specific plans to abolish the RRC, which it had never liked from the beginning. On April 25, three days before the restoration of full independence to Japan, the cabinet announced that the "complex and cumbersome" administrative agencies set up during the war and Occupation would be disbanded and their duties and powers transferred to the relevant ministries. The cabinet announced that it was taking this action in the interests of simplicity, efficiency, and "the principle of democracy." However, the way the statement lumps together "totalitarian" wartime and "democratizing" Occupation agencies suggests that the government simply sought to concentrate power in the bureaucracy and remove it from the hands of semi-independent agencies.

Once it became apparent that the RRC would cease to exist (the date was fixed at midnight on July 31), the commissioners had the option of bowing out of the licensing process altogether; by simply allowing their agency to expire, they could hand over these decisions to the Ministry of Posts and Telecommunications, which was to absorb the RRC's functions. Satō Eisaku, who had been minister of posts and telecommunications since July 1951, was known to be hostile to Shōriki and supportive of NHK. Satō later frankly expressed his views on the issue: "With regard to broadcasting, I was of the English school: I didn't approve of permitting commercial broadcasting. For that reason I was very distressed by the Yomiuri's Shōriki Matsutarō."[40] Thus, a failure to act by the RRC might mean the award of a television broadcasting monopoly to NHK.

On July 31—the RRC's last day of existence—the commissioners met to decide on the award of broadcast licenses. This event has passed into broadcasting lore as one of the most dramatic in Japanese television's history. The commission did not begin its session until 2 P.M., and the deliberations immediately ran into controversy. At least one commissioner, Segawa Masakuni, held out to the end for inaction: the RRC, he felt, should simply let itself lapse. In midafternoon Amishima received a phone call from Satō asking him to recess the meeting and "leave the decisions to your successors." Then, in the early evening, the commission's chief administrative officer inexplicably disappeared, leaving a resignation letter with the commission's secretary. A search party was sent out, and the errant bureaucrat was eventually rounded up and talked out of his decision. But the debate within the RRC was by no means concluded. At least three of the five commissioners were in favor of giving Shōriki a license, but Amishima wanted a unanimous vote. In the end this proved impossible to achieve, so the RRC finally issued a majority ruling just twenty minutes before its dissolution at midnight. The decision: Shōriki

Figure 5   Shōriki Matsutarō celebrates the award of a television license to his company, NTV, in early August 1952. Shōriki is the bald man holding his glass toward the camera. (Courtesy of Nihon Terebi Hōsōmō)

would receive a license. Two other applicants, NHK and Radio Tokyo, were left in limbo. The RRC claimed it was too early to pronounce on either—NHK had not yet received legal approval to charge license fees for television, and Radio Tokyo had only just gone on the air. Two other license applications were definitively rejected.

After the RRC decision, Segawa published a dissenting opinion: "We should have abandoned attempts to pass regulations as soon as the decision was taken to abolish this committee. As for the decision that was released today, considering the present system we have in Japan, it would seem on principle that NHK should be given precedence."[41]

The drama and significance of this last-minute decision by the RRC have been played up by Japanese historians of broadcasting and by the participants themselves. But did the RRC really change the course of history with these apparently brave actions? Important sections of the establishment had already decided by the end of 1951 that commercial broadcasting should be initiated as soon as possible in Japan, and Shōriki was the strong favorite to be the initiator, both because of his personal political clout and because he was in the best position to accelerate the process. Although Satō Eisaku portrays himself as an enemy of Shōriki, it is noteworthy that his administration did nothing to sabotage Shōriki's entry into television even after the Ministry of Posts and Telecommunications assumed jurisdiction on August 1, 1952. Indeed, the ministry proceeded to license numerous additional commercial television broadcasters, including Radio Tokyo. Meanwhile, it was clear that NHK, despite the RRC's pointed snub, would eventually receive a television license. Indeed, NHK quietly received its license in November 1952 and went on the air in February 1953, six months ahead of Shōriki's NTV.

MANUFACTURER STRATEGIES

By the end of 1951, it had become apparent that television would be introduced into Japan in the near future using the format of the U.S. industry. It was around this time that the major Japanese radio manufacturers made commitments to build televisions for the Japanese market. What made these hard-headed businessmen think they could make money on television sets? After all, the required investments were very large, and the economic conditions of Japan still seemed to militate against the spread of such an expensive product.

No Japanese company had yet taken serious steps toward the manufacture of television, although most large makers of electrical goods had produced a handful of experimental sets. Japan still lacked production facilities for many key components, including the picture tube. And although a half-dozen major companies had entered into technology assistance agreements with leading Western companies, these pacts were aimed at radio manufacturing and had not yet led to the transfer of television technology.

On October 30, 1951, the *Nikkei* published an analysis of the prospects for manufacturing. The article estimated it would cost ¥2 billion ($5.6 million) to create a manufacturing capability, assuming adoption of the six-megacycle standard and the import of American technology. This investment broke down into ¥100 million for research and development; ¥400 million to establish picture tube production facilities; ¥400 million to establish receiver production facilities; ¥100 million for parts production facilities; and ¥1 billion working capital. Another ¥1 billion would be required to set up an installment financing system for 2,000 sets a year (about 10 percent of total sales). MITI's sales projections were modest at best: 22,500 sets in the first year, 42,500 in the second year, and 140,000 in the third year. MITI's wireless section head, Araya Seizō, commented: "Japan can't catch up with America's 12 million sets, or with the UK's 700,000 sets. But I think we can easily overtake France's 50,000 sets."[42]

The initial assumption was that household demand would be almost nil. A Matsushita internal planning document assumed that early purchasers would include large department stores, restaurants, government offices, schools, theaters, and wealthy families (defined as "owning some property and having monthly income of over ¥50,000"). These last were expected to account for less than a quarter of the projected 18,500 units sold by all companies.[43] (Even the optimistic Shōriki Matsutarō planned to rely on placing large-screen television sets in public places, much as Senator Mundt proposed, in order to garner viewers.) Matsushita estimated that imports and do-it-yourself kits would account for a good half of sales, leaving Japanese manufacturers to divide up a market of fewer than 10,000 buyers. Moreover, Matsushita planners were very hesitant to project large increases in future years. The plan tentatively suggested a doubling of demand in the second year but made no bets beyond that.

With such high investment costs and such modest expected returns, it is not surprising that few companies made a major commitment to television manufacturing at this stage. MITI assumed that only two or three companies—specifically Matsushita, Toshiba, and Nippon Denki—would take the plunge, and MITI assigned most of its modest subsidy funds to them (direct MITI subsidies amounted to ¥128 million in 1950–52).[44] But even these companies were to some extent paying lip service to the idea of manufacturing. None of them took serious measures to set up production facilities prior to the launch of television.

The commitment to domestic television manufacturing was not, therefore, as wholehearted as it might at first have appeared. When television broadcasting began in February 1953, only one of the three companies targeted by MITI—Matsushita—was actually making televisions, and its output was very low—about forty sets per month—while prices were extremely high, at some ¥290,000 per set. Quality was also poor. By August Matsushita had given up manufacturing its own sets and had resorted to selling imports.

VISIONS AND REALITIES

Headlines blaring "THIS IS THE YEAR OF TELEVISION" ushered in 1953 in Japan. The new MITI minister, Ogasawara Sankurō, said in the trade journal *Denpa shinbun* (Radio News) that manufacturers must make every effort to close the technological gap in television, radar, and tubes because "electric communications are the symbol of a modern civilized country." Reflecting a parallel theme of the new political economy, Toshiba president Ishizaka said: "I believe that every person's goal is a better life (*betaa raifu*). I have very strong hopes for the use of electricity. Japan is poor in other raw materials, but we are wealthy in electricity."[45]

Amid fanfare, banners, and speeches, NHK went on the air with full-time programming on February 1, 1953. After all the bickering over licensing, NHK still beat Shōriki's NTV by a full six months. But with the agonizing decisions over format and licensing over, it remained to persuade the public to watch the expensive new medium.

In some respects, the launch of television had proceeded roughly according to plan—at least, according to the plans of the mandarins in MITI. Imports of nonessential items and completed receivers were severely restricted or banned outright. The conditions were in place to nurture a domestic industry and promote television watching. After all the rhetoric, the reality had arrived in the form of a rather fuzzy square gray-and-white screen.

However, many of the plans of the previous two years simply did not materialize. Despite two decades of research, none of the established manufacturers had a viable product to offer by the time television programming began. Those companies with the longest research histories—Toshiba, Nihon Victor, Nippon Denki, and Nihon Columbia—seemed to be the slowest in bringing a product to the market. Nihon Victor was the furthest behind; Takayanagi Kenjirō, head of the company's television division, apparently never regained his momentum after the defeat over broadcast standards. By February 1953, Victor was the only major player that had not yet concluded a license agreement with RCA—a step that was by now universally acknowledged as essential. Indeed, by the end of the year Nihon Victor faced severe management and financial difficulties, necessitating a humiliating takeover by Matsushita Denki in 1954.

On the plus side, a number of new companies were stepping into the television market. Once MITI had made it clear (in mid-1951) that it would permit Japanese companies to sign license agreements for the import of television technology, a spate of would-be entrants took the initiative and entered into negotiations with key patent owners, particularly RCA. That company assisted by offering access to its patents (for a fee) to all comers. Although MITI envisioned that only a handful of companies would license foreign television technology, by June 1953 some forty-two companies had applied to the FIC for approval. The majority of these agreements were apparently negotiated quite independently of MITI and the FIC, and MITI was more or less forced to consent to them. MITI placed a cap of thirty-seven on the number of licenses it would approve, but in the end this covered all the serious applicants.

Having gained access to foreign technology, several smaller companies aggressively began manufacturing televisions. Hayakawa Denki, owned by feisty entrepreneur Hayakawa Tokuji, was making two hundred sets a month by the beginning of 1953, making it by far the largest television producer in Japan. Moreover, Hayakawa's sets, which it sold under the brand name Sharp, were priced much more attractively than the limited offerings of its more established competitors, retailing for around ¥175,000.

Paradoxically, Hayakawa's lack of a long research tradition seems to have worked to the company's advantage. Hayakawa imported many of its television components and farmed out production of those parts that were readily available in Japan. Its specific expertise was in efficient, low-cost assembly, giving it a great advantage over other Japanese television makers. Hayakawa Tokuji had toured RCA's production facilities in 1952 and recognized the importance of importing not only parts and technologies but also mass production techniques. Hayakawa Denki broke ground on a new ¥107 million television factory in April 1953, giving the company the most advanced assembly facilities in Japan. It is worth noting that Hayakawa was much more willing to take risks than its better-established competitors. The company's total capital in mid-1953 was only ¥120 million.[46]

The Yao company began manufacturing television sets in March 1953, also relying for the most part on imported parts. Yao sold under the brand name General (reputedly named for General MacArthur), and with Hayakawa (Sharp) it was to capture 33 percent of the market in 1953, 36 percent in 1954, and 40 percent in 1955. By contrast, Nippon Denki never gained a foothold in the black-and-white television market, and Nihon Victor never succeeded in gaining more than 5 percent of the market (see Table 2, p. 244).

The most successful companies in the early years of Japanese television were those that most closely followed the Shōriki vision. Bringing television to Japan was as simple as importing kits from the United

States and assembling them. But what of MITI's vow to restrict imports to the bare minimum? Like the major electrical goods companies, MITI found that the realities of the world of television were very different from its initial vision. In addition to licensing far more companies than originally projected, MITI found itself in the unpleasant position of having to approve imports on a much larger scale than it had planned.

In 1950 and 1951, the combination of direct U.S. aid and procurement orders for the Korean War masked Japan's underlying trade imbalance. These forms of assistance, however, were known to be temporary; in 1953 U.S. aid came to a near-complete halt, and although U.S. procurements remained strong, Japanese imports soared. As a result, Japan began running a trade deficit, and foreign exchange reserves began to drain out of the country at the rate of $20 million a month. Moreover, imports of machinery, including radio- and television-related machinery, were climbing steadily as a proportion of all imports. Machinery imports made up 9 percent of total imports in 1953, versus only 3 percent in 1951, and electrical goods imports soared from ¥24 million in 1950 to ¥1.1 billion in 1952.[47]

In 1953 the demand for imports increased still further. In effect, the Shōriki plan was coming to fruition. Shōriki had forced an early start to television premised on the ease of importing from the United States (he imported some two hundred large sets himself and set them up in public places around Tokyo), and MITI, which wanted to promote television's popular acceptance, had to permit those imports to occur. Yet the worsening foreign exchange situation made it a particularly inauspicious time to engage in an overseas buying spree. MITI was caught between two irreconcilable goals, and as a result its policy at this time was characterized by sudden about-faces and private actions that contradicted public posturing.

The ambiguity of MITI's position came across in a *Denpa shinbun* article from February 7, 1953:

> A rumor is circulating that there are close to 2,000 imported sets now sitting in a certain warehouse in Yokohama. Of course we think this is just a rumor, but let us introduce you to another rumor: there is a strange story circulating that MITI will easily allow you to bring in foreign sets under the foreign exchange allocation "miscellaneous." It seems quite obvious to us that a television set is a communications device and not "miscellaneous," but perhaps if you disassemble it, then legally it becomes "miscellaneous."

Officially, MITI allowed the import of 5,300 television sets in 1953. However, it planned in subsequent years to limit imports to important components such as picture tubes. Later in 1953, the tightening foreign exchange crisis caused MITI to reverse itself and restrict imports even more severely than originally planned. Imports of picture tubes smaller than 17 inches were totally banned, making domestic television manufacture all but impossible (there was as yet no domestic picture tube industry). The resulting parts shortage forced MITI to unlock the import gates again, approving the import of 82,000 picture tubes of 14 inches or more.[48]

For the broadcasters, too, television got off to a slow start, falling far short of Shōriki's initial expectations. Indeed, Shōriki had overestimated at every turn. For startup capital he raised not the ¥1 billion he had confidently predicted (and with which all his biographies seem even now to credit him) but just ¥250 million (about $700,000). Nor did he borrow anything like the additional ¥1 billion he had sought. Loans at the end of 1953 totaled just ¥100 million.[49]

CONCLUSION

After much fighting, debate, maneuvering, and consensus-building, Japan by the end of 1953 had both television broadcasting and a domestic television industry. Both were established much more rapidly than an observer in 1950 could possibly have anticipated. Television was now ready to take its privileged position; the nation turned to it for the great serial dramas of high economic growth, the consumer revolution, and the arrival of the "middle mass" society.

By all rational calculations, television should not have begun in Japan for another several years. What made this early debut possible? Two explanations are frequently put forward, both for the successful launch of television and for the success of the electrical goods industry as a whole. One is that Japan had a long tradition of research, including pioneering efforts by leading scientists such as Takayanagi Kenjirō. In the case of television, this argument can easily be dismissed. Quite to the contrary, Japan's television research establishment, if left to itself, would have delayed the medium's arrival by at least several more years. The companies most effective in gaining a share of the new industry were those most willing to discard the efforts of the past and to rely wholeheartedly on foreign imports and foreign technology.

Another common argument credits the rapid introduction of television to MITI's prescient industrial targeting. This argument, too, fails to stand on its own. If MITI did see potential in a domestic television industry, it certainly failed to envision the development of an export powerhouse. A few bold people both inside and outside MITI may have mentioned export potential as one justification for establishing a television industry. But none of the participants seriously imagined that Japanese companies could compete in the foreseeable future against the American and European giants of the industry. Nonetheless, other measures of support by MITI—most notably its policy of import restriction—were undeniably critical to the establishment and eventual success of the Japanese television industry.

Ultimately, an understanding of the precipitous rise of Japanese television rests not on possible rational explanations but on the economic *irr*ationality of the process. With the exception of highly risk-oriented entrepreneurs such as Shōriki Matsutarō and Hayakawa Tokuji, all parties involved in the birth of the industry agreed in the early 1950s that the economics of television were difficult at best. But each of these parties came around to the view that, in spite of the economics, Japan *should* have television broadcasting and a domestic television industry. Some, such as Prime Minister Yoshida and the members of the Radio Regulatory Commission, were swayed by concerns about public demand, public morale, and "raising the level of national culture." This kind of view is perhaps best expressed in a letter to the *Denpa Jihō* in October 1952: "Right now, we are struggling just to return to our prewar standard of living. If we wait for Japan to catch up to the American standard, it may take a hundred years for us to get television. But for that very reason, I believe that people should be allowed to raise their cultural level at least a little by acquiring one of the major implements of twentieth century civilization."

At MITI, national pride, the lure of a high-technology industry, and the issue of "national culture" prompted officials to overlook the significant drain on foreign exchange resources—in clear contravention of the spirit of the Foreign Exchange Law—that television inevitably caused. For others—particularly Shōriki's American supporters—a more important consideration was the power of television as a weapon against communism. None of these arguments changed the fact that, economically, television made no sense for Japan.

Shōriki Matsutarō's powerful campaign acted as a stimulus to all of these themes. Shōriki was possessed by a vision of television's immense potential for profit, influence, and power. He said at one point: "There is no business that will make as much profit as television. Unlike newspapers, it needs no paper and no delivery staff. They say that being a

Buddhist monk [*bōzu*] is pure profit, but monks have nothing on this."[50] Of all the participants in the drama, Shōriki perhaps saw most clearly how television would serve as an integral part of a new era of prosperity. Because he expected to reap a great harvest of gain himself, Shōriki may have encouraged overoptimism in his rosy economic projections for television. But in the long term, his vision was realized.

It is ironic, but not altogether surprising, that this vision belonged not to one of the young pioneers of the "new Japan" but to a bastion of the old regime. Volker Berghahn, in a study of German postwar business elites, comments on the importance of examining the attitudes and values of entrepreneurs if we are to understand the dynamic of the postwar economy. "I was struck time and time again," he writes, "by the reappearance of many names of people who had undergone their tertiary socialization in the interwar period and who had risen to leading positions in the Nazi economy."[51] Clearly, the case of Japan was not very different.

Like his contemporary Yoshida Shigeru, Shōriki understood that the new contained many features of the old. Shōriki had lived through the first flush of mass culture in the 1920s and helped harness the power of the media to the cause of mass mobilization in World War II. These experiences would stand him in good stead in his nurturing of the "middle mass" consumer society. Like Yoshida, Shōriki was entrenched in the very warp and woof of Japan's institutional structure. He knew as well as anyone in Japan how to get what he wanted. Much of the story of Japan's early embrace of television can be explained by the power of his vision.

4

The Technologies of Desire

Technological creativity has, according to Joel Mokyr, been "the lever of riches" in the history of the Western world. "Without it," he adds, "we would all still live nasty and short lives of toil, drudgery, and discomfort."[1] This would actually be a fair description of the lives of many Japanese at the turn of the 1950s, although it hardly applied to Shōriki Matsutarō, Matsushita Kōnosuke, Morita Akio, and the other heroes of the Japanese electrical goods story.

A decade later, at the turn of the 1960s, the Japanese economy was growing at 10 percent annually, and households were filling up with the hardware of late modernity. Japan had not only discovered the lever of riches but was pulling on it for all it was worth. To what extent was technology responsible for this newfound prosperity? What was the mechanism that converted diodes and circuit boards into such amazing wealth? More important, how did this technology affect the lives of ordinary Japanese people? Was it the key to prosperity for them, too?

The impact of technological change on Japan's economic growth is indisputable. Japan during the 1950s and 1960s embarked on what was at that time perhaps the biggest orgy of technology importation in history. Every survey of the Japanese economy at that time and since acknowledged this importation as one of the key stimuli for rapid economic growth. One well-known econometric study concluded that improvements in technology accounted for 22.4 percent of Japanese economic growth between 1953 and 1971, even using the most limited definition of "technology." Adding scale economies, which arguably are the result of technological advance, raises technology's contribution to 45 percent of growth.[2]

The electrical goods industry was one of the prime beneficiaries of technology importation, accounting for about one quarter of all technology purchases during the 1950s (see Table 3, p. 245). This investment appears to have generated a very high return. Electrical goods companies spent ¥128 billion on imports and research and development (much of which may have supported the development of imported technology) between 1950 and 1960. During the same period, the output of the electrical machinery industry grew by ¥1,130 billion (from ¥162 billion to ¥1,292 billion).[3] If roughly one-quarter of this growth came from improvements in knowledge (a conservative assumption, as this was essentially a knowledge industry), then a ¥128 billion investment begat at least ¥280 billion in returns.

But to state simply that technology begat growth is to evade the important question of *how* technology and growth are related. Although economists have, since the pioneering work of Robert Solow in the 1950s, come far in their ability to measure technology's contribution to growth, such measurement remains an exercise in elimination: "technology" remains the unexplained residual.[4] This formulation fails to gauge the mechanisms by which technology creates economic growth. Simply importing the designs and specifications for television sets, vacuum tubes, and transistors is not in itself a sufficient condition to create wealth. At the very least, these designs and specifications must be turned into products and sold. Yet Japan in the early 1950s had no market for expensive new products such as televisions and washing machines—both because the products were new and because most Japanese were too poor to buy them. Japanese entrepreneurs solved this problem at least in part through technology—not the technology of products but the technologies of production and marketing.*

For all the attention it has received, importation of product technologies represents only a part of Japanese technological advance during the 1950s. Equal or greater gains occurred vis-à-vis the enabling technologies of mass production, distribution, and marketing. It is as

---

*I have adopted a very broad definition of "technology," for reasons discussed later in this chapter (pp. 132–36).

though two concurrent, massive, and equally important feasts of technology importation took place during the 1950s. One encompassed product technology, which is what most analysts refer to when they discuss Japan's technological dependence on the West. The other centered on the methods, philosophies, and structures of Western—particularly American—management.

Both of these feasts took place with the encouragement of American businessmen and bureaucrats. The relatively low price Japanese companies paid for product technologies has spurred a long-running debate: whether or not Japan got a free ride at American expense. Nothing raises the blood pressure of critical U.S. policy analysts so much as the "giveaway" of technologies that later were used as lethal weapons against American companies. One study estimated, for example, that Japan's total payments for foreign technology between 1951 and 1984 were only $17 billion—a fraction, several analysts have pointed out, of a single year's trade surplus with the United States.[5]

But the other great feast—the massive importation of American management methods—has received relatively little attention. The irony is that, aside from personnel expenses, these technologies cost the Japanese little or nothing. Indeed, the U.S. government actively sponsored and helped pay for the transfer of this knowledge with the explicit motive of helping Japanese businessmen understand the basis of American prosperity. The process of technological importation was in essence a massive, bilateral project between Japan and United States—the project of providing Japan with the material benefits of late modern civilization.

PRODUCT TECHNOLOGIES

Japanese businessmen have created their own myth of the process of product technology importation; I call it the Myth of the Electronics Samurai. The Japanese, in this telling, started the postwar at a severe disadvantage; the "blank space" of the war had put them at least ten years behind the world's technological leaders. Nevertheless, Japanese engineers had a high level of native technical prowess that enabled them to catch up rapidly. Through dedication, hard work, and a modicum of trickery they succeeded in getting vital technology from the United States—much more than the providers had intended. Using that as a base, Japan's electronics wizards succeeded in developing highly innovative new products such as the transistor radio. Eventually, they built up their industry into a position of world leadership, while American industry went into a long-term decline. This is a story I have heard from dozens of executives in the electrical goods industry. It is particularly apparent in a highly acclaimed television documentary series on Japan's transistor industry, *Autobiography of an Electronics Leader, Japan.*[6]

Though based in understandable pride, this myth ignores or hides several important aspects of the story of Japanese electronics. One is the extremely important role of the war, which was by no means a "blank space" but rather a period of very rapid development and learning. Another is the importance of Japan's primary resource in the electronics industry of the 1950s: cheap female labor (an issue discussed in much more detail in Chapter 6). A third is the importation of management and marketing technologies. Nevertheless, for better or worse the story of electrical product technology importation remains the domain of the Electronics Samurai. To a great extent, we continue to rely on their own testimony as evidence. And the story they tell is by no means a trivial one.

Renewal of Prewar Ties

Japanese business leaders entered the 1950s with a vision of where technology might take them but little suspicion of how extensively and how rapidly they would be able to realize that vision. Business leaders and MITI officials initially hoped for a return to something like the status quo ante. During the 1930s, Japan's major electronics companies had been closely allied to Western mentors until government policy forced the dissolution of those ties. The essence of these relationships—which included substantial shareholdings by the foreign partner—was that the Western companies provided technology and management know-how, and the Japanese companies offered a local manufacturing capability and a domestic, and sometimes an Asian, sales and marketing network.[7]

In the early postwar years, the greatest hope of electrical goods business leaders was to recreate these prewar ties and thus benefit once again from the flow of advanced technology. Entering into such ties was a little like selling one's soul: the Japanese companies would get comprehensive access to the technologies of their mentor but would lose much of their independence. Indeed, before the war Nippon Denki and Toshiba had been regarded as little more than local production and marketing subsidiaries of their American patrons.

During the first years of the 1950s, the major Japanese electrical goods companies succeeded in entering agreements that would provide them with up-to-date electronics technologies (see Table 4, p. 245). These contracts applied mainly to radio technology—Japanese companies were particularly in need of advanced vacuum tube designs—but the clear understanding was that as new applications such as television became viable in Japan, these technologies would also be available as needed. For example, Nippon Denki's agreement with International Standard Electric (ISE, an affiliate of AT&T) reportedly provided that "Nippon Denki would have the right to use *all* ISE patents, and would also be given access to manuals relating to design and production."[8]

Several companies were entering into technology assistance agreements for the first time: Hitachi, Kōbe Kōgyō, and Matsushita had all grown into major players during the period of Japanese isolation. But their bargaining position was similar to that of the established companies: in order to gain access to needed technologies, they would have to accept a subordinate position in an exclusive, dependent relationship.

Televisions, Transistors, and Japan's Technological "Feast"

In 1952 and 1953, Japan's technological relationship with the outside world changed dramatically. In spite of MITI's prediction that only three or four companies would import television technology, a total of thirty-seven entered into contracts for television technology licensing.

The patent situation with regard to television was complex. An analysis in the *Nikkei* on January 9, 1952, counted 351 patents relating to television, as well as 105 utility models (*jitsuyō shin'an*), for a total of 456 protective measures. Of these, 47 were deemed essential to a would-be television manufacturer. The most vital patents belonged to RCA, but the widespread practice of cross-licensing entitled a variety of other Western firms to offer television technology as a part of an overall package. Moreover, other firms owned essential patents for television—notably Westinghouse and Britain's Electric and Musical Industries (EMI). Again, these patents were frequently available through cross-license. Yet another complicating factor was that EMI preferred to negotiate exclusive agency agreements that permitted a single company in a given nation to sublicense its patents (in Japan, it chose Nippon Denki), whereas RCA preferred to negotiate an individual licensing deal with each user company, regardless of nationality.

By late 1951 it was apparent that in order to compete in the industry envisioned by the RRC and MITI, a company had to conclude an agreement with RCA. For Kōbe Kōgyō this was simply a question of extending its original agreement to include television, which it did in November 1951. Toshiba followed with a similar agreement soon after. Also in November, Mitsubishi Electric extended its contract with Westinghouse, becoming the sole Japanese licensee of that company's television technology. Rounding out the first phase of major-company deals, Hitachi in March 1952 finalized a television technology assistance agreement with RCA.[9]

By August 7, 1952, the *Nikkei* could assert that "the process of technology importation is almost finished." This turned out to be an overoptimistic conclusion. The agreements were only the beginning. But the *Nikkei*'s judgment reflected the consensus thinking of the time, which was that television manufacturing would be concentrated in a very small number of companies. However, views on the importation of television technology underwent drastic modification as it became apparent that a large number of companies wanted to do so. Because MITI had designated television as a desirable technology, manufacturers felt free to negotiate contracts directly with American companies (particularly RCA) in the expectation that these deals would be ratified. In the end, MITI and the Foreign Investment Committee were forced to meet this expectation.

One of the main reasons for this unexpected surge in patent license agreements was RCA's liberal licensing posture. Far from demanding an exclusive parent-subsidiary relationship, RCA insisted on *non*exclusivity. Any company was free to purchase its black-and-white television patents for a more or less standard fee. This policy was designed to counter the threat of antitrust action, which constantly haunted pioneering electronics companies in the 1950s. RCA had already lost a long and bruising battle over radio patents, and it expected a similar fight over television. RCA would, in fact, be sued by the Justice Department in 1954 and reach an expensive settlement in 1957. Under these circumstances, it hardly seems surprising that RCA would make its patents available to Japanese companies. This was merely an extension of its domestic policy, under which it had already offered technology to hundreds of American firms. Competition from Japan must hardly have seemed an issue for RCA when it was already facing stiff, and to some extent coerced, domestic competition. Moreover, Japanese firms, because of their relatively weak bargaining position, were willing to pay higher licensing fees than RCA could expect from American buyers. Initial contracts with Japanese firms called for a fee equal to 2.75 percent of sales, whereas from early 1953 American companies paid only 1.75 percent.[10]

The feast of product technology importation had as its main course the transistor. Almost all American manufacturers of transistor technology adopted an open licensing policy. As a result, Japanese companies were able to participate in the transistor boom after only a short time lag. They took full advantage of their partners' dispensations. Several of the larger companies entered into agreements providing full access not only to product patents and designs but also to the detailed how-to's needed for rapid assimilation of new technologies. Even smaller companies such as upstart Tōtsūkō (precursor to Sony) could gain access to basic transistor technologies with relative ease.

The quest for the transistor constitutes the defining episode in the Myth of the Electronics Samurai. They are justifiably proud of their achievement. Out of nowhere, Japan became the world's largest producer of germanium transistors by the turn of the 1960s. In subsequent decades the transistor has become ever more important as a fundamental building block in the world's most advanced technologies—and Japanese companies have remained leading participants. This dramatic story had modest enough beginnings. In the early 1950s a handful of companies were carrying out transistor research in Japan. Several entered negotiations to purchase basic transistor technology starting in 1953 (Sony was one, but only one, of these applicants—see Chapter 6 for a more detailed discussion).

Two vitally important developments occurred in the mid-1950s. First, American improvements in transistor technology made it apparent that the transistor would remain a core component of the next generation of electronic products. Second, it became clear that American companies were more than willing to provide transistor technology to foreign buyers. Thus began one of the great technology transfers of all time. Japanese engineers flocked to the United States to drink directly from the fountain of knowledge. They visited the great leaders of the global electronics industry—RCA, General Electric (GE), and Western Electric (manufacturing arm of AT&T)—and exerted every means in their power to acquire the information necessary to manufacture transistors and incorporate them into other products.

Kimura Ichitarō, a young employee of the trading company Marubeni-Iida, recalls hosting at least three hundred researchers between 1954 and 1956. Kimura recalls the austere living conditions some researchers endured in order to get the most out of their meager budgets:

> At the time, the limit for carrying out of the country was $500, and most people stayed as long as they could for the money. Some people would run out after about ten days, while others would stay in really cheap places, and would see everything they possibly could for their money. A cheap place was about $30 for a week. They had to eat and drink too, so it wasn't possible to stay longer than eight or ten weeks. The braver types stayed two months in those kinds of places. That was about the lowest existence you could imagine.[11]

Flights from Tokyo to the United States would sometimes contain several researchers from different companies all bent on the same objective: to bring home as much information about transistor technology as they could gather. Kimura recalls the spirit of cooperation and mutual assistance between these rival compatriots:

> [A researcher called Miyagi] was sent to RCA by Hitachi. Even when I took someone to RCA from one of Hitachi's rivals, I would ask Miyagi *san* to make arrangements, and he would take us out to dinner together. He helped out a lot of Japanese. . . . It's rather shameful to say this now, but he allowed us to use him. Even though we were taking rivals to visit, we'd call Miyagi and tell him what time we wanted to visit the following day, and ask him to check up if there was anyone who was in charge of this or that area—we'd ask him all these selfish things.

Nippon Denki's Nagafune Hiroe spent two months traveling all over the United States in 1957. He was amazed at how easily one could get permission to visit factories even without a technology assistance contract: "America at that time was proud, or magnanimous, I don't know which . . . they'd show you anything. It was a kind of boasting. They'd say, 'This is really good too, come and look at this,' or 'Let's go and look there.' I never even dreamed [I could see so much]." During his American sojourn, Nagafune landed an invitation to a supposedly top-secret military conference in Colorado on new transistor applications. He was there as a guest of Western Electric's plant manager, Andy Anderson, who had taken a personal liking to him. Anderson not only got Nagafune into the conference but also arranged a seat for him in the very front row of the crowded room because his English was so shaky.

Another fact-finding visitor to the United States was Iwase Shingō, who joined Sanyō in 1957 and shortly thereafter crossed the Pacific to negotiate transistor contracts with Western Electric and RCA. "Actually," he recalls, "I visited the RCA factory before we had a contract. I was a research type, so I really wanted to learn. And I found that if

asked, people for the most part responded. I was raising debating points
between researchers, and they couldn't go saying it was a company secret or something. . . . Well, it's best to ask, isn't it? If they don't answer
you're just back where you started, so you can only gain by asking."

Nippon Denki's Nagafune entered a contract with GE in 1958:

> I knew that GE were developing some technologies that weren't in the con-
> tract—for example, I knew they were working on a concept similar to the
> integrated circuit. I tried to learn about these from them. I felt I had to get
> access to this technology as soon as possible because of the pace of change in
> industry. But . . . when I tried to negotiate for products or know-how related
> to this, they said, "We can only give a know-how contract for something
> we're already manufacturing." In the world of semiconductors, something
> that's already being manufactured is about to go out of date. If you don't get
> hold of the very latest technology then you will lose the race.
>
> Even if their position was reasonable, it was a problem for me. . . . So I
> went to meet the person in charge of development directly, and I became
> friendly with him, and I got my hands on all the know-how. It was fine that
> there was nothing in writing. It's enough if I can just get it into my head. If
> you gossip with those researchers enough, you'll get whatever you want.
> You know, all researchers are the same: they want to boast about what
> they've done. I interpreted the know-how contract as including that kind of
> thing. It was only the administrative types who had a different interpreta-
> tion. . . . Of course, I didn't get the information for nothing. We were paying
> a great deal of money, so it would be stupid not to get the most out of it.

Nagafune was accompanied by Suzuki Masao, a manufacturing specialist who recalls the strong sense of mission felt by those who went on
overseas trips: "At that time, if you said you were going to America,
they would make banners to see you off. It was just like sending a sol-
dier off to war. . . . It was equivalent to being given three banzais and
told, 'Come back a hero or don't come back at all.'"

A number of Americans commented on the propensity of the Japanese to draw pictures of the machinery they were viewing (in most cases,
photography was not permitted inside transistor plants). Informational
drawings have a long tradition in Japan, dating back to the Edo era.
Fukuzawa Yukichi included his detailed travel sketches of Western
things in the compendium *Conditions of the West*. Americans found
these drawings rather quaint, but Japanese researchers attest to their
importance in transferring detailed information. Suzuki recalls:

> I took huge amounts of notes, and drew pictures. . . . Photos were not al-
> lowed, so I'd make sketches on the spot. Then when I got back to the hotel
> I'd stay up late making fair copies. . . . They were miserable pictures, but
> when I got back I found these had all became manufacturing appliances. All

of them. Even if I just sent the main points, the people in Japan could make one machine after another. Just using the sketches, no explanation needed. . . . It's not that my team were particularly outstanding, but the Japanese are just like that . . . The people back home and I were all of the same spirit. With just a little explanation, they could extract the mechanism that lurked in the back of the pictures.

Another information gatherer, Toshiba researcher Muraoka Hisashi, was responsible for producing crystals for the company's planar transistor. In a reminiscence, Muraoka recalled one visit in which note-taking was forbidden:

> I did my best to remember as much as I could, but if an important piece of data seemed as though it was about to leave my head, I'd get up and go to the toilet. In the toilet I'd take notes like crazy, and then I'd nonchalantly come back and resume the conversation; but then by and by some other piece of vital information would come out—so back to the toilet. Since I was running to the toilet so often, the person I was talking to looked concerned, and my colleague asked: "Is something wrong with your stomach?" I excused myself, saying, "American water's really bad, isn't it?" It really was an effort. Then when I got back to the hotel at night, I looked at those notes and feverishly wrote out all the information.

These war stories create a charming image of dedicated Electronics Samurai struggling to get the maximum mileage from their hosts. The reminiscences are mixed with pride, a little sheepishness, and real gratitude for the assistance received. Certainly, we should not underestimate the achievement involved in reproducing technologies developed in a far-off nation. Nathan Rosenberg has referred to the "host of difficulties—institutional and otherwise—which hamper the successful adoption of foreign technology."[12] In particular, Rosenberg stresses the importance of individuals in the transfer of knowledge. Technological development can be seen as "a continuous stream of innumerable minor adjustments, modifications and adaptations by skilled personnel. . . . The skills are inevitably embodied in the human agent and not the machine."[13] Japanese engineers benefited from their long backgrounds of electronics research (including wartime research) and by the availability in Japan of capable support industries, particularly the machinery industry. Even so, the Electronics Samurai stress the difficulties they had to overcome, including unsympathetic executives, befuddled subcontractors, inflexible bureaucratic procedures, and reluctant suppliers. So extensive were the hurdles, indeed, that frustrated middle-ranking managers complained of a "wall of misunderstanding" when it came to transistors. Nippon Denki manager Suzuki Masao illustrates:

> The semiconductor industry depends on supplies from countless related industries . . . but at that time those industries didn't exist. . . . That was the age of "heavy, hot, long, and big," so [suppliers] didn't want to be involved with a nit-picking industry like ours.
>
> For example, the final stage in the assembly of a transistor was the attachment of gold wire, and at the time there was no one who would make us such fine wire. When we went to our suppliers, they would ask, "How many tons do you need?" We'd reply, "Actually we just need a few kilograms," and that was the end. So we had to import it. . . . But in order to import, we had to get a special foreign exchange allocation from the Ministry of Finance [MOF], so I had to go to MOF and explain why we needed gold wire. They would say, "In this time of foreign currency shortage, why do you need to import a luxury item like gold?" Even if I explained transistors to the MOF bureaucrats, it didn't sink in.[14]

Yet these tales tell only a part of the story of Japan's importation of technologies during the 1950s.

The American Push to Introduce Technologies to Japan

Economists, historians, and politicians wage an ongoing debate over whether Japanese electronics companies enjoyed a monumental free ride at American expense. Of course, American companies did not literally give away technology free of charge. Patent and license fees ranged widely, with the specific figure depending on such factors as the extent of assistance provided and the nature of and demand for the technology. As a general rule, Japanese companies paid more in the 1950s, when Japan was considered a far-off and risky place, and less in the 1960s, when American companies recognized the profit potential of licensing to Japan and were more actively competing to transfer technologies.[15] In the 1950s, fees ranged from around 2 percent of revenues for the basic Western Electric transistor patent to 4 percent or more for a more complete package of assistance that included manufacturing know-how (see Table 5, p. 246). Sometimes several licenses had to be purchased, and it was by no means unknown for the total cost to Japanese companies to exceed 10 percent of sales.[16]

A 1953 article in *Fortune* commented on the willingness of Japanese companies to pay for technology they urgently wanted to acquire:

> The total amount of foreign exchange remitted [from Japan to U.S. companies] as royalties for 1951 came to $3,700,000, while for 1952 the figure rose

close to $15 million. Capitalizing the royalties at a modest 6 percent, the value of the technical assistance contracts might be reckoned at $250 million in 1952. Thus this is no shoestring program. It is about equal in magnitude to the entire Point Four program for all of Asia and the Middle East.

Jerome Cohen, the article's author, was one of the few commentators to examine whether it was truly advisable for American companies to provide technology to potential Japanese competitors. He asked: "Will not revitalized Japanese industries cut into the U.S. market abroad, and increasingly in our domestic market?" But his conclusion was sanguine:

> In the context of a static world trade volume, Japanese expansion would, of course, come at the expense of the U.S. and Britain, especially of the latter. But if Stalin's prediction that the Western trading bloc cannot absorb the export capacities of Japan and West Germany is to be thwarted, every measure must be taken to expand the volume of free world trade, and if this is done there will be ample room for expansion of Japanese trade. If it is not done, the U.S. could lose much more than markets.[17]

The fees paid by Japanese and other foreign companies represented a valuable source of income for American companies, which had to squeeze their innovations for revenue as quickly as possible. The brief shelf life of new product technologies is a recognized feature of today's electronics industry, and the situation was no different in the 1950s. Commenting on the short time RCA had to realize profits from product innovations, *Business Week* in 1953 commented: "Often, this doesn't give RCA much of a head start—but it is a start. The company's production, sales, and research teams use it for all it's worth."[18]

RCA saw constant pressure on its profit margins from the early 1950s onward. In 1948–51, RCA's pretax margin on all sales (including military) was 12.5 percent. By 1956 this had dropped to 7.1 percent, and a *Fortune* article talked of "the problem facing the whole electronic industry—how to make miracles pay."[19] *Business Week*, commenting on the "infinitely fragmented" business that electronics had become, observed of television that "the ratio of net to sales is constantly shrinking."[20] A 1957 *Fortune* article mentioned the chaotic conditions affecting the black-and-white television industry. Commenting that 51 of 101 television set makers had "thrown in the sponge" in 1956 alone, the article commented: "[The electronics business is] running on three different clocks. One part of the industry is already 'old' enough to have seen severe competition, strong forces toward concentration, and a number of business casualties; this is the world of the TV and radio manufacturers—a mature, dangerous jungle."[21]

Foreign sources of income were particularly favorable to American companies because they maximized returns from the competitive consumer electronics business without threatening the more lucrative military business. Understandably, American companies tended to concentrate their efforts in the latter area while milking the consumer cash cow as much as they could. Alps Denki founder Kataoka Katsutarō comments: "U.S. manufacturers were always focused primarily on military and government applications—space, aircraft, weapons, and professional communications. That's where they put their best engineers. But in Japan, we couldn't make those things. So our best people went into the consumer area."[22] Sony veteran Kanoi Nobuo adds: "Think of it this way: in military applications, the American military would pay even for the failures. If only 1 out of 100 transistors worked, the military would still pay for the other 99. That's why a single transistor might end up costing thousands. In our case, on the other hand, the consumer will only pay for that one transistor. All the rest is loss. You can see why the Americans didn't want to bother with that."[23]

The other factor motivating foreign companies to license in Japan was the generally poor outlook for the Japanese economy, which persisted well into the second half of the 1950s. This environment made American companies unwilling to invest directly in Japan, even where Japanese government policy permitted such investments. A 1953 article in *Business Week*, for example, concluded: "It's clear that U.S. business regards investment in Japan as risky." The article cited Japan's proximity to Communist China and Russia, uncertain balance of payments prospects, scarce raw materials, and hostility to foreign investment.

In part, American distrust of the Japanese business climate reflected lack of knowledge. There were very few business reporters stationed in Japan, and articles of astonishing inaccuracy sometimes appeared in print. A 1956 *Business Week* article referred to the "feudal" conditions faced by workers, which caused them to "plod along and show no initiative." Because of a "caste system," supervisors would "never dirty their hands in a factory." Citing the paucity of management skills, the article commented: "Instead of three shifts they have two twelve-hour shifts, but they put two people on each shift in case one of them falls asleep." New machines, according to the report, were not installed "because of an almost childish desire to hold them in reserve as symbolic insurance against bad times." The article detailed one incident in which

American technicians providing assistance to a Japanese company asked for copies to be made of their saws, which had worn down. "When [the new saws] arrived they had been carefully filed down tooth by tooth to match the discarded blades."[24]

Such negative perceptions did not belong solely to American reporters, however. Another *Business Week* article cited a Japanese journalist in 1954 as saying: "I fear for my sons who four years from now must go out to make a living. I can see no future for them."[25] Given the overwhelming negativity of reporting and analysis about the Japanese economy, it is not surprising that American companies opted for a relatively low-risk licensing approach rather than committing to major direct investments.

However, we should not underestimate the importance of the good will and genuine admiration many Americans felt for the aspirations of the hard-working Japanese. James Arlie of Bell Laboratories hosted many Japanese visitors:

> The Japanese would come in formal suits and white shirts. Ordinarily, they would always have cameras and notebooks. But in Bell Laboratories you were not permitted to take cameras, so they would only bring a camera if they had prior permission. But they would take notes like crazy, and one noteworthy thing was that they would diligently draw pictures. In the 1950s and early 1960s, the Japanese visitors would work very hard not to miss any detail. A particularly conspicuous feature was that they would come after making meticulous preparations. They would make detailed preparations about what they needed to see or hear, and what they needed to study. Compared with that the Americans were [the] worst—they came on a whim, and spent most of the time boasting about themselves. . . . The Japanese visitors were clearly the most systematic and hard-working, and they were the ones who appeared most capable of reproducing the experiments.[26]

Andy Anderson, plant manager at Western Electric, also formed a highly favorable impression of the Japanese visitors.

> After the 1956 seminar, Japanese visitors came from almost all the Japanese companies. All were very keen to learn, and knowledgeable, and not arrogant. It was a pleasure to be with them.
>
> You know, we wanted Japan to recover from the bottom of our hearts. We tried very hard to help Japan recover and once again enjoy an age of prosperity. Our efforts bore fruit, and Japan has become a wonderful industrial nation. That makes me very happy indeed.[27]

Another strategic factor helps explain American companies' willingness to provide technology, whether through licensing or direct investment, to Japanese companies: Japanese companies could hire labor more cheaply and thus make items such as black-and-white television sets less expensively than could manufacturers in the United States. Ultimately, this cost advantage spurred American companies to subcontract assembly operations to Japanese partners, thereby gaining a competitive advantage over their higher-cost rivals. Even in Asian markets, the strategy of exploiting Japanese cheap labor made economic sense. *Electronics* explicitly stated this rationale in a 1954 article, though in relation to technology licensing with Italian companies: "The agreements are to give the Italian company's plants the benefit of US progress and at the same time to allow US firms to supply the Italian and other markets with products identical to those produced here at considerable dollar saving and a reasonable rate of return."[28]

MANAGEMENT TECHNOLOGIES

The story told by the Electronics Samurai represents half of the saga of technology introduction in the 1950s. The other half involved the diffuse area of Western management. It included marketing, production management, organization, and administration.

Japanese businessmen recognized from the beginning that product technologies on their own would not produce American-style prosperity. Indeed, the success of American corporations reflected a much wider range of technologies, including "rational" or "scientific" management, office automation, quality control, and marketing. These men defined "technology" in its widest possible sense, taking it to mean the whole organization and guiding principles of American society.

Using this wider definition of technology, which encompasses processes and ideas well outside the scope of patent protection, Japanese technology importation can be seen in its fullest sense. It can be seen in the ever-increasing number of visits to the United States and Europe by executives and specialists. It can be seen in the flood of literature on management, marketing, and the secrets of American prosperity. It can be seen in the increasing involvement of Japanese companies, including electrical goods companies, in the U.S. military procurement network. And it can be seen in U.S. and Japanese government initiatives, particularly the jointly established Japan Productivity Center (JPC, also Nihon Seisansei Honbu).

Production Management

Analysts of the gap between Japanese and American industrial power focused in the early postwar years on one thing above all else: the superiority of American productivity. Then, as now, productivity was widely considered the key to economic growth and prosperity. In its simplest terms, productivity can be measured as the value created by each individual worker.

In subsequent decades, Japanese industry has made extraordinary advances in productivity, achieving a strong advantage over the West in some areas of manufacturing. Studies of the automobile industry, for example, showed that in the mid-1980s Japanese firms could build a car in eighteen worker hours, whereas their American rivals required up to forty-one worker hours—and the Japanese vehicles had fewer defects.[29] As a result of this extraordinary progress, analytical attention has come to focus on the secrets of Japanese manufacturing productivity and quality.

Many of the techniques of lean production, zero-defect manufacturing, and production management in general were adapted from methods brought to Japan by the United States. In Chapter 2, I described how U.S. administrators revived the prewar quality control movement to facilitate the recovery of industries vital to the Occupation's strategic goals, including the electrical goods industry. American support for the Japanese productivity movement climbed continuously throughout the 1950s. Some of this support was purchased by Japanese firms. Technology license agreements often included know-how support in the form of plant layouts, production machinery design (or import), and training. Television manufacturer Hayakawa Denki (owner of the Sharp brand) grabbed an early lead over its Japanese rivals by building a mass-production assembly plant modeled closely on an American facility—so closely, in fact, that the work benches were placed at a height appropriate for American rather than Japanese women, forcing the company to adopt a minimum height requirement when hiring female workers. But much state-of-the-art production technology was freely available through textbooks and trade journals, and U.S. bureaucrats directly supported Japanese efforts to import these techniques.

The first great stimulus to American promotion of Japanese production management—particularly quality control—was the Korean War. Japanese companies became major local suppliers for the voracious U.S. forces in East Asia. The war exposed Japanese companies directly to the standards and testing methods that had aided American companies so much during World War II—a system developed by W. Edwards Deming, among others, based on the statistical sampling techniques of Walter Shewhart of Bell Laboratories. U.S. military buyers ordered large amounts of electrical equipment from Japan and subjected it to strict standards of quality. These standards were both an educational tool—the military trained Japanese engineers and sent them around to educate suppliers—and a demanding requirement.

Masujima Shō, a top executive of TDK (Tokyo Denki Kagaku Kōgyō, or Tokyo Electrical Science Manufacturing), recalls the shock of his first exposure to quality control techniques and the difficulty of implementing them:

> I graduated from university in 1952. I majored in production engineering, but at that time there was literally no mention of quality control in the curriculum. After graduating, I attended many lectures on quality control, mostly by Japanese experts. I realized that I would have to completely rethink the way I had been taught at university.
>
> But once I was put in charge of a production line, these new techniques were not at all easy to implement. In Japan at the time people still worked as craftsmen. They were accustomed to being responsible for their own output, including checking for defects. It was very difficult in the 1950s to convince people like that to accept outside supervision, such as quality inspections. I had to persuade them to work as a group and not as individuals. It was not easy.[30]

One of the reasons for Masujima's struggle was that at the turn of the 1950s, mass production—in the sense of the manufacture of large numbers of identical, generally consumer-oriented goods—existed in Japan only in a very limited sense. The techniques pioneered by Henry Ford in the second decade of the twentieth century—which by 1950 had undergone considerable enhancement in the United States—had yet to make a major impact in Japan. As a result, Japanese companies could implement methods of assembly plant management, statistical quality control, production machinery, and work-flow management only after overcoming considerable worker resistance.[31]

Deming's quality control regime has become the defining symbol of Japan's more-than-successful adoption of American production technologies. Although he had played an important role in developing the military's quality control system during World War II, Deming was a relatively marginal figure in the United States. In Japan, by contrast, he became a revered leader after whom the Japan Union of Scientists and Engineers (JUSE) named its most sought-after prize. Deming did indeed receive a much more enthusiastic reception in Japan than he had been given at home. He reportedly was amazed that his first JUSE-sponsored lecture was attended by the presidents of no fewer than forty-five major companies.[32] However, it would be a mistake to overemphasize Deming's influence. William Tsutsui has convincingly argued that Deming was more important as a figurehead and public relations symbol than as a technological leader. Indeed, the scope of the Japanese movement to import production management techniques was far too wide for any one figure to occupy a monopoly role.[33] That program involved massive and comprehensive efforts that included the introduction and elaboration of academic theory, the institution of training facilities, the translation of foreign textbooks and consulting literature, lecture tours by foreign academics and businessmen, the importation of production machinery, the development of a domestic machine tool industry, study tours to the United States and Europe, the burgeoning of a Japanese consulting industry, and specific know-how agreements with foreign firms.

Beginning in the mid-1950s, the Japanese production technology effort centered on the Japan Productivity Center (JPC), a semipublic agency established with financial and administrative support from both the Japanese and U.S. governments. The mutual security agreement concluded between Japan and the United States in 1954 explicitly linked the strengthening of Japan's military capabilities with the strengthening of the economy. One of the four major objectives outlined in the pact was: "Improvement of the managerial and marketing efficiency of Japanese industrial enterprises through, among other means, technical assistance."[34] Within Japan, the JPC was widely perceived as having a civilizing mission and an important role in exploring and reproducing the secrets of American-style prosperity. The JPC's executive director, Gōshi Kōhei, argued that the productivity movement was "the only way to modernize Japan, to make the lifestyle of the Japanese people wealthy and bright" (*yutaka ni shi, akaruku suru*).[35]

There was extensive precedent for the JPC program. By the time the JPC was founded in 1955, some 16,000 European and 1,000 non-European managers, technicians, and labor leaders had already visited the United States under the auspices of the Foreign Operations Administration (precursor to the International Cooperation Administration [ICA], which supported the Japanese program). The Anglo-American Council of Productivity, financed by U.S. aid, had also prepared a large series of reports on American productivity.[36]

The JPC was (and, indeed, still is) active in organizing lectures, training courses, and publications. But it is best known for the large numbers of study groups it sent during the 1950s to foreign countries—

most to the United States—to study productivity. In 1955, the first year of the JPC's operation, fifteen study groups totaling 174 people traveled to the United States. In 1956, twenty-seven groups totaling 307 people made the trip, and by the end of the program in 1961, some four hundred study groups totaling 4,000 people had gone overseas. The pilgrims included business leaders, small business representatives, technical specialists, academics, and labor leaders, and their missions covered a variety of topics, from top management to the nuts and bolts of assembly line management.[37]

Alps Denki founder Kataoka Katsutarō traveled to the United States under the auspices of the JPC in 1957. He recalls the generosity of the program: "We contributed just $5 a night for hotels. No matter what quality of hotel we stayed in, ICA paid for the rest. Of course, we stayed in top-class places." The JPC paid for travel and incidental expenses, leaving the participants responsible only for some meals and private spending.[38]

The JPC also coordinated visits to Japan by American specialists and general managers. In July 1955, shortly after the creation of the JPC, a group of four top American managers—including Arthur Nielsen, vice president of the A.C. Nielsen public relations firm—visited Japan and, after extensive visits to factories and workplaces, offered an analysis of the needs of Japanese business. The group concluded that "labor relations and marketing are the two biggest top management problems in Japan." According to the group, "Japanese executives were visibly startled to learn of the dominant role of the marketing function in American industry. Many Japanese directors tend to regard their sales departments as mere collection agencies, instead of the most vital profit-earners of their companies." The observers concluded: "If increased per worker output is to do any good, it must be accompanied by vigorous sales promotion."[39]

Marketing

Among the JPC's most important activities was the promotion of marketing. It may sound surprising that marketing should fall within the purview of an agency dedicated to productivity, but the concept enjoyed a much broader definition in the 1950s than it does today. The breadth of the Productivity Center's self-perceived mission is indicated by the title of its monthly magazine, *Manejimento* ("Management"). This magazine contained articles on a wide variety of management is-

sues, including office automation, quality control, marketing, and finance. Japanese business leaders recognized marketing as an essential
technology offering a solution to a problem that had plagued Japan
throughout its modern history: how to find domestic outlets for the nation's growing industrial capacity. Of all the elements to reproducing
American industrial success, marketing was considered among the most
important.

Perhaps the most influential of all the JPC study missions was the top
management group headed by Ishizaka Taizō, president of Toshiba,
which left for the United States on June 9, 1955. Its expressed mission
was to investigate "why the U.S. economy continues to be so prosperous, and what are the underlying causes [of the continuing prosper-
ity]."[40] On its return, the group offered the following analysis:

> One major reason [for American prosperity] is the ability of American in-
> dustry to open new markets. . . . The noteworthy point about American
> companies' market development is that it is based on the creation of mass
> markets for new products that previously did not exist, or additions to mass
> produced products that had previously been standardized. . . . As for Japan,
> the reason our high population is a burden is because the people's buying
> power is poor. It is often said that our country is small, and this really refers
> to the lack of purchasing power. But what we wish to emphasize is the un-
> skillfulness of our industry's market-opening ability. Competition in our
> country is based not on opening new markets but on struggling [for existing
> markets]. . . . Moreover, our businessmen are lacking in the skills of market
> studies in general. This is one of the main reasons for unnecessary competi-
> tion and unplanned investment. Even if you are opening up new markets, it
> is necessary to carry out a detailed market study.[41]

In March 1956, a study group traveled to the United States under
JPC auspices specifically to study marketing. This group published a
very detailed report on American marketing techniques. The report
treated marketing as a technology that could (and should) be imported
in a manner similar to manufacturing technologies. Sections of the report dealt with the concept of American marketing, the status and organization of American marketing divisions, distribution channels,
market studies, advertising, and marketing education. In its introduction, the report commented:

> If you simply adopt a sales-oriented philosophy and believe that it's enough
> to make and sell goods, at a discount if necessary, then you will fall behind
> the times and perish. Marketing was born of the needs of a new age, an age
> represented by the advanced economy of the United States. It is a new tech-
> nology, founded on a new way of thinking. Introducing this technology will

undoubtedly cost a little money, but if our corporate executives recognize the importance of this technology, and both introduce and sufficiently implement it, they will obtain results worth many times their investment.[42]

Manejimento also carried regular features and instruction on marketing. Consultants, marketing executives, and top managers frequently commented on the need for improved marketing capabilities, often emphasizing techniques to create markets and demand. For example, the president of Mitsubishi Denki contributed the following comments:

> According to a recent magazine, research is underway to use atomic power to fit the entire electrical equipment of a house into the size of a matchbox. Since this is American research, it will immediately be mass-produced.
>
> Why is this? Since manufacturing automation has reached a high level in the United States, rather than the previous philosophy of just maximizing profits, the new management thinking is that the only way to make profits is to expend all possible efforts on making products that enhance customer satisfaction. . . .
>
> Compared to this, how is Japan at present? We too have introduced mass production and automation, but it's hard to say that products have been prepared well enough to sell sufficiently. Given our shallow economic base and poor political power it's perhaps natural, but our main topic is how to overcome this situation by making salable as well as buyable products.[43]

The notion that marketing might be at the heart of the United States's sudden and—after a decade of depression—quite unexpected new prosperity was just coming into widespread circulation. Americans themselves were bedazzled by marketing's apparently unlimited potential for wealth creation. American magazines from the 1950s are full of reports on the nation's unexpected prosperity. With titles like "The New American Economy," "Selling to an Age of Plenty," and "Preaching a New Consumer Economic," the articles describe the rapid rise in American incomes, the awesome spending power of the middle class, and the fabulous output of the mass production machine.

In particular, these articles dwell on what was seen as a fundamentally new, surprising, and revolutionary aspect of the U.S. economy: the power and wealth of the mass market. "All history," puffed *Fortune*, "can show no more portentous economic phenomenon than today's American market," at the heart of which lay "the rise of the great mass into a new moneyed middle class." *Fortune* pointed out that the number of families in the mid-range $4,000–$7,500 income bracket had increased by 44 percent between 1947 and 1953 and now accounted for 35 percent of all families. Other characteristics of the new mass market included rapid (and unexplained) population growth, a marked trend toward homogeneity of taste, and a huge exodus to the suburbs, the population of which had increased by 17 million since 1947.

What dynamic stood behind these amazing changes? *Fortune* placed primary emphasis on the rising productivity of American industry, "that cachet of efficiency without which no nation today is civilized or even modern." *Fortune* offered several additional explanations for the mass market's rise. First was the "basic cultural restlessness of the American people"; the "desire for the new" led people to invent and purchase new products, resulting in an expanded market. Second was the leveling of U.S. incomes as a result of rising productivity, union bargaining, social legislation, and wartime inflation. Whereas in 1929 the top 1 percent of income earners took 19 percent of total income, the proportion in 1946 was only 8 percent. A third factor was the homogenization of cities, which now offered "the same chain stores, liquor stores, candy stores, department stores, shoe stores, and the same prices." *Fortune* also pointed to the soaring population. Demographers were said to be "flabbergasted" by the continuing baby boom, which, combined with the accelerating breakup of families, caused unprecedented household formation. Then there was the growing power of the media and the "booming circulation of fashion, home, and 'consumer' magazines." Finally, *Fortune* commented on the "science of consumption" that was becoming a key feature of corporate activity. "By now, it should be clear, nothing is more important than the inclinations of the consumer. He has money, he has a big choice, he can buy as he desires, and he can stop buying many things for quite a while." His "habits have accordingly become a major preoccupation of American economists."[44]

Japanese observers devoured such analyses of the United States's unimagined prosperity. The concept of marketing was certainly not unknown to Japanese businessmen. Most large companies established advertising departments before the war, and universities and businesses studied advertising. Japan's major advertising agencies—Dentsū and Hakuhōdō—were established early in the century. W. D. Scott's seminal work *The Psychology of Advertising* (1908) was translated into Japanese in 1915 and received widespread attention.[45] However, the postwar period saw a massive importation of Western—particularly American—concepts and methods of marketing that extended far beyond simple advertising.

Among the first books actually using the term "marketing" was *Maaketingu* by Hamano Tsuyoshi and Kamioka Kazuki, published in 1953. Hamano introduced the book as follows:

Marketing is now taking its place on the stage of the new era. [Nowadays] companies are prospering, and they are moving from political transactions to the question of how they can most quickly meet market demand, establish long-lasting goodwill among the masses, and increase profits through mass sales. . . . Marketing refers to a comprehensive range of activities from procurement to sales. In order to understand these issues, it is necessary to have long experience, as well as extensive theoretical and practical research. We are, of course, nowhere near that stage.[46]

The latter half of the 1950s brought a veritable flood of texts and treatises on marketing, many of them of great sophistication. For example, a well-known marketing consultant, Hayashi Shūji, wrote texts on corporate and brand image creation, marketing plans, marketing and the Japanese firm, the "distribution revolution," and market structures.[47] Major companies rapidly implemented these techniques and carried out their own studies and training programs without waiting for the appearance of Japanese-language textbooks. Matsushita, for example, upgraded its advertising department to a "PR headquarters" in 1956. The revamped unit engaged in extensive market research, brand analysis, corporate image creation, focus group studies, product packaging, marketing planning, publicity surveys, and other activities using information supplied by foreign partners, executives returning from foreign travel, and foreign and Japanese consultants.[48]

At precisely the same time that U.S. business journals were describing their nation's prosperity with a mixture of disbelief and self-congratulation, social commentators were placing the phenomena of mass consumer demand, marketing techniques, and high economic growth in sharp critical focus. For example, in 1957 Vance Packard published *The Hidden Persuaders*, a critique of the insidious methods by which marketers created desire. Packard paid full tribute to the extraordinary power of the U.S. market; quoting a business leader who says: "Capitalism is dead—consumerism is king!" But Packard emphasized what he saw as a darker side to this phenomenon. "One way of viewing this rich, full life the people were achieving was the glowing one that everyone could enjoy an ever higher standard of living. That view was thoroughly publicized. But there was another way of viewing it: that we must consume more and more, whether we want to or not, for the good of our economy."[49] Marketing professionals, according to Packard, were becoming more and more aware of the limitations of traditional demand and consumption analyses, which saw the consumer as essentially rational. According to Packard, recent empirical studies demonstrated that consumers were *not* driven by rational impulses. On the contrary, it was precisely their *ir*rationality on which marketing specialists focused.

Packard described in sinister detail the new field of "motivation research," or "depth marketing," which was increasingly being used by major corporations. Psychiatrists and research bodies with esoteric names such as the Institute for Motivational Research were examining people's reactions to advertising and promotions through focus groups and surveys. They did not ask direct questions, assuming that people would be unable or unwilling to express their underlying motivations. But through clever indirect questioning, these researchers concluded that people were actually driven by deep-seated fears and insecurities. It was essential, they told their corporate clients, for advertising to reassure by playing subtly on these insecurities.

Packard compared the idealized version of the American housewife portrayed in television and magazine commercials—a "pert, alert gal, very wise and competent"—with the reality that marketing men sought to manipulate. The real middle-class housewife "works harder than other women, her life has very narrow routines, she likes to deal only with familiar things and tends to view anything outside her narrow world as dangerous and threatening. . . . Her imaginative resources are highly limited." Mrs. "Middle Majority," as Packard referred to women of the lower-middle and upper-lower income segments, possessed "a strong moral code and a deep sense of guilt when she deviates from it."

Also highly influential was David Riesman's *The Lonely Crowd*, a sociological analysis that identified a new American social type. In contrast to the "inner-directed" pioneers who had built the nation, Americans of the current generation were "outer-directed"; that is, they based their behavior on the actions of others—or on the suggestions of clever marketers. This outer-directed psyche was receptive to the techniques of mass persuasion and market creation. According to Riesman, "[P]eople learn early to accept their directions in the game of leisure and life from their peers—that is, their age-mates, job mates, and playmates—to whom they respond with radar sensitivity."[50]

Packard followed *The Hidden Persuaders* with *The Waste Makers*, published in 1960. *The Waste Makers* lodged an outspoken attack on the philosophy and methods of corporate marketing, describing in detail the techniques used by companies to encourage waste and excess.

The economic theory supporting these popular volumes was itself supplied in a popular package: John Kenneth Galbraith's 1956 work

The Affluent Society. This book attacked the notion that economic growth should be pursued by foisting unneeded products onto the public. Galbraith said of advertising and salesmanship that "their central function is to create desires—to bring into being wants that previously did not exist." Galbraith pointed out the absurdity of a system in which "production, not only passively through emulation, but actively through advertising and related activities, creates the wants it seeks to satisfy."[51]

All of these works were rapidly translated into Japanese, so there can be no doubt that their significance was apprehended. *The Waste Makers*, translated by Ishikawa Hiroyoshi, was published in 1961, one year after its U.S. appearance. Ishikawa added the following comments:

> Today's consumer revolution is both an economic revolution and a human revolution. The development of the consumer economy not only changes the nation's economic structure, it also results in profound changes in the psychology of consumers living in that nation. In cases where the economy is sustained by excessive consumption or even waste, consumers must lead wasteful lifestyles whether they like it or not.
>
> Looking at the situation in Japan, we must look carefully at the views of someone like Packard—although he is writing about his own country—and there are many lessons we must learn from him. This book tells of the endeavors of American consumers to change their economy from a waste economy to a correct consumption economy, and this should be an effective clue in showing us Japanese how to deal with our own problems.[52]

Ishikawa later commented wryly that Japanese marketers actually embraced his book as a compendium of techniques of waste creation. The book stimulated Japanese marketing consultants to propose strategies for encouraging excess in Japan. Their ideas included:

> Develop throw-away products—e.g. ¥100 underwear, ¥1,000 watches.
> Create new gift-giving opportunities—for example, Maruzen's Valentine's Day sale.
> Make people hoard by creating concepts that require excess purchases—for example, fully stocked home bars.
> Make add-on products: for example, leather cases for cameras.
> Make people differentiate products more: for example, different vitamin compounds depending on age
> Promote "seconds": e.g. second radio, second camera.
> Make people feel possessions are out of date, so that their owners will replace them even though they are still functional.[53]

The degree of referentiality and self-consciousness with which Japan imported not only marketing technologies but also debates on and critiques of those technologies undeniably sets its process of mass market creation apart from that of the United States.

CONCLUSION: TECHNOLOGY AND THE PROJECT OF PROSPERITY

For Japan's leading electrical goods companies and for their owners, technology was undoubtedly one of the levers of riches in the 1950s. But to understand the relationship between technology and the massive growth of electrical goods firms, two points must be held firmly in mind. First, "technology" did not just refer to product designs and specifications; Japanese companies also imported production technologies and marketing technologies on a grand scale. Second, the transfer of these technologies was by no means a one-sided affair; it succeeded largely because the U.S. government and American businesses gave their full cooperation.

However, crediting technology for the prosperity of a handful of companies and their owners is very different from assigning it a determining role in *national* prosperity. What was the effect of technology, particularly electrical goods technologies, on the ordinary people of Japan? Was technology the key to prosperity for them also? Analyzing this issue is problematic at best. Of the vast number of changes that helped Japan achieve a kind of prosperity by the end of the 1950s, which were caused at least in part by technology and—perhaps an even harder question—which were not?

Joseph Schumpeter was one of the first economists to focus on the effects of technology on economic development. He argues that innovation is the primary force moving an economy out of steady-growth equilibrium. Innovation is, according to Schumpeter, "the outstanding fact in the economic history of capitalist society."[54] Each innovation, great or small, generates a wave of energy that resonates throughout the economy. At the longest extreme are the great technological breakthroughs that spur countless related innovations and work themselves out over a period of decades. The industrial revolution of the late eighteenth and early nineteenth centuries and the power revolution of the turn of the twentieth century are examples of these long-term cycles. At the shortest extreme are tiny, incremental advances that might cause only a ripple in a larger current of innovation-induced expansion.

In *Business Cycles: A Theoretical, Historical and Statistical Analysis of the Capitalist Process,*[55] Schumpeter develops an economic model of how innovation spurs economic expansion (and, eventually, contraction). He uses a very broad definition of "innovation" that includes "technological change in the production of commodities already in use, the opening up of new markets or of new sources of supply, Taylorization of work, improved handling of material, the setting up of new business organizations such as department stores—in short, any 'doing things differently' in the realm of economic life."[56] Schumpeter postulates that the initial effect of any innovation is to spur entrepreneurs to invest in the plant and machinery necessary to exploit it; extension of credit and fulfillment of orders in response to this demand constitute the first iteration of innovation-driven growth. The second iteration comes as other entrepreneurs rush to take advantage of the innovation, causing a general boom in the economy, much of it based on secondary demand—that is, on the expansion of businesses that have nothing to do with the original innovation. The quantity of goods in circulation increases as the innovation and its spinoffs spread throughout society.

Schumpeter's analysis focused mainly on the leading economies in which innovations first appeared. But in a case such as Japan's, in which a technically backward society makes a concerted effort to catch up with advances made elsewhere, the effects described in Schumpeter's model might be even more strongly felt. Given the widespread and iterative effects of even a single technology introduction, it is not hard to see how the simultaneous introduction of many new, well-developed technologies could produce truly explosive economic effects. Moreover, this growth would not be confined to a single industry; it would take place in waves, creating a general prosperity marked by high economic growth rates and an across-the-board rise in incomes.

Schumpter's framework also proves useful in looking at the composition of technology imports, particularly given his very wide interpretation of "innovation." As noted, technological importation in Japan's electrical goods industry was extremely wide in scope. Electrical goods companies imported not only product technologies but also manufacturing technologies such as production machinery, factory layouts, quality control methods, statistical sampling methods, and shop floor organizations. For the most part, these systems had been widely introduced in the United States before and during World War II. They were, indeed, similar to the "Taylorization" mentioned by Schumpeter. The third group of imports related to management, particularly to the technologies of demand creation. All these types of technology were entering a new phase in the postwar United States. Thus, Japan was simultaneously introducing the results of not one but *three* separate technological revolutions, which in the United States had occurred over a period of almost half a century. In Schumpeter's framework, this level of innovation would be expected to fuel an extraordinary economic expansion.

Indeed, the Schumpeter model underscores the danger of focusing solely on the actual products Japanese firms were importing. These products, and the process by which Japanese firms developed them, have been assigned an inordinate degree of importance. Indeed, the transistor is the core piece of hardware in what is sometimes termed the final paradigmatic phase of twentieth-century technology development: the information and communications age.[57] Although Schumpeter did not live to see all the applications of the transistor, he would surely have credited it with a central role in a long wave of innovation-induced growth similar to the industrial and electrical revolutions. But for Japan in the 1950s, the short-term effects of the transistor were minimal—confined mainly to making smaller, more energy-efficient radios. The introduction of mass production and marketing technologies undoubtedly had a much greater impact.

What does Schumpeter's model suggest about the relationship between technology-driven growth and prosperity? Schumpeter himself is quick to point out the uneven distribution of benefits from innovation-related economic growth. Indeed, one of his most famous insights is the essentially destructive nature of technology-driven growth, which howls through the interstices of established interests in a "perennial gale of creative destruction."[58] Certainly, technological advance created corporate losers in Japan. More to the point, it produced an uneven distribution of gains among people. For example, the production of televisions and radios brought large numbers of new workers into electrical goods factories. Most were young women working for extremely low wages, roughly $0.10 per hour. These poorly paid employees can hardly be seen as beneficiaries of technology-induced prosperity (see Chapter 6).

To understand technology's effect on the prosperity of ordinary Japanese people, we must recognize that there are dimensions to the impact of technology, and to the nature of prosperity, that go beyond economics. Schumpeter, indeed, pays little attention to the actual content of the technology. Peter Drucker writes that "technology is not about tools. It is about how Man works."[59] For a historian, the challenge is to understand how technology has affected how Man *lives*. Technologies have a significance that goes beyond the statistics of growth; the uses to which they are put also matter.

Commentators of the late 1950s, when challenged to pick out the greatest social changes of the decade, almost invariably remarked upon the widespread ownership of electrical goods. Indeed, simply owning these goods was often equated with economic progress and well-being. The products people bought fell into two broad categories of function: televisions and radios were used to connect with the outside world, whereas electric fans, vacuum cleaners, washing machines, and refrigerators increased convenience and saved labor for housekeepers. Clearly, these changes affected ordinary people's lives; but the question of whether or not they represented *prosperity* is open to dispute. The broadcast media, in particular, have been widely accused of reducing the quality of everyday life for ordinary people—robbing them of their culture, draining their minds, turning them into passive objects of an industry whose single dominant message was: consume! (This issue receives more detailed scrutiny in Chapter 5.) The same criticism might be applied to the mass phase of modernity as a whole: has it brought us benefits, or has it subjected us to an unprecedented level of control? This question comes close to the heart of the issue of technology and social change. Perhaps both interpretations possess a degree of validity.

Nor are the convenience goods of the household free from dispute in interpretation. One effect of filling the home with labor-saving technologies has been to reinforce the ideology of the housewife, by which women belong to a separate, mainly domestic social sphere. Critics have argued that this ideology has served to rob women of their independence and forced them into a passive role in which their main social function is to consume.

The question of the passivity of consumers is an important one for this study. In the next chapter I examine in detail the ways in which electrical goods companies worked to *create* demand in the face of considerable public skepticism. Schumpeter once again provides a useful insight in this matter, stressing that the effect of consumer demand in stimulating innovation, or economic change in general, is minimal.

> Railroads have not emerged because any consumers took the initiative in displaying an effective demand for their service in preference to the services of mail coaches. Nor did the consumers display any such initiative wish to have electric lamps or rayon stockings, or to travel by motorcar or airplane, or to listen to radios, or to chew gum. The great majority of changes in commodities consumed has been forced by producers on consumers who, more

often than not, have resisted the change and have had to be educated up by elaborate psychotechnics of advertising.[60]

Of course, advertising also falls within Schumpeter's definition of innovation. We thus have the paradoxical result that technology introduction both creates the problem—lack of innate meaning or desire—and provides the solution.

In discussing Japan's rapid assimilation of advanced technology, it is useful to look at what did *not* change. The glamorous new technologies of the promised age of prosperity tended to throw forth a glare, blinding many to the enduring essentials of their own society. By the end of the 1950s, the lives of many Japanese remained fraught with drudgery, toil, and discomfort—and remain so today, for that matter. Technology did not make the Japanese home any larger, nor did it significantly expand lifestyle or career choices for most Japanese. Indeed, some would argue that technology has been used to preserve long-standing rigidities in the Japanese social order.[61]

5

Creating the "Bright Life"

For the rest of Japan the people who have been able to become salary men are symbols of the *akarui seikatsu* (bright new life), the life with leisure time, travel and recreation, and few binding obligations and formalities. . . .

This is how Ezra Vogel introduces his chapter on "The Bright New Life" in his 1961 study *Japan's New Middle Class*. "The excitement of the consumer has been enormous," continues Vogel:

Before the war, electricity, the sewing machine, irons, and the radio were already widespread, but all other electric equipment, like refrigerators, heaters, toasters, washing machines, fans, and the like have become common in Japan only in the last decade. . . . These new goods were at first available only to the wealthy, but now they are within the reach of the average salary man.[1]

Vogel makes an explicit link between the "bright new life" and the ownership of electrical goods. He was not alone among his contemporaries in doing so. By the turn of the 1960s in Japan, the "bright life" (a more accurate translation of *akarui seikatsu*) was a common shorthand for an ill-defined but widely held set of attributes. The term implied a level of affluence sufficient to transcend the daily struggle for survival. It implied a "modern" home with a middle-class standard of living. It implied a nuclear family with a housewife at its center. And it implied ownership of certain talismanic possessions, notably electrical goods such as a television, washing machine, and refrigerator.

Figure 6 A family watches television, c.1956. (Courtesy of Nippōsha)

Vogel may not have been aware that the concept of the bright life had a history—one that included its share of conflict. Much of that history has subsequently been buried in the long postwar celebration of Japanese material wealth. Indeed, despite Japan's high savings rate, consumption is one of the nation's defining postwar features. The ebullience of this consumption has given rise in some circles to a deterministic interpretation of Japanese history by which, following a period of aberrant military adventure, Japan returned to the right and proper course of beneficent modernization.

Historians often point to the rapidity with which Japanese people filled their homes after the war with the accoutrements of affluence, even when incomes were low. The apparently spontaneous, even festive nature of these purchases is captured by the slogans attached to successive waves of consumption: the "three sacred treasures" of the 1950s (television, electric washing machine, and refrigerator); the "three Cs" of the 1960s (car, room cooler, and color television); and the "three Js" of the 1980s (jewels, jet travel, and *jūtaku*—i.e., home ownership).[2]

But neither ebullience nor consumerism was remotely in evidence in the early 1950s; indeed, as described in Chapter 2, they were little more than a dream in the minds of a few farsighted businessmen. The bright life was a creation of the 1950s, one that in its own way was just as impressive and dramatic as the creation of the transistor radios, televisions, and stereos that were to set Japan's electronics industry on the path to worldwide success.

HARD TIMES: EVERYDAY LIFE IN THE EARLY 1950S

In the early 1950s, consumption had more to do with putting rice on the table than with the pursuit of pleasure. By any comparative statistic, the Japanese people still lacked many of the bare essentials. Caloric intake in Japan remained far below that of affluent Western countries. The housing situation remained atrocious. Victims of wartime bombings were still crowded into urban housing with returnees from the lost empire. Families of six or seven lived in a single room, with no running water and only communal cooking and toilet facilities.

The word *seikatsu* (life, or lifestyle) had bitter overtones during these years; in the press, it was usually paired with *mondai* (problems). Indeed, for most Japanese everyday life remained problematic at least through the first half of the 1950s. Magazines carried anguished articles about the difficulties of making ends meet. A typical case was "Mr. C," a forty-two-year-old man who worked for a publishing firm. His monthly after-tax income of ¥15,400 was close to the urban average. Mr. C supported a wife, four children, and two parents on his salary. After paying for food, utilities, doctors, and school meals, Mr. C had only ¥2,000 left for entertainment and savings. Of this, he spent ¥1,000 on tobacco and ¥300 on newspapers. By the end of the month, Mr. C was lucky to have saved even ¥300 ($0.80).[3]

Ronald Dore, who lived in a typical Tokyo neighborhood in 1951, described the living conditions of Mr. O, a policeman with a wife and three children.

> The five of them have one "four-and-a-half mat" room, that is, a room about nine feet square with one large recessed cupboard to contain the bedding, which is rolled up and stored away in the daytime. The *tatami* mats are yellowed and frayed and bear the distinctive musty odour of mats which should long ago have been renewed. Apart from a table, the only other furniture consists of two large chests-of drawers. On the top of one of these chests is a wireless. There is one gas ring on which Mrs. O cooks for the whole family. One sink with a single cold tap, and one lavatory are shared with three other families. There are no baths, but Mrs. O takes the children to the bath-house every other day and Mr. O goes regularly once a week. In winter a brazier burning charcoal or anthracite produces fumes but probably less heat than

five human bodies. In the dark and cold evenings the children have to be indoors long before their energies are exhausted.

Mrs. O's greatest dream, according to Dore, was to own an electric fan for the stifling summer nights.

A decade later, both the C and the O families most likely owned not only electric fans but also electric washing machines and televisions. Television ownership had reached 55 percent of the urban population by 1960; by 1964 it was 95 percent. (See Table 6, p. 247, for nationwide television ownership figures.) This phenomenal growth in the domestic market has been widely acknowledged as the single most important factor in the success of the Japanese electrical goods industry. Domestic sales, not exports, fueled growth throughout the 1950s and well into the 1960s—indeed, for the whole first decade of explosive growth. It was domestic demand that allowed Japanese companies to increase manufacturing volumes to the point where they could compete against the high-volume, low-cost producers of the West. And their experiences with the domestic market enabled Japanese firms to build technical skills, sharpen product designs, and become competitive in world trade by the 1960s (see Table 7, p. 247).[4]

Where did this homegrown demand come from? How did the grim world of "lifestyle problems" suddenly metamorphose into the butterfly world of the bright life? Of course, real incomes almost doubled during the 1950s in conjunction with high economic growth, but by the end of the 1950s the average urban family was still only earning about ¥35,000 ($100) a month, a level that scarcely qualified as affluence. One fact often overlooked in the general celebration of the "consumer revolution" of the late 1950s is that budgets continued to be extremely tight. Indeed, though a segment of the press exulted in the bright life (the *Asahi shinbun*, for example, retitled its Sunday family section "The Bright Life" in April 1959), articles on lifestyle problems continued to outnumber celebratory pieces by a wide margin. Reality did not change dramatically during the course of the decade.

Made in Nippon

Nor were the Japanese themselves so sure they wanted the newfangled products of the electrical age. Throughout the 1950s, a lasting note of skepticism accompanied outpourings of celebration over televisions, washing machines, and refrigerators. People were unsure about the functions and benefits of these products—even aside from their astro-nomical prices. Indeed, magazine articles—particularly earlier in the decade—tended to express suspicion of the goods being thrust on the public by an industry in which consumers had little faith.

Kurashi no techō (Handbook of Living) was founded at the end of the 1940s in emulation of American consumer magazines. It included product tests and reviews of the choices available. Throughout the 1950s, its prevailing tone was one of deep skepticism. For example, the magazine had a regular feature entitled "Made in Nippon" that was en-tirely devoted to the faults of Japanese products: suitcases that fell to pieces, door handles that stuck, razors that wouldn't shave. This cau-tious approach extended to reviews of electrical products. The maga-zine commented in a study of electric washing machines:

> An electric washing machine is certainly convenient, but it cannot do every-thing. . . . [For example] if you only have one or two items to wash, they'll be rubbing against water and won't get clean, as well as its being uneco-nomical. For that reason, it is not very profitable for a couple to buy a wash-ing machine. . . . [A washing machine] is just a machine that goes round, so it's hard to allow for the characteristics and dirt conditions of your area. . . . Home spun, woolen, and synthetic fabrics are not strong and are li-able to shrink, and the movement of an electric washing machine is too strong for them, it seems.[5]

Another article concluded that refrigerators might not be useful for everyone.

> However convenient a tool it may be, it's not equally useful to all families. Everyone's lifestyle is different. For example, some families are able to live entirely through deliveries, buying every day exactly what they need for that day. It's not in every country that you can get even small items with one phone call. Families that use this method don't need to spend a lot of money on an electric fridge. Also, if you just want to cool things down for enjoy-ment, an ice box is just as effective.

The article also commented on the drawbacks and problems of refrig-erators: they tended to dry food out, had to be defrosted regularly, suf-fered from numerous manufacturing defects, and added to the electric-ity bill. The article concluded that refrigerators were most useful for two-worker families or large, busy families.[6]

Fujin no tomo (The Woman's Friend) was another independent mag-azine that took a highly critical view of extravagant and sometimes faulty consumer goods. Like *Kurashi no techō*, *Fujin no tomo* carried out product tests, but perhaps more revealing was the magazine's detailed focus on household budgets—the vast majority of which simply did not include room for unneeded products.

Japanese people might choose not to buy electrical goods for any number of reasons, apart from the hard reality of low purchasing power. One related issue was the very low cost of labor in the 1950s. Even at the end of the decade, unskilled workers earned only in the neighborhood of ¥40 ($0.11) an hour. With labor available at that price, the incentive to purchase labor-saving goods was commensurately reduced. An electric washer, for example, cost about ¥20,000 to purchase, and interest and running costs might add ¥2,000 per year. Using Hitachi's own estimates (see below), hand laundry for the average family of five required a daily average of about forty minutes of labor; the cost of hiring that labor would be no more than ¥30 per day, or a maximum of ¥10,000 per year. (Although I have not been able to find the prices charged by professional washer-women, I assume they were very low.) Cheap labor also made affordable the delivery of all sorts of goods, including food, undercutting the need for each family to have its own refrigerator.

Moreover, family heads—who continued in most cases to be older men—needed a lot of convincing that it was worth dipping into the family hoard merely to save the labor of young women in the family. Hard work was expected of most Japanese in the 1950s, particularly of young females.

Yet another factor limiting the domestic demand for electrical products was sheer unfamiliarity. In 1955 most Japanese had still never seen a washing machine, refrigerator, or even television. People did not well understand the rationale for purchasing these products, nor did they know how to operate them. Indeed, electricity remained a little-used and rather alarming commodity, deterring many Japanese from purchasing the wondrous products of modern industry.

All these doubts and criticisms added to the challenge for the electrical goods industry, which had to educate, persuade, and incentivize its customers. It is perhaps not surprising that leaders of the industry attempted to do so at the highest and most persuasive level of popular discourse: the level of ideology.

THE IDEOLOGIES OF PROSPERITY

In Chapter 2, I described how ambitious and farsighted entrepreneurs and businessmen formed a vision of Japan that mirrored the image of the United States. The immediate goal was to expand the frontier of the domestic market. This daunting task clearly could not be achieved with the tools available at the time. For this reason, Japanese companies devoted major resources to importing technologies of demand creation, including advertising, marketing, and management techniques, as described in Chapter 4.

But the process of demand creation involved more than a vision realized through technology acquisition, even using the widest possible definition of technology. Creating a mass consumer market in Japan required changes in the very structure of Japanese society—particularly the structure of the family. Corporations attempted to stimulate such changes in part by using technological resources to disseminate potent ideological symbols.

Three successive ideological constructs have exerted such power in Japan that analysts have labeled them "hegemonic." In the premodern era, according to this analytical tradition, "Confucianism" dominated the ideological landscape. From the later Meiji era until 1945, the dominant ideology was the "emperor system." The third dominant ideology, that of the postwar, is "democracy."[7]

All of these dominant themes possessed a chameleon-like ability to blend seamlessly into the social fabric: "[C]onsent so permeates the society that to many it seems commonsensical, natural, and at times invisible."[8] But if democracy, with all its confusion and contradictions, permeated the air that Japanese people breathed in the 1950s and after, it was surely not the only element in the compound. In recent years scholars have analyzed at least three related hegemonies that have exerted their own extraordinary influence in postwar Japan, coexisting uneasily at times with the discourse of democracy. Andrew Gordon, for example, has described a "reconstruction of workplace culture" during the 1950s intended to "make the enterprise a hegemonic institution whose interests were seen by most people as congruent with the natural, national interest as well as the personal interests of all Japanese."[9] Congruently, women became segregated into the roles of housewife and child-minder, leaving husbands free to pursue the goals of the enterprise.[10] A third theme running parallel to democracy has been that of the "middle mass" society. Since the late 1960s, the vast majority of Japanese have identified their social position as being in the "middle," even though objective measures of social equality appear to contradict this claim. As a result, many analysts have come to view the "middle mass" as an ideological construct.[11]

Arguably, these themes stretch the definition of ideology somewhat: exhortations on the roles of men in the company and women in the home clearly do not in themselves represent "the integrated assertions, theories, and aims that constitute a sociopolitical program."[12] But the theory of ideology itself has stretched to meet a more expansive definition. Building on the work of Jürgen Habermas and Louis Althusser, John Thompson argues that "the most effective ground of ideology is not the domain officially defined as 'politics,' but rather the domain of everyday life—the home, the workplace, the school, the media."[13] Key to Thompson's interpretation is the role of ideology in perpetuating relations of dominance.

Moreover, the themes of democracy, the "middle mass," and gender-based social norms run so closely together and are so clearly interdependent that it can be hard to tell which is the dominant and which the supporting theme. Democracy as constructed by many in postwar Japan may have as much to do with owning televisions and Toyotas as with the ownership of government. Carol Gluck has interpreted Japan's postwar democracy as closely linked with equality of access to material welfare.[14] Another common characteristic is that all of these dominant themes emerged only after a great deal of conflict and debate. The 1950s in particular were a time of uncertainty during which ideological boundaries remained blurred and malleable. Was the company a harmonious institution of mutual welfare or a ruthless exploiter? Was the government a benevolent guardian of the people's interests or a militaristic bureaucracy based upon the prewar order? These conflicting interpretations existed side by side in 1950s Japan, creating paradoxes so striking that they demand examination.

One particularly notable feature of that decade's ideological discourse is the remarkable consistency of terminologies. Indeed, it is sometimes hard to distinguish mere code words from themes that can actually lay claim to ideological meaning. "Democracy," for example, appears within all of the discourses, with greater or lesser effectiveness. Often the same words connote near-opposite meanings in different contexts, another paradox that haunts the creation of ideologies in the postwar.

Thompson emphasizes the importance of "symbolic forms" in the establishment and sustenance of relations of domination. Symbolic forms include "a broad range of actions and utterances, images and texts, which are produced by subjects and recognized by them and others as meaningful constructs."[15] I would identify the concept of the bright life as such an ideological symbol, albeit one with a tenuous relationship to the maintenance of political domination. Electrical goods companies were, of course, involved in ideology creation at many levels. Several suffered serious labor unrest during the late 1940s and were highly committed to securing the cooperation of employees. The bright life was in many ways a distillation of the major themes, implying as it did the housewife-centered family and the dominance of the middle class. Like the other themes, however, the bright life did not take hold without considerable dispute.

Raw Materials: A New Life For Japan

The leaders of electrical goods companies, whether consciously or not, used the bright life and other ideologically charged symbols to effect the fundamental changes in values and social structure needed to create demand for their products. But industry leaders were by no means the only group interested in such changes. A widespread feeling already existed among the Japanese that they must alter their lifestyle—that they needed, in essence, a "new life" (*shin seikatsu*). There was, however, a great deal of disagreement about what kinds of change were most appropriate. For some, "new life" meant a sober era of thrift and honesty. For others, it meant an end to sharp political practices; to others still, the improvement of productivity and product quality. Those who saw their salvation in the acquisition of televisions, washing machines, and refrigerators were probably in a minority.

Much of the language of these debates had a long currency in Japan. Phrases such as "new life," "lifestyle improvement" (*seikatsu kaizen*), and "lifestyle rationalization" (*seikatsu no gōrika*) appeared as motifs at least as early as the 1920s, and they continued in circulation despite radical shifts in interpretation. The first official "lifestyle improvement" campaign, for example, was launched by the Ministry of Education in 1920. It combined traditional exhortations to improve morality with programs to simplify life, limit the expense of ceremonies, and otherwise economize (see Chapter 1). A 1930s reincarnation focused on a "buy Japanese" drive.[16] The concept of "rationalization" of lifestyles has an even more involved history.

By the 1950s, the concept of the new life had a legacy of historical antecedents and multiple meanings. The first new life movements appeared in China in the 1930s under the Nationalist government of Chiang Kai Shek. The Chinese versions aimed primarily at alleviating the poor living conditions of the potentially revolutionary rural masses. Campaigns focused on specific goals such as the eradication of flies and mosquitoes. In Japan, calls for a new life emerged in the immediate aftermath of defeat in World War II, generally with the encouragement of the Occupation authorities, whose own agenda for a new life included democratization and the reduction of state intervention in everyday life. A "new Japan construction movement" (shin Nihon kensetsu undō) was launched by the conservative socialist government of Katayama Tetsu in 1949. Although Katayama's movement officially died with his premiership, it was survived by a number of more or less contemporaneous regional initiatives. For example, Kanagawa prefecture launched its own new life movement in September 1949 with the goal of "raising morality, rationalization of lifestyles, promotion of industrial economy, nurturing of healthy entertainment, and promotion of the peace, culture, and human rights movements."[17] Other local movements were known as "lifestyle scientification" (seikatsu kagakka) or "lifestyle improvement" movements.[18]

These currents of thought came together in the "new life" movement launched by the Hatoyama cabinet in August 1955, just months after Hatoyama Ichirō assumed the premiership from Yoshida Shigeru and during negotiations for the creation of the Liberal Democratic Party. Hatoyama first proposed the movement in January 1955 as a part of his general election campaign (much of its content was planned prior to that date by the Ministry of Education, which has an equal claim to the movement's parentage). The overall theme of Hatoyama's election campaign was the creation of a "bright Japan" (akarui Nihon).[19] In publicizing the new life movement, Hatoyama was apparently searching for a formula that could link the identity of the emerging political order to the aspirations of the electorate.

In a speech introducing his initiative, Hatoyama described the goals of the movement as "raising the standard of daily life through rationalization, cultural enhancement, and mutual harmony." This statement might be taken as a validation of modernization, technology, and the peaceful pursuit of wealth—the elements of what we now recognize as the "Japanese miracle." But Hatoyama saw the new life movement as something very different—indeed, as something opposed to the increasing modernization, Westernization, and materialism of Japanese society. "Since the war," he pontificated, "such lamentable tendencies as irresponsible freedom and laissez-faire, the lack of a spirit of idealism and progressiveness, and a trend toward negativity can be seen to be spreading as society modernizes in response to the opportunity presented by stable living standards." Hatoyama, it seems, adhered to the traditionalist implications of "lifestyle improvement." In the new life, he was looking for the restoration of the old. Nor is it surprising that Hatoyama should have taken this conservative approach: he had been a leading figure in the prewar and wartime political establishment.[20]

Although his introductory speech gave some clues to Hatoyama's conception of the "new life" movement, he deliberately refrained from outlining specific activities, insisting that the movement should be of the people and not "descended from heaven." Hatoyama went no further than to appropriate ¥50 million for the program and to form an organizing committee. The money was eventually entrusted to a New Life Movement Association (*Shin Seikatsu Undō Kyōkai*), which held its first meeting in November 1955 under the chairmanship of none other than Maeda Tamon, the chairman of Tōkyō Tsūshin Kōgyō (later Sony).

Because the prime minister declined to specify the activities of the new life movement, it was up to the people to do so. There was no shortage of opinions, and their bewildering variety attests to the inchoate nature of the key words under discussion. The New Life Movement Association received (among many others) the following suggestions, which it reviewed at its inaugural meeting:

The new life movement should carry out the following activities:

1. Using every means available, extermination of flies and mosquitoes in cities.
2. Drive away beggars from Ueno Park, Asakusa, and other places where they flourish, and find suitable work for them.
3. Clean stray dogs out of the cities.
4. Abolish permanent waves for ordinary women (*ippan josei*).

This movement should aim at abolishing the extravagance of the upper classes. For us lower class types, this movement is already a daily practice— if it wasn't, we couldn't live.

New life movement, go to it! I realize the new life movement is government-run, but the new Tokyo city office buildings are too fine. It's not necessary to use the high taxes paid by ordinary people for such splendid buildings. If foreigners visit, I think it's best for them to see well-ordered, simple buildings.

I believe that the goal of the new life movement should be the reduction of prices.

[The new life movement should]: stop people from making gorgeous clothes; instead of building conspicuous wooden houses, make them from concrete as much as possible; choose food which does not lack nutrition.

Together, preserve courtesy, help each other with all our hearts, reduce time-wasting, and focus on moral instruction at school.
Let us absolutely give up Christmas parties.[21]

In a discussion of the movement's goals published in *Shakai kyōiku* (Social Education), opinions on the meaning of "rationalization" and "cultural enhancement" were equally wide-ranging. A leader of the Association of Women's Groups singled out milk prices as the most pressing issue; another women's group leader called for political reform. Several participants emphasized the need for basic reform of "irrational" attitudes and social structures. For example, a female youth group leader commented: "We are about to become young wives. . . . Well, what is a young wife? She is called a wife, but as soon as she enters that position she immediately has to lead the life of a cow or a horse. The change we have to strive for is simply to be able to lead a human life." Another commentator added: "As goals for the New Life Movement, people often mention the improvement of morality, the promotion of industrial economy, lifestyle rationalization, the promotion of healthy entertainment, and the encouragement of religious movements for peaceful culture. But all of these are really based on democracy. . . . The New Life Movement can basically be explained as democracy."[22]

The "new life" movement provoked strong criticism from some quarters. The very notion of "rationalization" was abhorrent to the left wing, who associated it with layoffs and the strengthening of managerial control (the same critique was made of the productivity movement). A Sōhyō union leader commented:

> The idea of the new life movement came from the rich, not the poor. It came because the capitalist system feels danger from out-of-control expenses, corruption, and incipient collapse. Moreover, it will be used as a tool for lowering already low wages, and restructuring by firing workers. . . . In a country that treated individual profit and national profit the same, the new life movement would succeed. For example in China there are no flies, and even when there are no teachers in the exam room, nobody cheats.[23]

Amidst this cacophony, it is not surprising that the *Nippon Times* gloomily concluded the "new life" movement would not amount to much:

> Prime Minister Hatoyama first suggested the movement during the February political campaign, and the title caught on with a lot of voters, who put his party in power. "New Life" meant many things to different persons. To some it was the end of bureaucratic waste in government and business alike—no

more geisha parties, mahjong and golf during working hours. To others it was modernizing the kitchen and installing flush toilets. And there were yet many other ideas. But the whole thing to this day remains nebulous. . . . The fact remains that only Mr. Hatoyama seems to know what the movement is. Or does he?[24]

The Bright Life

It was from the assorted notes of this cacophony that electrical goods companies took the raw materials for their version of the new life. They had powerful weapons on their side, notably their ties to the media and the innate attractiveness of their products. Moreover, the Japanese business world as a whole was endeavoring to reconstruct workplace culture during the same period, and the ideals involved in this effort—the benevolent but hegemonic enterprise, the separate spheres of male workers and female housewives, and the "middle mass" society—were clearly related to the specific agenda of the electrical goods industry.

Electrical goods companies seized in particular on the concept of the bright life (*akarui seikatsu*), which seemed ideally suited to the products they were selling. The fluorescent light bulb was one of the new products that spread rapidly throughout Japan in the 1950s. Its purveyors were literally bringing brightness to the Japanese home, which until had then only been lit by dingy 20-watt incandescent bulbs. Several major electrical goods companies seized on "brightness" as a theme for advertising, promotion, and sloganeering. In 1955, Matsushita's National brand adopted the slogan "Bright National," which many people still remember as its defining image (the same can scarcely be said of Hatoyama's "bright Japan" campaign). The image of brightness clearly registered among ordinary people. Forty years later, former assembly-line worker Hanada Mitsue recalled that she was attracted to join Matsushita by the "Bright National" slogan. A women's-group diary eloquently sums up the desire evoked by the bright life to escape the grim present: "When we look at the lights of the Occupation soldiers gleaming on the hilltop, and compare them with our own dim lives, we feel we must act to make our lives brighter: for if we don't, who will?"[25]

The "rational lifestyle" was another potent symbol for electrical goods companies. Of all the terms in the ideological cauldron of the 1950s, "rationalization" is perhaps the most fraught with ambiguity—and with irony. It is probably impossible to unravel all the influences affecting the word, which William Kelly has aptly labeled an "ideologically potent and semantically slippery rubric."[26] The word was first used extensively in the 1920s in the context of "industrial rationalization," a government- and business-inspired movement that borrowed concepts both from Taylorist scientific management in the United States and from statist industrial policies in Germany. Ironically, given its cosmopolitan background, the concept of "industrial rationalization" was to become one of the great rallying cries for economic nationalism and autarky. In the postwar era, the definition of "rationalization" has been further nuanced by the term's inclusion, following Weber, as one of the criteria of modernization theory.[27] Even before the war, "rationalization" was used in a loose sense to refer to modernization, Westernization, and "sweeping away the evil customs" of the feudal era. In this context, it entered the discourse on the reform of lifestyles; once again, though, its precise meaning remained unclear. For some, rationalization meant reducing extravagance and prioritizing saving over expenditure, but the term could also be commandeered to promote a reordering of the household through electrical goods. Rationalization had strong overtones of Westernization and a scientific approach to living (often connected to life in the West). Because new products such as television were the product of modern scientific advance, the term was doubly applicable to them under this rubric.

One of the heavy ironies of the electrical goods companies' support for rationalization is that it coincided with an increasing appreciation for the spontaneity and lack of planning that lay behind many purchase decisions. Consumer research by Matsushita revealed that whereas families might spend hours planning small purchases such as food so as to achieve the maximum economy, the decision to purchase a television was typically made on impulse—and it was often precipitated by the least "rational" members of the family, the children.

A related component of the bright life was the Western-style nuclear family home with a housewife at its center. Electrical goods companies emphasized this ideal to tie the ideology of the bright life directly to a larger discourse that occupied center stage throughout the high-growth era: the transformation of Japanese society into a Western-style advanced industrial economy. As we saw in Chapter 1, the model of the Western-style home had a substantial history in Japan, dating back at least to the 1920s. But it was during the 1950s and 1960s that this idea became validated as the norm throughout urban and, increasingly, rural Japan.

Less Work for Mother?

The bright life, with its attendant themes of "rational" housewives and managed consumption, may well sound familiar; indeed, the creation of rational consuming housewives has appeared at times to be one of the great projects of twentieth-century modernity. From the beginning of the century, American and European wives were cajoled into a well-defined place inside the middle-class home, where they were surrounded by convenient appliances and household goods. Thomas Edison himself described his vision of household electricity in a 1901 interview with *Good Housekeeping:*

> The housewife of the future will be neither a slave to servants nor herself a drudge. She will give less attention to the home, because the home will need less; she will be rather a domestic engineer than a domestic laborer, with the greatest of all handmaidens, electricity, at her service. This and other mechanical forces will so revolutionize the woman's world that a large portion of the aggregate of woman's energy will be conserved for use in broader, more constructive fields.

If this sounds like emancipatory thinking, Edison revealed the limits of such a conception when he went on: "[Electricity] will develop woman to that point where she can think straight. Direct thought is not at present an attribute of femininity. In this woman is now centuries, ages, even epochs behind man. That it is true is not her fault, but her misfortune, and the misfortune of the race."[28]

In the United States, the concept of the housewife originated with the upper-middle-class family, where women managed servants but did little physical labor. With the dramatic spread of the middle class during the 1920s, however, the ideal of the housewife came to encompass a large segment of the American population. And, as in Japan, a part of the ideal in the United States was the ownership of labor-saving household appliances. Ruth Schwartz Cowan has chronicled some of the ironies of this process, which promised to emancipate women from the drudgery of household work but actually added many tasks that women had not previously performed. As a result, the housewife of the 1960s actually worked *longer* hours than her predecessor of 1900.[29]

In Europe, too, the ideal of the rational housewife was already being vigorously promoted by the 1920s. In Weimar Germany, conservative housewives' organizations and radical socialist groups alike endorsed the rationalization of household life. The latter tended to support cooperative household maintenance, which would allow women to work on a more equal footing with men. The former, by contrast, idealized the housewife as a rational director of an "efficiently managed home business" in which "the full significance of the economic principle takes hold for consumption as it has for production." This approach was supposed to free up time for the housewife to fulfill her appointed duty as "the preserver and inspirer of spiritual values." The household electrical goods industry naturally supported the movement and incorporated the theme of rationalization in its messages.[30]

The United States, Europe, and Japan were clearly similar not only in the form taken by the ideology of the rational consuming housewife but also in the process of ideological formation. Rationalization was the focus of different and disputed opinions in Weimar Germany, as it was in postwar Japan. American electrical goods companies, like their Japanese counterparts, promoted idealized images of young, pretty housewives effortlessly performing housework. Perhaps the most notable similarity is the gap that continued to exist between the ideal as expressed in advertising images and the reality as lived by most Americans, Germans, and Japanese. American family life was far more diverse than the homogeneous portrayal of it in advertisements and soap operas. And in Japan in the early 1950s, the housewife was still the exception rather than the rule. In 1955, 57 percent of Japanese women aged fifteen or older continued to be employed. Women accounted for one-quarter of the manufacturing work force, a third of the service industry work force, and half of the agricultural work force. In the countryside, the nonworking housewife was a great rarity.

For all their similarities, the experiences of Japan, the United States, and Europe differed in important ways—most notably in the extent of the gap between ideal and reality. In both Germany and the United States, a substantial percentage of the population lived in middle-class, housewife-centered households by the 1950s. In Japan, the percentage of families in which women actually fulfilled the exclusive role of housewife was much lower. Ezra Vogel makes this point clear in discussing women from Mamachi who were not the wives of salarymen: they faced lives of hard work, economic insecurity, and limited opportunity. Vogel understood that in 1960, Japan's "new middle class" still only represented a small minority of the population.

But the gap between Japan and the West was not only quantitative; it was also qualitative. For example, housing conditions for most Japanese, even those who qualified as middle class, were very far removed from the idealized homes portrayed in advertising materials. Even the privileged salaryman families of Mamachi lived in housing that would have been considered barely livable by American standards.

ADVERTISING, EDUCATION, AND DEMONSTRATION

During the latter half of the 1950s, Japanese electrical goods companies put their studies of U.S. marketing to good use. Their efforts to promote, distribute, finance, and sell their products were truly vast: Japan had seen nothing like it before. The marketing efforts of Japanese companies in the 1950s were comprehensive, and they included far more than just advertising. In Japan, much more than in the United States or Europe, consumers had to be educated, cajoled, even shown how to use and how to purchase electrical products.

Advertising the Bright Life

The 1950s were a golden decade for Japanese advertising. The growth rate of the industry puts even the most high-flying of the manufacturing industries to shame. Total national expenditures on advertising grew from ¥9 billion in 1953 to ¥146 billion in 1959, totaling 1.5% of gross domestic product in that year.[31] The 1960 *White Paper on National Life* specifically singled out advertising in its analysis of the consumer revolution that was suddenly sweeping over Japan: "Today, there is even a view that the demand for luxurious or cultural goods is actually created by the manufacturers, who, together with retailers, are putting their efforts into advertising and other means of selling new products. The development of television, radio, newspapers and magazines—the so-called mass communication media—has lent a great deal of strength to this effort."

Electrical goods companies made vast investments in advertising during the 1950s. As Matsushita Electric's sales rocketed into the stratosphere—quadrupling in the four years from 1955 to 1959—its advertising expenditures grew even faster, from less than 4 percent of sales in the early 1950s to 8.7 percent in 1959.[32] Ad spending far surpassed expenditures on research and development, which averaged a mere 2 percent of sales for electrical goods companies in the 1950s.

Advertising was a powerful medium for promoting the bright life, which several companies took explicitly as their theme. For example, a Sanyo advertisement headed "Sanyo electrical products for a Bright Life" offers a romantic sketch superimposed on a soft-focus picture of a Western-style young mother:

A white frosty morning
A lively evening meal
A rainy day, a windy day
Overflowing laughter
You are the sun of the family
A soft loving hand to the children
To father, just one person
Mother
This year too, bright, beautiful!

This advertisement combines several of the key themes of electrical goods advertising, all under the parasol slogan of the bright life. The housewife-mother is portrayed as "the sun of the family," an explicit link to the theme of brightness. To her husband she is "just one person," indicating a nuclear household without intrusive parents-in-law. The advertisement implies a marital relationship based on love, and it suggests that the housewife is a beautiful woman and not a drudge.

A Matsushita advertisement for National brand goods opens, "Of the world's 1.4 billion women, the one woman you chose as your wife." The advertisement, which features an image of a tired (but still pretty) housewife carrying a heavy metal bucket, goes on: "Since the war, Japanese women have been liberated from the feudal system, and their status within the family has also risen. How is it with your family? Is your wife still tiring herself out with housework, losing her youth and beauty?"

The advertisement displays graphs comparing housewives' labor in the "cultural nations" of Europe and America (Ōbei bunkakoku) to the workload of Japanese women. By these figures, an American housewife spent only four hours on housework and enjoyed nine hours of leisure and eight hours of sleep per day. By contrast, a Japanese salaryman's wife had ten hours of housework per day, with only two hours of leisure and seven hours of sleep. The advertisement appeals to husbands: "For the sake of your busy wife, won't you add electrical goods to your household, even a little at a time? For example, if you only bought a National electric rice cooker, your wife would be able to sleep an extra thirty minutes per week." The advertisement also adds economic arguments, calling on husbands both to value their wives' labor and to reduce food bills by relieving wives of calorie-consuming labor:

Compared to the two hundred hours per month that a salaryman works, a wife works for three hundred hours. Since that is 1.5 times the working hours of a typical female factory hand who earns ¥8,300 per month, your

Figure 7 A "scientific" illustration of the need to reduce the housewife's labor. The caption reads: "Of the world's 1.4 billion women, the one woman you chose as your wife." (Courtesy of Matsushita Denki Sangyō)

wife's work is worth some ¥12,500 per month. These statistics do not include the 1,502 calories that your wife consumes just from doing housework, which is 70% of her total caloric intake of 2,200 calories. It is not unreasonable that your wife should become thin and haggard.

In their efforts to reproduce the American suburban ideal in Japan, electrical goods companies sometimes got themselves into deep water. The American families portrayed in television dramas and sitcoms had lifestyles that were sometimes hard to understand, let alone imitate, in Japan. For example, the vast majority of urban Japanese seldom or never received social visitors at home. The Matsushita Company, perhaps driven by Matsushita Kōnosuke's vision of an American-style middle-class society, launched a campaign to persuade Japanese people to invite their friends home. A 1958 Matsushita advertisement features, next to a picture of a young, smiling, Western-dressed family, the slogan:

This year's resolution: Let's bring guests to our home.

In Japan today social intercourse mainly takes place outside the home, and it is only the husband who participates. As a result, husbands are coming home later and later, and the families are left lonely. All sorts of prob-

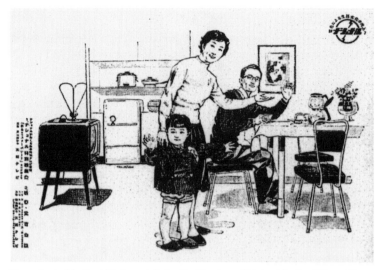

Figure 8   An idealized Western-style family. (Courtesy of Matsushita Denki Sangyō)

lems have arisen from this situation. Won't you please consider entertaining guests at home as a new year resolution, for the sake of your family?

The campaign can hardly be called a success (it is still quite rare to see the inside of a friend's home in Japan), probably because most homes were simply too shabby and cramped for entertaining.

Nor do husbands come home from work any earlier today, despite another enticing Matsushita advertisement in which a boy in shorts (itself a symbol of middle-class aspiration)[33] temptingly holds up a cold beer—chilled, of course, in a Matsushita refrigerator—next to the slogan "Father—Beer!" and the commentary: "Please come home early. Your sweet child and your lovely wife are keeping your beer cold in a National refrigerator."

Education and Scientific Rationality

Advertising played an important part in electrical goods companies' efforts to stimulate consumer demand. But marketers in Japan had to do much more than simply advertise. To a much greater extent than their U.S. counterparts, Japanese companies had to teach people *why* they needed expensive products such as washing machines and refrigerators (U.S. electrical goods companies faced a similar situation, and adopted similar strategies, in the 1920s). They did so through a wide variety of educational, demonstration, and promotional efforts. Educational campaigns included lectures, published explanations, scientific analyses, and the sponsorship of clubs for the investigation of electrical goods. Demonstration was pursued via door-to-door sales, showrooms, traveling displays, lecture-demonstrations, and special exhibitions.

The overriding theme of these efforts was that electrical goods represented *rational* purchases. The "electrification lifestyle" was set forth as a new field of knowledge steeped in the authoritative language of Western science. Explanations of electrical products were laced with statistics designed to show the benefits the items offered. In general, these benefits fell into two categories: benefits of health and welfare, and economic benefits based on the saving of labor. An article on Matsushita refrigerators, for example, includes detailed charts and diagrams of the perishability of food, showing how food kept in different compartments of the refrigerator retains its freshness much longer than food kept in ice boxes or storage jars. The health benefits of the refrigerator are definitively established and represent the main argument in favor of a purchase. The ability to enjoy a cold beer is thrown in almost as an afterthought.[34]

Health benefits, economic benefits, and the ideology of the Western middle-class housewife run together in a long article published by Matsushita in 1955 for its independent retailers ("so that you can kindly inform your customers"). The article, by Ogiwara Gunji, a professor of medicine at Osaka University, is headed "The Housewife Is Getting Too Tired." It opens: "The Japanese woman ages as soon as she has married and had children. This is because she is constantly harassed by excessive housework, placing too heavy a burden on her body. If she could reduce the burden just a little, what a bright life might she enjoy." The article provides a detailed statistical analysis (using the "R.M.R. method") comparing the calories women consume while performing traditional tasks versus those consumed while performing the same tasks using electrical goods. Photographs depict women wearing masks attached to "Douglas bags" strapped to their backs to measure the calories consumed during activities such as washing clothes, sewing, and drawing water from a well. In one example, four women between seventeen and twenty-three years old washed five shirts in a wooden tub and five shirts using a National brand washing machine. On average, the subjects consumed an additional 30 to 40 calories by using the tub. "From these calculations," the article concludes, "it is clear that the person who uses a tub must take in the equivalent of an additional bread roll, or her body will not hold out."

The author adds emphasis by stressing the difference between the "blue-collar" nature of clothes-scrubbing and the "white-collar" nature of using a washing machine: "If you consider the hardness of the work, using a tub is equivalent to operating a crane or turning a lathe, while operating an electric washing machine uses only about the same labor as using an abacus, doing office work, or operating a telephone switchboard."[35]

A Hitachi advertisement finds an even greater caloric demand from the rigors of washing in a tub and makes the economic argument more explicit still:

> For family life, the time and effort spent on washing is amazing. According to a study, in a family of five the average daily washing time is thirty to forty minutes, or 5 percent of all the energy consumed in one day. . . . Therefore, washing is a major issue for the improvement of lifestyles. For a 100- to 200-watt washing machine, the cost of electricity is ¥1 to ¥1.60 an hour. On the other hand, if you do your own washing, you will use 150 to 200 calories an hour, which if you look at the current cost of food comes to ¥20 to ¥25, or fifteen to twenty times the cost of electricity.[36]

Educational efforts were backed up by enormous demonstration campaigns. Because most Japanese had no familiarity with electrical products, direct experience and proactive sales efforts were considered essential. These sales efforts would, in turn, often dwell on the scientific benefits of the products. Yamada Shōgo, a Toshiba salesman, describes the showmanship he used to persuade buyers of their need for new electrical products,

> I decided to copy the techniques of the street entertainers and sellers of Taiwanese bananas, who would entertain their audience by telling stories. . . . I came up with idea of a performance focusing on "sen-ta-ku" ["many agonies of washing," a pun on the Japanese word for laundry, sentaku]. I would use vivid illustrations to show what agony washing was for the typical housewife. For example, I would show that the annual weight of washing for a family of five was equivalent to the weight of Hanako, the new elephant in the Ueno zoo.[37]

Personal visits from sales representatives accounted for the majority of electrical product sales in the 1950s. These traveling vendors usually carried models with which they would conduct demonstrations on the spot, sometimes leaving samples with customers for a home trial. Sales departments used this approach not only because of the perceived need

Figure 9 A woman wears a gas mask and Douglas bag to measure caloric consumption. (Courtesy of Matsushita Denki Sangyō)

to educate customers but also because of the rundown appearance and small size of many retail outlets, which had often started as radio repair shops using little more than a single room. Ōtake Chikayuki, owner of an electrical shop in Fukuoka, described his strategy for selling televisions: "My most effective method is leaving a set with the family. Of course, it's no good to do that indiscriminately, but I have found that once you leave a set with them, customers usually buy it."[38]

Electrical goods companies created alliances to facilitate demonstration of their wares. As early as 1948, fourteen electrical goods companies joined forces with a group of electrical power companies to form the Household Electrical Culture Society (Katei Denki Bunka Kai).[39] The Electrical Products League (Denki Shōhin Renmei), a group centered on the Tokyo Electric Power Company, formed in 1955 and shortly thereafter launched a magazine, *Denki Shōhin* (Electrical Products), to spread the gospel of modern technology. These joint efforts produced educational demonstrations and lectures throughout the country. Like so many of the comprehensive efforts at market creation in Japan, this initiative followed a U.S. model. In the first two decades of the twentieth century, American electric utilities, manufacturers, distributors, and retailers formed industry groups such as the National Electric Light Association and the Society for Electrical Development. These groups launched publicity campaigns, traveling demonstrations, exhibits, and school contests.[40]

Electrical goods companies also worked hard to create powerful alliances with local organizations, particularly women's groups, parent-teacher associations, and agricultural cooperatives. This activity represents an intriguing parallel with the "new life" movement, which relied heavily on the cooperation of these same groups. Some of these civic organizations were reluctant to admit to a direct involvement in the promotion of electrical products, in part because Occupation legislation specifically prohibited them from participating in such activities.[41] Yet it is clear that electrical goods companies made concerted efforts to co-opt local associations. Yamada Shōgo, a Toshiba veteran, recalls that his company sponsored agricultural and women's association events.[42] A diary kept by a Kawasaki women's group also records strong links with electrical goods producers. In March 1951, for example, Toshiba invited this group to tour its factory and sent the women home with gifts of light bulbs. In July 1953, the same organization staged a play entitled "The Electrical Family's Afternoon" (Denka katei no gogo). The script had been written by a Toshiba employee.[43]

On top of retailers' efforts to demonstrate electrical goods, manufacturers organized their own large-scale campaigns, both for publicity and for educational purposes. Matsushita operated a helicopter that would fly to cities and smaller towns, usually landing on the grounds of a school, where Matsushita representatives would demonstrate and lecture on washing machines and refrigerators. Matsushita also created the "mobile electrical classroom" (*hashiru denka kyōshitsu*), a truck equipped with a model kitchen and living room, which toured Japan in the second half of the 1950s.[44]

Electrical goods companies also mounted large numbers of special exhibitions. For leading technologies such as television, these were often held in department stores, continuing a long tradition dating back to the prewar period and earlier. For more prosaic products, such events took place in hotel banquet rooms and other rented spaces. In 1960, for example, Matsushita held the "Key to Happiness" exhibition in a total of 104 locations throughout Japan. This road show was designed to promote Matsushita refrigerators, which were equipped with key-shaped door handles. Retailers sent out 90,000 invitations to this exhibition, targeting higher-income households. Invitations came with a golden key and the motto, "Please open up your happiness with the key to happiness." The campaign drew 110,000 attendants, a measure of the public's receptiveness to such exhibitions. It cost ¥14.65 million, the equivalent of about 500 refrigerators.[45]

Manufacturers also sponsored societies and publications specifically devoted to promoting their product line. An example is Matsushita's Fountain of Living Club (*Kurashi no Izumi Kai*), founded by the company's advertising department in August 1956. Retail stores were encouraged to begin local Fountain of Living clubs at their own expense. One Matsushita-affiliated shop reported that its club had eighty-four members (twenty-five men and fifty-nine women). The club met once a month, with up to twelve members invited at a time. At the first meeting, the store owner demonstrated rice cookers, electric mixers, and electric irons. The cost of the meeting totaled ¥3,700, and it included a meal for the participants. However, the store owner claimed, four of the attendees returned the next day to buy rice cookers.

In 1957, Matsushita launched an associated magazine, *Kurashi no Izumi* ("Fountain of Living," subtitled "The guide to creating a bright electrical lifestyle"), which ran for more than a decade. A glossy publication with a sleek, modern appearance, *Kurashi no Izumi* generally featured a television personality on the first page, always permed and wearing Western clothes. The magazine featured articles and discussion groups on Matsushita products, accompanied by glossy color photographs. Although it was pure propaganda, *Kurashi no Izumi* was a good imitation of the Western-style fashion and lifestyle magazines that were becoming popular in Japan in the latter half of the 1950s. Matsushita's PR department described the goals of the magazine as follows: "Since the magazine is aimed at housewives, the editorial plan is to offer practical articles above all, featuring aspects of daily life that are often overlooked, as well as spotlighting the rationalization of lifestyles, and logical explanation of the need for electrical goods."[46]

Sports Mad: Selling Television

Of all the electrical products of the postwar era, television was perhaps the least justifiable in terms of "rational" explanation. What is the value of television? How can one logically justify spending several months' income on such a product? Today we might say that television has entertainment value and leave it at that. But in 1950s Japan a television cost too much for such a frivolous justification. Entrepreneurs such as Shōriki Matsutarō had invoked the threat of communism to help them get licenses for television broadcasting, but no one was going to buy a television based on that logic. There were many pious comments in the press about the educational value of television, particularly in rural communities. But farmers were most unlikely to spend their meager savings on such an expensive educational tool.

Yet televisions were the first products that flew out of the electrical goods stores. Although the price of a television set was about three times that of an electric washing machine, by 1960 more than 9 million Japanese households had bought television sets, versus 6 million for washing machines. Refrigerators trailed far behind—a mere 2 million sold by 1960. The popularity of televisions, which had no obvious use, over very practical items such as washing machines remains something of an enigma. However, this phenomenon has been repeated in many other developing societies, where television antennas (and, more recently, satellite dishes) rise in neighborhoods with the most primitive housing and living conditions. The 1994 Chinese film *Ermo* portrays a village woman who is so determined to buy a television that she sells her own blood (as often as twice a day), leaves her husband in order to toil long hours in a menial city job, and eventually enters a compromising relationship with a local truck driver. Her motive for buying a television is apparently invidious—Ermo hates the wife of the village head, who owns the only other television set in the village. In spite of her husband's plea that they use the money to buy a house ("a house is a hen, but a television is only an egg," he argues), Ermo finally buys an enormous color television, which she installs on the only surface big enough to hold it: her own bed.[47]

Japanese television buyers seem to have been motivated less out of envy than out of love for popular pastimes, particularly sports. Almost universally, Japanese television owners mentioned sports as the key reason for their purchase. Hanada Mitsue, for example, bought a television despite extremely straitened family circumstances (see Chapter 6), saving the money for a discounted set from her salary of ¥8,000 a month because her father loved sumo. "Father's business [carving personal seals] hadn't been going well, and his health wasn't good. His one pleasure in life was watching sumo. He used to go to the local café to watch on their television. But I felt it would be such a pleasure for him to watch it at home."

Of course, the dream of television in Japan was linked to sports from the very beginning: Takayanagi Kenjirō fantasized about watching the Olympics on television. No one made the connection between the emerging mass media and sporting events more effectively than Shōriki Matsutarō, who as a newspaper owner had brought Babe Ruth to Japan and who as a television station owner now broadcast baseball, sumo, and professional wrestling. A true phenomenon of the 1950s, wrestling gave Japanese television its first superstar: Riki Dosan. His fights attracted hundreds of thousands of viewers, who watched both at home and in public places. In partial fulfillment of Karl Mundt's original plan, Shōriki's NTV had installed some 200 large-screen television sets in prominent places around Tokyo. So thick were the crowds in front of these sets during popular sports events that television announcers had to issue regular safety warnings, advising people not to climb telegraph poles or power lines and to keep the road clear for passing traffic.

Hasegawa Kikuyo, whose husband managed a troupe of traveling actors in Saitama prefecture, describes the very real tradeoffs that her husband's television purchase involved:

At that time, there wasn't a single television anywhere near us, and if we wanted to watch television, we had to go to the town which was two or three leagues away. My husband was a wrestling fan, and for no other reason he bought a large television for his theater. It cost ¥180,000, near ¥190,000.

As a matter of fact, since my family house in Tokyo was destroyed in the air raids, what I really wanted was to buy a house. At that time, where we were living in Saitama, land cost ¥2,500 or ¥3,000 per *tsubo* [3.3 square meters], or if you paid ¥5,000 you could get a really well-located piece. In order to buy the land and an older house for about ¥85,000, I was working myself to the bone [as a recycler of discarded goods]. When my husband

Figure 10   Pro boxing fans watch television in front of a
newspaper office, 1956. (Courtesy of Asahi Shinbunsha)

said he was going to use that money to buy a television, we fought over it.
Even so, once we'd bought a television I thought it was really wonderful.

Hasegawa and her husband took the television with them when they
went on tour around the villages of Saitama.

Wherever we went, the old people would say to us, "I never thought I would
see television in my lifetime, but thanks to you I've been able to. Thank you,
thank you." On days when there was wrestling, we'd say, "If there's time
after the wrestling, then we'll put on a play for you," and the actors would
make the arrangements, and all the audience would watch the wrestling together. At the end, there'd be no time for acting. But still, the audience was
satisfied. . . .

  In the morning, as we bicycled home through the rice fields, the farmers
working on their plots would shout to us, "Thanks for last night!"

I laugh sometimes thinking that if we had bought land instead of that television, we'd now be fat plutocrats![48]

The tradeoff between a television and a home is not as far-fetched as it may sound. Even in the six largest cities in Japan, a modest home with land could be purchased for ¥200,000 (a comfortable middle-class urban home, with land, cost around ¥600,000 in the mid-1950s).[49] By contrast, a television in 1955 cost about ¥140,000.

In the Ozu Yasujirō film *Ohayō* (1957), two young boys are so desperate to watch sumo wrestling on television that they go on strike against their parents, refusing to talk or cooperate in family life until their parents break down and buy a television. Although the film is a satire, the primitive process of television purchasing is well illustrated here. In fact, market studies of the time indicate that the decision-making process depicted in the Ozu film was not so unusual.

Ohayō illustrates how far the ideology of electrical goods had already permeated Japanese society and how much ambivalence it provoked in observers and participants. The families portrayed in the film are by no means wealthy—they belong to the lower ranks of the middle class—yet it seems that electrical goods are the main topic of their lives (by contrast, Ozu's *Tokyo Monogatari* [1954] is steeped in the languor of a former age). For the residents of the shabby neighborhood depicted in the film, ownership of electrical goods seems, in spite of its glamour, to be connected to a breakdown of morality and of the established order. A woman who has just purchased a washing machine is suspected of having stolen funds from the women's society to pay for it. And the only people who own a television at the beginning of the film, a young neighborhood couple, are the subjects of much local gossip:

"I've heard that the pair of them wear Western nightclothes from noon onward. . . . "
"Well, it's understandable, since they say she used to be a cabaret dancer in Ikebukuro."
"Really? That class of person, is she? Well, then it makes sense. . . . "[50]

The stage directions, though, make it clear that this is an attractive, fun-loving, apparently happy couple. For example, they make their first appearance "singing *chansons* companionably."

So powerful was the appeal of televised sporting events that manufacturers scarcely had to justify the purchase of television rationally. Nevertheless, they paid lip service to the rational ideal. Manufacturers advertised the cultural benefits of television, using appealing images of families seated around the television in harmony and togetherness. And they emphasized the monetary value of the entertainment provided by television. Sharp claimed, for example: "You can enjoy ¥300,000 worth with one television set." The advertisement, which features a pair of sumo wrestlers literally throwing each other out of a television screen, supports its assertion by noting that attending all the sports and theatrical events broadcast on NHK in a single year would cost ¥300,000 ($800) per person. "If you add the cost of food, travel etc. that really comes to a large amount. If you have a Sharp television then you and your family can enjoy wrestling, sumo, plays and music at your leisure for years. Maintenance costs are low, so it's very economical." At the time (1957), a Sharp television cost ¥84,500.

Learning Sales Techniques

Education extended not only to end users but also to the retailers who bore the ultimate burden of convincing the customer. During the 1950s electrical goods companies, led by Matsushita, increasingly brought retailers into the fold in an attempt to create nationwide brand networks. Matsushita, for example, greatly expanded its prewar network of affiliated retail stores: from 6,000 in 1950, the number of *renmeiten* ("league stores") grew to 40,000 by 1956. This network gave Matsushita coverage throughout Japan, with outlets even in small communities not penetrated by other electrical goods makers. From 1957 Matsushita began designating "National Shops" from among the league stores. Whereas league stores were only loosely tied to the company's National brand, National Shops exclusively sold Matsushita merchandise. Also in 1957, Matsushita teamed up with leading wholesalers to launch jointly capitalized regional sales companies, which replaced Matsushita's own regional sales offices and offered a full range of distribution, maintenance, and support services to retail stores.[51]

Matsushita provided extensive support to its retail network. In addition to holding training courses and seminars, Matsushita published *Nashonaru shoppu* (National Shop), a magazine distributed to independent retailers. *Nashonaru shoppu* contained a wealth of educational materials on the benefits of various Matsushita products, sales techniques, market research methods and results, and economic and market analyses. These materials explicitly stressed the importance of ideology as a marketing instrument. A 1956 article by Yamada Masaharu, a marketing consultant, exhorts retailers: "Electrical goods shops, sell

テレビ買ってくれなければご飯たべない

Figure 11   The cartoon caption reads: "If you don't buy a
television, I won't eat." (Source unknown)

culture!" The article opens: "It's old-fashioned to think that 'I'm a
shopkeeper so it's enough just to sell goods.' The mission of your shop,
and indeed the best plan for prosperity, is to sell a 'joyful life' to customers."[52]

Matsushita also emphasized the need for market research and provided instruction in *Nashonaru shoppu* on how to conduct and inter-
pret surveys. Some of the magazine's own research provides interesting
insights into the nature of electrical goods purchases. For example, one
study revealed that the initiators of electrical goods purchase decisions
were for the most part children (in 57 percent of cases); moreover, the
larger the contemplated purchase, the more likely children were to initiate it. Trying to explain this seeming paradox, the magazine specu-
lated that "various unimagined convenience goods have entered the
market. They are scientific and complex, and can't be evaluated with
existing knowledge. Thus the voice of young people is stronger." However, the family head made the ultimate decision—and paid for the
goods—in some 60 percent of cases, and discussion involved the whole
family in 85 percent of cases. This broad participation was noted to be
a major change from the prewar era, when men and women alike
tended to purchase items without consultation—but when few families
had the means to buy consumer durable goods.[53]

Matsushita researchers also commented upon the surprising spontaneity of electrical goods purchases. A survey found that, once they had decided to buy an electrical product, 79 percent of households bought the item immediately. Only 21 percent waited to save more before making the purchase.[54] Later in the decade, retailers were increasingly exhorted to focus on housewives—in part because housewives had leisure and control over increasing amounts of disposable income, but also because, after televisions, the second most popular products were washing machines, which primarily benefited women.

Creating Credit

The final piece of the marketing puzzle was the establishment of installment loan subsidiaries to finance purchases of big-ticket items. In the case of Matsushita, these loan companies were also retail outlets: they both sold and financed Matsushita products. By 1960, Matsushita's installment loan subsidiary network accounted for some 25 percent of the company's sales.[55] Installment payment plans have a long history in Japan, dating back as far as the premodern period. But that credit system was highly fragmented and generally limited to minor purchases such as clothes and food. During the 1950s personal finance witnessed massive growth, providing a vital spark to the "consumer revolution."

According to Toshiba's Yamada Shōgo, his was the first company to begin offering installment purchases after World War II. In August 1950, Toshiba made credit terms available for purchases of radios, washing machines, and refrigerators. Matsushita subsequently took the lead and forced other makers to create their own national finance networks. Banks also joined in the consumer credit game: Kangyō Bank pioneered "cultural savings" accounts (*bunka yokin*) and an "easy payment system" (*iijii peimento no shisutemu*).[56] By 1960, the *White Paper on National Life* was able to say of the installment system: "Currently, 50 percent of television and sewing machine purchases and 30 percent of refrigerator and fan sales are on this system. Moreover, MITI estimates annual expenditure on monthly payments at ¥500 billion, or 5 percent of GDP. On top of that, the city banks are now actively preparing to introduce new types of consumer finance such as auto loans, credit cards etc."[57]

Private consumer credit companies and retail consortia also became major players in the installment loan game. The largest, a company called Nihon Shinyō Hanbai (Japan Credit Sales), started in 1951. In its first year it had 20,000 borrowers and a total lending outlay of ¥60 million. By 1959 the number of borrowers had grown to 300,000, with ¥4 billion in loans. An alliance of retailers formed a rival group, the Nihon Senmonten Kai Rengō (Japan League of Specialist Stores). Some retail chains, notably Marui, also launched aggressive installment programs.

Finance charges varied with the length and amount of the loan, averaging about 5 percent for a ten-month loan. However, for larger purchases such as televisions, loans tended to be for eighteen months or more, and the finance charge was typically 9 to 15 percent. In addition, retailers paid the finance company a fee of 4 percent, much as merchandisers now pay credit card companies. The finance companies would generally lend only to consumers who had salaried employment, with the payments automatically deducted from the borrower's bank account. Marui was an exception: it lent directly to housewives and sent its representatives to the home for collection. The majority of monthly installment payments were less than ¥3,000, although some 10 percent exceeded ¥5,000. Many small electrical retailers also extended credit to their customers.[58]

The 1950s saw a substantial increase in spending on electrical goods as a proportion of income, even as incomes rapidly rose (as Table 8, p. 248, demonstrates). Several studies commented on the high "income elasticity" of electrical goods—i.e., an increase in income tended to trigger an even greater increase in electrical goods spending. It is important to account for debt payments in analyzing electrical goods spending: although not all consumer lending was for electrical goods, television and appliance purchases were the major targets of the installment system in the 1950s.

An internal Matsushita survey conducted in 1960 confirmed the extremely high proportion of household expenditures devoted to debt repayment. The survey found that even in the most affluent households, with over ¥55,000 per month in expenditures, an average of 9 percent of total spending went toward installment payments. Mid-range families (¥16,000–¥25,000 expenditures, accounting for 37 percent of all households) spent the highest proportion on installment loans—up to 14 percent of total expenditures, with an average over 10 percent (see Table 9, p. 249).

From this data, Matsushita concluded that the greatest opportunity for expanding credit still further lay in the middle and lower income ranges. At the time, Matsushita's typical credit plan for television purchases stipulated twelve monthly installments. With a ¥13,400 down payment, this meant payments of ¥3,800 per month (based on a purchase price of ¥49,000 and interest and fees of ¥10,500). However, the report recommended extending the repayment period to sixteen months with no additional interest charge. This would reduce monthly installments to less than ¥3,000, bringing about a million households into the market. Matsushita noted that government regulators as well as labor unions were opposed to repayment schedules lasting longer than twelve months, but the report concluded: "[S]ince other companies are offering sixteen and even twenty installments, we will have no choice but to follow in their footsteps."[59]

The Japanese appeared to be critical of installment lending, even as they availed themselves of it. There was a widespread feeling that borrowing for the sake of consumer purchases was undermining to the lifestyles and morality of society. The magazine *Shūkan josei jishin* (Women's Own Weekly) published the following cautionary tale:

> Saitō Ryōko was thrilled when her husband was promoted last April, and as a first step to the coveted "electrical lifestyle," she bought an electric washing machine on the installment system. For just one-twentieth of the price, they had the satisfaction of having a top maker's machine in their kitchen. They hated the shabbiness of their company housing, but now they felt that their kitchen had become *o-nyū* (new).
> Mrs. Saito's purchase encouraged neighboring housewives to buy goods on installment, so now she felt "everyone else is doing it, so we can relax—it must be all right." Up till then, there had been something embarrassing about borrowing. Well, once she had learned that borrowing wasn't a big burden, she no longer felt satisfied with just a washing machine. She couldn't lose out to the neighboring wives. So she started rapidly buying household goods, including a television, refrigerator and vacuum cleaner.
> Of course, it's clear that even if you succeed in rationalizing your lifestyle, your household finances may not be very well rationalized. The monthly expenses eventually came to a little over ¥10,000. That was about half their income of ¥23,000. Suddenly her husband, who never talked about the household finances, started getting angry. In the end she left a note to her husband apologizing, and went back to her family in Saitama. According to neighbors, even his two annual bonuses weren't enough to pay off the loans.

Another problem cited by the article was the rapid introduction of new products at lower prices, before buyers had finished paying for the older product:

> You have only just bought an electric washing machine on installment when a new product is launched, which is not only better but costs the same. Nakasato Fumiko, an office worker from Osaka, says, "Since a new product has come out, it seems stupid to be paying the loan. It's like piling one loss

on top of another. Of course if you paid cash, it would also hurt if a new product came out. But it is particularly annoying to see the ads singing the praises of the new machine, when you are still paying for the old one."[60]

Nevertheless, installment purchases became integrated into Japanese lifestyles on an unprecedented scale during the 1950s.

THE POWER OF THE MEDIA

Like their counterparts in the United States and Europe, Japanese electrical goods companies promoted their ideal of an appliance-owning society with considerable help from an increasingly influential mass media. The links between electrical goods companies and the media were close, although complex. These firms were among the largest advertising customers of television and radio stations, magazines, and newspapers. They were also prominent sponsors of commercial programming.

This symbiosis is well illustrated by a small episode related by Shibata Hidetoshi. When a group of American experts visited Osaka in 1952 as the personal guests of Matsushita Kōnosuke, he presented each of them with a miniature portable radio. They switched on their radios and listened together to the first broadcasts of Osaka's new commercial radio station. Matsushita was a major shareholder in the radio station. The program they listened to was sponsored by the Matsushita company.

An internal report prepared by Matsushita in 1963 reported sponsorship of fifty-two radio programs and thirty-three television network programs, including *National Tuesday Nighter* (NET), *National Sunday Theater* (TBS), *National Kid* (NET—a serial drama), and *Bonanza* (NTV).[61] One of Matsushita's most successful sponsorships was of the long-running radio show *The Pop Song Without a Song* (*Uta no nai kayōkyoku*), which for each of its daily fifteen-minute runs was preceded and followed by a Matsushita message such as the following:

> All you have to do is attach a cord to your light socket, flick the switch, and your National electric washing machine will clean your washing beautifully. The mechanism is scientifically set to protect fibers, and to use only a small amount of soap and electricity. Housewives, please use the superb National electric washer in order to keep yourselves ever young and beautiful, and to have plenty of time for self-improvement and leisure.[62]

Cultural historians have painted a generally dark picture of the mass media's influence on society. According to this view, the media, particularly television, have had a crucial role in spreading a deadening ideology of passive consumption. As a result, concludes Salvador Giner, "the chief processes of overt communication in a given society always take place through technological devices, which favor a one-way flow of communication from a relatively small number of people at the transmitting (and producing) end, while an immense audience lies at the receiving end."[63] The content of this communication, according to critics, is liable to be excessively homogeneous and of a uniformly low level. Echoing Joseph Goebbels, Bensman and Rosenberg comment that the mass communicator seeks "the lowest common denominator of a general program, commercial entertainment, or propaganda appeal; by finding themes accessible to everyone he cuts through the social, economic, regional, occupational and individual bases of differentiation."[64] In this interpretation, the spread of commercialized messages into the home bring leisure and private life into the realm of marketable commodities. Horkheimer and Adorno developed a critical analysis of the "culture industry" in the early 1940s.[65] This analysis is closely identified with a Marxist critique of the increasing intrusiveness of capitalism, which "must invade the spaces of the good life and seek to control them for its accumulation. Trying to hold on to our leisure as our free time, we discover it time and again to be poisoned by the ugly irrelevancies of overproduction."[66] In Japan, the power and ambivalence of mass communications are perhaps best illustrated in the career of Shōriki Matsutarō, who appeared to understand thoroughly the relationships among mass entertainment, mass mobilization, and massive profits.

More recent research has tended to question this dark assessment of the trajectory of consumer culture. On one hand, McKendrick and others have argued persuasively that a vibrant consumer culture existed in England in the eighteenth century, before the arrival of mass media and theories of propaganda. On the other, a number of scholars have argued that the influence of the media, particularly through advertising, is much weaker than might have been assumed. These analysts have argued that consumers are more skeptical, more certain of what they want, and less apt to be manipulated than the critics (and even the apologists) of advertising, propaganda, and the media have maintained.[67]

But whatever effect the media had in reorienting Japanese social attitudes toward consumption and the bright life, there can be no doubt that the symbols of a new consumer culture were very much on display in the media during the 1950s, nor that the presentation of these symbols was intimately linked with the market-creating efforts of the electrical goods companies.

The 1950s saw an extraordinary flourishing of broadcasting and publishing in Japan. Beginning with a single national radio station in 1950, Japan acquired a wide variety of commercial and noncommercial broadcast outlets by the turn of the 1960s, becoming a nation of avid radio listeners and television watchers. Newspapers grew from four or six pages of muddy print to twenty pages of features including living, fashion and consumer tips. Starting in the middle of the decade there came a flood of new, glossy magazines aimed at the growing urban middle class. Weekly magazines, a rarity before the mid-1950s, rapidly overtook monthly magazines in circulation (see Table 10, p. 250). Whereas the Japanese family of 1950 might have read only one meager newspaper regularly—and considered it a luxury—the same family in 1960 spent hours every week absorbing images and information from a wide variety of sources. In particular, housewives—newly "liberated" by the acquisition of labor-saving household appliances—took in an ever-increasing amount of material. The average apartment-dwelling housewife, according to one study, by 1960 spent five hours per day watching television (two hours seven minutes), listening to the radio (one hour thirteen minutes), and reading newspapers and magazines (one hour forty-one minutes).[68]

It would be impossible to isolate the dominant themes within this vast outpouring of print and broadcast materials, let alone those that explicitly promoted electrical goods consumption. But a study of print media does reveal an abiding interest in lifestyles far removed from those of most readers. Some of these, such as apartment living, were to become the dominant lifestyles of middle-class Japan. Other subjects, such as the royal wedding of 1959, have come in retrospect to hold a talismanic status in the story of the development of postwar mass culture.

The Royal Wedding

The April 1959 wedding of the crown prince, Akihito, to Masada Michiko, the daughter of a textile company president and a commoner, was Japan's great media event of the 1950s. The wedding was announced in November 1958 and immediately became the single greatest topic of interest in Japan. Michiko (the present Empress of Japan) was a glamorously understated figure: trim and athletic, she looked her best in the tennis clothes she wore on the courts where the couple romanced. Suddenly the magazines were full of pictures of Michiko, analyses of her clothes and styles, and tips on where to buy similar items. The "Michie boom" was a collaboration between a public hungry for celebrities and an information industry that thrived on meeting that demand.

The images of the wedding were packaged for mass consumption in a vast organizational effort. The royal couple's parade in central Tokyo was covered by 108 television cameras and 1,200 television personnel at a cost of ¥23.5 million. Other aspects of the wedding lent to its symbolism of Westernized modernity. The marriage was said to be a love match. This was still unusual even for ordinary people in Japan, let alone the imperial family. Michiko's clothes and fashions were uniformly Western, and the wedding itself combined elements of the Shinto ceremonies of old with traditions of European royalty—pomp, circumstance, and horse-drawn carriages. The magazines made much of the fact that, after their marriage, the royal couple would set up an independent household, away from the forbidding gaze of the stern Empress. They were to be, indeed, Japan's model nuclear family.

Shūkan josei jishin was launched just in time for this event. The first issue appeared on December 12, 1958, barely too late to cover the wedding announcement (another new weekly, *Shūkan Myōjō* [Star Weekly], scooped the story by translating an unauthorized *Life* magazine article on the engagement). Its inside cover carried a romantic shot of a young man sitting on a wall beside a fashionable shop window, a cigarette hanging out of his mouth, with a girl in a chic outfit looking into the distance. The picture was captioned: "West Ginza Evening: strolling in the evening, looking in shop windows. Young, carefree ennui."

The next issue of *Shūkan josei jishin*, however, was full of stories on the royal engagement. There were articles about the glamorous Michiko, her family, and other young members of the imperial family. The following week's edition carried a feature on Michiko's clothes (as worn at tennis matches and other public appearances), with details on where readers could buy Michi-style tennis sweaters for less than ¥3,000. From that point on, the new princess was a major subject of every issue until the wedding. The Masada family received over 10,000 new year's greeting cards for 1959, and *Shūkan josei jishin* devoted a two-page feature to the post office's travails in delivering them. The magazine also reported on the appearance of commemorative stamps, commemorative cigarettes, and commemorative savings accounts.

The wedding took place on April 10, 1959. The royal couple paraded through central Tokyo, with some 540,000 people reportedly watching on television. Popular legend has it that the royal wedding caused a huge surge in television purchases—even that it spurred the Japanese to near-universal television ownership. Such stories are apocryphal: television sales were increasingly brisk throughout 1959, but I have not found evidence of a peak early in the year. Surveys reported that the 24 percent or so of the population who did own televisions, however, spent an average of ten hours and thirty-five minutes watching television that day.[69]

Commentators frequently associate the royal wedding with the maturation of mass culture in Japan. Matsushita Keiichi stated at the time that it marked the birth of a "mass emperor system" (taishūtennōsei) based on the central image of a nuclear family and a love match with a commoner.[70] This image was clearly a creation of the media, which stressed that Michiko was a commoner princess—giving readers, listeners, and viewers the feeling that they, too, might someday stand in her white satin shoes.

Working Couples

Another phenomenon that seemed to appear in the media much more frequently than in real life was that of the working couple (tomo kasegi). Such couples emanated an aura of glamour because they often had greater spending power than one-worker families; because they appeared to put the excitement of a career ahead of humdrum domesticities such as housework and children; and because they tended to live very "rational" lives, often in modern apartments fully equipped with electrical conveniences.

One article in Shūkan josei jishin features a husband and wife who both work for the travel company that manages the "Hato bus" tours of Tokyo. The husband is a driver, and the wife is in administration. Explaining why they both work, the wife says: "It's not only for economic reasons. Through my work, I can understand my husband. This helps us have a fresh-feeling married life. . . . If we want to build a human lifestyle, then we must work together in spite of the obstacles. . . . In Japan, in order to have a cultural lifestyle, you must both work."[71]

Another article, entitled "Uneconomic Couple," features two newlyweds who both work for a television company. So busy are their lives that they seldom spend any time together—they are lucky to share a meal once a week. The article emphasizes how much of their income they spend on unnecessary items such as leisure and entertainment (each month, the husband spends ¥13,000 of a total combined income of ¥38,000 on "personal" items). Almost as an aside, the article adds that the couple owns such electrical items as a washer and refrigerator. The wife comments that they only partially own these items (presumably since they are paying installments for them), but adds, "We do not grudge spending for the sake of lifestyle rationalization."[72]

It may seem paradoxical that while companies were pouring vast resources into creating idealized images of a nuclear family with a housewife at its center, magazines were promoting two-income marriages. But the two models are not as incompatible as they at first seem. The working couples are usually young and invariably childless, with the implication that, once they have children, the women will take up their position at the center of the family. Moreover, by earning extra income for discretionary spending and by pursuing rational lifestyles, the working couples represented an ideology that encouraged electrical goods purchases. Indeed, Sandra Buckley, discussing the dramatic increase in the number of salaried women workers in subsequent decades, argues that the "expense of furnishing and maintaining a high-tech household" actually perpetuated the need for women to remain in the work force.[73]

The question of working couples gave rise to a rancorous debate in Japan beginning in the mid-1950s. Conservative opinion leaders, particularly those affiliated with the corporate ideal of a dedicated working husband, denounced the trend of women in the workplace. The *Asahi,* for example, argued in an editorial:

> One specialist has estimated that housewives perform as many as thirty-seven separate jobs in the home. When one adds up the chores of cooking, washing, cleaning, child-rearing, education, caring for the sick, and shopping, one realizes how impressive the wife's work is. Moreover, families are beset by various economic problems, and it is not an easy thing [for the wife] to manage these. Society, children, and husbands should recognize what an all-around player the housewife is. But even more important, the housewife herself does not realize this enough, or value it sufficiently.[74]

Women themselves, judging by the views they expressed in women's magazines, were divided on the issue. But some prominent apologists defended women's right to work on the grounds of equality and democracy in home life. Nishi Kiyoko wrote in *Fujin Kōron:* "Women who refuse to quit their jobs when they marry are not necessarily doing so because of poverty. Rather, they are thinking in terms of nurturing an equal, independent lifestyle. The meaning of dual-job families is therefore changing."[75]

Surveys, however, indicated that most dual-income families worked not out of lifestyle considerations but for economic reasons—often out of necessity. Although the most frequently cited motivations were saving for children's education and saving for a home purchase, it is not unreasonable to assume that the purchase of expensive household appliances also played a role.

Apartment Life

Another role model that frequently appeared in the popular press was the apartment dweller. The focus fell particularly on those who lived in the *danchi* apartments built from 1955 on by the Japan Public Housing Association (Nihon Jūtaku Kōdan), other cooperative enterprises, and private companies. The *danchi zoku* ("danchi tribe") was first labeled by the magazine *Shūkan Asahi* in 1956,[76] and the name stuck. The 1960 *White Paper on National Life*, comparing the *danchi* to "American suburbia," described the *danchi zoku* as "psychologically influenced by their small homes and group lifestyle," noting: "In the *danchi*, a new lifestyle consciousness has been born, based on the need for simplification and rationalization. [Danchi dwellers use] standardized modern equipment and enjoy a rational, cultural lifestyle rather than emphasizing thrift and saving."[77]

The *danchi* housing developments (which were, incidentally, far from comparable to the American suburbs) received a great deal of attention during the 1950s, arguably out of proportion to their importance as a form of housing. By 1960 no more than 140,000 of Japan's 20 million households were living in the *danchi*. Yet they were a favorite topic of magazine and newspaper articles, which emphasized the demographic and lifestyle differences between *danchi* dwellers and ordinary Japanese. *Danchi* households tended to have younger heads and fewer members than average, with high incomes and a high proportion of white collar and managerial workers. They were also better educated, owned more consumer durable goods, ate more Western foods, and, according to the *White Paper*, enjoyed substantially more leisure than their traditional counterparts. The typical *danchi* housewife spent only six hours and fifty-two minutes per day on housework, compared to nine hours and two minutes for other Tokyo housewives.[78]

Today the *danchi* are often thought of as cheap urban apartments built in response to Japan's severe postwar housing shortage. Indeed, the buildings were generally simple and functional, the apartments small and economically constructed. For most people, however, the *danchi* represented a considerable investment in upgrading the quality of life. Although their incomes were somewhat higher than the Tokyo average, *danchi* dwellers spent 16 percent of their earnings on rent, versus only 3 percent for the average Tokyoite. In exchange they were able to enjoy a convenient life in new premises equipped with stainless steel kitchen sinks, baths, and toilets.

The *danchi* are also widely credited with stimulating durable goods purchases, as residents fitted them out for convenient lifestyles.[79] However, 1960 statistics indicate that *danchi* occupants were only marginally more likely than the average Tokyo resident to own advanced consumer goods (although the *danchi* had a greater lead in previous years). Most notable are the higher penetrations of washing machines and rice cookers (see Table 11, p. 250). In any case, the *danchi* undoubtedly had value as symbols of a Western, rational lifestyle.

Magazines of the late 1950s were by no means wholehearted in their praise of apartment living, for all its "rationality." The criticisms most frequently raised against it were the expense, the cramped conditions, and the loneliness.

One article contrasts two extremes of apartment living. On one hand, it portrays a wealthy bachelor who lives in the luxurious nine-story Tōkyū apartments in Mita. He pays a staggering ¥35,000 a month in rent, in addition to a twice-yearly "key money" payment of ¥200,000. "In exchange" says the renter, "I get a bath, toilet, telephone attached, and hot running water." The charm of this life, he says, is that "with one key, I can enter a separate world." On the other hand, the magazine presents the case of a 24-year old, low-income married woman who lives in a small, inexpensive apartment. She comments: "Although my main room is six mats, it feels like five or less because of our furniture. And we have to go downstairs to the toilet." She also complains about the loneliness of apartment living and the unfair conditions imposed by landlords—for example, vaguely worded rental agreements that fail to specify that if a tenant has a baby, the rent goes up. The dissatisfied renter concludes: "In America, even people on welfare have showers and toilets in their apartments. Here in Japan, we still live poky and cramped lives."

INTO THE COUNTRYSIDE

Even more dramatic than the transformation of urban society in the 1950s was the transformation of the Japanese countryside. Although rural sales of electrical goods lagged behind urban figures, by the end of the decade the countryside had become a vital target of the electrical goods manufacturers. The same households that just a few years earlier had been worrying about installing a first window in the kitchen were now among the most avid buyers of electrical goods.

Change in the countryside was desired by everyone—the Occupation, which wanted to democratize the *ie* (traditional household) and free tenants from feudal oppression; Americans like Karl Mundt, who saw progress in the countryside as key to fighting communist influence; Japanese politicians, who saw the tremendous power of the rural vote; and educators at home and abroad, who saw their mission as bringing light to the rural darkness. In particular, the idea of using television as an educational tool—expounded eloquently by Mundt—was taken up and promoted by developmental organizations.

An example was the UNESCO experiment of 1956–57, a follow-up to a similar experiment in France in 1953–54. A UNESCO team installed public-viewing television sets in sixty-four rural communities in twenty-six Japanese prefectures. The villages, UNESCO, and the Japanese government each contributed one-third of the cost of the television sets. The villagers watched communally and gave comments to the researchers on the merits of the programming and the good and bad points of communal viewing. The shows were generally educational in content, with offerings such as "Rural Life in Japan," "Why Doesn't She Want to Become a Wife?" "Tomorrow's Villages," and "What Will Happen to our Second and Third Sons?"[80]

These pious efforts bore little relation to the profit-oriented mechanisms that ultimately placed television sets in most rural households. The creation of a rural market was intimately bound up with the ideologies of change that were being promoted throughout the 1950s. In particular, the electrical manufacturers took advantage of the various educational movements and community programs launched throughout the decade, using them as podiums from which to "educate" rural communities about their products. Toshiba salesman Yamada Shōgo describes a joint effort between electrical appliance makers and the newly privatized rural power companies, which also were working actively to promote greater electricity use.

> We didn't necessarily expect to get direct sales, but we needed to do public relations in expectation of a future boom. The power companies arranged lectures in public halls, schoolrooms, and so on. It was impossible to use cars in the rural areas, so we had to improvise transport—by sidecar, jeep, or

Land Rover. It makes my heart palpitate to remember the terrible roads we drove over. . . .

Sometimes the lectures counted as classes in the schools. The more old-fashioned teachers were still terrified of electricity, so they were glad to let the appliance makers take charge of teaching it. Of course, we couldn't just go and advertise our own products—we had to be more public-minded. So we often took the products of rivals too. The lecture halls were usually tatami style, so we sat in the middle surrounded by the audience so we could show them the products more closely. . . .

Lots of people would bring children, who would run around making a big din, swallowing up our explanations. At a time like that it's impossible to restrain them, so we got them to help with making dumplings for the meeting. We also got local teachers in to teach cooking, but most of them had no experience with electric appliances, so they weren't much use.

We had to be very careful to make sure that our lectures didn't have the reverse effect and make people think electric appliances were useless. We were always being asked questions like: can you get the stains out of collars, or out of *tabi* (Japanese cloth shoes)? At times like that, if I didn't explain very carefully, they'd conclude that the machine was useless. I would say, "Of course if you use a washing machine, they will get clean," but using charts to explain the principle of the washing machine, I'd add, "It would be better for you to wash just these things yourselves," and I'd actually show them how to wash a pair of *tabi* with soap. . . .[81]

Matsushita's marketing department began to turn its attention to the countryside from the middle of the 1950s. In addition to low incomes and lack of understanding about electrical goods, these remote areas had few retail outlets or other distribution channels. In a 1955 discussion, the owner of a provincial clock shop described his efforts to handle National washing machines. "I have to go out to the villages and sell door to door," he said. "Usually I focus on the village leader, but lots of other people usually turn up for demonstrations of washers and mixers. When the people first saw it in action they asked, 'Does steam come out?'" A 1957 Matsushita survey added that because of the lack of sales outlets, rural families often had friends or relatives in towns or cities buy electrical goods on their behalf. The report noted: "Rural people visit the city extremely seldom. For this reason, they have few opportunities to connect with actual electrical products."[82]

Matsushita at first pursued a strategy of cooperation with local organizations, in particular local chapters of Nōkyō, the national farmers' cooperative. In addition to giving Matsushita an instant chain of retail outlets, an affiliation with Nōkyō would "provide a tie-in with the lifestyle improvement movement, through the positive promotion of

Figure 12   A rural family uses a washing machine. (Courtesy Matsushita Denki Sangyō)

electrical goods." However, the sudden growth of the rural market and Nōkyō's demand for deep discounts prompted Matsushita eventually to develop its own retail network.[83]

As electrical goods companies became more involved in selling in the countryside, they grew increasingly sensitive to the complex cultural considerations that seemed to prevent rural families from purchasing. A focus group convened by Matsushita in 1956 concluded that rural incomes were not a serious obstacle to sales: "In this area there are no families that don't have three or four bicycles. Personally, I still use the one I bought before I was twenty, even though it has lost its shape. But farming families buy a new one every two years." However, traditional family attitudes regarding the role of women seriously hindered sales of labor-saving products such as washing machines: "In one family, the wife said, 'We have two daughters in this house, and if we let them use an electric washer, then they won't be able to do the washing when they marry.'"

Other barriers included fear of electricity, and the reluctance of farmers to be seen buying something that others in the village did not own: "I have heard that even when farmers buy a washing machine, they ask for it to be delivered in the night, so no one will see. There's still a strong feeling that a branch family may not own something that the main family doesn't have." Another participant commented on the hesitancy of farming wives to put dirty objects in something as beautiful as a new washing machine, adding: "When I was a bride, we weren't supposed to wash women's things with men's things. There was an upper and a lower washtub, and the elders would be furious if you tried washing an upper garment in the lower tub. That kind of thinking is hard to change."[84]

This perceived irrationality led the focus group participants to conclude that fundamental reforms in the lifestyles of farmers were needed before electrical goods sales could spread. For example, the tendency of parents to spend large sums on bridal kimonos—when they could be sending their daughters off with a washing machine instead—was unanimously derided. Another criticism charged: "If [farmers] make a little money, the first thing they always do is make a bath-place. Or they'll replace their thatched roof with tiles." In a similar vein, a 1956 article in *Nikkei shinbun* reported that:

> The rural use of money is certainly without planning. In one village of forty-five households, eighteen had purchased washing machines. Of these, at least ten were simply decorating the *tokonoma*, or were placed in a corner of the porch. Clearly, they were not being used. According to the owners, an electric washing machine is not a tool of living: rather, it is a family asset. That is a barometer of the value of money for those people.[85]

The desire to reform extravagant and allegedly irrational spending habits illustrates how the apparently antithetical goals of the thrift-minded new life movement and the consumer-oriented electrical goods companies actually worked in tandem. One participant in Matsushita's discussion group explicitly stated the link: "The new life movement has been focusing mainly on reducing wedding and funeral expenses. But I think it really needs to work toward promoting the improvement of living conditions rather than farmers wasting their money on tile roofs."[86]

The concordance between the thrift and consumer movements is further illustrated by this letter from a farming wife, who uses the logic of household planning (a theme of the new life movement) to justify purchase of a washing machine:

> My husband and I have been thinking about how to achieve a bright and affluent ideal lifestyle. We have developed a long-term family improvement plan, one part of which was, first, to get running water, and then to improve the kitchen. Then as the next step we bought a National washing machine. I had been doing my children's, father's, and husband's washing daily, and the simple operation and automatic movement of this machine saved me time and trouble, and so I have been able to think about general education instead. My household efficiency has greatly increased.[87]

By 1958, the potential of the rural market was becoming more and more apparent. Washing machines had gained much wider acceptance and were rapidly becoming a common wedding gift. A 1958 Matsushita analysis commented on the progress of the "lifestyle improvement movement" and its impact in rural communities:

> According to the Ministry of Agriculture and Forestry's "*Kamado* [cooking stove] Improvement Statistics," 37.8 percent of rural households improved their *kamado* in the last year alone. Perhaps one can not claim that just by improving the *kamado*, rural households are raising their standard of living, but this does directly indicate the economic power of rural households, and it also indicates that the structure of rural lifestyles has changed a great deal.[88]

Yet many problems remained. In a discussion group, a rural retailer lamented: "In my area the people are very religious, and they believe that to suffer is beneficial; if people don't suffer they will not become wise. It's very tough for me."

All the discussants agreed on the importance of going door to door and actually demonstrating the benefits of electrical products to rural families. Because the traditional family system persisted in the countryside, it was considered particularly important to gain the consent of the household head: "There is no other way but to demonstrate to and persuade the father's generation. . . . It's important to find out who makes the decision and approach them directly. In most rural families the household head system still remains, so it's usually the father."[89]

In 1960 the penetration of washing machines in the countryside was still only 8.7 percent (versus 45.4 percent for cities), whereas televisions were at 11.4 percent (54.5 percent for cities).[90] It was not until the 1960s that the trickle of sales to the countryside turned into a flood.

That development was accompanied by massive changes in the lifestyles of country people, as millions of villagers abandoned farming to take up work in the factories of the cities—the very factories that were producing goods to revolutionize the lifestyles of those left behind. Rural consumption was to provide the fuel for sustained rapid growth in the electrical goods industry in the 1960s.

THE PARADOXES OF PLENTY

The creation of Japan's mass consumer market in the 1950s was fraught with paradoxes. How could "household rationalization" encourage both thrift and consumption? How could the new life mean both a return to traditional Confucian morality and a break with the old order? How was it possible to promote "economy" while asking families to spend several months' income on electrical goods? I have attempted in this chapter to demonstrate that the fluidity and plasticity of ideological formation allowed for conflicting interpretations to coexist, even when there was general agreement on the basic terminology. But some of these contradictions have never fully resolved themselves, and they account today for some of the austerity and bitterness that persist in Japanese society even in the midst of plenty.

High Savings and Consumption

Perhaps the most intriguing of all the paradoxes associated with consumption in the 1950s is the remarkable way in which it grew side by side with savings. As consumer spending and borrowing soared in the latter half of the 1950s, Japan's savings rate also climbed ever upward, reaching a plateau far above savings rates in the rest of the industrialized world. In 1960 the average Japanese family was saving close to 20 percent of its disposable income. How was it possible simultaneously to consume and to save with such abandon?

Recent studies of ideological formation in the 1950s have tended to emphasize the exhortations toward thrift emanating from the "new life" movement and from the various organs of "moral suasion" in the arsenal of conservative bureaucrats.[91] This interpretation of government-sponsored thrift seems to be consistent with the common wisdom that consumers were to some extent sacrificed during the 1950s to the cause of industrial growth, which did indeed depend on the mobilization of household savings. But the emphasis on thrift ignores not only the alternative interpretations of rationalization and brightness but also the reality of the consumer revolution, which was already an acknowledged fact by 1960.[92]

How was it possible for both consumption and savings to grow so rapidly? The simplest answer is to point to the rapid decline in spending on certain essential items, most notably food, as a share of overall expenditures. Food expenses declined from 40 percent of the total in 1953 to only 31 percent in 1960, providing a ready reserve for other types of consumption and for additional savings (see Table 12, p. 251). Clothing costs also declined as a percentage of expenditure, and the tax burden decreased beginning in the middle of the decade. Meanwhile, important costs such as housing remained a very small component of Japanese family budgets.

Another approach is to look more closely at who was consuming and who was saving. This analysis makes it clear that whereas higher-income families had little difficulty maintaining both high consumption and high savings, those in the lower income echelons were doing considerably less saving (see Table 13, p. 252). Indeed, for poorer families, average monthly expenditures substantially *exceeded* earned income. The difference was made up by drawing on family assets and borrowing additional funds (see Table 14, p. 252).

But perhaps the most rewarding approach is to look at the common ground between those urging consumption and those urging saving. Advocates of both consumption and saving were calling for a new, more scientific approach to household management. The leaders of the savings drives called on families to keep detailed account books as a method of gaining greater control over expenses. Electrical goods companies similarly emphasized the new and the scientific in their ideology, even supporting the keeping of account books on the same grounds as the savers: more careful household economy would result in a greater surplus, which then could be used for durable goods purchases.

Similarly, both consumers and savers called for the elimination of traditional family structures. The savers objected to the tendency of traditional family heads to throw all their surplus cash into new tiled roofs or expensive kimonos for their daughters; the electrical goods companies wanted to get more financial decision-making power into the hands of younger people and wives, who were more likely to embrace new products. And consumers and savers were united in their abhorrence of the wasteful practices that prevailed in Japanese society, particularly in the countryside. Expensive wedding ceremonies, mid-year and new year's gifts, and lavish funerals took up large amounts of disposal income that could be used for rational activities such as buying electric washing machines—and saving.

Thus, to view the 1950s as a tug-of-war between diehard thrift advocates and devil-may-care consumerists is to misrepresent the vision of policy makers, businessmen, and the Japanese people themselves. Their vision of the changes needed in Japanese society was flexible enough to accommodate both saving and consumption. Concepts such as "lifestyle rationalization," the "bright life," and "raising the level of culture" were indeed fought over by groups trying to attach radically different ideological meanings to them. But these debates were not resolved into any neat closure. The concepts were wide enough, and visions of Japanese society complex enough, to accommodate multiple interpretations. The result has been a paradoxical social phenomenon that continues to puzzle.

The Ambiguous Role of Government

Another apparent paradox lies in the role of the Japanese government. Important bureaucratic agencies and the Liberal Democratic Party have frequently been seen as hostile to consumption during Japan's high-growth period, at least until the Ikeda Income Doubling Plan (1960) gave an official nod to the importance of the consumer. But the government in fact played an ambiguous and complex part in Japan's postwar economic development.

Many have argued that bureaucrats concerned with reforming Japan's industrial structure revered growth and production at the expense of consumer gratification. However, these officials in fact thought long and hard about the role of consumption. In the immediate postwar chaos, the primary concern of economic bureaucrats was controlling inflation and stabilizing the economy. Once this was accomplished through the brutal mechanism of the Dodge Line, questions of democracy, rationality, and consumption entered economic policy debates. The United States offered a model of economic prosperity and consumer-oriented industry (for a discussion of government debate during the Occupation, see Chapter 2). Accordingly, the government took some concrete measures during the 1950s to promote consumption. Most notable of these was the Kishi administration's tax cut of 1957, which halved a typical white-collar worker's income tax rate from 40 percent to 20 percent. The 1958 *White Paper on National Life* identified this tax initiative as a major factor in that year's extraordinary surge of consumer spending. For a family at the average income level of ¥30,940 per month, the tax burden fell by ¥3,310 per month. Those in the highest income bracket saw their income tax rate fall from 16.2 percent to 11.2 percent.

It is tempting to discern a clear mandate for consumption in this policy. But this story, too, is fraught with contradictions and confusions. Most notably, the tax cut was not an initiative of the Liberal Democratic Party nor any of its members. Indeed, the elected government representatives seem to have treated the proposal with a great deal of suspicion throughout.

The idea began when Hatoyama Ichirō's finance minister, Ichimada Hisato, created a committee in August 1955 to study how to *increase* taxes in response to the 1954–55 economic slowdown.[93] The committee had no party politicians or members of the taxation bureaucracy, presumably because the government sought a broad consensus for whatever changes might be recommended. Its members included the chairman of the Sōdōmei labor union and Tokyo University academic Arisawa Hiromi; its chairman, Hara Yasusaburō, was head of a pharmaceutical company.

While the committee deliberated, Hatoyama stepped down as prime minister and was replaced by Ishibashi Tanzan, who in turn resigned because of ill health in favor of the arch-conservative Kishi Nobusuke. The committee made its final recommendations just as Kishi appointed his cabinet, which included Ikeda Hayato as finance minister. But instead of proposing ways to increase taxes, the committee called for a major reduction in tax rates. In spite of his reputation as a friend of the consumer, Ikeda initially responded warily. But once he became convinced that much of the tax loss could be replaced through the rapid growth of the economy, Ikeda accepted the recommendations, and shortly afterward they became official government policy.

Rather than touting the tax break as a major pro-consumer initiative, the government, as reflected in newspaper comment, regarded it with a remarkable blend of suspicion and resignation. According to the *Asahi,* most party politicians still believed they could gain more votes by "building one more bridge or laying down one more railway line" than by cutting taxes. There was also hostility to the idea of further increases in consumer spending, which already was growing more quickly than many politicians wished.[94] The tax reduction ultimately was greeted with no more than a whisper of faint praise; no one stood up to claim its parentage.

By contrast, Ikeda's 1960 Income Doubling Plan continues to be seen as the government's ultimate acknowledgment of the importance of the consumer—both for political peace in the wake of the security treaty riots of 1960 and for the benefit of the economy. But the plan, for all its specific measures, should not be credited with the doubling of incomes that actually took place over the following seven years (three years ahead of the plan's timetable). High income growth was already well under way in Japan and would undoubtedly have continued with or without the Income Doubling Plan. The plan was in fact launched provisionally by Ikeda in 1959, before the security treaty riots and while Ikeda was still finance minister. Nor can Ikeda even take full credit for the plan, since it was actually conceived as early as 1957, when the Kishi cabinet asked the preparers of the long-term economic plan if "it would not be possible to use the expression 'doubling?'"[95]

Moreover, many analysts have pointed out that however successful the plan may have been in meeting its economic goals, the nation's welfare needs, particularly for economic equalization and prevention of pollution, were grossly underachieved.[96] What the Income Doubling Plan illustrates best is the power that can accrue to an ideological slogan if used shrewdly and at the right time. In terms of concrete government policies, the 1957 tax cut was the more important of the two.

The "Unbalanced" Life

A final paradox, which continues to haunt Japanese society even forty years later, involves the phenomenon of the "unbalanced life." This term was used in the 1960 *White Paper on National Life* in reference to the fact that, despite very high levels of ownership of consumer durable goods relative to their incomes, Japanese people were far behind Western Europe—let alone the United States—in several of the measures considered basic to human welfare, including food and housing.[97] The study found, for example, that Japanese people only derived 6 percent of their calories from animal protein, compared with 42 percent in the United States and more than 30 percent in most Western European countries. Overall caloric intake remained substantially lower in Japan than in the West. Infrastructural amenities were also severely lacking: roads were in terrible condition, and a mere 13 percent of urban Japanese households were connected to sewer mains. The abominable housing situation represented perhaps the largest concern. An objective study showed that 63 percent of Japanese families lived in crowded conditions (i.e., households with more than 1.5 people per room), compared with only 4 percent in the United States and 11 percent in Great Britain. Even this statistic, however, failed to capture the poor quality of housing for the majority of urban Japanese. During the 1950s a revolution did indeed occur in consumer habits and the purchase of electrical goods, and the food situation did improve, but the other basic conditions of living did not change nearly as much. At the end of the 1950s, as at the beginning, most people lived in cramped accommodations, lacked amenities, and worked long hours for low pay.

The 1960 *White Paper* also found cause for concern in the widening wealth gap in Japan. Although assets became more equitably distributed after the war because of land reform and other forms of wealth confiscation, by 1960 the income gap was widening. As much as high earners were experiencing high income growth, low income families faced low growth. For example, in 1957 the disposable income of the lowest income group grew 3.7 percent, whereas that of the highest group grew by 12.6 percent (from a much higher base, of course).

Not mentioned by the *White Paper*, but perhaps most serious in its consequences for many Japanese, was the steep increase in the price of land during the 1950s. This may be seen as a direct consequence of high economic growth. While incomes more than doubled between 1950 and 1960, urban land prices rose by a horrifying fifteen times. During the following decade residential land values gained by another six times while incomes again more than doubled. Of course, this trend benefited the large proportion of the population who owned property, but it also served to widen the gap between the haves and have-nots of Japanese society—a gap that, despite the "middle mass" rhetoric, remains wide today. It is ironic that the very phenomenon that gave the appearance of affluence—mass purchases of electrical goods—served to fuel the boom that helped put the security of a home forever out of the reach of many.

CONCLUSION

During the 1950s, Japanese companies launched new products based on exciting new technologies, and technology has since come to be seen as the defining feature of Japan's great electrical goods corporations. But new product technologies were meaningless without users willing to purchase the products. The project of creating new markets was at least as important as that of creating high-tech goods. Domestic demand, even during a period of relative poverty, laid the foundations for the Japanese electrical goods industry's subsequent rise in the global marketplace.

The extent to which companies actively created demand rather than simply fulfilling spontaneous or existing demand is highly contentious. Michael Schudson has argued that the brash claims of advertising executives have been taken too much at face value, that consumers are more likely to be guided by broader social conditioning than by the narrow dictates of corporate message merchants.[98] However, a formidable array of analysts from widely divergent critical traditions seem to agree on the insidious, exploitative, and deceptive nature of corporate demand-creating activities.[99] At their most extreme, these critiques would have us believe that every small pleasure in life has by now been appropriated, commodified, and culturally molded by an unholy alliance of state ideologists and profit-seeking corporations.

Some critics overestimate the power of corporations to manufacture desire and the willingness of consumers to be led by the nose. But of one fact there can be no doubt: Japanese electrical goods corporations were doing their best to perform exactly those feats in the postwar era. Their leaders, intensely aware of the Japanese public's lack of buying power, used all means at their disposal to stimulate demand. Whether or not they succeeded in this enterprise, they most certainly tried.

Although unadulterated opinions of ordinary people are hard to assess with any certainty, would-be consumers appear to have regarded electrical goods with a great deal of skepticism. My own judgment is that corporate demand-creating activities were an essential, though clearly not the only, ingredient in the rise of mass markets for expensive durable goods in Japan. Schudson himself concedes that some groups of people are more vulnerable to advertising than others. Among the most vulnerable are children and people "who are relatively new to the world of mass marketed consumer goods."[100] Japanese consumers in the 1950s would surely fit into this last category, and I have described how companies aimed many of their advertising messages at children. Moreover, I have highlighted demand-creating activities that extended far beyond simple advertising. Indeed, the ideology-creation efforts of electrical goods companies tied in directly to a broad reconstruction of Japanese social ideals, one that clearly had the support of both the state and big business and has made a lasting impact on Japanese society.

One of these linked ideals was that of the middle-class housewife. The ideal of the nuclear family with a housewife at its center was already well established by the end of World War II, but with the expansion of the middle class (or those who considered themselves to be such) in the 1950s this ideal hardened into something resembling a hegemonic social construct. Electrical goods companies by no means achieved this feat alone. Andrew Gordon has argued convincingly that the child-minding household manager was a necessary counterfoil to the extraordinary demands made on male workers in large enterprises—demands that amounted to co-option of male workers into the "corporate family" at the expense of the biological family.[101] But the "bright life," with its idealized housewife-centered nuclear family (in stark contrast to the "feudal" family model of patriarchal family heads and tyrannical mothers-in-law), certainly played its part in consolidating this ideology.

It is hard to separate how much electrical goods companies promoted this ideal out of narrow self-interest and how much they simply were part of a larger process. Arguably, electrical goods companies perceived that a relatively passive housewife who spent several hours a day absorbing media messages was more likely to respond to suggestion than was a working husband or wife. Also, Japanese companies were probably influenced to a considerable extent by the images generated in the American mass media, where the idealized home with its pert and pretty housewife had for some time been a standard image in advertising, magazine features, and radio and television dramas.

Nevertheless, if there were marked similarities between Japanese and American ideals of the home, there were significant differences in the outcomes in the two countries. In Japan, the gap between the model of the nuclear family with a housewife at its center, on one hand, and the social reality of extended families and working women, on the other, was much wider than in the United States. The housewife in Japan remained a relatively small minority even as the ideal of the housewife took firmer hold. Over time, the constructed role of housewife has—with the institutional support of companies and the government—displayed remarkable staying power in Japan. Forty years later, the model of the nuclear family with the housewife at its center retains its hegemonic status, although this ideal continues to be elusive for the large number of women who still perform menial work for low wages.[102]

Similarly, the consumer revolution in Japan was different from those taking place in other countries. Throughout the 1950s, Japan was by any objective measure an underdeveloped nation. Incomes in Japan were a fraction not only of American incomes but also of those of Western Europe, including the defeated Germany. In the United States, the issue in creating demand in the 1950s was not lack of means; rather, it was how to keep stimulating the surfeited appetites of consumers. In Japan, by contrast, making electrical products affordable was a key issue.

Moreover, American consumers by the 1950s were already well acquainted with most electrical goods (the exception was microwave ovens, which took several decades to catch on). In Japan, by contrast, people not only had to be educated about the functions and benefits of these products but also in some cases had to be persuaded that the products were superior to traditions that had stood the test of centuries.

An even more significant difference is the extraordinary degree of self-referentiality that characterized the Japanese introduction of mass consumption. Japanese analysts and marketing managers were attempting to stimulate a mass consumer market while such markets were flourishing overseas. The Japanese thus could observe the effect of corporate efforts on mass consumption in other countries and heed the criticisms of analysts such as Vance Packard and John Kenneth Galbraith. And while they watched these phenomena unfold elsewhere, Japanese managers and consultants were also consciously introducing those same phenomena, criticisms and all, into Japan. This self-referentiality is one of the key differences marking off Japan's experience of mass-consumer modernity from those of other countries—a point to which I shall return in the conclusion to this book.

The successful creation of a mass consumer market did not come without costs. Left-wing critics were not the only ones concerned about capitalist manufacturers' increasing hold over the everyday lives of Japanese people. The government, too, worried that even as they spent ever-increasing amount on household appliances, the Japanese people continued to lack many amenities considered essential by all accepted measures. Chief among these was the quality of housing, which remained abysmal in spite of fifteen years of postwar reconstruction.

6

Nimble Fingers

THE STORY OF THE TRANSISTOR RADIO

In an April 1950 article on the outlook for Japanese manufacturing, the *Oriental Economist* quoted the following expert opinion: "The only course open to Japan in the way of promotion of her export trade is the production of articles having features all to her own, articles of exquisite workmanship not capable of being mass produced; something unsuitable for American production methods."

With hindsight, the pessimism of this analysis seems ironic and rather quaint. Within a short decade, Japanese companies were in the midst of an export boom driven by high-value-added products such as ships and electronics goods. In subsequent decades, Japanese companies excelled precisely in the mass production of standardized goods. In 1960, the number-two export product after ships was transistor radios. Very shortly thereafter, Japan was to extend its export success to black and white televisions. In both cases, the principal market was not the developing economies of Southeast and East Asia but the developed nations of the West.

How did Japanese companies overcome the barriers to export competitiveness that seemed insurmountable to the eminent business executive of 1950? And how did they gain a leading international position in a high-technology industry such as electrical goods within such a short space of time?

The majority of analysts have pointed to technology as the key, referring to the long background of development described in Chapter 1, or to the extensive importation of technology described in Chapter 4.[1] More recently, the learning skills of Japanese companies have come under intensive study: organizational learning capabilities, innovative manufacturing practices based on improvement of foreign models, and quality management based on adaptation of U.S. techniques combined to make Japan "consistently first in being second," as Peck and Tamura put it.[2] There are also those who ascribe Japanese competitive success to innovation, pure and simple. The transistor radio, which is the subject of this chapter, is a good example.

All of these factors contributed to the growth and competitive success of Japanese companies at the turn of the 1960s. But in all the excitement about Japanese organizational capabilities, the "national system of learning," and the "capitalist developmental state," it is easy to lose track of the single most important factor in Japan's early export successes: cheap labor.[3] This chapter is about the development of the transistor radio as a Japanese export staple, a success that, despite the technological marvels the radio embodied, I attribute primarily to an abundant supply of dexterous, very cheap, young female laborers.

FROM TŌTSŪKŌ TO SONY

The story of the transistor radio is inseparable from the saga of Sony, one of the world's greatest business successes. Sony was the first Japanese company to launch a transistor radio and has with increasing frequency come to be misidentified as the inventor of the transistor radio. Sony's development of a Japanese transistor radio was indeed a pioneering technological achievement and the main force behind its emergence as a major global corporation. But it was *not* the key to Japan's successful export of transistor radios.

In 1952, Tōtsūkō (the precursor of Sony) was a successful company with an outstanding product—Japan's first reel-to-reel tape recorder (see Chapter 2)—and a solid reputation in Japan. But that was not enough to reassure its founders, Morita Akio and Ibuka Masaru, about the company's prospects. They had two major problems on their minds. First, no matter how good Tōtsūkō's technology, it was only a matter of time before much larger companies such as Toshiba and Matsushita used their marketing muscle to dominate the tape recorder business. The second problem was more specific to the circumstances of the moment. In order to carve out a niche in Japan's competitive electronics industry, Morita and Ibuka had hired large numbers of talented engineers. They had been able to do this because of the unique conditions at the end of the war, when opportunities in large companies were severely limited. But now that the economy was booming in the flush of money from the Korean War, Morita and Ibuka worried their expert employees would find better opportunities elsewhere. More than 30 percent of Tōtsūkō's staff were university graduates—an unheard-of ratio at the time. Ibuka later recalled: "These people expected to become managers, then executives. So I couldn't sleep worrying about what to do with them."[4]

Ibuka discovered a possible solution to the problem during a study trip to the United States in March 1953. Most of the U.S. electronics companies he visited were working on consumer applications of an exciting new device: the transistor.

Although the original invention, announced with much fanfare by Bell Laboratories in 1948, had been too delicate for commercial production, the ensuing five years have brought substantial improvements in transistor design. Transistors were increasingly being used in telephone and computer circuitry, as well as in military applications. What had at first been an exotic if exciting oddity was now a growing part of everyday life for electronic engineers.

The problem—and the opportunity—was that transistors in 1953 were not yet reliable or powerful enough to handle the requirements of radio. Western Electric, the leading manufacturer of transistors in the United States, was warning patent licensees that its transistors were not appropriate for consumer applications. But American companies were rapidly making improvements in transistor design, and most had transistor radios on their drawing boards. Indeed, these experimental models are probably what prompted Ibuka to think seriously about the transistor radio. The literature of the time reflected great anticipation of the age of the transistor radio. How soon it would come remained open to question.

Back in Japan, Morita and Ibuka held long strategy sessions on the transistor. With or without the transistor, the trend in radio was toward miniaturization and portability. In Japan, portable radios still had not cracked the consumer market, but in the United States sales of portables were outpacing those of traditional console sets. The portable radios made use of tiny vacuum tubes, which consumed less power and less space than conventional tubes. Portable radios had inferior sound quality, but they ran on batteries, and American families enjoyed the convenience of carrying them on picnics and installing them in bedrooms as second and third sets.

Japanese manufacturers were just beginning to manufacture portable radios. It had taken a decade for the industry to recover from wartime shortages of technology and materials and to satisfy the domestic demand for higher-quality "superheterodyne" sets. But by the mid-1950s most radio manufacturers were investing heavily in portable set assembly, with a view specifically to the export market. Tōtsūkō could jump on this bandwagon, but it had little chance of competing with the giants of the industry, all of which had powerful sales organizations. Transistor radios offered a much better opportunity; if the technology improved enough, they might leapfrog the miniaturized vacuum tube models. They promised to be much smaller and lighter, and they would offer far longer battery life. Moreover, transistor radios played to Tōtsūkō's strength as a research-intensive organization. If Tōtsūkō were first in Japan with a transistor radio, it might carve out a permanent place for itself in the electronics industry.

Of course, investing in transistors represented a big risk. To this point, transistor research and manufacturing had been the preserve of large, well-financed American companies. Although start-up American companies would eventually prove that size was not a prerequisite for transistor manufacturing, this fact was not yet evident. Moreover, there was still no proof that transistors could be made with the frequency capacity needed for radio. In addition to the challenge of transistor manufacturing, there was also the challenge of the circuitry and parts for an ultra-small radio. The speaker, coil, battery and condensers would have to be designed from scratch either by Tōtsūkō or by its suppliers.

Access to existing transistor technology was not, in principle, a serious issue: the basic transistor patents were available to all comers. Western Electric, the owner of Bell Laboratories and hence of the patents, would license the technology for $25,000 up front, with a 1 percent royalty payable on sales. For most American companies, $25,000 was a negligible fee; for Western Electric, it was just enough to ward off frivolous license applications. But for Tōtsūkō, $25,000 was equivalent to the company's entire 1952 profits. And because it had to be paid in dollars, the transaction had to be authorized by the government.

The Tōtsūkō team decided to go ahead with the transistor radio project. In August 1953 Morita signed a provisional contract with Western Electric, subject to final MITI approval. The deal called for Western Electric to supply Morita with its transistor "bible," a two-volume set called *Transistor Technology*. Although essential to would-be transistor manufacturers, *Transistor Technology* was a small return for a $25,000 payment. The first applicants to Western Electric, in 1950 and 1952, attended week-long seminars detailing the manufacturing process for transistors. *Transistor Technology*, by contrast, was rapidly losing its value, as its contents became outdated and as unauthorized versions proliferated. By 1954 pirated copies were available in Tokyo for as little as ¥6,000.[5] Western Electric therefore had little to lose by entrusting Tōtsūkō with the information the books contained.

However, when MITI learned that Tōtsūkō had signed a contract without its approval, a major fracas ensued. MITI officials summoned Ibuka to their offices and shouted at him that Tōtsūkō's act was "inexcusably outrageous." Although intimidated, Ibuka stuck to his guns, and after six months of persuasion and a personnel change in MITI, the contract finally received bureaucratic sanction.[6]

This spat has come to be seen as a classic faux pas in MITI's industrial planning approach. Morita recalls that "the MITI bureaucrats could not see the use for such a device and were not eager to grant permission."[7] But there is no question that MITI perceived the importance of transistors: Denki Shikenjo, a MITI research institute, had been carrying out transistor research since 1948. In 1953 several major Japanese electronics companies were in the process of negotiating for transistor patent licenses, and MITI approved these contracts without delay. The real issue was MITI's reluctance to authorize a small and relatively unknown company to spend precious foreign exchange on a technology it might not be able to exploit effectively.[8]

While the standoff with MITI dragged on, Tōtsūkō began research in earnest on transistors. The company entrusted the project to technical director Iwama Kazuo. Iwama set up a study team in Tokyo in the summer of 1953 and charged it with reading materials on transistors. The basic texts were William Shockley's *Electrons and Holes* and Western Electric's *Transistor Technology*. The latter contained detailed information about the processes of manufacturing transistors—a more generous provision than many corporate licensing arrangements offered—but it also left a good deal out. In particular, the manual assumed that the user had access to a large amount of specialized equipment that did not exist in Japan.

Accordingly, Iwama set out for the United States in early 1954 to study manufacturing techniques in person. Staying in a $3.50-a-night hostel, he made regular visits to Western Electric's factory, making copious notes and sketches after each visit. Although Western Electric welcomed visitors, the company sought to share only an overview of its manufacturing activities, not detailed specifications. Western had a strict policy prohibiting the taking of photos during visits. Nevertheless, Iwama gained enough information from these visits to prepare detailed specifications for reproducing Western's production machinery.

Iwama sent a total of seven memos back to Tokyo. On balance, he was optimistic that Tōtsūkō could manufacture transistors of a similar quality to those made in United States. In a memo written shortly before his return, Iwama wrote: "There are no new technologies of the kind that we couldn't have thought of from our study of *Transistor Technology*. Progress in America has been stagnant for the last year. I think it's quite feasible for us to catch up to the American level within the next year." In this respect, Iwama was probably overconfident. U.S. firms were in fact making rapid strides in transistors, although Western Electric may not have been at the cutting edge. RCA in 1953 had patented the alloy-type transistor, which in time would be refined to meet all the specifications for radio manufacturing. Indeed, despite Western Electric's pessimism, American electronics companies were already coming close to the goal of a commercial transistor radio.

Back in Tokyo, Iwama's colleagues set about applying their theoretical knowledge to the construction of an actual transistor. The "grown-junction" transistor (developed by Bell Laboratories as an improvement on its initial "point-contact" version) required exceptionally pure germanium derived through the "zone refining" process (also developed by Bell). Although *Transistor Technology* described these methods, the manual assumed that the user owned appropriate machinery for them. For example, zone refining required a germanium oxide reductor, a highly controlled furnace, and an extremely precise slicing machine. Tōtsūkō had none of this equipment, nor did *Transistor Technology* contain information on how to construct it. The engineering team, led by Akanabe Sukemi, had to rely on drawings sent back by Iwama, along with their own inspiration, to design and build their own machinery. Their efforts were severely hampered by lack of machine tools. Iwama therefore considered it something of a miracle that, upon his return, his team already had a working point-contact transistor and was on the point of making an experimental grown-junction transistor.[9] Rosenberg has commented that even when a company or country willingly provides technology, its successful adoption by others is far from a foregone conclusion. It is not enough simply to provide blueprints and charts: "Only a part, and mainly the broad lines, of technical knowledge is codified by non-personal means of intellectual communication or communicated by teaching outside the production process itself."[10] Tōtsūkō's ability to make production machinery is an impressive example of the use of organizational skill to overcome the boundaries of the printed word.

Tōtsūkō spent another year working on development of its transistor radio. The company's engineers had to develop production machinery, perfect designs, organize suppliers, and solve the myriad small problems related to a product for which there was no precedent and no established parts supplies. Kanoi Nobuo, a young engineer on the circuit design team, recalls: "We worked on that with tremendous enthusiasm. Most days I would work up until 10 P.M. When I got home I would do my chores such as clothes washing, then I would study, usually American periodicals and texts. I'd study until 2 A.M., and then go to work the next morning and repeat the whole round. There were plenty of times when I stayed at the company for two or three days." He adds:

> You mustn't forget that the transistor itself was only a part of the radio. We had to introduce a wide range of new parts to meet the demands of this miniaturized piece of equipment. For example, it required development of a special battery [the 9-volt battery, still in use today]. . . . The speaker had to be shrunk to a much smaller size, and the magnetic power of the speaker coil consequently had to be magnified. I spent a lot of time going around the parts companies getting them to work with us on this. I think perhaps one reason for the success of Japanese companies [in transistor radios] was that we had a very well-established parts industry. This was also a business opportunity for us in the future. For example, we found that there was no company in Japan that made a glue capable of sticking together a Bakelite circuit board to its copper circuitry. We ended up importing this from the United States, and we set up a company to do the importing. Later, other Sony subsidiaries undertook manufacturing. At one time we were providing 85 percent of the adhesive used in Japanese circuit boards.[11]

Technical challenges were not the only ones Tōtsūkō faced. The transistor research effort involved a sizable proportion of the company's staff of 400. Tōtsūkō in 1955 was still capitalized at ¥100 million ($280,000), an insufficient amount for its transistor research project (even when subsidized by profits from tape recorder sales). However, the executives of this "unknown" company very much belonged to the Japanese establishment. Bandai Junichirō, a board member of Tōtsūkō, was one of Japan's most respected bankers and a former president of Mitsui Bank—which, not surprisingly, provided the company with substantial funding.

Figure 13   The Sony TR-55 transistor radio. (Courtesy of Sony Corporation)

Tōtsūkō completed its first transistor radio, the TR-52, in January 1955. Morita Akio traveled to the United States in February 1955 to begin marketing this product, for which the name "Sony" had been chosen. He was more successful that he dreamed: the Bulova watch company was impressed by the radio and placed an order for 100,000 sets. According to Sony legend (and Morita's own memoirs), the young executive refused the order because Bulova wanted to affix its own brand name to the radio. In reality, Sony probably could not have fulfilled even a fraction of the order. Nor, as it turned out, was the quality of the sets remotely adequate for commercial sales. Indeed, shortly after Morita's April return to Japan, the one hundred sets so far made began literally to disintegrate in the early summer heat—forcing Tōtsūkō to call off the planned Japanese launch of the radio.[12]

Tōtsūkō's first transistor radio to reach the marketplace, the TR-55 "Sony," was launched in August 1955. Although the sound quality was poor compared to that of portable vacuum tube radios, Tōtsūkō advertised its long battery life, dubbing it "the radio that pays for itself in two years." In spite of its high price tag (¥18,900), the product became a hit in Japan during the summer of 1956. Tōtsūkō began mass production of the radio to meet the growing demand, churning out 300,000 transistors a month by year's end.[13] The Sony legend had begun.

The First Transistor Radio?

One aspect of the Sony legend has in recent years become pervasive: that the company invented the transistor radio at a time when Western companies had no interest in, or even conception of, such a product. For example, Tom Forester's *Silicon Samurai* opens one chapter: "Back in 1955—when the rock 'n' roll revolution was getting underway and America was the greatest country in the world—an unknown Japanese company by the name of Sony introduced the US public to something called a 'transistor radio.'"[14]

Sony executives themselves have supported the establishment of this myth. Although admitting that theirs was not the very first transistor radio on the market, they acknowledge only one predecessor, the "Regency," which they claim was an inferior product that lacked the commitment of management. In his reminiscences, Morita Akio writes:

> An American company called Regency, supported by Texas Instruments, and using TI transistors, put out a radio with the Regency brand name a few months before ours, but the company gave up without putting much effort into marketing it. As the first in the field, they might have capitalized on their position and created a tremendous market for their product, as we did. But they apparently judged mistakenly that there was no future in this business and gave it up.[15]

Transistor radios were, as I have noted, in experimental production from the very beginning of the transistor era. Indeed, it was probably exposure to such prototypes that first stimulated Ibuka's interest in the idea. Although early transistors could not handle the high frequencies needed for radio, by 1954 Texas Instruments was making grown-junction transistors (the same type licensed by Sony) with relatively high handling capabilities. The alloy transistor also promised good frequency handling. As early as May 1954 the U.S. trade magazine *Electronics* could comment: "The next step that may take place this year is the commercial introduction of a transistorized portable. Many of the components necessary for such a set are available now. GE has demonstrated an experimental vest pocket portable radio, weighing about 5 oz., that uses transistors and diodes and is powered by two penlight cells. Raytheon has also shown an all-transistor experimental receiver that may be marketed in 1955."

By late 1954, a number of companies were making serious progress toward bringing transistor radios to the market. The first product to make a formal debut was indeed the Regency, the brand name of a small company called Industrial Development and Engineering Associates (IDEA) of Indianapolis. IDEA developed its radio in partnership with Texas Instruments (TI) and used TI transistors. The radio went on the market in January 1955, as acknowledged by Sony.

Shortly thereafter, in March 1955, Raytheon launched a transistor radio using alloy transistors. The Raytheon radio weighed five pounds, making it rather heavy as a portable set; its main advertised attraction was its long battery life. The Raytheon set sold for $79.95. In June 1955 Emerson announced a mixed tube and transistor radio weighing less than one pound and selling for $44. The following month Mitchell Manufacturing, a maker of air conditioners, introduced a transistor radio priced at $49.95 and weighing 12 ounces. Thus, by the time of the August 1955 launch of the Sony TR-55 in Japan, at least four transistor radios had already appeared on the U.S. market. Moreover, the Sony TR-55 was not marketed in the United States; it was purely a domestic product.

In September 1955 RCA announced the release of two transistor radios, both selling for $79.95. In early 1956, *Electronics* estimated that half of the projected 11 million transistors made that year would be for radios. That summer, *Electronics* surveyed forty-two radio manufacturers and found that sixteen had transistor radios on the market. The magazine commented that "nearly every major radio manufacturer has a transistorized receiver available."

It was not until mid-1957, with the launch of an ultra-small "pocketable" radio (the TR-63), that Tōtsūkō began successfully selling this niche product in the United States. By that time, rival Japanese companies were also offering transistor radios for the home and export markets. Sony's launch in the United States was hardly the pioneering gambit that many have portrayed it to be.[16]

Sony had competitive products and introduced them relatively early in the race, but it was still just one contender in a fairly large pack. By the time Sony began marketing its goods in the United States, the transistor radio was already an established product. Nor is it clear that Sony had any particular advantage over its competitors at this early stage. As Aida's study makes clear, Tōtsūkō did not overcome the very high reject rate for usable transistors until 1957 at the earliest. The major breakthrough came in 1958, by which time there were a number of superior technologies available in the United States.[17]

There is a footnote to the story of *Electronics* and the Sony transistor radio. In July 1956, when the Sony radio was still unknown in the

United States, *Electronics* published an article entitled "Transistor Circuitry in Japan." The article relies on information provided by Tōtsūkō (Iwama Kazuo and another company engineer are explicitly credited) and includes circuit designs and photographs of the Sony transistor radio. Most of the description is matter-of-fact and technical, although the Japanese receivers are credited with "novel circuits that seem to be high in signal-handling efficiency." But the article attests to Tōtsūkō's publicity skills and to the curiosity in America about developments in far-off Japan. Indeed, *Electronics* in its August issue published a small item headed "DEMPA GIZITSU":

> Words were added to our vocabulary when we received the material for the article on Japanese transistor techniques that appeared in the July issue. Some of the data was enclosed in an envelope on which the words "dempa gizitsu" appeared in Arabic [*sic*] letters. Checking with the New York representative of a Japanese company, we find that these words can be translated as "literature" or "manuscript" in our editorial language.

This translation is wrong. *Denpa gijutsu*, as it would be romanized today, means "radio technology." In November, *Electronics* corrected itself. Next to a photo of the envelope, the magazine explained that Tōtsūkō executive Morita Akio had visited the editors and over lunch had confirmed the correct meaning of *denpa gijutsu*. The editors also noted with evident gratification that Tōtsūkō had *Electronics* air-mailed to Japan at a cost of $120 a year (the regular subscription price was just $6.95 per year). Morita and Tōtsūkō garnered a modicum of publicity (within the industry, at least) before they had even launched their radio in the United States.

Sony's Technological Breakthrough

In 1957 Sony made the technological breakthrough that consolidated its position as a transistor industry leader—a position it has never relinquished. Throughout 1956 and into the first half of 1957, Tōtsūkō made each radio and each transistor virtually by hand. The reject rate for transistors (i.e., those incapable of handling the demanding reception needs of a radio) remained at or above 90 percent—precisely the conditions that Western Electric had warned Ibuka about. Moreover, the variability in performance even among transistors made in the same batch required a separate test for each unit. A single radio therefore required an inordinate amount of time and labor—so much so that the words "mass production" scarcely seem appropriate. Indeed, Tōtsūkō managed to keep its production line running only by designing separate circuitry for various different grades of transistor performance. The company's circuit designers produced twelve major configurations, and the appropriate one would be chosen after each transistor was individually tested.[18]

Tōtsūkō's early success therefore had less to do with technological superiority than with its willingness to live with manufacturing conditions that others found unacceptable. The difference seems mainly to have been one of perception. What Western Electric saw as an insurmountable obstacle, Ibuka saw as a competitive challenge:

> The fact that defects are high means that if you can reduce them, then you'll profit tremendously. In that sense, a high defect rate is an opportunity. Some problem was making the defect rate high, so if we could identify and eliminate that, then I believed we would start to make huge profits. At first our defect rate for grown transistors was 99 out of 100. With that kind of failure rate, no one had the nerve to start making radios. But I am ignorant, so I went ahead and did it, and that's the reason Sony is here today.[19]

Sony carried out detailed tests of its manufacturing process in the spring of 1957 and found that the main problem lay in the first stage of the manufacturing process. This step called for the creation of a "sandwich" of pure and adulterated germanium, a result achieved through the addition of controlled amounts of an impurity. Following the recommendation of Bell Laboratories, Sony was using antimony as the impurity. But its tests revealed that the antimony was spreading into the germanium crystal and destroying the carefully controlled layering. In response to this discovery, technical director Iwama experimented with phosphorus as an alternative to antimony. This turned out to be a much more effective impurity—although Bell Laboratories had apparently experimented with it and found it wanting.

Iwama obtained such promising results using phosphorus that he confidently switched the entire production line over without further ado. In the process, he almost ruined the company. His testing was woefully insufficient; thousands of transistors were manufactured under the new method, but not a single one of them worked, and Sony had to stop shipping radios altogether. The problem lay in the ratio of phosphorus to tin, which had to be added for stability. The volatility of phosphorus made a workable formula almost impossible to obtain. Only after several months of further study, during which Sony researcher Esaki Leona discovered the effect that was to win him the

Nobel Prize, did the team came up with a solution: replacing tin with indium and mixing it 50–50 with the phosphorus. This, finally, was the breakthrough Sony had been looking for. The reject rate fell from 90 percent to 10 percent, and Sony's profits soared, as Ibuka had anticipated.[20]

Sony's new production method helped establish it as one of the world's leading manufacturers of transistor radios and formed the basis for its future successes. But it is important to see this breakthrough in the context of global developments in the transistor radio industry. By 1957 the grown-junction transistor method developed by Bell Laboratories at the turn of the decade and licensed to Sony in 1953 was widely acknowledged to be out of date. Although the alloy method developed by RCA at first produced transistors with inferior handling capabilities, by the mid-1950s alloy technology had radically improved, and high-performance alloy transistors were becoming readily available, with Texas Instruments as the leader. New developments were taking place with the rapidity that has consistently characterized postwar electronics technology. The surface-barrier transistor, developed by Philco in 1954, used jet etching techniques to achieve high-frequency capabilities, and the diffusion method developed by Western Electric in 1956 dramatically improved manufacturing quality and reject rates.[21] These techniques were in wide use among leading American transistor makers at the time that Sony achieved its breakthrough using the older grown-junction method. Moreover, Sony's Japanese competitors purchased the later technologies and incorporated them in their manufacturing processes by the late 1950s. Even Sony entered into a comprehensive technology licensing agreement with General Electric in 1958.[22]

EXPORT SUCCESS AND MASS PRODUCTION

Japanese radio exports hit the United States with the suddenness of a hammer blow. In the late 1950s the Japanese economy was growing at a rate of 10 percent a year, the dire crises of the postwar decade had been overcome, and Japan was rapidly being transformed into the middle-class nation of the industrialists' dreams. Although the electrical goods industry was hardly excluded from this newfound prosperity, *exports* of electrical products were negligible. For example, 1957 exports of radios totaled less than a million dollars.

Through the efforts of Japanese researchers and the willing participation of American companies, by the end of 1957 all of Japan's radio manufacturers had transistor radios on the market, and most were beginning to export to the United States. The larger companies were able to use new transistor designs as they emerged, whereas Sony relied on improving the original Western Electric design. Both strategies were reasonably successful. In 1958 exports suddenly took off (see Table 15, p. 252). This increase was not just attributable to Sony; a market survey conducted in 1959 found no fewer than 130 Japanese companies making transistor radios, including ten that also manufactured their own transistors. By 1960 Japan was the largest manufacturer of germanium transistors in the world. Radio exports that year totaled ¥50 billion ($140 million), making radios Japan's second-biggest export product, after ships.

The transistor radio put Sony, Toshiba, Hitachi, and Japan itself on the industrial map. Westerners, however, were not unduly impressed. Gen. Charles de Gaulle summed up the West's amused contempt for Japan's modest success when he dismissed visiting prime minister Ikeda Hayato as a "transistor radio salesman"—a quip that has never been forgotten in Japan.[23]

It takes a major initiative to turn a successful domestic industry into an export powerhouse. For all its glamour and growth, Japan's domestic electrical goods industry was heavily protected. Imports of televisions, washers, refrigerators, radios, and other household electrical goods were virtually banned on the assumption that Japanese companies could not compete against powerful foreign rivals. In the export market, however, Japanese companies had to compete not only against each other but also against the full array of American electronics companies, in all their might. These American competitors already had established retail networks, brand recognition, and plenty of domestic publicity—all the advantages that should have guaranteed them a leadership position. How did it come to pass, then, that Japanese electrical goods manufacturers became so successful in overseas markets? The transistor industry was characterized by extremely rapid technological diffusion caused primarily by the pace of development, which made leading companies anxious to squeeze additional profits from obsolescent technologies through the sale of know-how. As a result, the playing field in terms of technology was relatively even at the end of the 1960s. Although U.S. companies remained ahead in the most advanced transistor technologies, they did not necessarily use these technologies for radio production; in fact, they were much more likely to use them in military applications.

This rapid dissemination of technology enabled various Japanese companies to begin large-scale manufacturing of transistors and transistor radios. Large companies such as Toshiba, Hitachi, Matsushita, Fujitsu, and Nippon Denki achieved this swift development with extensive—even comprehensive—assistance from American and European firms. The greatest provider was RCA, which offered not only its own alloy transistor but also, through cross-licensing, many of its competitors' advances in transistor technology. As a result, transistor factories established from 1957 to 1960 were fully adequate to the task of producing high-frequency transistors for use in radios. Although Sony supplied rival companies with transistors in the early years of radio production, by 1958 Toshiba was already more than doubling Sony's output, having invested ¥1.3 billion in plant facilities.[24]

In an environment of technological parity, the low-cost producer possesses a decisive advantage. American companies had invested large amounts in automation of production but with very limited results; because transistors continued to be plagued by high reject rates, they still required laborious assembly by hand. Indeed, for all its miraculous advances the transistor industry did not, in many of its essentials, employ high technology. Rather, it relied on labor-intensive manufacturing of the type at which Japanese companies excelled.

The same is even more true of the transistor radio industry. Once the basic product line was established, transistors and other components could be bought off the shelf from any number of sources. To make radios, one only needed to put the parts together in a box. The difficulties in automating this kind of work meant that American companies were unlikely to have a significant advantage in labor productivity. Transistor radio was precisely the kind of mechanical assembly operation that could be assigned to dexterous manual workers, of which Japan had an abundant supply.

It is to that labor, which I believe constituted Japan's true advantage in transistor radios, that I now turn.

Transistor Girls

A Matsushita advertisement from 1961 offers the following interpretation of Japan's sudden export success in transistor radios:

> Let's Praise the Dexterity of the Japanese!
>   The Japanese race are famous for their dexterity. Their feelings for beauty may be said to surpass those of other races, and now Japanese fine arts and

crafts, as well as architecture, have become sought-after by westerners, and Japanese traditional designs have become a part of western lifestyles.

But even if they want to, westerners cannot imitate Japanese dexterity. . . . We must wake up to the fact that this dexterity, passed down to us by our ancestors, is responsible for the creation of scientific products that could only be made in Japan. . . . The National transistor, which is famous throughout the world, owes its expansion to the divine fingers of young Japanese women.

For all its patriotic bravado, this explanation probably gets closer to the truth of Japanese export success than the Myth of the Electronics Samurai. At the heart of Japanese mass production of transistors—and, in large companies, transistor radios—stood a cadre of young girls, many of them teenagers, who were paid extremely modest wages to sit for long hours in front of microscopes assembling components with pairs of tweezers. They, more than any other factor, spurred Japanese companies' sudden rise to global dominance in the transistor radio industry.

Indeed, Toshiba's Nishijima Teruyuki recalls that the two keys to success in the transistor business were the improvement of the reject ratio and the hiring of "transistor girls." At its peak, Toshiba employed 3,000 female assembly workers in its Tamagawa plant alone. Most of them were middle school graduates hired straight out of school at the age of fifteen. "Since the girls would only work four or five years," Nishijima says, "we had to ensure a large supply. We ran all over the country looking for them, from Hokkaido to Okinawa."[25]

Tōtsūkō began hiring young women for its assembly lines in November 1956. Because of the sudden surge in domestic demand for Tōtsūkō's transistor radio, the need for workers fell outside the traditional hiring season. The majority of middle-school leavers looking for factory work had already signed on with textile mills, which were well-established employers of young female labor. As a result, Tōtsūkō managers had to scour the countryside for the workers they needed. General affairs manager Tachikawa recalls that the problem was solved by the bad harvest in Hokkaido that year. Girls who had been planning to go on to high school had to abandon their hopes and find work to help the family. In order to make the position with an unknown company sound a little more glamorous, Tōtsūkō advertised openings not for the traditional "female factory hand" (*joshi kōin* or *jokō*) but for "transistor girls" (*toranjisuta gaaru*). Tachikawa recalls that Tōtsūkō representatives interviewed the girls in the presence of their parents. "The quickest way to judge the daughter," he felt, "was by her parents."

In April 1957 a group of Tōtsūkō managers traveled up to Hokkaido and collected the girls upon their graduation from middle school, putting them all together on a night train to Ueno. In future years, Tōtsūkō would send female escorts and nurses with the male managers to escort the girls. Tōtsūkō also provided taxi fare for the parents to see the girls off at Hakodate or Sendai and, after treating the parents to lunch, promised: "We'll take good care of your daughter."[26]

Like the textile factories, Tōtsūkō housed its women workers in a dormitory (in fact, a renovated paint factory). Indeed, the similarity between the female workers in transistor and radio factories and those who had traditionally constituted the foundation of the textile industry is striking. Indeed, as Tōtsūkō's Tachikawa comments, electrical goods companies competed directly with textile factories for young female labor. Herein lies an important clue to the conundrum of Japan's extraordinary success in one of the "highest" of high-technology industries. Underneath the apparent revolution in technology development and industrial structure lay a profound continuity based on the abundance of extremely cheap, relatively docile female labor. It was this supply of young women laborers that fed the growth of the textile industry in the prewar era, prompting bitter criticism abroad of the "social dumping" of goods on the export market. Low wages are the most important point of similarity between textile workers and women workers on the electrical goods assembly lines. In April 1960 the average woman textile mill worker made ¥8,534 for 215 hours of work (¥39.7 per hour), while the average woman electrical machinery worker made ¥8,604 for 204 hours of work (¥42.2 per hour).[27] These wages were startlingly different from those paid adult workers, particularly males. In the same industries, a salaried male received ¥27,115 and ¥27,759, respectively. The average industrial wage in Japan for male and female workers of all ages was ¥22,630 per month.

Electrical goods workers in 1960 were apparently not much better paid than textile mill workers in the 1920s. According to one study, female factory hands at Kanebo (a major textile company) were paid an average ¥1.20 per day in June, 1924, or ¥31.20 for a twenty-six-day month.[28] Based on the movement of the consumer price index, ¥31.2 in 1924 was worth some ¥8,300 in 1960, making the salaries of prewar and postwar workers comparable in terms of spending power.[29] This statistic, however, ignores the longer hours worked by prewar factory hands, who generally toiled for twelve-hour shifts. It also does not take into account the many compulsory deductions made to prewar workers' paychecks. Overall, the electrical goods workers may have been marginally better off. But it was not a large margin.

Before the war, the low wages of textile workers prompted international criticism of what was called "social dumping": the export of goods made through the exploitation of people earning less than a subsistence wage. Similar complaints came from within Japan. Critics decried the extremely low wages, sometimes brutal exploitation, dismal living conditions, poor health, and early death of these women workers. Their plight was most eloquently expressed in *Jokō Aishi* (The Sad Story of Women Factory Workers), a book written by Hosoi Wakizō, who was himself a textile factory worker for fifteen years. Hosoi wrote with poetic pathos of the diseases, the frustrations, the calamities, the fetters, and the meager pleasures of women factory workers. In one passage Hosoi illustrates the psychological strains experienced by these workers in a catalogue of their distinctive mannerisms:

1) Their faces are extremely somber.
2) They are extremely timid, and they show a listless condition when they try to do anything.
3) When they get upset by some trifling matter, they look about twice as mean as ordinary people. And if the issue involves someone else, they will scowl balefully at that person for a long time. Indeed, that scowl is what makes their expression so heavy.
4) They will laugh like crazy people at something that isn't the least bit amusing.[30]

To be fair, girls from the countryside often considered themselves much better off working in the textile mills than sharing the hardships of their farming families: at the mills, at least, they had rice three times a day. A retrospective survey of 580 former silk-filature workers found that 90 percent of them had thought the factory-provided food "good"; only 3 percent found the work "hard."[31] Moreover, although many girls were recruited in the countryside through traditional channels, a significant number found work directly at the factory gates, often having moved from other factories.[32]

Still, international complaints about social dumping in the Japanese textile industry continued into the 1950s. A Canadian spokesman, for example, charged in 1955 that textiles from Japan represented "unhealthy competition" because of the inferior "living, working, and financial conditions" of Japanese workers.[33] Female electrical goods workers in Japan were paid at a level similar to that of the average worker in India, one of the poorest countries in the world.[34]

It would be easy to take the comparison between prewar textile and postwar electrical goods workers too far. In addition to important similarities, there were also important and revealing differences between the two groups. For example, the gravest problems of the prewar mills included crowded living conditions, poor nutrition, long working hours, and fast-moving machinery. Tuberculosis and beriberi haunted the early-twentieth-century silk and cotton mills. According to one estimate, every year some 15 percent of workers had to quit their jobs because of ill health. Many were sent home to their villages to die. The mortality rate for textile workers was three times the rate for their age group in the population at large.[35] By contrast, health conditions for "transistor girls" seem to have been quite good. In a 1962 survey of 2,004 electrical goods factory workers aged eighteen years or younger, only 1.3 percent had taken eight days or longer off during the prior year. Complaints about health and well-being were extremely muted: less than 10 percent of respondents had any such grievances, and the most common were mere tiredness and irritability.[36]

Work conditions were also better for postwar electrical goods workers. Occupation-sponsored legislation limited working hours for women; whereas the prewar textile worker typically worked a twelve-hour shift, alternating weeks of day and night shifts, the electrical goods worker generally worked an eight-hour day shift, albeit with occasional overtime. Thus, the typical electrical goods worker worked 215 daytime hours per month, compared to the prewar mill worker's 300-plus day and night hours.

Another important difference was in the composition of workers. Most accounts state that the majority of prewar mill workers came from rural districts, where there was a perennial surplus of labor. The case of Tōtsukō, which scoured the Hokkaido countryside for recruits, affirms that many electrical goods workers also came from outlying areas. But a 1962 survey found that electrical goods factories in Tokyo hired two-thirds of their young workers from Tokyo, Saitama, and Kanagawa.[37] In such cases, hiring generally took place directly out of school and without the assistance of professional recruiters. Workers from Hokkaido, Aomori, Iwate, Miyagi, and Akita—the rural northern provinces—made up only 14 percent of the Tokyo work force. Overall, only 24 percent of the workers came from agricultural families.[38] Seventy-one percent of the 2,004 workers surveyed lived at home with their families; only 21 percent lived in company dormitories. Even among large companies with more than 500 workers, only 24 percent lived in dormitories.[39]

Finally, although the wages of prewar mill workers and postwar electrical goods workers were equally low, the latter seem to have had more spending money in their pockets. Hosoi describes how a woman textile worker, out of her monthly salary of ¥41, took home only ¥9 after compulsory savings, repayment of loans, and compulsory remittance to her family.[40] By contrast, electrical goods factory workers surveyed in 1962 had few compulsory deductions, and those living in dormitories were able to spend at least ¥2,000 per month on clothes and entertainment.[41] It is somewhat surprising that girls from rural families were least likely to contribute to the support of their families. Those living at home were expected to contribute at least 25 percent of their salary to the family budget, whereas those living in dormitories sent home only an average ¥400 per month.[42]

These subtle differences go some way toward explaining one of the paradoxes of the role young women workers played in postwar Japan: despite being exploited and underpaid, they were among the earliest and most dedicated participants in the mass consumer society. In 1962, 69 percent of electrical goods factory workers spent at least some time every day watching television, and 89 percent of girls resident in dormitories said their main reading was weekly magazines.[43] Because most of these women came from urban families, they presumably had little difficulty adjusting to the culture of consumption and desire. Indeed, in spite of their low wages many purchased electrical goods, including televisions, at discounted prices from their employers.

None of the differences between prewar textile workers and postwar "transistor girls" is attributable to high technology. Rather, the differences reflect changes in the social climate that affected all workers. Indeed, electrical goods workers benefited from reforms—shorter hours, fewer deductions, and less coercive employment contracts—that were probably targeted at the textile industry. The Labor Standards Law of 1947 included provisions limiting women's working hours, prohibiting night-shift work for women, and providing mandatory leave before and after childbirth and during menstruation.[44] Japanese society had indeed changed, but the fundamental social conditions that allowed companies to hire young women workers at very low wages had not.

These generalizations about factors affecting all electrical goods workers mask substantial diversity in their individual experiences. Whether rural or urban, some came from conditions of bitter family hardship, forcing them to make great sacrifices; others, by contrast, had easy lives and could use most of their salaries for personal consumption. Two former Matsushita line workers, Hanada Mitsue and Morimoto Keiko, present such a study in contrast.

Matsushita recruited exclusively from Osaka-area schools. The company had no dormitory for women; all its women workers lived with their families. For Osaka middle-school graduates, a job with Matsushita was considered very desirable. Many applied, but only a few passed the rigorous manual dexterity tests that qualified them for employment. Morimoto recalls that of fifteen applicants from her school, only two received job offers from Matsushita. Those hired were put on three months' trial and faced dismissal if their dexterity and pliability were judged inadequate.

Morimoto came from a relatively affluent family; her father worked for Kanebo's trading subsidiary, and the family lived in company housing. Much of Morimoto's ¥8,000 monthly paycheck from Matsushita was available for discretionary spending. She put some of her money into a corporate saving plan and gave her mother money for living expenses. Still, she was able to spend about half her salary. "It was quite an easy life," she recalls. "I was able to buy clothes and entertain myself [as] much as I felt like it."

Hanada, by contrast, joined Matsushita out of sheer necessity. Her father was a carver of personal seals (*hankō*), but his business was unstable and subject to long periods of inactivity. Her mother worked as a restaurant waitress, and all five of Hanada's brothers and sisters went to work as soon as they were able to do so.

"I worked from elementary school on," recalls Hanada. "In my first job, I worked as delivery girl for evening meals (*zangyō shoku*), and then I worked as errand girl for a clothes shop. I used to come home from school by 5:00, and go straight to work until 8:00. Then I would do my homework for two hours; but at 10:00 I would go back to the shop to help them close up. That's the work I did throughout junior high school." Hanada's salary came mainly in the form of clothes. "It took me a month of work to earn a beautiful white sweater that I had longed for. I was so happy to get that."

Once Hanada went to work for Matsushita, she handed her entire salary of ¥6,000 over to her mother, who used it for bare necessities such as food and rent. The family lived in a market area in a tiny two-room house, with a six-mat room upstairs and another downstairs; Hanada's father's shop was downstairs. The rent was a burden, even for such a small dwelling. Hanada's only brother suffered from a bad leg, which prevented him from working; her elder sister ran away from

1957-3-22 新制中学定期採用者入社記念撮影

Figure 14 Middle-school leavers entering the Matsushita Company. Hanada Mitsue is third from left, second row. (Courtesy of Hanada Mitsue)

home, as did a younger sister. Only Hanada and her other younger sister went on working to help support the family. Even with this contribution, the family struggled to maintain its stability and find a modicum of pleasure.

After starting at Matsushita, Hanada continued to work at part-time jobs in the evenings. For fifteen years she worked every evening from 8 until 11 P.M. in a shoe repair shop. "With my sisters gone, I had to help take care of my family," she says. "Then in 1965 my father died, and my responsibilities were even greater." However, the additional work also helped pay for a few recreational activities, her greatest pleasures in life. A sports lover, Hanada played volleyball and went mountain climbing with her male and female colleagues.

Eventually Hanada earned enough money to purchase a few elements of the new, electrical lifestyle. She bought a television set for her family in 1961, after four years with the company. "For us, a television came before anything else," she says. Hanada obtained the television at a discount, and the company offered credit assistance. Nevertheless, the purchase amounted to several months' salary. Hanada's next acquisition was a washing machine, which lightened the burden of washing for her large family—previously, the family only had access to inconvenient communal facilities.

Morimoto, by comparison, was able to afford a television as early as 1955 (two years after joining Matsushita), and she bought a washing machine at roughly the same time. She later purchased an electric fan, a refrigerator, and an electric rice cooker.

The working hours at Matsushita were 8 A.M. till 5 P.M., with forty minutes for lunch and two ten-minute rest periods. Although the eight hours a day of assembly work were hard, the workers do not remember them as being a great burden. Hanada's job involved plugging some twenty components into a printed circuit board, a process that took about one and a half minutes. When she finished one board, the next was always waiting on the conveyor belt. In a typical day, Hanada assembled between 300 and 400 circuit boards. "The time certainly passed very quickly," recalls Hanada. "But it was not a terribly hard job." The girls were put on the assembly line for the first three years or so, but they could look forward to supervisory roles after that, testing and checking the work of the newer recruits. Moreover, the scale of the factory was quite human: a typical staffing level for an audio products assembly line was between twenty-five and thirty women. On hot summer days, the company placed large blocks of ice on the floor of the wooden factory building so that workers could cool their tired hands and drink cold barley tea in their brief rest breaks.

The company encouraged productivity and suggestions for process improvement by offering rewards. Output was monitored and tallied on a monthly basis, and productive workers were presented with dolls. Employees whose suggestions were adopted received cash awards based on the amount their idea was judged to save the company. But the greatest motivation of all was peer pressure. "I wanted to do a good job, and I did not want to fall behind the others," says Hanada. "Those were my strongest incentives."

Indeed, despite the many hardships she faced at the time, Hanada remembers her early years at Matsushita as the happiest time of her life. She enjoyed close friendships with many of the other female workers. She was able to indulge her passion for sports, even engaging in quick volleyball sessions during the ten-minute rest periods. And she lived for the many excursions and activities that she shared with her fellow workers.

Morimoto resigned from her job after ten years when she married an employee from the same factory. In quitting to get married, she was sharing the experience of the majority of her fellow workers. However, Matsushita did not enforce resignation upon marriage or childbirth, and there were women who continued working throughout their married lives. For those who retired upon marriage, the union agreement guaranteed their rehiring within ten years. Morimoto returned to work after the deadline; she had to retake the entrance exam but had no difficulty in passing it. Hanada never married and is now in her fortieth year at Matsushita.

Both Morimoto and Hanada emphasize the benefits of working for a large company such as Matsushita. "The working hours were short, and the pay comparatively good," says Morimoto. "And the company treated us well. It was much tougher for the people who went to work for small or medium-sized companies." The company also provided annual bonuses equivalent to 2 months' salary, plus six paid holidays per year, in addition to Sundays and national holidays (Matsushita introduced a five-day work week in 1965). Neither Hanada nor Morimoto considered her salary excessively low, nor did either resent the higher salaries paid to men. "We were brought up to think that men are superior," says Hanada.

Indeed, in some ways the factory workers of giant companies such as Matsushita, Toshiba, and (by the end of the 1950s) Sony were fortunate, at the top of their profession. Conditions undoubtedly were less desirable at smaller companies. This rule probably applies as much to the prewar textiles industry as to the postwar electrical goods industry. At the bottom of the totem pole sat the many families, both rural and urban, who took in piecework for subcontractors. Such work often found its way into brand-name goods sold in the West; but the final destination did little to improve conditions for the workers.

A 1968 survey of 2,020 electrical goods companies that farmed out work to some 25,000 mainly urban families found that pieceworkers were assembling transistors, winding coils, assembling transformers, and soldering parts. For an average 119 hours of work per month, the average income was ¥8,820, or ¥74 per hour. Forty percent of the workers made less than ¥60 per hour. In 1960 money this was equivalent to ¥40, or roughly the same amount the young assembly line workers made. In addition, pieceworkers sometimes had to pay for their own tools and transportation and guarantee product quality.[45] Clearly, this was very inexpensive labor, and the workers lacked any of the benefits enjoyed by full-time employees in well-known companies. For the most part these were not young women but mothers with child care responsibilities who took advantage of the flexibility provided by piecework. Nevertheless, the working conditions for these women were often as poor as in the worst factories, with substandard lighting, inadequate ventilation, and long working hours.

According to the *Census of Manufactures*, in 1960 the average Japanese radio and television production worker (male or female) received ¥18,000 ($50) per month, including bonuses, and produced output of ¥419,000 ($1,164). Labor costs therefore equaled only 4.3 percent of total revenues. A separate survey specifically on transistor radios found a lower wage scale. Large transistor radio makers in 1959 paid their line employees ¥12,032 per month, and revenues generated per worker were ¥331,166, a ratio of 3.6 percent. By contrast, the average American factory worker earned $329 per month and produced revenues of $2,546, for a labor cost equaling 12.9 percent of revenues.[46]

U.S. labor generated higher revenues per worker, which tends to indicate that U.S. companies did indeed enjoy higher productivity and hence could remain competitive even while paying higher wages. Indeed, value added per worker was ¥156,000 ($433) per worker in Japan, $1,028 per worker in the United States. But value added was higher in the United States in part because American manufacturers charged substantially higher prices for their goods than Japanese firms did. Although MITI acted to maintain prices of Japanese exports in order to avoid allegations of dumping, in 1958 the average Japanese transistor radio cost $15 on the U.S. market, whereas U.S.-made radios typically sold for $40 or more.[47] If, for the sake of argument, U.S. makers were forced to cut their prices in half to compete against Japanese companies, then labor costs would rise to 26 percent of revenues, and value added per worker would fall to minus $245. In other words, American companies would be losing money.

This hypothesis admittedly ignores the difficult issue of quality. American radios and televisions tended to include more features and may have been somewhat more reliable than Japanese makes, particularly those from smaller manufacturers, which dominated Japanese exports. Although there were higher-quality Japanese sets, they tended to sell for higher prices; Sony radios, for example, sold for up to $40. But

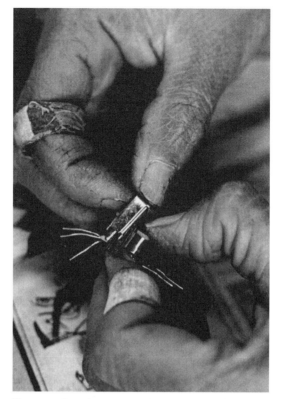

Figure 15 A rural woman assembles transistor radio components in her home. (Courtesy of Hanabusa Shinzō)

as general indicators of the benefit Japanese companies gained from cheap labor, these statistics are telling. Their importance is confirmed by the developments that actually followed. U.S. radio makers did indeed plunge into the red during the 1960s and rushed to outsource their manufacturing operations to Japanese firms. According to one study, there were no domestic radio manufacturers left in the United States by the end of the 1960s.[48]

The transistor radio represented the kind of product sought by the *Oriental Economist*'s commentator at the turn of the 1950s: an article "of exquisite workmanship not capable of being mass produced." It was notoriously difficult to harness to mass production techniques, and Japanese female workers—who tended to come from disciplined family backgrounds, to be well educated, and to work with diligence and dexterity—were ideally equipped to assemble them by hand. Indeed, superior dexterity was long considered a racial trait of the Japanese. For a while, Japan's labor advantage would be enough to propel it to export competitiveness.

American Buyers

Japan's early export success with transistor radios was aided by American entrepreneurs who saw a unique opportunity in the nation's skilled, low-cost labor force. While Sony gained fame for its technological prowess, dozens of small Japanese companies quietly offered cheap labor and a modicum of reliability to aggressive American "buyers" seeking to outsource assembly operations.

In 1959, for example, of the estimated 4.9 million transistor radios manufactured in Japan, only 2.1 million—43 percent—were made by the largest twelve manufacturers. The remaining 2.8 million sets were assembled by 118 small and medium-sized companies employing an average of under 100 workers per factory. Indeed, the smallest recorded factory occupied only 99 square meters, the size of a single floor of a suburban house. When it came to exports, smaller companies accounted for an even higher proportion; the largest twelve companies manufactured only 29 percent of the 3.3 million sets sold overseas.[49]

None of these smaller companies made their own transistors. As in the United States, most Japanese transistor radio manufacturers purchased their transistors from specialized providers. At first they used American-made transistors, as Japanese companies were unable to manufacture enough to meet the demand. However MITI, concerned about the effects of massive imports on the domestic transistor industry, brokered an agreement in 1958 that guaranteed supplies of Japanese-made transistors to domestic assemblers.

Nevertheless, the overwhelming impetus for smaller companies came from orders placed by American purchasing agents, known in Japan as *baiaazu* (buyers), who provided anything from designs and financing to full knock-down kits. The initiative in the overwhelming majority of these cases came from the American side. American trading companies recognized the relative simplicity of transistor radio assembly and saw the benefits of exploiting cheap Japanese labor. The American buyers provided their Japanese partners with capital, designs, parts, and marketing facilities. The value added by the Japanese companies was undoubtedly low, but it came in the form of precious export dollars.

MITI identified approximately twenty major American companies that contracted for Japanese transistor radio manufactures. These included trading firms that specialized in radio, such as Longwood and Channel Master; general trading companies such as Continental Merchandising; trading companies that previously had dealt in Japanese textiles and now were diversifying; retail chains such as Macy's and Woolworth; and large manufacturers such as RCA that had recently begun contracting for production in Japan. In addition, a large but unspecified number of small American trading operations were involved in contracting for radios or radio parts.[50]

Egawa Toshiō worked for a small Japanese trading firm at the turn of the 1960s. Later, his company would enjoy substantial growth as the sole Japanese sourcing representative of Admiral, a major American radio distributor. But in its early years the company sold "anything—cigarette lighters, wire coils, radio parts, toys—you name it." Egawa recalls the communication process between Japanese sellers and American buyers:

> There was a magazine in those days called *Baiaazu gaido* (Buyers' Guide). Actually you couldn't really call it a magazine, since it was just a few sheets mimeographed by hand. I doubt if you could find a single copy of it in any library today.
>
> Well, this magazine came out weekly, and it contained a list of all the American buyers currently in Tokyo. The people who prepared the magazine would go the rounds of the hotels—there weren't many in those days—and they would look at the guest lists and see who had arrived, and from what companies.
>
> So we would consult this magazine, and see who might be a potential customer. Then we would go to see the buyer in the Imperial Hotel or wherever he was staying. There were no appointments—not many of us had access to telephones. Everyone would just turn up, and they'd wait in a line outside the buyer's hotel room, holding samples of their wares. Sometimes there'd be as many as thirty people lined up in the corridor outside the room! And when your turn came, you would show him your sample, and if he liked it, he'd order a certain quantity on the spot.[51]

Egawa comments that technology was hardly an issue in the majority of these transactions.

> Most of these [Japanese assembly] companies were very small indeed. Just a family, working in a shop on the bottom floor of their house. At the most, they might have twenty or so workers, but none of them would be particularly skilled. The managers weren't trained engineers, either. After all, what they were being asked to do was very simple. Making a coil, for example, just involved winding the wire around the coil. If there was a more complex operation involved, the buyer would provide the manufacturer with detailed specifications and drawings. But it usually wasn't that complicated.[52]

The Japanese government, curiously, was torn about how to deal with this type of commerce. On the one hand, the American buyers provided export earnings and financial support for small enterprises that might not be able to survive otherwise. But on the other, the simple operations entrusted to the Japanese firms cut out many value-added activities. Indeed, imported American parts could be interpreted as competing with Japan's emerging transistor radio parts industry. Moreover, there had been complaints that American buyers provided inferior components and then forced the Japanese to swallow losses from defective finished products. Even more worrisome, a few cheap or defective product lines might damage the reputations of *all* Japanese manufacturers. MITI harbored great concern over the resumption of "bad practices" that had characterized prewar trade, and it feared that the country's inspection system and price maintenance agreements would fail to prevent poor-quality goods from leaving the country.

MITI believed Japan should compete not by offering low prices but by finding an appropriate niche in foreign markets. The ministry identified that niche as pocket radios, which were not at the time being manufactured in the United States: "Just as the European car industry has found a special niche in the US, we must do the same for radios, based on specializing in ultra-small products that don't compete with US makers."[53] MITI justified this choice by arguing: "It's not that [pocket radios] cannot be made abroad. But the fine, close-packed wiring assembly is not an easy thing to do. This is one of the reasons for the success of the Japanese transistor radio industry with its skillful, cheap labor."[54]

CONCLUSION: JAPAN'S PLACE IN THE WORLD, WOMAN'S PLACE IN JAPAN

Cheap labor was the final piece in the puzzle of Japan's rise to postwar prosperity. The combination of new technologies, vigorous demand stimulation, and cheap manufacturing inputs helped Japan's electrical goods companies succeed domestically and in the export market. Of course, the major beneficiaries of this success were the owners of the electrical goods companies. Salaried male employees also benefited from substantial income increases as a result of this newfound prosperity. But the people who made the miracle possible—the young women toiling on the assembly lines—did not receive many of the rewards of the prosperity. Although hourly wages have, of course, increased substantially since the 1950s, women remain Japan's primary source of cheap domestic labor. As women have become more likely to receive secondary and higher education, the focus has shifted somewhat from school leavers to mothers reentering the work force part-time after their children reach school age. These workers earn less per hour even than eighteen-year-old high school graduates. Many of these women undoubtedly are working because they have come to see the consumption items of the age—electrical goods, foreign travel, and entertainment—as essentials without which they cannot live. Japanese working women continue to have second-class status; indeed, in the long recession of the 1990s the job market closed up even for women with university degrees.

Eric Hobsbawm has observed that a "decisive innovation" of the 1950s was that third world countries began to supply the world market, "becoming part of a transnational process of manufacture."[55] Giovanni Arrighi notes a similar theme when he comments on the trajectory of late-twentieth-century capitalism: "[T]he main structural feature of the emergent regime remains the provisioning of wealthy markets with products that embody the cheap labor of poor countries."[56] My intent is not to provide a critical analysis of the Japanese capitalist system's co-optation and exploitation of women. For that, I would point the reader to existing studies.[57] Rather, I wish to examine the paradoxes revealed by this analysis and to understand the interactions among business, technology, and social change.

First, Japan's place in the world was ambiguous during this phase of economic development. Japan was indeed providing wealthy markets, particularly the United States, with products made with cheap labor. That labor was a precious resource to Japanese electrical goods companies, to the point that analysts commonly referred to rural teenagers as "golden eggs."[58] Yet that cheap labor helped fuel a sustained industrial expansion that quickly resulted in a consumer revolution and a "first world" standard of prosperity. Was Japan in 1960 a poor country that happened to have a high level of television ownership? Or was it a wealthy country that happened to have a class of workers willing to accept low wages? The answer, of course, is that Japan was both. The prosperity of the 1950s and 1960s was not evenly distributed, nor were lifestyles even among the middle classes uniformly prosperous. As hourly wages rose in response to economic growth, and as more and more women went on to high school and university education, companies searched harder and harder for low-cost laborers. Increasingly, Japanese electrical goods manufacturers have moved their production overseas in order to benefit from the much cheaper labor of East and Southeast Asia, focusing on high-value-added activities in Japan. But within Japan, young women continue to be a primary source of relatively low-cost labor. Companies have increasingly looked to part-time female workers returning to the labor force after child-rearing. These workers remain shockingly underpaid and vulnerable to arbitrary treatment.

Japan's postwar economic focus on high-technology industries apparently contradicted the traditional theory of comparative advantage.[59] Japan's primary competitive resource compared with other industrial nations was cheap labor. Why, then, did Japanese businessmen and industrial planners focus so much on developing high-technology industries? At least in the case of transistors and transistor radios, the two were not necessarily incompatible. Japan's comparative advantage remained in cheap labor, even when manufacturing products that embodied high technologies.

Related to the paradox of Japan's place in the world is the paradox of women's place in Japan. Young women in the mid-1950s were expected to work with docile subservience for minimal wages. But as Japan's consumer revolution unfolded, it became apparent that young women also had another vital role to play: as consumers. Increasingly, women's magazines, cosmetics companies, and even electrical goods companies targeted unmarried working women as prospective customers. Their enlistment in the system of consumption was particularly important, as many of them would eventually marry and aspire to own the full panoply of possessions associated with the ideal home. How did these young women who earned a below-living wage manage to become consumers? The cases of Hanada Mitsue and Morimoto Keiko provide some insight. Although extravagant consumption was out of the question for workers like Hanada, Morimoto's family conditions allowed her to keep—and spend—a high percentage of her salary. At a time when households were hard-pressed to save a few thousand yen a month out of salaries averaging ¥20,000 to ¥30,000, Morimoto was able to allocate at least ¥4,000 per month for personal expenditure. This placed her spending power quite high up the scale in comparative terms. Of course, if Morimoto had wanted to set up house independently, such a level of spending would have been impossible. But because she lived with her family, she had few financial responsibilities beyond a basic contribution to the household budget.

In a third paradox, the use of young women workers on the electrical goods assembly lines simultaneously upheld long-standing traditions and represented a break with the past. Young women have been mainstays of industrial expansion throughout modern Japanese history, fueling export growth and profitability from the time of the prewar textile industry through the export heyday of the electrical goods industry. The exploitation of women continues up to the present day: for the most part they remain economically dependent in Japanese society, and the financially successful career woman remains a comparative rarity. But the postwar also presented a decisive break with the past. Occupation reforms dramatically increased the protection of women from abusive work practices. Moreover, young women increasingly acted as consumers, giving them unprecedented economic power: the power to buy or not to buy.

Conclusion

The Japanese electrical goods industry appeared on the world scene, apparently from nowhere, at the turn of the 1960s. Within a little more than a decade Japanese companies such as Sony, Matsushita, Hitachi, and Toshiba became household names throughout the world—and emerged as feared competitors to their international rivals. How did this juggernaut suddenly emerge?

TRADITION AND TRANSFORMATION

Continuities

The high-growth electronics industry did not emerge out of nowhere. It was part of a continuum stretching back to the beginning of Japan's modern history. The continuity of Japanese technological development has been to some extent obscured by the two great caesuras of modern Japanese history—1868 and 1945—which made it convenient for Japanese and foreigners alike to forget prior capabilities. But in both cases, Japanese scientists entered the new era with a greater accumulation of knowledge than was usually recognized. This was particularly true in the aftermath of World War II, when Japanese electrical engineers had substantial expertise in advanced technologies such as radar, television, and microwave applications (the exception was semiconductors).

Japanese leaders unwaveringly supported the development of electronics and communications technologies. The government perceived the defense implications of such technologies as early as the civil war of 1877, which it won with the aid of the telegraph, and it consistently encouraged and sponsored research for defense purposes. The government also supported radio for national propaganda purposes, a reflection of the Nazis' growing influence in Japan. And its "domestication of production movement" (*kokusanka undō*) called for technological development in the name of national defense, national pride, and national economic power.

In the nineteenth century the government founded research institutions within universities and ministries, and in the twentieth century these came to be mainstays of Japan's technological establishment. It is often commented that Japan's successful system of innovation owed much to the large numbers of engineers emerging from the educational system. They, in turn, owed their educations to the elite institutions established in the nineteenth century and to a large number of new academies founded during the period of militarism.

Rapid growth itself has a long tradition within the Japanese electrical goods industry. Indeed, available statistics indicate that production growth was actually *more rapid* during the war years (1932–42) than during the "high-growth" era of 1955–1970. This growth not only provides a new perspective on the origins of the high-growth era but also helps account for the ability of postwar Japanese companies to take on large development projects. During the prewar years of high growth, electrical goods companies acquired the financial and technical critical mass to compete in the postwar era.

At least as important as these institutional, human resource, and policy continuities—already the subject of a growing number of weighty studies—are continuities in the evolution of Japanese society. Just as the postwar electrical goods industry did not emerge full-grown from the womb of a defeated nation, so the "bright life" of electrical goods ownership had its infancy in prewar social trends, the memory of which has been almost obliterated by the craters of war and defeat. Many of the ideals used with such effectiveness in the postwar development of a mass consumer market were already in circulation by the 1920s and 1930s. These concepts—including "lifestyle improvement," "rational" and "scientific" lives, and a private home at the center of a happy family life—were generally associated with the Western-style, nuclear family with a housewife at its center. They enjoyed broad support across a spectrum of political and institutional affiliations and effected real changes in Japan's social structure. The 1920s saw the emergence of a significant class of urban white-collar households—perhaps half a million all told—that occupied suburban-style homes, had wives who lived at home, and could afford the modest range of home comforts widely available at the time. The image of such a lifestyle was propagated in mass circulation magazines and, increasingly, radio broadcasting.

The prewar period was in some ways an era of shadows, in which the outlines of postwar Japan's "middle mass" society became discernible. As so often throughout Japan's modern history, this social change followed a model already established in other countries. Indeed, these models became in some ways self-fulfilling prophecies. A few people of vision and personal dynamism set forth on far-sighted ventures that were to have wide-ranging repercussions in the postwar. Shōriki Matsutarō's newspaper publishing enterprise, Matsushita Kōnosuke's fledgling bicycle-parts company, and Takayanagi Kenjirō's television research project are examples.

The war itself had curious and distorting effects on these continuities. In some cases, the war forced a painful retreat; household electrical goods ownership, for example, might have grown much faster had the demands of the military not choked off the consumer market. But in other areas, the war had exactly the reverse effect. The influence of the media, for example, increased dramatically during the war, creating one of the many paradoxes of the postwar era, as wartime villain Shōriki Matsutarō was able to reconstitute himself as a postwar "man of the masses." Still other areas remained remarkably consistent in spite of the extreme swings of war, defeat, and occupation—for example, the government's steadfast support for the radio industry. Nevertheless, the war was a major watershed in one way: never again would the government attempt to cut Japanese technology off from the mainstream of world developments.

The Keys to Prosperity

In the aftermath of defeat, a massive process of soul-searching got underway in Japan. What had gone wrong? And what was the way out of the dark wood in which the Japanese people now found themselves? People from all walks of life searched for answers to these questions, none more earnestly than the leaders of the electrical goods industry, whose role as apostles of modernity was now open to interpretation as a deadly betrayal.

Japan had lost the war in part because domestic technology failed, and it was to the United States that industrial leaders now turned for a formula for recovery. This quest was rendered all the more urgent by the extraordinary and unprecedented prosperity of the United States, which seemed to place it on a trajectory altogether different from Japan's. What were the keys to this prosperity? This question preoccupied Japanese industry leaders and entrepreneurs at the turn of the 1950s. And, broadly speaking, they found the answers. Each individual pursued the leads that seemed most appropriate to his or her own goals, but collectively business leaders and entrepreneurs focused on four major themes.

The first was the media, particularly broadcasting. Shōriki Matsutarō, a prewar and wartime newspaper tycoon, understood the importance and influence of mass communications and their enormous money-making potential. In this, he was guided by television's success in the United States. Shōriki allied himself with a cross-section of Japanese politicians, bureaucrats, and investors. Between them, these groups succeeded in bringing television to Japan much sooner than conventional economic logic would have suggested.

The second was technology. The 1950s witnessed a great wave of technology importation, as Japanese engineers filled the flights across the Pacific to learn from the great electronics companies of the United States. This importation program included not only product technologies but also the latest technologies of production, management, and marketing. The U.S. government actively promoted the transfer of these latter technologies, which it regarded as nonproprietary resources that could strengthen the economies of political allies.

The third theme was the domestic market. As early as 1951, Matsushita Kōnosuke envisioned a broad, consuming middle class in Japan. Within little more than a decade he would see that vision largely realized. Japanese companies applied an unprecedented amount of resources to the program of market creation, utilizing newly imported technologies to the fullest. At the highest level, companies engaged in a large-scale program of ideology creation, one effect of which was the widespread acceptance of the ideal of the "bright life."

The final theme was Japan's traditional comparative advantage in low-cost labor. Despite subsequent grandiose claims, the Japanese at the turn of the 1950s had no plans to compete in export markets on the basis of superior technology or quality. On the contrary, they generally expected Japanese technology and quality to remain inferior for the foreseeable future. But Japan's vast supply of extremely cheap labor, particularly of young female workers, was a formidable asset at least until the late 1960s. High-technology products such as transistors, transistor radios, and televisions still required painstaking manual assembly, and Japanese companies excelled at finding inexpensive, nimble hands to do the job.

Continuity and Difference

What factors set the postwar period apart from the prewar? I have stressed continuities, and these were undoubtedly central to the story. Ultimately, however, Japan's postwar success resulted from a new vision, formed in the aftermath of defeat. Although all of the elements of this vision were present before and, in some cases, during the war, there were some key differences in the postwar era.

One was the political environment in which the vision was formed. In the prewar, political considerations guided the electrical goods industry to a large extent. Government policy favoring defense applications worked to the disadvantage of consumer-oriented companies, at times actively obstructing them. Moreover, the government's *kokusanka* policy closed the doors to vital developments abroad. In the postwar, the government played a much less central role.

Another key difference lay in the American model. From the moment Commodore Perry set up his telegraph machine in a field at Uraga, Japanese leaders had sought to emulate the United States in terms of technological achievement. But the awesome prosperity represented by the United States in the 1950s was something entirely new. One company president who visited the United States in the early 1950s recalls: "I wondered what on earth made us think we could fight this country."[1] This seemingly boundless affluence was based on the vast expansion of middle-class purchasing power. Some American intellectuals were uncomfortable with such conspicuous consumption, but it acted as a powerful draw to Japanese companies.

Finally, the United States's direct intervention and support constituted a clear break with the prewar. During the Occupation, Americans provided Japanese researchers with direct access to the great technological breakthroughs of the war and postwar. U.S.-inspired reforms radically changed the institutional framework of Japan's political economy. At a more visceral level, ordinary Japanese could see the amazing affluence of the victors, who lived in a world of twinkling hilltop lights and easy comfort. Moreover, as the cold war began, the United States actively supported technology transfer to allied countries in order to help them shore up their economies. Finally, American companies provided technology and know-how to Japanese buyers on a much greater scale after the war than in the prewar.

Paradoxes

A number of seemingly irresolvable paradoxes hover around this story. The first is the paradox of consumption and saving. By the end of the 1950s, Japanese people were spending a large percentage of their incomes on electrical goods—more than, by most measures, they should have been able to afford. Yet by 1960 Japan had the highest savings rates in the industrialized world. Moreover, government agencies and private organizations were sponsoring organized savings drives, often using the very same slogans and ideals employed by the electrical goods industry to promote consumption. Concepts such as "lifestyle rationalization," for example, could be interpreted as a call both for severe thriftiness and for devil-may-care spending.

The second paradox juxtaposes growth and success. Laura Hein raises the issue in *Postwar Japan as History*. Like many researchers, Hein challenges the large and admiring literature that equates Japan's high GNP growth rate with success. She calls for an evaluation of success that includes "some measure of economic growth with some measure of economic justice."[2] The 1950s did indeed bring success for a small number of Japanese manufacturers that have since become household names throughout the world. I have highlighted Sony and Matsushita in particular, but Toshiba, Hitachi, Mitsubishi, Nippon Denki, Oki, Sharp, Fujitsu, Sanyo, and Nihon Victor, together with a larger number of parts manufacturers, also rode the wave of growth. But failures also abounded. The torrid pace of investment, severe price competition, and rapid product changes overwhelmed all but the strongest and best-managed companies. For example, MITI estimated that the sudden replacement of miniature tubes by transistors in 1957 put a large number of portable set makers out of business, as the manufacture of sets using vacuum tubes declined by 70 percent.[3] Most of the victims have sunk into oblivion.

Nor did ordinary people benefit uniformly from the remarkable growth of the electrical goods industry. Some families sacrificed necessities—in particular, adequate housing—in order to buy television sets and other products of debatable utility. And the electrical goods industry's success rested on the backs of thousands of young and older women working for very low wages on the assembly lines and in their homes.

The third paradox is the combination of high technology and cheap manual labor that drove Japan's electrical goods industry. The transistor represented the acme of technological achievement in the early 1950s. By 1960, Japan was the world's largest producer of germanium transistors, and ever since Japanese companies have been formidable competitors in the never-ending war to bring out denser, more powerful transistor-laden chips. There is a school of thought that Japan's mastery of this key technology places it in a position to lead the next phase of global capitalist development. Indeed, Japanese learning skills, shop-floor flexibility, and production-line innovations have been credited with shifting the geographic focus of world capitalism. But Japan's success in the 1950s derived not from the technological content of the products produced—that remained largely irrelevant—but from the availability of cheap labor to make products that did not easily lend themselves to automated manufacturing techniques.

These paradoxes cannot be resolved neatly. They are potent examples of the chaotically tangled fabric of history. But the tangles illustrate that Japanese history defies easy interpretation. Even today, consumption and thrift continue to go hand in hand, and rich Japan continues to harbor millions of poor Japanese. And although most labor-intensive tasks have been relocated overseas, Japan still has a supply of inexpensive labor in the form of married women, who often work part-time at very low-technology tasks in the midst of Japan's dazzling high-technology economy.

The Role of the Government

The discourse on the postwar Japanese economy has been dominated by a range of academic models that for the most part are intended to explain "success." Some of these, such as Chalmers Johnson's *MITI and the Japanese Miracle*, have been extraordinarily influential, both inside and outside Japan, in promoting the idea of Japanese difference. Johnson argues that Japan's high-growth era was created by perceptive bureaucrats who, acting as an "economic general staff," targeted certain industries (including electronics) for nurturing. Johnson even credits MITI with "creating" the industry through the Temporary Measures for the Promotion of an Electronics Industry of June 1957.[4] Influential analysts of technology have also focused considerably on the role of the government.[5]

Johnson points out MITI's "virtuoso" use of a specific group of tools, including foreign exchange and foreign capital control, cartelization, bank-centered business groups, industrial location subsidies, direct government finance, tax incentives, and economic "nationalism." However, many of these tools had little relevance to consumer electronics. Cartels, banking arrangements, industrial location packages, and government subsidies played virtually no role in spurring Japan's consumer electronics industry to high growth. Far from creating the electrical goods industry, MITI seems to have played the role of anxious referee and, occasionally, coach. The industry seems to have been very much the master of its own destiny.

Indeed, everywhere I have looked for evidence of direct government intervention, I have found that less than I expected. The 1957 Temporary Measures law, often misidentified as the starting point of Japanese electronics, primarily targeted industrial electronics and computers—areas in which Japan was not to gain a significant advantage for decades, if ever. MITI seems to have consistently underrated the importance and potential of consumer electronics. As I showed in Chapter 2, MITI's policy toward the creation of a domestic television industry was ambiguous. Though it supported the industry by allowing technology imports and restricting imports of finished goods, the agency leveled a grievous blow at established Japanese companies by encouraging the use of American standards at the expense of native technology two decades in the making.

There are other examples. With its calls for "lifestyle rationalization" and "raising the level of culture," the government-sponsored new life movement might be taken as a blueprint for a modern, consumption-oriented life; in fact, however, it had much in common with Tokugawa sumptuary edicts. Similarly, the drastic income tax cut of 1957—which on the surface looks like a powerful statement favoring personal consumption—was passed almost in spite of the wishes of the government. And the famous Income Doubling Plan of 1960 had much less influence on the promotion of consumption than is commonly thought.

Even in the area of technology, where the government has received much praise for its liberal attitude toward imports and its emphasis on strategic technologies, Japan is the only country in the capitalist world to have imposed controls on technology importation. As Peck and Tamura point out, technology imports in 1960 accounted for only 1.8 percent of Japan's total foreign exchange outflows.[6] Yet MITI commented in 1960 that "as much as the importance of technology import is great, so on the other hand is the problem of excessive dependence on foreign technology; as we move towards trade liberalization, we may expect these problems to become even more urgent than before."[7] Peck and Tamura conclude that the controls were intended to suppress imports of consumer-oriented technologies in favor of strategic industrial technologies such as chemicals and machine tools.[8] But television was a consumer industry and could scarcely be considered strategic. MITI eventually permitted thirty-seven companies to import television technology, when it originally thought three or four would be ample. On balance, MITI's import controls seem to have been neither excessively obstructionist nor prescient. Perhaps in the end MITI did little more than follow the trend of the market.

Overall, the government played a supportive role in the development of the consumer electrical goods industry in the 1950s. MITI's controls on imports of foreign products were probably the most important single measure of the government's effectiveness, but technology policy, a beneficent income tax structure, and a relatively free and competitive business environment all helped. Given the alternative models of government economic management in the twentieth century, simply avoiding active obstruction of industrial and market development is a considerable achievement.

JAPAN IN THE LATE TWENTIETH CENTURY

I do not wish to make excessively radical claims for the significance of electrical goods in Japan's postwar history. But certain features of the story cry out for interpretation within a larger context. The first of these is the extraordinary pervasiveness of electrical goods in the records of the 1950s and 1960s. It was no accident that Ezra Vogel picked out electrical goods ownership as one of the symbols of the "bright new life" that salaried Japanese were suddenly enjoying. The "three sacred treasures" of the 1950s (television, electric washing machine, and refrigerator) and the "three Cs" of the 1960s (car, room cooler, and color television) have acquired near-iconic status as emblems of the age. Social commentators were stunned by the "consumer revolution" of the late 1950s. Electrical goods, and the "bright life" they symbolized, surely meant more than entertainment and convenience.

Second is the importance the companies involved in this story came to have in later years. For Sony, Matsushita, Toshiba, and others, the domestic electrical goods market in the 1950s was the stepping stone to global conquests from the 1960s through the 1980s. The explosive domestic growth of the later 1950s was a phenomenon in its own right. Electrical goods were an integral—even a paradigmatic—component of the "Japanese miracle."

Third is the extremely rapid pace of social change that accompanied—and to some extent were symbolized by—the purchase of electrical goods. These changes included the decline of traditional household ties and the rise of the nuclear family, with its female household manager; the emergence of a middle class comprising salaried male white-collar workers and, increasingly, factory workers in large companies; and the greatly increased amount of time that people spent reading, listening to, or watching the vehicles of mass communication.

Eric Hobsbawm refers to the early postwar era as a golden age of economic growth and prosperity in the industrialized world. Hobsbawm identifies five essential components of this golden age: the economic and political hegemony of the United States; the rapid development and introduction of new technologies; active economic management and planning even in free market economies; the worldwide spread of "Fordist" production and management techniques; and the development of a transnational system of manufacture that allowed third world countries to supply cheap products to the advanced economies.[9]

Several of these features are notably relevant to the case of Japanese electrical goods. During the 1950s and 1960s, Japan experienced an explosive economic growth rate founded on cheap labor; the implementation of standardized mass production procedures; the strong impact of new technologies on the lives of people; and the rise of a mass consumer market. I have discussed the complex role of technology at some length in Chapter 4 (and I return to it later in this discussion). The economic and political influence of the United States—the effects of the Occupation-mandated political economy, the role of American anti-communism in promoting television in Japan, the American model of the consumer society, the transfer of technologies to Japan by American companies, and the direct procurement by American buyers of Japanese electrical components—has also been a constant theme throughout this study.

Hobsbawm's last two points are much more subject to dispute than the others. The model of Fordism as a description of mid-twentieth-century industrialism has been seriously disputed in recent years; scholars have argued that standardized mass production never attained the hegemonic systemic status the model implies (many successful American firms, for example, remained committed to "flexible" production methods even in the Fordist heyday).[10] Nevertheless, Fordism remains a powerful model to which a large number of scholars still adhere.[11]

While I have no wish to endorse Fordism as a hegemonic model, the Japanese electrical goods industry strikingly fits its broad outlines. Definitions of this Fordist system vary, but common features include the implementation of standardized mass production systems, the employment of large amounts of fixed capital, a commitment to increasing economies of scale, the growth of homogeneous markets for standardized products, a concern for scientific rationality, and a stable and conservative political power structure. According to this analysis, the high-technology marvels of transistorization, communications, and computers were less responsible for the industrial boom of the 1950s than was the implementation of scientific management and mass production methods—which were largely developed during the first two decades of the twentieth century. Although it may seem surprising that the world should have benefited in the 1950s from the innovations of thirty years earlier, Paul Krugman has articulated a wide consensus in his comment that "a new technology, no matter how marvelous, may have only superficial effects for decades, then flower as it finally reaches critical mass."[12]

A more difficult question is whether the technologies of mass demand creation also belong to this paradigm. Hobsbawm, among others, includes the need to foster demand as a key feature (and central problem) of the postwar political economy. He argues that "human beings were essential to such an economy only in one respect: as buyers of goods and services." More radical critiques refer to the near-coercive nature of demand creation as corporations pushed "to sustain sufficient buoyancy of demand in consumer markets to keep capitalist production possible." In this view, Fordism was "less a mere system of mass production and more a total way of life."[13]

Whether or not we include models of consumer culture under the general rubric of Fordism, the case of Japanese electrical goods also of-

fers intriguing resonances with widely used models of the consumer society. A full discussion of the many conflicts and debates within the vast
field of consumer and cultural studies is beyond the scope of this book.
But in very general terms, it is possible to portray a pair of contrasting
traditions in the analysis of consumer culture. Purely for the purpose of
a few general descriptive remarks, I will label these the "critical" and
the "liberal" traditions.

The critical tradition has its origins in the critiques of Marx and focuses on capitalism's constant need for new markets to absorb its ever-
expanding productive capacities. As developed in the twentieth century
by scholars such as Horkheimer and Adorno, Lukács, Marcuse, and
Lefebvre, this theory has focused on the absorption into the capitalist
framework of all social activities, including leisure and culture itself
(the "culture industry"). The mass media play a central role in this
process, producing a homogeneous mass culture in a one-way flow of
information.[14] A related school has added to this analysis by focusing
on the media's use of ideological symbols that lead people into accepting the existing social framework even though they are its victims. Mass
culture and mass consumption, in other words, work to hide inequalities of wealth and power.[15]

The liberal tradition, by contrast, is much more straightforward.
Based on classical economic theory, this school holds that consumers are
rational in their decisions—that they consume because they want to consume and that their purchase decisions (however irrational they may
seem to judgmental critics) are valid based on the only possible objective
standard: the opinions of the consumers themselves. "How forbidding
society would be," argues one apologist in this vein, "if one man's
aesthetic/moral preferences decided what goods his fellow consumers
might select. In open societies, human consumption choices share only
one characteristic—they are made in pursuit of happiness."[16] At its most
extreme, this school can appear to celebrate consumption for its own
sake.[17] But it is worth noting that even within the liberal tradition, a
number of economists have voiced serious doubts about the nature and
utility of twentieth-century consumption. Thorsten Veblen launched a
powerful, if idiosyncratic, attack on the invidious roots of consumer
choices, and John Kenneth Galbraith challenged the economic principle
that "more is better" in his influential 1957 work *The Affluent Society*.[18]

Both of these schools can cite ample case histories as evidence for
their outlook on consumption. In Japan, analysts of the liberal camp
often cite the ebullience of consumer electrical goods purchases to sup-

port their interpretation of a postwar history based on democracy and "the pursuit of happiness." The histories generated by companies within the industry uniformly support this view. But the concerns of the critical school have undeniable resonance in a study of electrical goods purchases in the 1950s. The Japanese electrical goods industry of the 1950s made an unprecedented effort to create consumer demand for products that were very expensive by the income standards of the time. Moreover, although corporate demand creation programs harped on the theme of "rationality," those corporations well understood that an irrational spontaneity, particularly on the part of children, served their real needs much better. Mass production and standardization of electrical goods resulted in a homogenization of purchases, as consumers were caught up in each successive wave of buying. Moreover, among the most popular uses of electrical goods was the transmission of mass entertainment, notably sports events, perhaps leading to the commodification and homogenization of leisure and culture. The television often took the place of traditional aesthetic symbols in the position of honor in the living room, and television viewing increasingly replaced traditional cultural pursuits such as local theater, cartoon plays, and traveling entertainments. Finally, the symbols embodied in the electrical goods industry ("rationalization," the "bright life") and broadcast by the products of that industry undoubtedly helped forge an ideological consensus during the 1950s—the consensus of the "middle mass" society, of the middle-class home with a durable-goods-owning housewife at its center. This ideological consensus arguably has served to hide real and widening inequalities in Japanese society, most notably in the ownership of and and the enjoyment of adequate housing.

In placing the Japanese electrical goods industry within the context of two highly contested models of late modernity, I have no wish to endorse these models as possessing any kind of universal validity. I share many of the serious doubts that critics have leveled against these models. At best, they seem to me overly generalizing. Nor do I mean to argue that the congruence of Japan's experience with those of the United States and Europe implies any sort of universality for these models or for any historical process. Indeed, the *differences* between Japan's experience and those of the West are more revealing about the nature of modernity as it has affected ordinary people in Japan, and it is to these differences that I now wish to turn.

First, the social consequences of consumerism were very different in Japan, a low-income country, than in the United States or even Western

Europe. In the United States, the major concern was the possible satiation of consumers who seemed already to have everything they needed. In Japan, by contrast, the 1950s remained a time of real shortage and want. The Japanese people's expenditure of large proportions of their incomes on durable goods created an imbalance in their lifestyles that has worried analysts and planners ever since. Japan was simultaneously a beneficiary of the golden age and its provisioner through the cheap labor of the Japanese people. Certainly, the phrase "golden age" would have sounded hollow to many Japanese during the 1950s.

Second, the consumer revolution in Japan was an unusually self-conscious event. Japanese marketing specialists, social critics, and popular journals feverishly studied developments in the United States, and this consciousness affected the course of the consumer revolution in Japan. Marketers imported the language of consumerism, including the language developed by critics of consumerism, in a conscious attempt to reproduce the phenomenon in Japan. I have referred to this self-referentiality at several points in this book. The conscious importation of foreign models relates to the well-established critical analysis of "late development" pioneered by Alexander Gerschenkron.[19] Gerschenkron points out that latecomers to industrial development are able—through study of foreign models, concentration of resources, and centralized planning—to absorb in a short space of time processes of development that took decades or centuries in the pioneering countries.

Such a process to some extent occurred in 1950s Japan, at least in the sphere of industrial policy. But the self-referentiality to which I have referred relates not only to the import of technologies and construction of factories but also to a conscious attempt to recreate in Japan complex cultural and social phenomena such as consumerism and the construction of a family-oriented middle class. Moreover, late development theory assumes that development itself is desirable. But in the case of 1950s Japan, the models that were being imported were contested. Although a consensus emerged in Japan during the 1950s in favor of economic growth, few would have advanced arguments in favor of conspicuous consumption or waste. Yet managers importing marketing technologies were aware that these were precisely the consequences American critics were harping against. The keys to prosperity as perceived by business leaders of the early 1950s were the keys to their own individual, or corporate, prosperity. And unlike Adam Smith's "invisible hand," these keys did not inevitably "[carry] the society to wealth and prosperity."[20] Rather, the consequences of technological advance were determined by a complex interaction of self-interested business activity and the social change produced by that activity. It is hardly surprising that the results were less than optimal by any objective measure of equity in welfare.

The question of late development raises another issue rooted in the difference between the experience of Japan and those of other industrial economies. The Japanese electrical goods industry enjoyed phenomenal success, becoming a global leader from the 1970s on. If the model of development was clear for Japanese business leaders, then it was equally clear for leaders from other countries. Indeed, Europeans were studying the secrets of American prosperity during the 1950s as assiduously as the Japanese. Why, then, did Japan acquire such a dominant role in the global electrical goods market when other low-wage countries were unable to match this achievement?

The answer must lie in conditions unique to Japan. As I made clear in Chapter 6, cheap labor gave Japan a decisive competitive advantage, *all other things being equal.* However, Japanese companies had to master product technology, production systems, quality control, marketing, and distribution before they could begin to benefit from this inherent advantage. In this context, Japan's long experience with electrical technologies (Chapter 1) was indeed a key prerequisite. Odagiri and Goto have argued that "technological capabilities cannot be developed simply by investing in technology importation and in education and training. There has to be a certain background facilitating the absorption of imported technology, and there has to be a willingness on the part of the industry to make necessary investments and innovate."[21] Concurring with this analysis, Richard Nelson suggests that there were five prerequisites for the success of Japanese industry in emulating and eventually, in places, surpassing Western technologies. They were:

1. A well-educated and technologically sophisticated population.
2. Subsequent high investments in human capital, matching those of the West.
3. Openness and creativity in searching out and learning to use modern technologies.
4. Entrepreneurialism, risk-taking, and intra-industry competition.
5. A strong supporting role by the government.[22]

My own analysis of the prewar and wartime development of the Japanese electrical goods industry supports this framework, with some exceptions. Clearly, the educational level of Japan's electrical elite was crucial, and the government took remarkably prompt steps to establish educational facilities. And although Japanese companies and research institutions showed few signs in the prewar era of the kind of creative adaptation for which they became renowned in the 1970s and later, they still introduced the latest foreign technologies with great speed, earning praise for being "consistently first in being second."[23] I am, however, rather less impressed by the level of competition and government support, at least before the war. As I argued in Chapter 1, the government's narrow focus on national defense purposes severely hindered Japanese companies in the race to keep up with electronics technologies, especially vacuum tubes.

The manufacture of transistor radios, Japan's first electrical goods export success story, required a rather low level of technological capability. Many of the basic components could be bought off the shelf, so Japanese companies only had to assemble the radios. The smaller makers did so using very cheap contract labor, the assembly often taking place in working-class homes. This achievement could, I believe, have been emulated by other low-wage countries (as indeed it subsequently has been by South Korea, Singapore, Taiwan, Malaysia, and China, among others). But Japanese companies—no doubt in the entrepreneurial and competitive spirit mentioned by Nelson—moved very rapidly to consolidate their hold on this new market, which appeared particularly suited to the country's mixture of technological and labor resources.

It is harder to explain how Japanese companies were able to maintain—and even, according to some analyses, increase—their competitiveness as labor costs rose steeply during the 1960s and 1970s.[24] Even as Japanese companies deluged the United States and Europe with inexpensive (but generally good-quality) products based on cheap labor, they were also expending vast resources to keep up with the latest technological developments and, at times, to initiate those developments. Industry executives repeatedly emphasize that the United States largely ignored the consumer electronics market, which was highly competitive and often unprofitable, to focus on military hardware. Japanese companies, which had no domestic military market to fall back on, put their best people into the development of consumer applications, which may have given Japan a measure of leadership in product technologies by the turn of the 1970s. Indeed, as early as 1962 Sony came out with the world's first fully transistorized television.[25] In addition, Christopher

Freeman has argued that Japanese companies were particularly adept at using and improving on the techniques of mass production they had imported during the 1950s.[26]

Finally, I return to the issue of technology and its role in the economic and social changes that took place during the 1950s. In Chapter 4, I employed a Schumpeterian model to illustrate the effects on overall economic growth of Japan's rapid introduction of product and management technologies. But, as I pointed out in that discussion, Schumpeter (and many other economists of technology) focus mainly on the economic effects of technology and innovation and not on the uses to which those technologies might have been put. In terms of understanding the role of technology in twentieth-century Japan, those uses are as important as the economic ripple effects measured in Schumpeter's model. And, as I pointed out in Chapter 4, in the case of electrical goods the effects of new technologies on everyday life were not necessarily all to the good.

Technology plays a vital role in the structures of late modernity. For example, it is accorded a central role in the critical analysis of consumer culture: the technologies of demand creation and the technology-derived manipulation of desire are seen in this tradition as key tools of control in late modern society. "Modern technology is the necessary and sufficient cause of mass culture," according to Bernard Rosenberg.[27] The technologies of mass communications, in particular, have been singled out as setting the late twentieth century apart from previous eras.[28]

Technology may therefore be seen as an enabler—or even a weapon—in the process of modernization. But technology was by no means unilaterally imposed on Japan (for better or worse) in some deterministic sense. It was as dependent on the processes of growth and social change, and on their economic and political contexts, as those processes were on technology. Television would have come to Japan in a quite different form—if it came at all during the 1950s—had it not been for the machinations of an ambitious entrepreneur building on American anti-communist sentiment. Mass purchases of labor-saving goods such as washing machines were (or were perceived as) dependent on sufficient change in traditional family structures to make the labor of women worth saving. And companies would not have been able to achieve labor-saving mass production without the emergence of mass demand. Again and again, this study has pointed to the complexity, and at times the paradoxes, of historical processes that ultimately produced a nation of television owners and an industry of undreamed-of prosperity.

If technological development and social change were locked in a mutually dependent relationship, that relationship was itself mediated by the activities of corporations. It may well be that, as Mokyr argues, technology-induced social change is not dependent on the capitalist system.[29] But in 1950s Japan, capitalism worked very effectively in mediating the dynamic relationship between technology and social change. Driven by their visions of corporate and personal prosperity, Japanese business leaders poured immense effort and resources into importing and developing technologies, creating markets, and promoting the social structures they saw as necessary to absorb their products. Those business leaders were equally dependent on the availability of new technologies, and on the effects of those technologies on society, for the success of their endeavors. The relationships among business, technology, and social change were dynamic, mutually dependent, and as complex as the labyrinthine workings of history itself.

An alchemy was at work in Japan in the 1950s and 1960s. From the raw materials of technology and business activity emerged a social revolution centered on mass consumption and the ownership of durable household goods. For Matsushita, Sony, and other electrical goods companies, this alchemy literally turned base elements into gold. The new media; the technologies of products, production, and marketing; the promotion of a lifestyle oriented toward electrical goods; and Japan's traditional resource of cheap labor set them on the road to prosperity. The changes unleashed in ordinary people's lives during the space of two decades were a consequence and an integral part of the much-lauded "Japanese miracle." Whether, for ordinary people, this miracle was the work of a divine being or an evil sprite, continues to be debated.

Appendix: Tables

TABLE I

COMMUNICATIONS EQUIPMENT GROWTH RATES, 1923–42

Year	Production of Batteries and Telegraph, Telephone, and Radio Equipment (¥000)	Growth Rate (percent)
1924	20,387	
1925	22,574	10.73
1926	26,341	16.69
1927	33,150	25.85
1928	25,232	-23.89
1929	34,102	35.15
1930	34,696	1.74
1931	24,281	-30.02
1932	28,155	15.95
1933	45,167	60.42
1934	52,631	16.53
1935	64,129	21.85
1936	87,240	36.04
1937	123,269	41.30
1938	164,288	33.28
1939	264,131	60.77
1940	301,180	14.03
1941	354,456	17.69
1942	525,721	48.32

Average growth in production, 1925–1942 (percent)	20.34
Average growth, 1932–1942 (percent)	32.25
Household electrical goods average growth, 1955–1970 (percent)	31.13
Communications equipment average growth, 1955–1970 (percent)	25.17

SOURCE: Tsūshō Sangyō Shō, *Kikai tōkei nenpō* (various years).

NOTE: Figures are expressed in current (not constant) values.

TABLE 2

MARKET SHARES FOR JAPANESE BLACK-AND-WHITE
TELEVISION PRODUCERS, 1953–56 AND 1958

Rank	1953 (percentage market share)	1954 (percentage market share)	1955 (percentage market share)	1956 (percentage market share)	1958 (percentage market share)
1	Hayakawa (22.9)	Hayakawa (25.4)	Hayakawa (24.5)	Hayakawa (16.9)	Toshiba (18.2)
2	Matsushita (21.8)	Toshiba (17.5)	Matsushita (16.9)	Matsushita (15.7)	Matsushita (17.3)
3	Toshiba (16.2)	Matsushita (16.0)	Yao (14.9)	Yao (12.7)	Hayakawa (16.9)
4	Yao (9.6)	Yao (11.6)	Toshiba (9.7)	Toshiba (12.6)	Hitachi (10.6)
5	Columbia (7.4)	Columbia (10.2)	Columbia (7.3)	Mitsubishi (10.6)	Mitsubishi (9.9)
6	Nanao (4.1)	Nanao (5.8)	Nanao (6.9)	Sanyō (10.0)	Sanyō (9.3)
7	Kyōritsu (3.3)	Mitaka (4.3)	Sanyō (6.0)	Columbia (5.6)	Yao (8.0)
8	Nippon Denki (1.5)	Yamanaka (2.5)	Mitsubishi (4.2)	Nihon Victor (3.3)	Nihon Victor (4.5)
9	Ichiban Denki (1.2)	Mitsubishi (1.5)	Nihon Victor (2.1)	Nanao (3.0)	Columbia (4.4)
10	Mitaka (0.8)	Sankōsha (1.2)	Sankōsha (1.6)	Hitachi (2.3)	Osaka Onkyō (0.9)
	Other (11.2)	Other (4.0)	Other (5.9)	Other (7.3)	Other (0.0)
Total Production	13,367	31,370	137,031	N/A	1,270,585
Number of Makers	23	17	25	N/A	10

SOURCE: Hiramoto, *Nihon no Terebi Sangyō*, 55.

TABLE 3

FOREIGN EXCHANGE REMITTANCES FOR ELECTRICAL EQUIPMENT
TECHNOLOGY ACQUISITIONS, 1950–60

Year	Remittances (¥ million)	Total R&D (¥ million)
1950	36	N/A
1951	281	N/A
1952	642	N/A
1953	1,062	N/A
1954	1,278	N/A
1955	1,553	N/A
1956	2,344	N/A
1957	3,042	N/A
1958	4,840	N/A
1959	6,792	N/A
1960	8,541	N/A
Total, 1950–60	30,409	97,330
Total, all industries 1950–60	121,104	260,537

SOURCE: Tsūshō Sangyō Shō, *Gaikoku gijutsu dōnyū no genjō to mondaiten* (Tokyo: Tsūshō Sangyō Shō kigyōkyoku, 1962).

NOTE: Total R&D excludes the remittances in the previous column.

TABLE 4

RENEWAL OF PREWAR TIES

Japanese Company	Foreign Company	Year (and new investment, if any)	Percent Ownership as of 1953
Nippon Denki	Western Electric	1950	32.8
Mitsubishi Denki	Westinghouse	1951 (¥100 million)	4
Toshiba	General Electric	1950	17
Fuji Denki	Siemens	1952 (¥90 million)	15

SOURCE: Tsūshō Sangyō Shō, *Gaishi dōnyū* (Tokyo: Tsūshō Sangyō Shō, 1953).

TABLE 5

TRANSISTOR PATENT LICENSE AGREEMENTS
AND ROYALTIES, 1953–60

Receiving Company	Providing Company	Year	Royalty (percent)
Kōbe Kōgyō	RCA	1951 *	3
Fuji Denki	Siemens	1952 *	3
Hitachi	RCA	1952 *	3
Matsushita Denshi	Philips	1952 *	4.22
Mitsubishi Denki	Westinghouse	1952 *	3
Toshiba	RCA	1952 *	3
Sony	Western Electric	1953	2
Toshiba	Western Electric	1953	2
Hitachi	Western Electric	1954	2
Kōbe Kōgyō	Western Electric	1954	2
Mitsubishi Denki	Western Electric	1954	2
Nippon Denki	ITT	1955	0.3
Nihon Musen	Telefunken	1956 *	2
Sony	RCA	1957	1
Fuji Denki	Western Electric	1958	2
Fuji Denki	RCA	1958	1.5
Nippon Denki	RCA	1958	1.5
Nippon Denki	General Electric	1958	3
Sony	General Electric	1958	3
Mitsubishi Denki	RCA	1959	1.5
Nihon Musen	Western Electric	1959	2
Nihon Musen	RCA	1959	1.5
Oki Denki	Western Electric	1959	2
Oki Denki	RCA	1959	1.5
Sanyō Denki	Western Electric	1959	2
Sanyō Denki	RCA	1959	1.5
Origin Denki	Western Electric	1960	N/A
Shin Denkō Kōgyō	Western Electric	1960	N/A
Shin Denkō Kōgyō	RCA	1960	N/A
Tōhō Sanken Denki	Western Electric	1960	N/A

*indicates the original year of the contract. Transistors were added to the contract at a later date.
SOURCE: Nihon Ginkō Kawase Kanri Kyoku, *Gaishi dōnyū kankei jūyō ninka anken ichiran.* Royalty percentages from Tsūshō Sangyō Shō Denki Tsūshin Ka, *Nihon no toranjisuta rajio kōgyō.*

TABLE 6

OWNERSHIP OF BLACK-AND-WHITE TELEVISION SETS, 1953–63

Year	Number of Households (000)	Household Penetration (percent)
1953	18	0.1
1954	54	0.3
1955	166	0.9
1956	450	2.3
1957	1,017	5.1
1958	2,088	10.4
1959	4,795	23.6
1960	9,259	44.7
1961	13,547	62.5
1962	17,616	79.4
1963	19,835	88.7

SOURCE: Hiramoto Atsushi, *Nihon no terebi sangyō*. Number of households calculated from household statistics, *Nihon chōki tōkei sōran*, vol. 1.

TABLE 7

HOUSEHOLD PENETRATION OF WASHING MACHINES
AND REFRIGERATORS (URBAN HOUSEHOLDS), 1957–60

Year	Washing Machines (percentage of households)	Refrigerators (percentage of households)
1957	20.2	2.8
1958	29.3	5.5
1959	36.7	10.1
1960	45.4	15.7

SOURCE: Keizai Kikaku Chō, *Kokumin seikatsu hakusho* (various years).

TABLE 8

HOUSEHOLD SPENDING ON FURNITURE AND UTENSILS
(INCLUDING ELECTRICAL APPLIANCES) AND DEBT PAYMENTS
(AS A SHARE OF TOTAL HOUSEHOLD INCOME), 1953–60

Year	Furniture and Utensils (percent of total income)	Interest and Principal on Debt (percent of total income)	Combined Furniture and Debt Payments (percent of total income)
1953	1.82	5.14	6.96
1954	1.55	6.12	7.67
1955	1.68	6.44	8.12
1956	1.87	7.15	9.02
1957	2.18	7.35	9.53
1958	2.68	7.34	10.02
1959	3.31	7.67	10.98
1960	3.28	7.64	10.92

NOTE: Spending on furniture and utensils represents cash spending.

TABLE 9
TELEVISION OWNERSHIP AND INSTALLMENT LOAN PAYMENTS (MARCH 1960)

Total Expenditures	Number of Households	Percentage of All Households	Television Penetration (000s)	Television Penetration (percentage of households)	Households Without Television (000s)	Monthly Installment Payments	Payments as Percentage of All Expenses
Over ¥55,000	256,000	1.4	212,000	82.7	44,000	Over ¥5,000	Under 9.1
¥46,000-¥55,000	275,000	1.5	207,000	75.3	68,000	¥4,600	8.3-10.0
¥36,000-¥45,000	823,000	4.5	558,000	67.8	265,000	¥3,400	7.6-10.0
¥26,000-¥35,000	2,950,000	15.8	1,537,000	52.1	1,413,000	¥2,750	7.9-11.0
¥16,000-¥25,000	6,950,000	37.3	2,030,000	29.2	4,920,000	¥2,050	8.0-14.0
¥11,000-¥15,000	4,820,000	25.8	593,000	12.3	4,227,000	¥1,210	8.0-11.0
Under ¥10,000	1,920,000	10.3	91,000	4.5	1,829,000	N/A	N/A
Unknown	618,000	3.4	220,000	35.6	398,000	N/A	N/A
Total	18,612,000	100.0	5,448,000	29.1	13,164,000	N/A	N/A

SOURCE: Matsushita Denki internal report.

TABLE 10

MAGAZINE CIRCULATION, 1956–60

	1956	1957	1958	1959	1960
Number of magazine titles	6,866	8,270	9,816	13,007	14,049
Women's magazines	17	30	42	43	43
Total magazine circulation (millions)	489	543	622	779	986
Weekly magazine circulation (millions)	110	110	270	320	520
Total magazine sales (¥ billions)	52.9	62.1	72.6	87.1	110.2
Magazine advertising revenues (¥ billions)	4.0	5.0	5.5	8.0	10.0

SOURCES: Serif Tōkei Kyoku, *Nihon Tōkei Sōran* (Tokyo: Nihon Tōkei Kyōkai), various years; Matsumoto Shō, ed., *Shuppan Nenkan 1960* (Tokyo: Shuppan Nyuusu Sha, 1960).

TABLE 11

OWNERSHIP OF GOODS, 1959

Item	Danchi Residents (percentage of households)	Tokyo (percentage of households)
Sewing machine	79.2	71.4
Radio	90.5	84.8
Transistor radio	22.5	22.0
Washing machine	76.0	49.2
Rice cooker	56.0	25.1
Refrigerator	20.5	13.7
Electric/gas heater	63.2	37.1
Electric fan	22.2	35.7
Television	61.1	60.6
Camera	69.6	59.2
8mm movie camera	3.6	3.8
Piano	1.6	3.1

SOURCE: Keizai Kikaku Chō, *Kokumin seikatsu hakusho, Shōwa 35*.

TABLE 12

ALLOCATION OF EXPENDITURES (AS A PERCENTAGE OF TOTAL EXPENDITURES)

Year	Food	Housing	Furniture and Utensils	Clothes	Other	Taxes	Savings/Insurance	Debt Payments
1953	39.69	2.64	1.82	10.86	22.33	6.62	6.43	5.14
1954	38.45	2.73	1.55	9.42	22.96	7.29	7.28	6.12
1955	36.46	2.74	1.68	9.02	23.43	7.57	8.92	6.44
1956	33.90	3.24	1.87	9.18	23.27	7.37	10.17	7.15
1957	33.61	3.19	2.18	9.15	23.64	5.97	10.97	7.35
1958	33.16	3.56	2.68	8.74	23.82	5.53	11.41	7.34
1959	31.73	3.42	3.31	8.74	23.99	5.03	12.51	7.67
1960	30.76	3.32	3.28	8.88	23.98	5.38	12.99	7.64

SOURCE: Sōmu Chō Tōkei Kyoku, *Nihon chōki tōkei sōran*, vol. 3.

TABLE 13
AVERAGE MONTHLY EXPENDITURES BY INCOME QUINTILE, 1960

	Top Income Quintile	Bottom Income Quintile
Total expenditures	¥87,208	¥21,763
Furniture Expenses (percentage of total)	¥2,856 (3.27)	¥591 (2.72)
Loan Repayment Expenses (percentage of total)	¥5,351 (6.14)	¥1,608 (7.39)
Combined Furniture and Loan (percentage of total)	¥8,207 (9.41)	¥2,199 (10.11)
Savings (percentage of total)	¥18,072 (20.72)	¥1,668 (7.66)

SOURCE: Keizai Kikaku Chō, *Kokumin Seikatsu Hakusho, Shōwa 36* (Tokyo: Keizai Kikaku Chō, 1961), 204–208.

TABLE 14
MONTHLY INCOME AND EXPENDITURES BY INCOME QUINTILE, 1960

	Top Income Quintile	Bottom Income Quintile
Total Earned Income	¥79,540	¥15,795
Total expenditures excluding savings	¥69,136	¥20,095
Net savings and insurance (percentage of income)	¥10,587 (13.3)	−¥130 (−.01)

SOURCE: Keizai Kikaku Chō, *Kokumin Seikatsu Hakusho, Shōwa 36* (Tokyo: Keizai Kikaku Chō, 1961), 204–208.

TABLE 15
EXPORTS, 1956–60 (ALL FIGURES IN ¥ MILLIONS)

Year	Total Exports	Total Machinery	Total Ships	Total Radios	Transistor Radios	Televisions
1956	900,229	174,095	93,590	1,708	N/A	22
1957	1,028,887	226,644	126,613	3,912	N/A	96
1958	1,035,562	225,849	120,517	12,194	N/A	312
1959	1,224,337	291,403	128,783	37,562	33,681	762
1960	1,459,633	334,174	103,726	49,945	42,652	1,046

SOURCES: Ōkurashō Shuzei Kyoku Zeikanbu, *Nihon gaikoku bōeki nenpyō* (various years); Nihon Ginkō Tōkei Kyoku, *Honpō keizai tōkei* (various years).

NOTE: Both ships and radios are grouped as "machinery."

Notes

INTRODUCTION

1. *Time*, February 23, 1962: 55.

CHAPTER 1

1. See, for example, Hiroyuki Odagiri and Akira Goto, *Technology and Industrial Development in Japan* (Oxford: Clarendon Press, 1996).

2. Francis L. Hawks, *Narrative of the Expedition of an American Squadron to the China Seas and Japan* (1856; London: Macdonald, 1954).

3. Michael Adas, *Machines as the Measure of Men: Science, Technology, and Ideologies of Western Dominance* (Ithaca: Cornell University Press, 1989).

4. H. D. Harootunian, *Toward Restoration: The Growth of Political Consciousness in Tokugawa Japan* (Berkeley: University of California Press, 1970). Quotations are from 171, 146, and 163, respectively. The final quotation is Harootunian, not Sakuma.

5. Teishin Shō, *Teishin jigyō shi*, Vol. 3 (Tokyo: Teishin Shō, 1940), 54–64.

6. Nihon Kagaku Shi Gakkai, *Nihon kagaku gijutsu shi taikei*, Vol. 19 (Tokyo: Dai Ichi Hōki Shuppan, 1969), 64.

7. Kudō Akira, *Nichidoku kigyō kankeishi* (Tokyo: Yūhikaku, 1992), 171.

8. Teishin Shō, 60.

9. Tokyo Shibaura Denki KK, *Tōshiba hyaku-nen shi* (Tokyo: Tokyo Shibaura Denki KK, 1977), 1–2.

10. Nihon Kagaku Shi Gakkai, Vol. 8, 341.

11. Nihon Kagaku Shi Gakkai, Vol. 19, 242.

12. Shirane Uyayoshi and Wakui Kōtarō, *Nihon no gijutsu 100-nen*, Vol. 5 (Tokyo: Chikuma Shobō, 1987), 43 (photo).

13. Basil Hall Chamberlain, *Things Japanese* (London: J. Murray, 1898), 1.

14. Richard J. Samuels, *Rich Nation, Strong Army: National Security and the Technological Transformation of Japan* (Ithaca: Cornell University Press, 1994).

15. See for example Odagiri and Goto, 7

16. Nihon Kagaku Shi Gakkai, Vol. 19, 183.

17. Sōmu Chō Tōkei Kyoku, *Nihon chōki tōkei sōran* (Tokyo: Nihon Tōkei Kyōkai, 1988), Vol. 2, 452; Vol. 1, 168.

18. David Harvey, *The Condition of Postmodernity: An Enquiry into the Origins of Cultural Change* (Oxford: Basil Blackwell, 1989), 122.

19. Quoted in Stuart Ewen, *Captains of Consciousness: Advertising and the Social Roots of the Consumer Culture* (New York: McGraw Hill, 1976), 53.

20. Ibid., 54.

21. Yokomitsu Riichi, quoted in Maruyama Masao, "Patterns of Individuation and the Case of Japan: A Conceptual Scheme," in Marius B. Jansen, ed., *Changing Japanese Attitudes Towards Modernization* (Princeton: Princeton University Press, 1965), 517.

22. Translated as Tanizaki Junichirō, *Naomi*, trans. Anthony H. Chambers (New York: Knopf, 1985).

23. Minami Hiroshi, *Taishō Bunka* (Keisō Shobō: Tokyo, 1965). Quoted in Jordan Sand, "House and Home in Modern Japan, 1880s–1920s" (dissertation: Columbia University, 1996), 4.

24. Sand, 41–45.

25. Maruyama, 518.

26. Sand, 90.

27. Ibid., 262–63.

28. Sheldon Garon, *Molding Japanese Minds: The State in Everyday Life* (Princeton: Princeton University Press, 1997) 133.

29. Ibid., 129. The final three quotations are from the Ministry of Education. The others are from Garon.

30. Rowland Gould, *The Matsushita Phenomenon* (Tokyo: Dayamondo Sha, 1970), 145.

31. Ibid., 146.

32. Matsushita Kōnosuke, "Watakushi no Rirekisho," in Nihon Keizai Shinbunsha, ed., *Watakushi no Rirekisho: Shōwa no Keieisha Gunzō* (Tokyo: Nihon Keizai Shinbunsha, 1992), 19.

33. Gould, 151. For more information on the life of Matsushita Kōnosuke, see John P. Kotter, *Matsushita Leadership* (New York: Free Press, 1997), and Matsushita Kōnosuke, *Quest for Prosperity: The Life of a Japanese Industrialist* (Tokyo: PHP Institute, 1987).

34. Samuels.

35. Nihon Hōsō Kyōkai, *Nihon hōsō shi*, Vol. 2. (Tokyo: Nihon Hōsō Kyōkai, 1965), 21.

36. Nihon Hōsō Kyōkai, *Nihon hōsō shi*, Vol. 1, 106. The Amishima quote is from *Denpa shinbun*, June 25, 1950, 2.

37. Gregory J. Kasza, *The State and Mass Media in Japan, 1918–1945* (Berkeley: University of California Press, 1988), 87.

38. Ibid., 73. The remark on bubonic plague was made by the first director-general of the BBC, as quoted in ibid., 82n.

39. Nihon Hōsō Kyōkai, *Nihon hōsō shi,* Vol. 1, 256.

40. Curt Riess, *Joseph Goebbels* (Garden City: Doubleday, 1948), 101; David Welch, *The Third Reich: Politics and Propaganda* (London: Routledge, 1993), 30, 148.

41. Inose Naoki, *Yokubō no media* (Tokyo: Shōgakkan, 1990), 17.

42. Quoted in Ewen, 83–84.

43. Ibid., 84.

44. Welch, 33. The quote is from the chief of Germany's national radio broadcasting company.

45. Inose, 98.

46. Nihon Hōsō Kyōkai, *Nihon hōsō shi,* Vol. 1, 476. The quote is of a senior Communications Ministry bureaucrat.

47. Ibid., 478.

48. Inose, 84.

49. Takayanagi Kenjirō, *Terebi kotohajime* (Tokyo: Yūhikaku, 1986), 57.

50. Shizuoka Daigaku Terebijon Gijutsushi Henshū Iinkai, *Shizuoka daigaku terebijon gijutsu shi* (Hamamatsu: Hamamatsu Denshi Kōgaku Shōrei Kai, 1987), 20–21.

51. Samuels, 41–42.

52. Nihon Kagaku Shi Gakkai, Vol. 19, 361.

53. Hasegawa Shin, "Gijutsu dōnyū to terebi kaihatsu," in Hashimoto Jurō, ed., *Nihon kigyō shisutemu no sengo shi* (Tokyo: Tokyo daigaku shuppankai, 1996), 171.

54. *Tōshiba hyaku-nen shi,* 47.

55. Takayanagi, 99.

56. Nakagawa Yasuzō, *Dokyumento Kaigun Gijutsu Kenkyūjo—erekutoronikusu shukoku no senshinsha tachi* (Tokyo: Nihon Keizai Shinbun Sha, 1987), 66.

57. Ibid., 86.

58. Ibid., 111.

59. Ibid., 128.

60. Ibid., 182.

61. Takayanagi, 148.

62. Charles Yuji Horioka, "Consuming and Saving," in Andrew Gordon, ed., *Postwar Japan as History* (Berkeley: University of California Press, 1993), 281.

63. See John W. Dower, "The Useful War," in Carol Gluck and Stephen R. Graubard, eds., *Showa: The Japan of Hirohito* (New York: Norton, 1992), 49–71. Also Earl Kinmonth, "The Impact of Military Procurements on the Old Middle Classes in Japan, 1931–1941," *Japan Forum* 4:2 (October 1992), 349–68.

64. Yoshiko Miyake, "Doubling Expectations: Motherhood and Women's Factory Work Under State Management in Japan in the 1930s and 1940s," in

Gail Lee Bernstein, ed., *Recreating Japanese Women, 1600–1945* (Berkeley: University of California Press, 1991), 278.

CHAPTER 2

1. Mark Gayn, *Japan Diary* (New York: William Sloane Associates, 1948), 46.
2. Ibid., 47.
3. W. G. Beasley, *The Rise of Modern Japan* (New York: St. Martin's Press, 1990), 213.
4. Kōdansha, ed., *Shōwa Nimannichi no Zenkiroku* (Tokyo: Kōdansha, 1989), Vol. 7, 159.
5. Ibid., Vol. 8, 32.
6. "Ie wo mitsukaru made," *Asahi shinbun*, February 17, 1948.
7. Kōdansha, ed., Vol. 7, 161.
8. Kōdansha, ed., Vol. 8, 114.
9. Nakamura Takafusa, *The Postwar Japanese Economy: Its Development and Structure* (Tokyo: Tokyo University Press, 1981), 21.
10. For duraluminum clogs, see Kōdansha, ed., Vol. 7, 265. For reminiscences on squid shoes and seaweed hats, I am indebted to Sakagami Hiroshi, president, Keio University Press.
11. Gayn, 47.
12. Kōdansha, ed., Vol. 8, 70–71.
13. Ibid., Vol. 7, 148, 154.
14. Ibid., Vol. 7, 154.
15. For example, Civil Communications Section Records, CCS 01179, unsigned memo to record, discusses the problem and reports on investigations, but apparently no concrete actions were taken.
16. Kōdansha, ed., Vol. 7, 155.
17. Ibid., Vol. 8, 312–13.
18. Ibid., Vol. 8, 136–37.
19. Aoyama Yoshiyuki, *Kaden* (Tokyo: Nihon Keizai Hyōron Sha, 1991), 50.
20. See, for example, Bruce Cummings, "Japan's Position in the World System," in Andrew Gordon, ed., *Postwar Japan as History* (Berkeley: University of California Press, 1993), 34–63.
21. Ibid., 39–41.
22. On Occupation policy toward cinema, see Kyoko Hirano, *Mr. Smith Goes to Tokyo: Japanese Cinema under the American Occupation, 1945–1952* (Washington: Smithsonian Institution, 1992).
23. Kōdansha, ed., Vol. 8, 131. For folk dancing, see Dorothy Robins-Mowry, *The Hidden Sun* (Boulder: Westview Press, 1983), 104–5.
24. Hideo Yoshikawa and Joanne Kauffman, *Science Has No National Borders: Harry C. Kelly and the Reconstruction of Science in Japan* (Cambridge: MIT Press, 1994), 6.
25. Memo from H. W. Miller, CCS, dated April 16, 1947, CCS 01179.
26. Supreme Commander Allied Powers directive, AG 676.3, November 13, 1945.
27. Memo from Paul F. Hannan, December 14, 1945, CCS 01179.

28. Unsigned "memo for record" dated November 4, 1946. Economic and Scientific Section Records, ESS (A) 00126.

29. For the denial, see memo to Dutch chargé d'affaires dated January 24, 1947 (CCS 01179). Superheterodyne set production increased from 120 a month in early 1946 to more than 25,000 a month by 1949 ("Vacuum Tubes," ESS [D] 12934).

30. See Michael A. Cusumano, *The Japanese Automobile Industry: Technology and Management at Nissan and Toyota* (Cambridge: Harvard University Press, 1985), 321–32; Ishikawa Kaoru, *Nihonteki hinshitsu kanri* (Nihon Kagaku Gijutsu Renmei, 1981); Chalmers Johnson, *MITI and the Japanese Miracle* (Stanford: Stanford University Press, 1982), 216–17; Mark Fruin, *The Japanese Enterprise System* (Oxford: Clarendon Press, 1994), 172–73; David Halberstam, *The Reckoning* (1986; New York: Avon, 1987), 312–20; Wada Toshihiro, "The Introduction of Quality Control in the Communications Equipment Industry, 1945–1955," *Japanese Yearbook on Business History* 12 (1995), 73–98.

31. William M. Tsutsui, "W. Edwards Deming and the Origins of Quality Control in Japan," *Journal of Japanese Studies* 22:2 (1996), 295–325.

32. Ishikawa Hiroyoshi, *Yokubō no sengoshi* (Tokyo: Kōsaidō Shuppan, 1989), 72.

33. Aida Yutaka, *Denshi rikkoku Nihon no jijoden* (Tokyo: NHK, 1993), Vol. 1, 103.

34. Nakagawa Yasuzō, *Nihon no handōtai kaihatsu* (Tokyo: Kōdansha, 1985), 30–31.

35. See Yoshikawa and Kauffman.

36. Nakagawa, *Handōtai*, 32.

37. *New York Times*, January 21, 1949, 4.

38. Nakamura, *Postwar Japanese Economy*, 39.

39. *Oriental Economist*, April 8, 1950.

40. Tsūshō Sangyō Shō, *Tsūshō sangyō shō nenpō* (Tokyo: Tsūshō Sangyō Shō, 1950), 149.

41. Ibid., 221.

42. See Richard J. Samuels, *Rich Nation, Strong Army: National Security and the Technological Transformation of Japan* (Ithaca: Cornell University Press, 1994).

43. Tsūshō Sangyō Shō Kōgyō Gijutsu Chō, *Gijutsu hakusho* (Tokyo: Kōgyō Shinbun Sha, 1949), 17.

44. Laura Hein, "Growth versus Success," in Gordon, ed., 109.

45. *Denpa shinbun*, February 5, 1951, 1.

46. Nihon Seisansei Honbu, *Seisansei undō 30-nen shi* (Tokyo: Nihon Seisansei Honbu, 1985), 111.

47. Katō Naofumi, ed., *Hanbai, kōkoku* (Tokyo: San'ichi Shobō, 1988), 202–4, Vol. 6 of *Nihon keiei shiryō taikei*.

48. Matsushita Kōnosuke, *Quest for Prosperity: The Life of a Japanese Industrialist* (Tokyo: PHP Institute, 1987), 255.

49. Ibid., 255.

50. Ibid., 251–53.

51. Ibid., 260.

52. *PHP*, May 1951, 28–31. The following quotations from Matsushita are from the same source.

53. Carol Gluck, *Japan's Modern Myths* (Princeton: Princeton University Press, 1985), 24.

54. Nihon Denshi Kikai Kōgyōkai, *Denshi kōgyō 30-nenshi* (Tokyo: Nihon Denshi Kikai Kōgyō Kai, 1978), 37.

55. Sony Corporation, *Genryū: Sony Challenge 1946–1968* (Tokyo: Sony Corporation, 1986), 18–19.

56. Ibid., 78. For the account of the "anarchist," see Akio Morita, *Made in Japan: Akio Morita and Sony* (New York: Dutton, 1986), 40.

57. Sony, 36–37.

58. Ibuka Masaru, "Watakushi no Rirekisho," in Nihon Keizai Shinbunsha, ed., *Watakushi no Rirekisho: Shōwa no Keieisha Gunzō* (Tokyo: Nihon Keizai Shinbunsha, 1992), Vol. 7, 181–227.

59. Sony, 76–77.

CHAPTER 3

1. *Oriental Economist*, April 1, 1950, 302.

2. *Nippon Times*, September 20, 1950.

3. *Oriental Economist*, May 20, 1950, 506.

4. Nagao Kazurō, *Shōriki Matsutarō no Shōwa shi* (Tokyo: Jitsuyō no Nihon sha, 1982), 304.

5. Inose Naoki, *Yokubō no media* (Tokyo: Shōgakkan, 1990), 174.

6. Janet E. Hunter, *Concise Dictionary of Modern Japanese History* (Berkeley: University of California Press, 1984), 150.

7. Nagao, 81.

8. Sano Shinichi, *Kyokaiden: Shōriki Matsutarō to Kagemushatachi no Isseiki* (Tokyo: Bungei Shunju, 1994), 106.

9. Nagao, 125–27.

10. For details on political scandals and the relationship with Gotō, see Sano, chapter 3.

11. Supreme Commander Allied Powers records, LS 17505–6.

12. Ibid.

13. Ibid.

14. *Oriental Economist*, July 16, 1950, 725.

15. Details of Mundt's speech are from United States Congress, *Congressional Record*, June 5, 1950, 8021–30.

16. Inose, 210–19.

17. Civil Communications Section records, CCS 02745, report by U.S. Reorientation Division, dated August 20, 1951.

18. Nihon Hōsō Kyōkai, *Nihon hōsō shi*, Vol. 2, 49.

19. Shibata Hidetoshi, *Sengo masu komi kayūki* (Tokyo: Chūō kōron sha, 1985), 150.

20. Inose, 228.

21. Shibata, 169.

22. Ibid., 167.

23. *Nippon Times*, September 15, 1951.

24. Mark Mason, *American Multinationals and Japan: The Political Economy of Japanese Capital Controls, 1899–1980* (Cambridge: Harvard University Press, 1993), 155.

25. Nihon Hōsō Kyōkai, Vol. 2, 141.

26. Tsūshō Sangyō Shō, *Gaishi dōnyū* (Tokyo: Tsūshō Sangyō Shō, 1953), 28.

27. *Nikkei Shinbun*, January 9, 1953.

28. CCS 02745, memo dated December 6, 1950, by Albert Feissner to record.

29. CCS 02745, memo from R. N. Kunz to General Back, dated July 26, 1950.

30. CCS 02745, letter from Amishima to CCS, undated.

31. CCS 02745, copy of letter from General MacArthur to Prime Minister Yoshida, undated.

32. Amishima Tsuyoshi, *Hatō. Denpa to tomo ni gojū nen* (Tokyo: Denki Tsūshin Shinkōkai, 1992), 373.

33. Nihon Hōsō Kyōkai, Vol. 2, 49.

34. Tsūshō Sangyō Shō, *Tsūshō sangyō shō nenpō* (Tokyo: Tsūshō sangyō shō, 1951), 215.

35. Matsushita Denki Sangyō internal archives.

36. Amishima, 376.

37. Amishima, 390.

38. Sano, 443.

39. Quoted without attribution in Inose, 247.

40. Quoted without attribution in ibid., 245.

41. Nihon Hōsō Kyōkai, Vol. 2, 53.

42. *Asahi shinbun*, December 21, 1951.

43. Matsushita Denki Sangyō internal archives.

44. Hashimoto Jurō, "Kikai denshi kōgyō no ikusei," in Tsūshō Sangyō Chōsa Kai, ed., *Tsūshō sangyō seisaku shi*, Vol. 6 (Tokyo: Tsūshō Sangyō Chōsa Kai, 1990), 591.

45. *Denpa shinbun*, January 3, 1953, 2.

46. Hiramoto Atsushi, *Nihon no terebi sangyō* (Tokyo: Mineruba Shobō, 1994), 39.

47. Statistics Department of the Bank of Japan, *Economic Statistics of Japan* (Tokyo: Bank of Japan, various years).

48. Hiramoto, 32.

49. Nihon Terebi Hōsōmō, *Taishū to tomo ni 25-nen* (Tokyo: Nihon Terebi Hōsōmō, 1978), end tables.

50. Sano, quote on dust cover.

51. Volker R. Berghahn, *The Americanization of West German Industry, 1945–1973* (Leamington Spa: Berg, 1986), 11.

CHAPTER 4

1. Joel Mokyr, *The Lever of Riches: Technological Creativity and Economic Progress* (New York: Oxford University Press, 1990), vii.

2. Edward F. Denison and William K. Chung, "Economic Growth and Its Sources," in Hugh Patrick and Henry Rosovsky, eds., *Asia's New Giant* (Washington: Brookings Institution, 1976), 94.

3. Hashimoto Jurō, "Kikai denshi kōgyō no ikusei," in Tsūshō Sangyō Chōsa Kai, ed., *Tsūshō sangyō seisaku shi,* Vol. 6 (Tokyo: Tsūshō Sangyō Chōsa Kai, 1990), 549–50.

4. N. Gregory Mankiw, *Macroeconomics,* 2nd ed. (New York: Worth, 1994), 115. See also Robert Solow, "Technical Change and the Aggregate Production Function," *Review of Economics and Statistics* 39 (1957), 312–20.

5. Cited in Victor Argy and Leslie Stein, *The Japanese Economy* (Basingstoke: MacMillan, 1997), 157.

6. See Aida Yutaka, *Denshi rikkoku Nihon no jijoden* (Tokyo: NHK, 1993), Vol. 1.

7. The relationship of Fuji Denki with Siemens is described in detail in Kudō Akira, *Nichidoku kigyō kankeishi* (Tokyo: Yūhikaku, 1992), chapter 6.

8. *Denpa shinbun,* August 5, 1950, 1. Italics added.

9. *Nikkei shinbun,* November 21, 1951; Tsūshō Sangyō Shō, *Gaishi dōnyū.*

10. RCA Annual Report, various years.

11. Unless otherwise stated, the following quotes are from Aida, Vol. 1, chapter 6. This is a precious source of oral reminiscence relating to Japan's transistor industry development. Because the quotes are in interview format (interspersed with questions), I have taken some liberties in rearranging the material to make it read smoothly. I hope I have not compromised accuracy in translation.

12. Nathan Rosenberg, *Perspectives on Technology* (Cambridge: Cambridge University Press, 1976), 151.

13. Ibid., 166.

14. Aida, Vol. 1, 290.

15. Merton Peck and Shūji Tamura, "Technology," in Patrick and Rosovsky, eds., 535–36.

16. Interview with Masujima Shō, Adviser, TDK Corporation, September 24, 1996; interview with Kanoi Nobuo, Statutory Auditor, Sony Corp., October 16, 1996.

17. *Fortune,* April 1953.

18. *Business Week,* February 28, 1953, 104.

19. William B. Harris, "RCA Organizes for Profit," *Fortune,* August 1957, 111.

20. *Business Week,* December 12, 1954.

21. William B. Harris, "The Electronic Business," *Fortune,* April 1957, 137.

22. Interview with Kataoka Katsutarō.

23. Interview with Kanoi Nobuo.

24. *Business Week,* October 6, 1956.

25. *Business Week,* August 28, 1954.

26. Aida, Vol. 2, 35.

27. Aida, Vol. 2, 37.

28. *Electronics,* September 1954.

29. James P. Womack, Daniel T. Jones, and Daniel Roos, *The Machine That Changed the World* (New York: Macmillan, 1990), 81.

30. Interview with Masujima Shō.

31. See Andrew Gordon, "Contests for the Workplace," in Andrew Gordon, ed., *Postwar Japan as History* (Berkeley: University of California Press, 1993), 373–94.

32. David Halberstam, *The Reckoning* (1986; New York: Avon, 1987), 318.

33. William M. Tsutsui, "W. Edwards Deming and the Origins of Quality Control in Japan," *Journal of Japanese Studies* 22:2 (1996), 295–325.

34. Sunaga Kinsaburō, "American Technical Assistance Programs and the Productivity Movement in Japan," *Japanese Yearbook on Business History* 12 (1995), 27.

35. Nihon Seisansei Honbu, 141. For European dissent, see Sasaki Satoshi, "The Emergence of the Productivity Improvement Movement in Postwar Japan and Japanese Productivity Missions Overseas," *Japanese Yearbook on Business History* 12 (1995), 45–46.

36. "The New American Economy," *Fortune*, January 1955.

37. Sasaki, 49. See also Nihon Seisansei Honbu.

38. Interview with Kataoka Katsutarō.

39. *Nippon Times*, August 10, 1955.

40. Nihon Seisansei Honbu, 202.

41. Katō Naofumi, ed., *Hanbai, kōkoku* (Tokyo: San'ichi Shobō, 1988), 202–4, Vol. 6 of *Nihon keiei shiryō taikei*.

42. Ibid., 207.

43. *Manejimento* 15:5 (May 1956), 61.

44. Gilbert Burck and Sanford Parker, "The Changing American Market," *Fortune*, August 1953, 98ff.

45. Yamamoto Taketoshi and Tsuganezawa Toshihiro, *Nihon no Kōkoku* (Tokyo: Nihon Keizai Shinbun Sha, 1986), 311. The work was published by Satō Shuppanbu as *Kōkoku no Shinrigaku*, posing not as a translation but as an original work.

46. Hamano Tsuyoshi and Kamioka Kazuki, *Maaketingu* (Tokyo: Maruzen, 1953), 1.

47. Hayashi Shūji, *Imeeji to kindai keiei*, 1960; *Maaketingu no keikaku*, 1959; *Nihon no kigyō to maaketingu*, 1959; *Ryūtsū kakumei*, 1962; *Kigyō to shijō kōzō*, 1961; *Kigyō to imeeji senryaku*, 1961. Tokyo University main library card catalogue.

48. Ample evidence of these activities is contained in the "PR Honbu" section of Matsushita's corporate archives.

49. Vance Packard, *The Hidden Persuaders* (1957; Harmondsworth, Penguin, 1981), 23.

50. Quoted in ibid., 147–48.

51. John Kenneth Galbraith, *The Affluent Society* (1956; Harmondsworth: Penguin Books Ltd., 1969), 149–50.

52. Vance Packard, *Rōhi wo tsukuridasu hitobito*, trans. Ishikawa Hiroyoshi (1960; Tokyo: Daiyamondo Sha, 1961), 375–76.

53. Ishikawa Hiroyoshi, *Yokubō no sengoshi* (Tokyo: Kōsaidō Shuppan, 1989), 89.

54. Joseph A. Schumpeter, *Business Cycles: A Theoretical, Historical and Statistical Analysis of the Capitalist Process*, abridged ed. (1939; Philadelphia: Porcupine Press, 1989), 61.

55. Ibid.

56. Ibid., 59.

57. Christopher Freeman, *Technology Policy and Economic Performance: Lessons from Japan* (London: Pinter, 1987), 60–80.

58. Joseph A. Schumpeter, *Capitalism, Socialism and Democracy* (New York: Harper, 1942), 84.

59. Peter Drucker, *Technology, Management and Society* (New York: Harper & Row, 1970), vii.

60. Schumpeter, *Business Cycles*, 47.

61. See Tessa Morris-Suzuki, *Beyond Computopia: Information, Automation and Democracy in Japan* (London: Kegan Paul, 1988).

CHAPTER 5

1. Ezra F. Vogel, *Japan's New Middle Class* (Berkeley: University of California Press, 1965), 71–72.

2. Citations of these "threes" are seldom the same. For example, even within a single volume, one contributor refers to the "three Ss" of the late 1950s—*senpūki, sentakki, suihanki* (electric fan, washing machine, and rice cooker)—while another refers to the "three treasures" of 1957—washing machine, vacuum cleaner, and refrigerator (Andrew Gordon, ed., *Postwar Japan as History* (Berkeley: University of California Press, 1993); the citations are from William Kelly and Carol Gluck, respectively). More traditionally, Yamada Shōgo refers to washer, television, and refrigerator as the *san shū no shinki* ("three sacred pieces of equipment"), apparently forgoing the benefits of alliteration. Actually, this lack of consistency is not surprising. The idea of grouping lifestyle attributes in threes appears to have originated some time before the television age, and to have proliferated much more than is generally acknowledged. Even within the short space of the 1950s, I have found a wide variety of threesomes that indicate the heterogeneity of desires, from the 1951 "3 Ps"—*parupu, pachinko, panpan* (pulp literature, slot machines, and prostitution)—to the 1956 "3 Bs"—*terebi, biniiru, bitamin* (television, plastic, vitamins)—and the truly ambitious "3 Cs" aspired to by a fashion model in 1959—"cash, Cadillac, and cultural home." (The "3 Ps" and the "3 Bs" are from Yamada Shōgo, *Kaden Konjaku Monogatari* [Tokyo: Sanseido, 1983]; the "3 Cs" are from *Shūkan josei jishin.*) What these portrayals have in common is the suggestion that consumer desires were spontaneous and that a new materialism was driving the social and economic developments of the era.

3. *Kurashi no techō* 24 (April 1954).

4. Hiramoto Atsushi, *Nihon no terebi sangyō* (Tokyo: Mineruba Shobō, 1994), 58.

5. *Kurashi no techō* 30 (July 1955).

6. *Kurashi no techō* 45 (February 1958). In a survey of 788 refrigerator owners, *Kurashi no techō* found that 70 percent of refrigerators bought within

the past three years had malfunctioned, as had more than 30 percent of refrigerators bought within the past year.

7. Carol Gluck, Lecture on the Intellectual History of Modern Japan, Columbia University, April 6, 1994. See also Gluck.

8. Gluck, 7, commenting on the analysis of Gramsci.

9. The first phrase is from Andrew Gordon, "Contests for the Workplace," in Gordon, ed., 385; the second is from Gordon, "Managing the Japanese Household: The New Life Movement in Postwar Japan," *Social Politics* (Summer 1997), 275.

10. Gordon, "Managing the Japanese Household." See also Sheldon Garon, *Molding Japanese Minds: The State in Everyday Life* (Princeton: Princeton University Press, 1997).

11. See William W. Kelly, "Finding a Place in Metropolitan Japan: Ideologies, Institutions, and Everyday Life," in Gordon, ed., 189–238, and Marilyn Ivy, "Formations of Mass Culture," in the same volume (239–258). Carol Gluck labels the "middle mass" a "hegemonic social mythology" as opposed to an ideology, though the distinction is not altogether clear to me.

12. "Ideology," Webster's Third New International Dictionary.

13. John B. Thompson, *Studies in the Theory of Ideology* (Cambridge: Polity Press, 1984), 83.

14. Gluck, Lecture on the Intellectual History of Modern Japan, Columbia University, April 13, 1994.

15. John B. Thompson, *Ideology and Modern Culture: Critical Social Theory in the Era of Mass Communication* (Cambridge: Polity Press, 1990), 59.

16. Jordan Sand, "House and Home in Modern Japan, 1880s–1920s" (Dissertation: Columbia University, 1996), 290n.

17. "Zadankai: Shin seikatsu undō no hansei to kadai," *Shakai Kyōkiku*, December 1958, 20–28. See also Kanagawa-ken Kyōiku Iinkai Jimukyoku, *Shin seikatsu undō no ayumi* (Yokohama: Kanagawa-ken Kyōiku Iinkai Jimukyoku, 1952).

18. Shin Seikatsu Undō Kyōkai, *Shin seikatsu undō yoron chōsa, dai isshū* (Tokyo: Shin Seikatsu Undō Kyōkai, 1956).

19. *Asahi shinbun*, January 3, 1955, 6.

20. *Asahi shinbun* (evening edition), August 22, 1955, 1.

21. Shin Seikatsu Undō Kyōkai, *Moriagaru shin seikatsu undō: shin seikatsu undō zenkoku kyōgikai kara* (Tokyo: Shin Seikatsu Undō Kyōkai, 1955).

22. "Zadankai: Shin seikatsu undō wa nani wo mezashi, dō susumetara yoi ka," *Shakai Kykōiku*, April 1955.

23. *Asahi shinbun*, September 2, 1955.

24. *Nippon Times*, editorial, September 6, 1955.

25. Onnatachi no Ima wo Tou Kai, *Jūgoshi nōto sengo hen,* Vol. 3 (Tokyo: Inpakuto Shuppankai, 1987), 34.

26. The quote is from William W. Kelly, "Rationalization and Nostalgia: Cultural Dynamics of New Middle-Class Japan," *American Ethnologist* (June 1986), 606.

27. See John Whitney Hall, "Changing Conceptions of the Modernization of Japan," in Marius B. Jansen, ed., *Changing Japanese Attitudes Towards Modernization* (Princeton: Princeton University Press, 1965), 7–41.

28. Edward Marshall, "The Woman of the Future [interview with Thomas A. Edison]," *Good Housekeeping*, October 1912, 436. I am indebted to Geoffrey Klingsporn for this reference.

29. Ruth Schwartz Cowan, *More Work for Mother: The Ironies of Household Technology from the Open Hearth to the Microwave* (New York: Basic Books, 1983).

30. Karen Hagemann, "Of 'Old' and 'New' Housewives: Everyday Housework and the Limits of Household Rationalization in the Urban Working-Class Milieu of the Weimar Republic," *International Review of Social History* 41 (1996), 308. The quotations are from a best-selling home economics handbook.

31. Keizai Kikaku Chō, *Kokumin seikatsu hakusho, Shōwa 35 nen* (Tokyo: Okurashō Insatsu Kyoku, 1961), 13–15.

32. Kohara Hiroshi, *Nihon maaketingu shi—gendai ryūtsū no shiteki kōzu* (Tokyo: Chūō Keizai Sha, 1994), 86.

33. I am indebted to Professor Kudo Akira for this observation.

34. *Kurashi no izumi* 27 (March 1960), 6–7.

35. *Nashonaru shoppu*, September 1955 (Matsushita Denki internal archives).

36. *Denki Shōhin* 1 (July 1955), 28.

37. Yamada, 74.

38. *Nashonaru shoppu*, April 1956.

39. Onnatachi no Ima wo Tou Kai, 33.

40. "Preparations for Electrical Prosperity Week," *Western Electric News* (October 1915), 25. I am indebted to Geoffrey Klingsporn for this reference.

41. J. E. Thomas, *Learning Democracy in Japan* (London: SAGE Publications, 1985).

42. Yamada, 89.

43. Onnatachi no Ima wo Tou Kai, 35.

44. Ishikawa Hiroyoshi, *Yokubō no sengoshi* (Tokuo: Kōsaidō Shuppan, 1989), 94–110.

45. Matsushita Denki internal archives.

46. Ibid.

47. Jacob Levich, ed., *The Motion Picture Guide 1996 Annual* (New York: Cine Books, 1996).

48. Onnatachi no Ima wo Tou Kai, Vol. 4, 47–49.

49. Kensetsu Jūtaku Kyoku, *Tochi oyobi Jūtaku Kakaku Chōsa Kekka Hōkokusho* (Tokyo: Kensetsu Jūtaku Kyoku, 1954).

50. Ozu Yasujirō, *Ohayō*, in Imai Kazuo, ed., *Ozu Yasujiro sakuhin shū* (1957; Tokyo: Tachikaze Shobō, 1984), Vol. 4, 185. Ozu's script is in Imai's book. I am very grateful to Scott O'Bryan for drawing my attention to this film.

51. Shimotani Masahiro, "The Formation of Distribution *Keiretsu*: The Case of Matsushita Electric," in *The Origins of Japanese Industrial Power*, ed. Etsuo Abe and Robert Fitzgerald (Ilford, Essex: F. Cass, 1995), 64–66; Son Il Sun, "Kōdō seichōki ni okeru kaden ryūtsū kōzō no henka," *Keizaigaku kenkyū* 35 (1992).

52. *Nashonaru shoppu*, September 1956.

53. *Nashonaru shoppu,* April 1956.
54. *Nashonaru shoppu,* April 1956.
55. Kohara, 74ff.
56. Yamada, 64.
57. Keizai Kikaku Chō, 13–15.
58. *Shūkan josei jishin,* January 30, 1959, 61–63.
59. Matsushita Denki Sangyō, internal archives.
60. *Shūkan josei jishin,* January 30, 1959, 61.
61. Matsushita Denki Sangyō, internal archives.
62. Ibid.
63. Salvador Giner, *Mass Society* (London: Martin Robertson, 1976), 168.
64. Joseph Bensman and Bernard Rosenberg, "Mass Media and Mass Culture," in P. Olson, ed., *America as a Mass Society* (London: Collier MacMillan), 166–84.
65. M. Horkheimer and T. Adorno, *Dialectic of Enlightenment,* trans. of 1944 (London: Allen Lane, 1973).
66. Fred Inglis, *Popular Culture and Political Power* (London: Harvester Wheatsheaf, 1988), 85–87.
67. Neil McKendrick et al., *The Birth of a Consumer Society: The Commercialization of Eighteenth-Century England* (London: Europa Publications, 1982); Roland Marchand, *Advertising the American Dream: Making Way for Modernity—1920–1940* (Berkeley: University of California Press, 1986); Michael Schudson, *Advertising, the Uneasy Persuasion: Its Dubious Impact on American Society* (London: Routledge, 1990 [1984]). See also Grant McCracken, *Culture and Consumption* (Bloomington: Indiana University Press, 1990); David Nasaw, *Going Out: The Rise and Fall of Public Amusements* (New York: Basic Books, 1983); and William Leach, *Land of Desire: Merchants, Power, and the Rise of a New American Culture* (New York: Pantheon Books, 1993).
68. Keizai Kikaku Chō, 145.
69. Sasaki Takeshi et al., eds., *Sengo shi dai jiten* (Tokyo: Sanseidō, 1991), 274.
70. Matsushita Keiichi, "Taishū tennōsei ron," *Chūō Kōron,* April 1959. See also "Terebi to 'kodoku na gunshū,'" *CBC Repōto,* June 1959.
71. *Shūkan josei jishin,* December 12, 1958, 81.
72. *Shūkan josei jishin,* February 20, 1959, 24.
73. Sandra Buckley, "Altered States," in Gordon, ed., 353. Buckley also provides the statistic cited on p. 349. Her references provide a useful bibliography to the debates on women in the work force.
74. *Asahi shinbun,* April 11, 1954.
75. *Fujin Kōron,* February 1955.
76. *Shūkan Asahi,* July 20, 1956.
77. Keizai Kikaku Chō, 137–45.
78. Ibid., 145.
79. See, for example, Aoyama Yoshiyuki, *Kaden* (Tokyo: Nihon Keizai Hyōron Sha, 1991), 98ff.
80. "Nōson to terebi," *Hōsō to senden: CBC repōto,* April 1958.
81. Yamada, 89–94.

82. "Nōson Hanbai Kaihatsu no Kentō to Jisshian," December 20, 1957. Matsushita Denki Sangyō internal archives.

83. Ibid.

84. *Nashonaru shoppu*, August 1956.

85. *Nikkei shinbun*, March 6, 1956, 11.

86. *Nashonaru shoppu*, August 1956.

87. *Nashonaru shoppu*, September 1957.

88. Matsushita Denki Sangyō, internal archives.

89. *Nashonaru shoppu*, September 1958.

90. Keizai Kikaku Chō, 123.

91. See, for example, Garon; Gordon, "Managing the Japanese Household."

92. For a representative analysis that includes a literature survey, see Charles Yuji Horioka, "Consuming and Saving," in Gordon, ed., 259–292.

93. *Asahi shinbun* (evening edition), August 26, 1955.

94. *Asahi shinbun*, December 22, 1956, 1.

95. Ishikawa, *Yokubō no sengoshi*, 86–88.

96. Sasaki et al, eds., 294.

97. Keizai Kikaku Chō, 20.

98. See Schudson.

99. See, for example, James Coleman, *The Asymmetrical Society* (Syracuse: Syracuse University Press, 1982) for a conservative critique; Galbraith for a liberal critique; Ewen for a left-wing critique; Cowan for a feminist critique. There are many, many more. Schudson analyzes the various strands of critical tradition (6–8, 250–255).

100. Schudson, xvi.

101. Gordon, "Managing the Japanese Household."

102. On the persistence of hegemonic social constructs in Japan, see ibid.

CHAPTER 6

1. See, for example, Hiramoto Atsushi, *Nihon no terebi sangyō* (Tokyo: Mineruba Shobō, 1994); Aida Yutaka, *Denshi rikkoku Nihon no jijoden* (Tokyo: NHK, 1993), Vol. 1.

2. Merton Peck and Shūji Tamura, "Technology," in Hugh Patrick and Henry Rosovsky, eds., *Asia's New Giant* (Washington: Brookings Institution, 1976), 583. For organizational learning, see Mark Fruin, *The Japanese Enterprise System* (Oxford: Clarendon Press, 1994); for quality management, see William M. Tsutsui, "W. Edwards Deming and the Origins of Quality Control in Japan," *Journal of Japanese Studies* 22:2 (1996); for flexible manufacturing, see David Friedman, *The Misunderstood Miracle* (Ithaca: Cornell University Press, 1988).

3. Japan's "national system of innovation" is the focus of Christopher Freeman, *Technology Policy and Economic Performance: Lessons from Japan* (London: Pinter, 1987), 61. The "capitalist develomental state" is a model proposed by Chalmers Johnson in *MITI and the Japanese Miracle* (Stanford: Stanford University Press, 1982).

4. Aida, Vol. 1, 314.

5. Ibid., 241.

6. Sony Corporation, *Genryū: Sony Challenges 1946–1968* (Tokyo: Sony Corporation, 1986), 99.

7. Akio Morita, *Made in Japan: Akio Morita and Sony* (New York: Dutton, 1986), 65.

8. For a discussion of the MITI decision, see Leonard Lynn, "MITI's Successes and Failures in Controlling Japan's Technology Imports," *Hitotsubashi Journal of Commerce* 29 (December 1994), 27–29.

9. Sony Corporation, 100–101.

10. Nathan Rosenberg, *Perspectives on Technology* (Cambridge: Cambridge University Press, 1976), 151.

11. Interview with Kanoi Nobuo, statutory auditor, Sony Corp., October 16, 1996.

12. Sony, 110–11; Morita.

13. Aida, Vol. 2, 8.

14. Tom Forester, *Silicon Samurai: How Japan Conquered the World's IT Industry* (Cambridge: Blackwell, 1993), 20.

15. Morita, 71.

16. *Electronics*, various issues, March 1954 to August 1956. The quotation is from the August 1956 issue. Information on Sony exports is from Sony, 120.

17. Aida, Vol. 1, 344.

18. Sony, 112.

19. Aida, Vol. 1, 320.

20. Sony, 144–45; Aida, Vol. 1, 336.

21. John E. Tilton, *International Diffusion of Technology: The Case of Semiconductors* (Washington: The Brookings Institution, 1971), 16–17.

22. Tsūshō Sangyō Shō Denki Tsūshinki Ka, *Nihon no toranjisuta rajio kōgyō* (Tokyo: Kōgyō Shuppan Sha, 1959).

23. Aida, Vol. 22, 29.

24. Sony, 142.

25. Aida, Vol. 2, 30.

26. Sony, 116–17.

27. Rōdō Daijin Kanbō Rōdō Tōkei Chōsabu, *Rōdō Tōkei Nenpō* (Tokyo: Rōdō Daijin Kanbō Rōdō Tōkei Chōsabu, 1961), 181–82.

28. Hosoi Wakizō, *Jokō Aishi* (1925; Tokyo: Iwanami Shoten, 1982), 146.

29. Sōmu Chō Tōkei Kyoku, *Nihon chōki tōkei sōran*, 5 vols. (Tokyo: Nihon Tōkei Kyōkai, 1988), Vol. 4, 332–33.

30. Hosoi, 349.

31. Yamamoto Shigemi, quoted in Mikiso Hane, *Peasants, Rebels and Outcastes: The Underside of Modern Japan* (New York: Pantheon, 1982), 283, note 33. The survey of prewar workers was carried out in the 1970s.

32. Barbara Molony, "Activism Among Women in the Taishō Cotton Textile Industry," in Gail Lee Bernstein, ed., *Recreating Japanese Women, 1600–1945* (Berkeley: University of California Press, 1991), 230.

33. *Nippon Times*, August 10, 1955.

34. Sōrifu Tōkei Kyoku, *Kokusai Tōkei Yōran* (Tokyo: Ōkurashō Insatsu Kyoku, 1962), 132, 169. Industrial wages in India, averaged for men and women, were the equivalent of ¥8,390 per month in 1959.

35. Hane, 190.

36. Rōdō Shō Fujin Shōnen Kyoku, *Denki Kikai Seizōgyō ni okeru Nenshō Rōdōsha no Rōdō Jittai Chōsa Kekka* (Tokyo: Rōdō Shō Fujin Shōnen Kyoku, 1963), chōsa tōkeihyō, 31.

37. Rōdō Shō, chōsa tōkeihyō, 22–23.

38. Ibid., 24.

39. Ibid., 40.

40. Hosoi, 180–81.

41. Rōdō Shō, chōsa tōkeihyō, 40.

42. Ibid., 30.

43. Ibid., 34–35.

44. Rōdō Shō, *Josei Rōdōsha no Jittai Chōsa* (Tokyo: Rōdō Shō, 1961).

45. Rōdō Shō Fujin Shōnen Kyoku, *Shōwa 43-nen Naishoku Kōchin Chōsa Kekka Gaiyō* (Fujin Kankei Chōsa Shiryō No. 48), 1968.

46. Tsūshō Sangyō Daijin Kanbō Chōsa Tōkeibu, *Kōgyō Tōkeihyō, Sangyō hen, Shōwa 35-nen* (Tokyo: Tsūshō Sangyō Daijin Kanbō Chōsa Tōkeibu, 1963), 332; Tsūshō Sangyō Shō Denki Tsūshinki Ka, 37; United States Department of Commerce, *Annual Survey of Manufactures, 1960* (Washington: US Government Printing Office, 1960), 42.

47. Tsūshō Sangyō Shō Denki Tsūshinki Ka, 56, 78–79.

48. Philip J. Curtis, *The Fall of the U.S. Consumer Electronics Industry: An American Trade Tragedy* (Westport: Quorum Books, 1994), 6.

49. Tsūshō Sangyō Shō Denki Tsūshinki Ka, 37, 45–46.

50. Ibid., 74–75.

51. Interview with Egawa Toshio, adviser, Konica Corporation, October 19, 1996.

52. Ibid.

53. Tsūshō Sangyō Shō Denki Tsūshinki Ka, 57.

54. Ibid., 16.

55. Eric Hobsbawm, *Age of Extremes: The Short Twentieth Century* (London: Michael Joseph, 1994), 275.

56. Giovanni Arrighi, *The Long Twentieth Century: Money, Power, and the Origins of Our Times* (London: Verso, 1994), 348.

57. Good examples are Itō Yasuko, *Sengo Nihon Joseishi* (Tokyo: Ōtsuki Shoten, 1974), and Kumazawa Makoto, *Portraits of the Japanese Workplace: Labor Movements, Workers, and Managers* (Boulder: Westview Press, 1996).

58. Itō, 119.

59. See, for example, Freeman, 97, and Terutomo Ozawa, *Japan's Technological Challenge to the West, 1950–1974* (Cambridge: MIT Press, 1974), Chapter 1.

CONCLUSION

1. Interview with Kataoka Katsutaro, chairman, Alps Electric, September 25, 1996.

2. Laura Hein, "Growth versus Success," in Andrew Gordon, ed., *Postwar Japan as History* (Berkeley: University of California Press, 1993), 100.

3. Tsūshō Sangyō Shō Denki Tsūshinki Ka, *Nihon no toranjisuta rajio kōgyō* (Tokyo: Kōgyō Shuppan Sha, 1959), 14.

4. See Chalmers Johnson, *MITI and the Japanese Miracle* (Stanford: Stanford University Press, 1982).

5. See, for example, Merton Peck and Shūji Tamura, "Technology," in Hugh Patrick and Henry Rosovsky, eds., *Asia's New Giant* (Washington: Brookings Institution, 1976); Terutomo Ozawa, *Japan's Technological Challenge to the West, 1950-1974* (Cambridge: MIT Press, 1974); and Christopher Freeman, *Technology Policy and Economic Performance: Lessons from Japan* (London: Pinter, 1987).

6. Peck and Tamura, 553.

7. Tsūshō Sangyō Shō, *Gaikoku gijutsu dōnyū no genjō to mondaiten* (Tokyo: Tsūshō Sangyō Shō Kigyō Kyoku, 1962), 1.

8. Peck and Tamura, 553.

9. See Eric Hobsbawm, *Age of Extremes: The Short Twentieth Century* (London: Michael Joseph, 1994).

10. See, for example, Philip Scranton, *Endless Novelty: Specialty Production and American Industrialization, 1865-1925* (Princeton: Princeton University Press, 1997).

11. See, for example, Hobsbawm; Giovanni Arrighi, *The Long Twentieth Century: Money, Power, and the Origins of Our Times* (London: Verso, 1994); Freeman; David Harvey, *The Condition of Postmodernity: An Enquiry into the Origins of Cultural Change* (Oxford: Basil Blackwell, 1989); and Miyoshi Masao and H. D. Harootunian, eds., *Postmodernism and Japan* (Durham: Duke University Press, 1989).

12. Paul Krugman, *Peddling Prosperity: Economic Sense and Nonsense in the Age of Diminished Expectations* (New York: Norton, 1994), 60. See also Drucker, 65.

13. Harvey, 61 and 134.

14. For summaries of this scholarly tradition, see Thompson; Don Slater, *Consumer Culture and Modernity* (Cambridge: Polity Press, 1997); and Mike Featherstone, *Consumer Culture and Postmodernism* (London: SAGE Publications, 1991). For critiques of this school, see Salvador Giner, *Mass Society* (London: Martin Robertson, 1976); Michael Schudson, *Advertising, the Uneasy Persuasion: Its Dubious Impact on American Society* (London: Routledge, 1990 [1984]); and G. Stauth and B. S. Turner, "Nostalgia, Postmodernism and the Critique of Mass Culture," in *Theory, Culture and Society* 5 (1988), 2-3.

15. See Antonio Gramsci, *Selections from the Prison Notebooks* (New York: International Publishers, 1971); and Jürgen Habermas, "Technology, Science and Ideology," in Habermas, ed., *Towards a Rational Society* (London: Heinemann, 1971). See also Thompson.

16. Stanley Lebergott, *Pursuing Happiness: American Consumers in the Twentieth Century* (Princeton: Princeton University Press, 1993), 11.

17. For accounts of this school, see Slater, as well as Ben Fine and Ellen Leopold, *The World of Consumption* (London: Routledge, 1993). For the celebratory analysis, see Lebergott.

18. See Thorstein Veblen, *The Theory of the Leisure Class* (New York: Mentor Books, 1953 [1899]); and John Kenneth Galbraith, *The Affluent Society* (1956; Harmondsworth: Penguin Books Ltd., 1969). For a more recent critical analysis in a similar vein see William Nordhaus and James Tobin, "Is Economic Growth Obsolete?" in Tobin, ed., *Essays in Economics: Theory and Policy* (New York: Basic Books, 1982), 360–439.

19. Alexander Gerschenkron, *Economic Backwardness in Historical Perspective* (Cambridge: Harvard University Press, 1962). For subsequent analyses in this vein, see Jansen, ed., and other works in the "modernization series"; and Alice H. Amsden, *Asia's Next Giant: South Korea and Late Industrialization* (New York: Oxford University Press, 1985).

20. Adam Smith, in *The Wealth of Nations* (Chicago: University of Chicago, 1976 [1776]), 49–50, wrote: "The natural effort of every individual to better his own condition, when suffered to exert itself in freedom and security, is so powerful a principle, that it is alone, and without any assistance, not only capable of carrying on the society to wealth and prosperity, but of surmounting a hundred impertinent obstructions with which the folly of human laws too often incumbers its operations."

21. Hiroyuki Odagiri and Akira Goto, *Technology and Industrial Development in Japan* (Oxford: Clarendon Press, 1996), 2.

22. Ibid., xi.

23. Peck and Tamura, 583.

24. Hiramoto Atsushi, *Nihon no terebi sangyō* (Tokyo: Mineruba Shobō, 1994), 205–6.

25. Sony Corporation, *Genryū: Sony Challenges 1946–1968* (Tokyo: Sony Corporation, 1986), 184–85.

26. Freeman, 40–52.

27. Cited in Giner, 160.

28. Thompson; see also Ruth Schwartz Cowan, *More Work for Mother: The Ironies of Household Technology from the Open Hearth to the Microwave* (New York: Basic Books, 1983).

29. Joel Mokyr, *The Lever of Riches: Technological Creativity and Economic Progress* (New York: Oxford University Press, 1990), 6.

Bibliography

Abegglen, James C., and George Stalk Jr. *Kaisha: The Japanese Corporation.* New York: Basic Books, 1986.

Adas, Michael. *Machines as the Measure of Men: Science, Technology, and Ideologies of Western Dominance.* Ithaca: Cornell University Press, 1989.

Aida Yutaka. *Denshi rikkoku Nihon no jijoden.* 4 vols. Tokyo: Nihon Hōsō Kyōkai, 1993.

Akatsuka Yukio. *Sengo yokubōshi: konran no 40, 50 nen dai hen.* Tokyo: Kōdansha, 1985.

Alford, Bernard W. E. "The Chandler Thesis—Some General Observations." *Management Strategies and Business Development.* Ed. Leslie Hannah. London: Macmillan, 1976.

Amishima Tsuyoshi. *Hatō. Denpa to tomo ni gojū nen.* Tokyo: Denki Tsūshin Shinkōkai, 1992.

Amsden, Alice H. *Asia's Next Giant: South Korea and Late Industrialization.* New York: Oxford University Press, 1985.

Anchordoguy, Marie. *Computers Inc.: Japan's Challenge to IBM.* Cambridge: Harvard University Press, 1989.

Aoki Masahiko and Ronald Dore, eds. *The Japanese Firm: The Sources of Competitive Strength.* Oxford: Oxford University Press, 1994.

Aoyama Yoshiyuki. *Kaden.* Tokyo: Nihon Keizai Hyōron Sha, 1991.

Appleby, Joyce. "Ideology & Theory." *American Historical Review* 81 (1976).

Arai, L. "Japanese Education and Economic Development." *The Economic Development of Japan and Korea.* Eds. C. H. Lee and I. Yamazawa. New York: Praeger, 1990.

Arendt, Hannah. *The Origins of Totalitarianism*. Cleveland: World Publishing, 1952.

Argy, Victor, and Leslie Stein. *The Japanese Economy*. Basingstoke: MacMillan, 1997.

Armstrong, John, and Stephanie Jones. *Business Documents*. London: Mansell, 1987.

Arndt, H. W. *Economic Development: The History of an Idea*. Chicago: Chicago University Press, 1981.

Arnold, E. *Competition & Technological Change in the Television Industry*. London: Macmillan, 1985.

Arrighi, Giovanni. *The Long Twentieth Century: Money, Power, and the Origins of Our Times*. London: Verso, 1994.

Arrighi, Giovanni, Terence K. Hopkins, and Immanuel Wallerstein, eds. *Antisystemic Movements*. London: Verso, 1989.

Asahi shinbun. Various issues.

Asahi Shinbun Sha, ed. *Sengo Nippon oboegaki 3*. Tokyo: Asahi Shinbun Sha, 1983.

Ashton, T. S. *The Industrial Revolution, 1760–1830*. Oxford: Oxford University Press, 1948.

Baron, Salo Wittmayer. *The Contemporary Relevance of History: A Study in Approaches and Methods*. New York: Columbia University Press, 1986.

Bartlett, Christopher A., and Sumantra Ghoshal. "Matsushita Electric Industrial in 1987." Harvard Business School Case Study, 1988.

Beechler, Schon Laureen. "International Management Control in Multinational Corporations: The Case of Japanese Consumer Electronics Subsidiaries in Southeast Asia." Dissertation: University of Michigan, 1990.

Bello, Francis. "Color TV: Who'll Buy a Triumph?" *Fortune* (November 1955).

Bensman, Joseph, and Bernard Rosenberg. "Mass Media and Mass Culture." *America as a Mass Society*. Ed. P. Olson. London: Collier MacMillan, 166–84.

Berghahn, Volker R. *The Americanisation of West German Industry, 1945–1973*. Leamington Spa: Berg, 1986.

Bijker, Wieber E., and John Law, eds. *Shaping Technology/Building Society: Studies in Sociotechnical Change*. Cambridge: MIT Press, 1992.

Bloch, M. *The Historian's Craft*. New York: Knopf, 1954.

Boger, Karl. *Postwar Industrial Policy in Japan: An Annotated Bibliography*. New York: Scarecrow Press, 1988.

Boorstin, Daniel J. *The Americans: The Democratic Experience*. New York: Random House, 1973.

Braun, Ernest, and Stuart MacDonald. *Revolution in Miniature: The History and Impact of Semiconductor Electronics*. 2nd rev. ed. Cambridge: Cambridge University Press, 1982.

Brewer, John, and Roy Porter, eds. *Consumption and the World of Goods*. London: Routledge, 1993.

Bright, Arthur Aaron. *The Electric Lamp Industry: Technological Change and Economic Development from 1800 to 1947*. 1949. Reissued by New York: Arno Press, 1972.

Brinton, Mary C. *Women and the Economic Miracle: Gender and Work in Postwar Japan.* Berkeley: University of California Press, 1993.

Bronner, Simon J., ed. *Consuming Visions: Accumulation and Display of Goods in America, 1880–1920.* New York: W. W. Norton, 1989.

Burke, Kenneth. *Attitudes Toward History.* Berkeley: University of California Press, 1984.

Business Week. Various issues.

Carlson, W. Bernard. "Artifacts and Frames of Meaning: Thomas A. Edison, His Managers, and the Cultural Construction of Motion Pictures." *Shaping Technology/Building Society.* Ed. Wieber E. Bijker and John Law. Cambridge: MIT Press, 1992.

Chamberlain, Basil Hall. *Things Japanese.* London: J. Murray, 1898.

Chandler, Alfred D., Jr. *Strategy & Structure: Chapters in the History of American Enterprise.* Cambridge: MIT Press, 1962.

———. *The Visible Hand.* Cambridge: Harvard University Press, 1977.

———. *The Coming of Managerial Capitalism: A Casebook on the History of American Economic Institutions.* Homewood, IL: RD Irwin, 1985.

———. *Scale and Scope: The Dynamics of Industrial Capitalism.* Cambridge: Harvard University Press, 1990.

Chiyotsuki Toshiaki. "Denki." *Sengo Nihon keiei shi.* Eds. Yonekawa Shinichi, Shimokawa Koichi, and Yamazaki Hiroaki. Vol. 2. Tokyo: Tōyō Keizai Shinpō Sha, 1991, 1–65.

Chūbu Hōsō KK. *Hōsō to senden: CBC repōto.* Nagoya: Chūbu Hōsō KK. Various issues.

Chūō Kōron. Various issues.

Civil Communications Section records. Various.

Cohendet, Patrick, Jean-Alain Heraud, and Ehud Zuscovitch. "Technological Learning, Economic Networks and Innovation Appropriability." *Technology and the Wealth of Nations.* Ed. Dominique Foray and Christopher Freeman. London: Pinter, 1993.

Coleman, James. *The Asymmetrical Society.* Syracuse: Syracuse University Press, 1982.

Cowan, Ruth Schwartz. *More Work for Mother: The Ironies of Household Technology from the Open Hearth to the Microwave.* New York: Basic Books, 1983.

Cumings, Bruce. "Japan in the World System." *Postwar Japan as History.* Ed. Andrew Gordon. Berkeley: University of California Press, 1993, 34–63.

Curtis, Philip J. *The Fall of the U.S. Consumer Electronics Industry: An American Tragedy.* Westport: Quorum, 1994.

Cusumano, Michael A. *The Japanese Automobile Industry: Technology & Management at Nissan & Toyota.* Cambridge: Harvard University Press, 1985.

———. *Japan's Software Factories: A Challenge to US Management.* Oxford: Oxford University Press, 1991.

Cusumano, Michael A., and Richard S. Rosenbloom. "Technological Pioneering and Competitive Advantage: The Birth of the VCR Industry." *California Management Review* XXIX:4 (Summer 1987), 51–76.

David, Paul. *Technical Choice, Innovation and Economic Growth*. Cambridge: Cambridge University Press, 1975.

———. "Clio and the Economics of QWERTY." *American Economic Review. Papers & Proceedings* 75:2 (1985).

———. "Path-Dependence: Putting the Past into the Future of Economics." *IMSS* 533 (1988).

Denison, Edward F., and William K. Chung. "Economic Growth and Its Sources." *Asia's New Giant*. Ed. Hugh Patrick and Henry Rosovsky. Washington: Brookings Institution, 1976, 63–153.

Denki Shikenjo. *Denki Shikenjo gojūnen shi*. Tokyo: Denki Shikenjo, 1941.

Denki shōhin. Various issues.

Denpa jihō. Various issues.

Denpa shinbun. Various issues.

Dentsū kōkoku ron shi. Various issues.

Dhawan, Kailash C. *Post World War II Marketing Policies and Practices of Japanese Consumer Goods Manufacturers: A Study of Consumer Oriented Characteristics and Their Cultural Explanation*. Dissertation: New York University, 1967.

Diamond, Larry, and Marc F. Plattner, eds. *Capitalism, Socialism and Democracy Revisited*. Baltimore: Johns Hopkins University Press, 1993.

Dore, Ronald. *City Life in Japan*. London: Oxford University Press, 1959.

———. *Flexible Rigidities: Industrial Policy and Structural Adjustment in the Japanese Economy, 1970–80*. Stanford: Stanford University Press, 1986.

Dosi, Giovanni. "Technological Paradigms and Technological Trajectories: A Suggested Interpretation of the Determinants and Directions of Technical Change." *Research Policy* 11 (1982), 147–63.

———. *Technical Change and Industrial Transformation: The Theory and an Application to the Semiconductor Industry*. Basingstoke: MacMillan, 1984.

Dosi, Giovanni, Renato Giannetti, and Pier Angelo Toninelli, eds. *Technology and Enterprise in a Historical Perspective*. Oxford: Clarendon Press, 1992.

Dower, John W. "The Useful War." *Showa: The Japan of Hirohito*. Ed. Carol Gluck and Stephen R. Graubard. New York: W. W. Norton, 1992, 49–70.

———. *Japan in War and Peace: Selected Essays*. New York: New Press, 1993.

———. "Peace and Democracy in Two Systems." *Postwar Japan as History*. Ed. Andrew Gordon. Berkeley: University of California Press, 1993.

Drucker, Peter. *Technology, Management and Society*. New York: Harper & Row, 1970.

Economic Planning Agency. *Economic Survey*. Tokyo: Economic Planning Agency. Various years.

Ekonomisuto. Various issues.

Ekonomisuto henshūbu. *Sengo sangyō shi e no shōgen*. Tokyo: Mainichi shinbunsha, 1977.

Electronics. Various issues.

Electronics and Communications in Japan. Various issues, 1963–1984.

Erekuturonikusu 50-nen to 21 seiki e no tenbō. Tokyo: Nikkei magurōhiru sha, 1995.

Ewen, Stuart. *Captains of Consciousness: Advertising and the Social Roots of the Consumer Culture*. New York: McGraw Hill, 1976.

Featherstone, Mike. *Consumer Culture and Postmodernism*. London: Sage Publications, 1991.

Feigenbaum, Edward A. *The Fifth Generation: Artificial Intelligence and Japan's Computer Challenge to the World*. Reading, MA: Addison-Wesley, 1983.

Fine, Ben, and Ellen Leopold. *The World of Consumption*. London: Routledge, 1993.

Forester, Tom. *Silicon Samurai*. Cambridge, MA: Blackwell Publishers, 1993.

Fortune. Various issues.

Foucault, Michel. *The Archaeology of Knowledge*. New York: Pantheon, 1972.

———. *The Foucault Reader*. Ed. Paul Rabinow. New York: Pantheon, 1984.

Fransman, Martin. *The Market and Beyond: Cooperation and Competition in Information Technology in the Japanese System*. Cambridge: Cambridge University Press, 1990.

———. *Japan's Computer and Communications Industry: The Evolution of Industrial Giants and Global Competitiveness*. Oxford: Oxford University Press, 1995.

Freeman, Christopher. *The Economics of Industrial Innovation*. Cambridge: MIT Press, 1982.

———. *Technology Policy and Economic Performance: Lessons from Japan*. London: Pinter, 1987.

Friedman, David. *The Misunderstood Miracle*. Ithaca: Cornell University Press, 1988.

Fruin, Mark. *The Japanese Enterprise System*. Oxford: Clarendon Press, 1994.

Fujin no tomo. Various issues.

Fukutake Tadashi. *Man and Society in Japan*. Tokyo: Tokyo University Press, 1962.

Furukawa Denki Kōgyō KK. *Sōgyō 100-nen shi*. Tokyo: Furukawa Denki Kōgyō KK, 1991.

Galbraith, John Kenneth. *The Affluent Society*. 1956. Reprinted by Harmondsworth: Penguin Books Ltd., 1969.

Garon, Sheldon. *Molding Japanese Minds: The State in Everyday Life*. Princeton: Princeton University Press, 1997.

Gayn, Mark. *Japan Diary*. New York: William Sloane Associates, 1948.

Gerlach, Michael. *Alliance Capitalism*. Berkeley: University of California Press, 1993.

Gerschenkron, Alexander. *Economic Backwardness in Historical Perspective: A Book of Essays*. Cambridge: Harvard University Press, 1962.

Giner, Salvador. *Mass Society*. London: Martin Robertson, 1976.

Gluck, Carol. *Japan's Modern Myths: Ideology in the Late Meiji Period*. Princeton: Princeton University Press, 1985.

———. "The Past in the Present." *Postwar Japan as History*. Ed. Andrew Gordon. Berkeley: University of California Press, 1993.

Gordon, Andrew. "Contests for the Workplace." *Postwar Japan as History*. Ed. Andrew Gordon. Berkeley: University of California Press, 1993, 373–94.

————. "Managing the Japanese Household: The New Life Movement in Postwar Japan." *Social Politics* (Summer 1997), 245–83.

Gordon, Andrew, ed. *Postwar Japan as History.* Berkeley: University of California Press, 1993.

Gotō, Akira. *Nihon no gijutsu kakushin to sangyō soshiki.* Tokyo: Tokyo University Press, 1993.

————. "Technology Importation: Japan's Postwar Experience." *The Japanese Experience of Economic Reforms.* Eds. Juro Teranishi and Yutaka Kosai. New York: St. Martin's Press, 1993, 277–304.

Gotō, Akira, and Hiroyuki Odagiri. *Innovation in Japan: Empirical Studies on the National and Corporate Activities.* Oxford: Oxford University Press, 1996.

Gould, Rowland. *The Matsushita Phenomenon.* Tokyo: Dayamondo Sha, 1970.

Gregory, Gene. *Japanese Electronics Technology: Enterprise and Innovation.* New York: John Wiley and Sons, 1986.

Grossman, G., and E. Helpman. *Innovation and Growth.* Cambridge: MIT Press, 1991.

Grumley, John E. *History and Totality: Radical Historicism from Hegel to Foucault.* London: Routledge, 1989.

Hagemann, Karen. "Of 'Old' and 'New' Housewives: Everyday Housework and the Limits of Household Rationalization in the Urban Working-Class Milieu of the Weimar Republic." *International Review of Social History* 41 (1996), 305–30.

Hakuhōdō Seikatsu Sōgō Kenkyūjo. *Bunshū no tanjō.* Tokyo: Nihon Keizai Shinbun Sha, 1985.

Halberstam, David. *The Reckoning.* 1986. New York: Avon, 1987.

Hall, John Whitney. "Changing Conceptions of the Modernization of Japan." *Changing Japanese Attitudes Towards Modernization.* Ed. Marius B. Jansen. Princeton: Princeton University Press, 1965, 7–41.

Hamano Tsuyoshi and Kamioka Kazuki. *Maaketingu.* Tokyo: Maruzen, 1953.

Hane Mikiso. *Peasants, Rebels and Outcastes: The Underside of Modern Japan.* New York: Pantheon, 1982.

Hannah, Leslie, ed. *Management Strategies and Business Development.* London: Macmillan, 1976.

Harootunian, H. D. *Toward Restoration: The Growth of Political Consciousness in Tokugawa Japan.* Berkeley: University of California Press, 1970.

Harris, William B. "The Electronic Business." *Fortune* (April 1957), p. 137.

————. "RCA Organizes for Profit." *Fortune* (August 1957), p. 111.

Harvey, David. *The Condition of Postmodernity: An Enquiry into the Origins of Cultural Change.* Oxford: Basil Blackwell, 1989.

Hasegawa Shin. "International Cartels and the Japanese Electrical Machinery Industry Until the Second World War: A Case Study of the Vacuum Tube Manufacturers." *Aoyama Business Review* (March 1995), 36–38.

————. "Gijutsu dōnyū to terebi kaihatsu." *Nihon kigyō shisutemu no sengo shi.* Ed. Hashimoto Jurō. Tokyo: Tokyo University Press, 1996, 159–204.

Hashimoto Jurō. "Kikai denshi kōgyō no ikusei." *Tsūshō sangyō seisaku shi.* Vol. 6. Ed. Tsūshō Sangyō Chōsa Kai. Tokyo: Tsūshō Sangyō Chōsa Kai, 1990, 549–615.

———. *Sengo no Nihon keizai.* Tokyo: Iwanami Shoten, 1995.

Hatoyama Ichirō et al. *Shin seikatsu ni tsuite 12 no iken.* Tokyo: Nihon Kyōbun Sha, 1955.

Hawks, Francis L. *Narrative of the Expedition of an American Squadron to the China Seas and Japan.* 1856. London: Macdonald, 1954.

Hayakawa Tokuji. *Watakushi to jigyō.* Tokyo: Ishokujū sha, 1958.

Hayashi Yoshikatsu. "The Introduction of American Technology into the Japanese Electrical Industry." Dissertation: University of California, 1986.

Heertje, Arnold, and Mark Perlman. *Evolving Technology and Market Structure: Studies in Schumpeterian Economics.* Ann Arbor: University of Michigan Press, 1990.

Hein, Laura E. *Fueling Growth: The Energy Revolution and Economic Policy in Postwar Japan.* Cambridge: Harvard University Press, 1990.

———. "Growth versus Success." *Postwar Japan as History.* Ed. Andrew Gordon. Berkeley: University of California Press, 1993.

Herbig, Paul A. *Innovation Japanese Style: A Cultural and Historical Perspective.* Westport: Quorum, 1995.

Hiramoto Atsushi. *Nihon no terebi sangyō.* Tokyo: Mineruba Shobō, 1994.

———. "Terebi sangyō ni okeru kasen taisei no keisei." *Kenkyū nenpō: keizai gaku.* Tōhoku Daigaku. 56:4 (January 1995).

Hirano, Kyoko. *Mr. Smith Goes to Tokyo: Japanese Cinema under the American Occupation, 1945–1952.* Washington: Smithsonian Institution, 1992.

Hitachi Seisakujo. *Hitachi Seisakujo shi.* 4 vols. Tokyo: Hitachi Seisakujo, 1949–1985.

Hobsbawm, Eric. *Age of Extremes: The Short Twentieth Century.* London: Michael Joseph, 1994.

Hopkins, Terence K., and Immanuel Wallerstein. *World-Systems Analysis: Theory and Methodology.* Beverly Hills: Sage, 1982.

Horie Yasuhiro. *Gendai Nihon keizai no kenkyū.* Tokyo: Tōyō Keizai Shinpō Sha, 1985.

Horkheimer, M., and T. Adorno. *Dialectic of Enlightenment.* Translation of 1944. London: Allen Lane, 1973.

Hosoi Wakizō. *Jokō Aishi.* 1925. Tokyo: Iwanami Shoten, 1982.

Ibuka Masaru. *Sōzō e no tabi.* Tokyo: Kōsei shuppansha, 1985.

———. "Watakushi no Rirekisho." *Watakushi no Rirekisho: Shōwa no Keieisha Gunzō.* Vol. 7. Ed. Nihon Keizai Shinbunsha. Tokyo: Nihon Keizai Shinbunsha, 1992, 181–227.

Ikeda Masajirō. *Hitachi gurūpu: teiseichō jidai o sakidorisuru keiei hōsoku: tettei kenkyū.* Tokyo: Sankei Shuppan, 1979.

Imai Kazuo, ed. *Ozu Yasujirō sakuhin shū.* Vol. 4. Tokyo: Tachikaze Shobō, 1984.

Imai Ken-ichi. "Patterns of Innovation and Entrpreneurship in Japan." *Evolving Technology and Market Structure.* Ed. Arnold Heertje and Mark Perlman. Ann Arbor: University of Michigan, 1990, 187–201.

Imatsu Kenji. *Karakuri Giemon.* Tokyo: Daiyamondo Sha, 1992.
Imazu, K. "Modern Technology and Japanese Electrical Engineers." *Development and Diffusion of Technology.* Ed. Akio Ōkōchi and Hoshimi Uchida. Tokyo: Tokyo University Press, 1980.
Inglis, Fred. *Popular Culture and Political Power.* London: HarvesterWheatsheaf, 1988.
Inkster, Ian. *Science and Technology in History.* Basingstoke: MacMillan, 1991.
Inose Naoki. *Yokubō no media.* Tokyo: Shogakkan, 1990.
Inoue Toshio. *Watakushi no Rirekisho.* Zaikaijin 7. Tokyo: Nihon Keizai Shinbun Sha, 1980.
Ishii Takemochi et al., eds. *A Look at Japanese Development.* Tokyo: Foreign Press Center, 1983.
Ishikawa Hiroyoshi. *Yokubō no sengoshi.* Tokyo: Kōsaidō Shuppan, 1989.
Ishikawa Kaoru. *Nihonteki hinshitsu kanri.* Tokyo: Nihon Kagaku Gijutsu Renmei, 1981.
Ito Masami. *Broadcasting in Japan.* New York: Routledge, Kegan, 1978.
Ito, Takatoshi. *The Japanese Economy.* Cambridge: MIT Press, 1993.
Itō Yasuko. *Sengo Nihon Joseishi.* Tokyo: Ōtsuki Shoten, 1974.
Ivy, Marilyn. "Formations of Mass Culture." *Postwar Japan as History.* Ed. Andrew Gordon. Berkeley: University of California Press, 1993.
Iwata Masami. *Sengo Nihon no kakei chōsa.* Kyoto: Hōritsu Bunka Sha, 1983.
Japan Electronics Almanac. Tokyo: Denpa Publications, 1981–.
Japan Fair Trade Commission. *Survey on Joint R & D.* Tokyo: Japan Fair Trade Commission, 1984.
Jitsugyō no Nihon. Various issues.
Johnson, Chalmers. *MITI and the Japanese Miracle.* Stanford: Stanford University Press, 1982.
Joseishi Sōgō Kenkyū Kai, ed. *Nihon Josei Seikatsushi.* 5: Gendai. Tokyo: Tokyo Daigaku Shuppankai, 1990.
Kaden ryūtsū nenkan. Various years.
Kagaku Gijutsu Chō. *Kagaku Gijutsu Chō nenpō.* Tokyo: Ōkurashō Insatsu Kyoku. Various years.
Kamatani Chikayoshi. *Gijutsu taikoku 100-nen no kei: Nihon no kindaika to kokuritsu kenkyū kikan.* Tokyo: Heibon Sha, 1988.
Kanagawa-ken Kyōiku Chō. *Shin seikatsu undō moderu chōson.* Yokohama: Kanagawa-ken Kyōiku Chō, 1954.
Kanagawa-ken Kyōiku Iinkai Jimukyoku. *Shin seikatsu undō no ayumi.* Yokohama: Kanagawa-ken Kyōiku Iinkai Jimukyoku, 1952.
Kassarjian, Harold A., and Thomas S. Robertson. *Perspectives in Consumer Behavior.* Fourth edition. Englewood Cliffs: Prentice Hall, 1991.
Kasza, Gregory J. *The State and Mass Media in Japan, 1918–1945.* Berkeley: University of California Press, 1988.
Katei Denki Bunka Kai. *Katei denki kiki hensen shi.* 2 vols. Tokyo: Katei Denki Bunka Kai, 1984.
Katō Masakuni et al. *Shōwa nichijō seikatsu shi.* 3 vols. Tokyo: Kakukawa Shoten, 1985–87.

Katō Naofumi, ed. *Hanbai, kōkoku.* Vol. 6. *Nihon keiei shiryō taikei.* Tokyo: San'ichi Shobō, 1988.

Keizai Antei Honbu. *Keizai hakusho.* Tokyo: Tōyō Shokan. Various years (until 1953).

Keizai Kikaku Chō. *Shōhisha dōkō yosoku chōsa.*

———. *Kokumin seikatsu hakusho.* Tokyo: Ōkurashō Insatsu Kyoku. Various years.

———. *Kokumin seikatsu henbō to jittai.* Tokyo: Keizai Kikaku Chō, 1956.

———. *Shōhi to chochiku no dōkō.* Tokyo: Keizai Kikaku Chō. Various years.

Keizai Kikaku Chō Tōkei Kyoku. *Kokumin seikatsu no genjō.* Tokyo: Keizai Kikaku Chō Tōkei Kyoku, 1957.

Keizai Shingi Chō. *Keizai hakusho.* Tokyo: Keizai Tōkei Kyōkai. Various years (from 1953).

Kelly, William. "Rationalization and Nostalgia: Cultural Dynamics of New Middle-Class Japan." *American Ethnologist* (June 1986), 603–18.

———. "Finding a Place in Metropolitan Japan." *Postwar Japan as History.* Ed. Andrew Gordon. Berkeley: University of California Press, 1993.

Kensetsu Jūtaku Kyoku. *Tochi oyobi Jūtaku Kakaku Chōsa Kekka Hōkokusho.* Tokyo: Kensetsu Jūtaku Kyoku, 1954.

Kikuchi Makoto. *Japanese Electronics: A Worm's-eye View of Its Evolution.* Tokyo: Simul Press, 1983.

———. *Nihon no handōtai 40 nen.* Tokyo: Chūō Kōron Sha, 1992.

Kimura, Yui. "Technological Innovation and Competition in the Japanese Semiconductor Industry." *Innovation in Japan: Empirical Studies on the National and Corporate Activities.* Ed. Akira Goto and Hiroyuki Odagiri. Oxford: Oxford University Press, 1996.

Kinmonth, Earl. "The Impact of Military Procurements on the Old Middle Classes in Japan, 1931–1941." *Japan Forum* 4:2 (October 1992), 349–68.

Kluback, William. *Discourses on the Meaning of History.* New York: P. Lang, 1988.

Kobayashi, Kōji. *Computers and Communications: A Vision of C&C.* Cambridge: MIT Press, 1986.

———. *The Rise of Nippon Denki.* Cambridge: Blackwell, 1991.

Kodama, Fumio. *Emerging Patterns of Innovation: Sources of Japan's Technological Edge.* Boston: Harvard Business School Press, 1995.

Kōdansha, ed. *Shōwa Nimannichi no Zenkiroku.* Tokyo: Kōdansha, 1989. Vols. 7 and 8.

Kōdo Seichō wo Kangaeru Kai, ed. *Kōdo seichō to Nihonjin. Part 2: katei hen.* Tokyo: Nihon Editaa Sukuuru Shuppanbu, 1985.

Kohara Hiroshi. *Nihon maaketingu shi—gendai ryūtsū no shiteki kōzu.* Tokyo: Chūō Keizai Sha, 1994.

Kokumin Seikatsu Kenkyūjo. *Dai toshi ni okeru shōhisha no ishiki oyobi kōdo ni kansuru chōsa.* Tokyo: Kokumin Seikatsu Kenkyūjo, 1962.

Komiya, R., et al. *Industrial Policy of Japan.* Tokyo: Academic Press, 1988.

Kosai, Yutaka. *The Era of High Speed Growth: Notes on the Postwar Japanese Economy.* Tokyo: Tokyo University Press, 1986.

Kotter, John P. *Matsushita Leadership.* New York: Free Press, 1997.
Krugman, Paul. "A Model of Innovation, Technology Transfer, and the World Distribution of Income." *Journal of Political Economy* 87 (1979).
————. *Peddling Prosperity: Economic Sense and Nonsense in the Age of Diminished Expectations.* New York: Norton, 1994.
Kubo Michio. *Kaden seihin ni miru kurashi no sengo shi.* Tokyo: Mirion shobō, 1987.
Kudō Akira. *Nichidoku kigyō kankeishi.* Tokyo: Yūhikaku, 1992.
Kumazawa Makoto. *Portraits of the Japanese Workplace.* Ed. Andrew Gordon. Trans. Andrew Gordon and Mikiso Hane. Boulder: Westview Press, 1996.
Kurashi no izumi. Various issues.
Kurashi no techō. Various issues.
Landes, David. *The Unbound Prometheus.* Cambridge: Cambridge University Press, 1969.
Lazonick, William. "Organizational Integration in Three Revolutions." *Evolving Technology and Market Structure.* Ann Arbor: University of Michigan, 1990.
————. *Business Organization and the Myth of the Market Economy.* Cambridge: Cambridge University Press, 1991.
Leach, William R. *Land of Desire: Merchants, Power, and the Rise of a New American Culture.* New York: Pantheon, 1993.
Levich, Jacob, ed. *The Motion Picture Guide 1996 Annual.* New York: Cine Books, 1996.
Levidow, Les, and Bob Young, *Science, Technology and the Labor Process: Marxist Studies.* 2 vols. London, CSE Books, 1981, and London, Free Association Books, 1985.
Lynn, Leonard. *How Japan Innovates.* Boulder: Westview Press, 1982.
————. "MITI's Successes and Failures in Controlling Japan's Technology Imports." *Hitotsubashi Journal of Commerce* 29 (December 1994).
Maaketingu shi kenkyū kai. *Nihon no Maaketingu.* Tokyo: Dōbunkan, 1995.
Majumdar, B. A. "Industrial Policy in Action: The Case of the Electronics Industry in Japan." *Columbia Journal of World Business* 23:3 (1988).
Malecki, Edward J. *Technology and Economic Development: The Dynamics of Local, Regional and National Change.* New York: Wiley, 1991.
Mandelbaum, Maurice. *The Anatomy of Historical Knowledge.* Baltimore: Johns Hopkins University Press, 1977.
Manejimento. Various issues.
Mankiw, N. Gregory. *Macroeconomics.* New York: Worth, 1994 (2nd edition).
Mannheim, Karl. *Man and Society In an Age of Reconstruction.* London: Routledge & Kegan Paul, 1949 (1940).
Marchand, Roland. *Advertising the American Dream: Making Way for Modernity—1920–1940.* Berkeley: University of California Press, 1986.
Marshall, Edward. "The Woman of the Future [interview with Thomas A. Edison]." *Good Housekeeping* (October 1912).
Maruyama Masao. "Patterns of Individuation and the Case of Japan: A Conceptual Scheme." *Changing Japanese Attitudes Towards Modernization.* Ed. Marius B. Jansen. Princeton: Princeton University Press, 1965, 489–531.

Marx, Karl. *Capital*. London: Lawrence & Wishart, New York: International Publishers, and Moscow: Progress Publishing, 1996. *Karl Marx, Frederick Engels: Collected Works*, Vol. 14.

Mason, Mark. *American Multinationals and Japan: The Political Economy of Japanese Capital Controls, 1899–1980*. Cambridge: Harvard University Press, 1993.

Matsuda Hiroshi. *Dokyumento hōsō sengo shi*. 2 vols. Zushi: Sōshisha, 1980.

Matsuda Shin'ichi. *Watakushi no ayunda michi*. Tokyo: Mitsuden Insatsu KK, 1991.

Matsushita Denki Sangyō KK. Internal archives.

———. *Matsushita Denki 50-nen no ryaku shi*. Osaka: Matsushita Denki Sangyō KK, 1968.

———. *Matsushita Denki no gijutsu 50-nen shi*. Osaka: Matsushita Denki Sangyō KK, 1968.

———. *Matsushita Denki eigyōshi (sengo hen)*. Osaka: Matsushita Denki Sangyō KK, 1979.

———. *Matsushita Denki senden 70-nen shi*. Osaka: Matsushita Denki Sangyō KK, 1988.

———.*Terebi jigyōbu shi*. Unpublished and undated ms.

Matsushita Kōnosuke. *Quest for Prosperity: The Life of a Japanese Industrialist*. Tokyo: PHP Institute, 1987.

———. "Watakushi no Rirekisho." *Watakushi no Rirekisho: Shōwa no Keieisha Gunzō*. Ed. Nihon Keizai Shinbunsha. Tokyo: Nihon Keizai Shinbunsha, 1992.

Matsuzaki Tadashi. "Technological Development and Economic Systems: Japanese Experience and Lessons." The 16th International Symposium of Hosei University. Tokyo: Hosei University, 1996.

McClelland, Peter D. *Causal Explanation and Model-Building in History, Economics, and the New Economic History*. Ithaca: Cornell University Press, 1975.

McCormack, Gavan. *The Emptiness of Japanese Affluence*. Armonk: M. E. Sharpe, 1996.

McCracken, Grant. *Culture and Consumption*. Bloomington: Indiana University Press, 1990.

McCraw, Thomas. *America Versus Japan*. Boston: Harvard Business School Press, 1986.

———, ed. *The Essential Alfred Chandler: Essays Toward a Historical Theory of Big Business*. Boston: Harvard Business School Press, 1988.

McKendrick, N., et al. *The Birth of a Consumer Society: The Commercialization of Eighteenth Century England*. London: Europa Publications, 1982.

Minami Ryōshin. *Power Revolution in the Industrialization of Japan: 1885–1940*. Tokyo: Kinokuniya, 1987.

Mitsubishi Denki KK. *Mitsubishi Denki shashi: sōgyō rokujū shunen*. Tokyo: Mitsubishi Denki KK, 1982.

Miyake Yoshiko. "Doubling Expectations: Motherhood and Women's Factory Work Under State Management in Japan in the 1930s and 1940s." *Recreat-*

ing Japanese Women, 1600–1945. Ed. Gail Lee Bernstein. Berkeley: University of California Press, 1991, 267–95.

Miyoshi, Masao, and H. D. Harootunian, eds. *Postmodernism and Japan.* Durham: Duke University Press, 1989.

Mokyr, Joel. *The Lever of Riches: Technological Creativity and Economic Progress.* New York: Oxford University Press, 1990.

Molony, Barbara. *Technology and Investment: The Prewar Japanese Chemical Industry.* Cambridge: Harvard University Press, 1990.

———. "Activism Among Women in the Taishō Cotton Textile Industry." *Recreating Japanese Women, 1600–1945.* Ed. Gail Lee Bernstein. Berkeley: University of California Press, 1991, 217–38.

Monbushō. *Annual Report of the Minister of State for Education.* Tokyo: Monbushō. Various years.

Morikawa Hidemasa. *Gijutsusha.* Tokyo: Nihon Keizai Shinbun Sha, 1975.

Morita Akio. *Made in Japan: Akio Morita and Sony.* New York: Dutton, 1986.

Moritani Masanori. *Gijutsu kaihatsu no Shōwa shi.* Tokyo: Tōyō Keizai Shinpō Sha, 1986.

Morris, Cynthia Taft, and Irma Edelman. *Comparative Patterns of Economic Development 1850–1914.* Baltimore: Johns Hopkins University Press, 1988.

Morris-Suzuki, Tessa. *Beyond Computopia: Information, Automation and Democracy in Japan.* London: Kegan Paul, 1988.

Motooka Tōru. *The Fifth Generation Computer: The Japanese Challenge.* Chichester, NY: Wiley, 1985.

Mowery, David C., and Nathan Rosenberg. *Technology and the Pursuit of Economic Growth.* Cambridge: Cambridge University Press, 1989.

Mumford, Lewis. *Technics and Civilization.* New York: Harcourt, Brace, 1943.

Nagao Kazurō. *Shōriki Matsutarō no Shōwa shi.* Tokyo: Jitsuyō no Nihon sha, 1982.

Nakagawa Yasuzō. *Nihon no handōtai kaihatsu.* Tokyo: Kōdansha, 1985.

———. *Dokyumento Kaigun Gijutsu Kenkyūjo—erekutoronikusu shukoku no senshinsha tachi.* Tokyo: Nihon Keizai Shinbun Sha, 1987.

Nakamura Seiji. *Sengo Nihon no gijutsu kakushin.* Tokyo: Ōtsuki Shoten, 1979.

Nakamura, Takafusa. *The Postwar Japanese Economy: Its Development and Structure.* (Translation of *Nihon keizai: sono seichō to kōzō,* 1980). Tokyo: Tokyo University Press, 1981.

———. *Kakeibō kara mita kindai Nihon seikatsu shi.* Tokyo: Tokyo University Press, 1993.

Nakayama, Shigeru. *Science, Technology and Society in Postwar Japan.* London: Kegan Paul International, 1991.

———. *Nihon no kagaku gijutsu.* 4 vols. Tokyo: Gakuyō Shobō, 1995.

Nakayama, Shigeru, David L. Swain, and Yagi Eri, eds. *Science and Society in Modern Japan: Selected Historical Sources.* Tokyo: University of Tokyo Press, 1974.

Narin, Francis, and J. Davidson Frame. "The Growth of Japanese Science and Technology." *Science* 245 (1989).

Nasaw, David. *Going Out: The Rise and Fall of Public Amusements.* New York: Basic Books, 1983.

Nashonaru shoppu. Various issues.

New York Herald. Various issues.

New York Times. Various issues.

Nihon Bikutaa KK. *Nihon Bikutaa no 60-nen.* Tokyo: Nihon Bikutaa KK, 1987.

Nihon Denshi Kikai Kōgyōkai. *Denshi kōgyō 20-nenshi.* Tokyo: Nihon Denshi Kikai Kōgyōkai, 1968.

———. *Denshi kōgyō 30-nenshi.* Tokyo: Nihon Denshi Kikai Kōgyōkai, 1978.

Nihon Denshi Kikai Kōgyōkai Denshi Kan Shi Kenkyū Kai. *Denshi kan no rekishi.* Tokyo: Oomu Sha, 1987.

Nihon Ginkō Kawase Kanri Kyoku. *Gaishi dōnyū kankei jūyō ninka anken ichiran.* Tokyo: Nihon Ginkō, 1961.

Nihon Ginkō Tōkei Kyoku. *Honpō keizai tōkei.* Tokyo: Nihon Ginkō. Various years.

Nihon Hōsō Kyōkai. *Nihon hōsō shi.* 2 vols. Tokyo: Nihon Hōsō Kyōkai, 1965.

———. *Fifty Years of Broadcasting.* Tokyo: Nihon Hōsō Kyōkai, 1977.

———. *Hōsō 50-nen shi.* Tokyo: Nihon Hōsō Kyōkai, 1977.

———. *Hōsō no 50-nen.* Tokyo: Nihon Hōsō Kyōkai, 1977.

Nihon Kagaku Shi Gakkai. *Nihon kagaku gijutsu shi taikei.* 22 vols. Tokyo: Dai Ichi Hōki Shuppan, 1969.

Nihon Keieishi Kenkyūjo, ed. *Sōgyō 100-nenshi.* Tokyo: Furukawa Denki Kōgyō KK, 1991.

Nihon Keizai Shinbunsha, ed. *Watakushi no Rirekisho: Shōwa no Keieisha Gunzō.* Vol. 7. Tokyo: Nihon Keizai Shinbunsha, 1992.

Nihon Musen Shi Iinkai. *Nihon musen shi.* Tokyo: Nihon Musen Shi Iinkai, 1950–1951.

Nihon Risaachi Sentaa. *10-nen go no kokumin seikatsu.* Tokyo: Nihon Risaachi Sentaa, 1966.

Nihon Seisansei Honbu. *Seisansei undō 30-nen shi.* Tokyo: Nihon Seisansei Honbu, 1985.

Nihon Terebi Hōsōmō. *Taishū to tomo ni 25-nen.* Tokyo: Nihon Terebi Hōsōmō, 1978.

Nikkei shinbun. Various issues.

Nippon Denki Corporation. *Nippon Denki Corporation: The First 80 Years.* Tokyo: Nippon Denki Corporation, 1984.

Nippon Denki KK. *Nippon Denki Kabushiki Gaisha 70-nen shi.* Tokyo: Nippon Denki KK, 1972.

———. *Nippon Denki monogatari.* Tokyo: Nippon Denki KK, 1980.

———. *Zoku Nippon Denki monogatari.* Tokyo: Nippon Denki KK, 1981.

Nippon Denki Kōgyōkai. *Nippon Denki kōgyō-shi.* Tokyo: Nippon Denki Kōgyōkai, 1956–79.

Nippon Times. Various issues.

Noguchi Yukio. *1940-nen Taisei.* Tokyo: Tōyō Keizai Shinbun Sha, 1995.

Nolan, Mary. *Visions of Modernity: American Business and the Modernization of Germany.* New York: Oxford University Press, 1994.

Nonaka Ikujirō. *The Knowledge-Creating Company.* New York: Oxford University Press, 1995.
————, ed. *Nihongata inobeeshon shisutemu.* Tokyo: Hakutō Shobō, 1995.
"Nōson to terebi." *Hōsō to senden: CBC repōto.* April 1958.
Nussbaum, Helga, Alice Teichova, and Maurice Levy-Leboyer, eds. *Historical Studies in International Corporate Business.* Cambridge: Cambridge University Press, 1989.
Nye, David E. *Electrifying America: Social Meanings of a New Technology, 1880–1940.* Cambridge: MIT Press, 1990.
Odagiri, Hiroyuki, and Akira Goto. *Technology and Industrial Development in Japan.* Oxford: Clarendon Press, 1996.
Okamoto Yasuo. *Hitachi to Matsushita.* 2 vols. Tokyo: Chūō Kōron Sha, 1979.
Okazaki Tetsuji and Masahiro Okuno. *Gendai Nihon keizai shisutemu no genryū.* Tokyo: Nihon Keizai Shinbun Sha, 1993.
Oki Denki Kōgyō. *Oki Denki 100-nen no ayumi.* Tokyo: Oki Denki Kōgyō, 1981.
Okimoto, Daniel I. *Between MITI and the Market: Japanese Industrial Policy for High Technology.* Stanford: Stanford University Press, 1989.
Okimoto, Daniel I., Takuo Sugano, and Franklin B. Weinstein, eds. *Competitive Edge: The Semiconductor Industry in the U.S. and Japan.* Stanford: Stanford University Press, 1984.
Ōkōchi Akio and Hoshimi Uchida, eds. *Development and Diffusion of Technology.* Tokyo: Tokyo University Press, 1980. Vol. 6 in the Fuji Conference Series.
Ōkurashō Shuzei Kyoku. *Nihon gaikoku bōeki nenpyō.* Tokyo: Ōkurashō. Various years.
Onnatachi no Ima wo Tou Kai. *Jūgoshi nōto sengo hen.* Vol. 3. Tokyo: Inpakuto Shuppankai, 1987.
Oriental Economist. Various issues.
Otsuka, K., G. Ranis, and G. Saxonhouse. *Comparative Technology Choice in Development: The Indian and Japanese Textile Industries.* London: St. Martin's Press, 1988.
Ouchi, William G. *Theory Z: How American Business Can Meet the Japanese Challenge.* Reading: Addison-Wesley, 1981.
Ozaki, Robert S. *The Control of Imports and Foreign Capital in Japan.* New York: Praeger, 1972.
Ozawa, Terutomo. *Japan's Technological Challenge to the West, 1950–1974.* Cambridge: MIT Press, 1974.
Packard, Vance. *The Hidden Persuaders.* London: Longmans, Green, 1957.
Pascale, Richard Tanner, and Anthony G. Athos. *The Art of Japanese Management.* New York: Simon & Schuster, 1981.
Patrick, Hugh, ed. *Japan's High Technology Industries: Lessons and Limitations of Industrial Policy.* Seattle: University of Washington Press, 1986.
Patrick, Hugh, and Henry Rosovsky, eds. *Asia's New Giant: How the Japanese Economy Works.* Washington: Brookings Institution, 1976.
Paul, David, and Julie Ann Bunn. "Gateway Technologies and the Evolutionary Dynamics of Network Industries: Lessons from the Electricity Supply Indus-

try." *Evolving Technology and Market Structure.* Ed. Arnold Heertje and Mark Perlman. Ann Arbor: University of Michigan Press, 1990, 121–56.

Peck, Merton, and Shūji Tamura. "Technology." *Asia's New Giant: How the Japanese Economy Works.* Ed. Hugh Patrick and Henry Rosovsky. Washington: Brookings Institution, 1976.

Penrose, Edith. "History, the Social Sciences and Economic 'Theory' with Special Reference to the Multinational Enterprise." *Historical Studies in International Corporate Business.* Ed. Helga Nussbaum, Alice Teichova, and Maurice Levy-Leboyer. Cambridge: Cambridge University Press, 1989, 7–15.

PHP. Various issues.

Prestowitz, Clyde V. *Trading Places: How We Allowed Japan to Take the Lead.* New York: Basic Books, 1988.

Radio Corporation of America Annual Report. Various years.

Rice, Richard Bruce. "Hitachi: Japanese Industry in an Era of Militarism, 1937–1945." Dissertation: Harvard University, 1974.

Riess, Curt. *Joseph Goebbels.* Garden City: Doubleday, 1948.

Robins-Mowry, Dorothy. *The Hidden Sun.* Boulder: Westview Press, 1983.

Rōdō Daijin Kanbō Rōdō Tōkei Chōsabu. *Rōdō Tōkei Nenpō.* Tokyo: Rōdō Daijin Kanbō Rōdō Tōkei Chōsabu, 1961.

Rōdō Shō. *Josei Rōdōsha no Jittai Chōsa.* Tokyo: Rōdō Shō, 1961.

Rōdō Shō Fujin Shōnen Kyoku. *Shōwa 43-nen Naishoku Kōchin Chōsa Kekka Gaiyō.* Fujin Kankei Chōsa Shiryō No. 48, 1968.

———. *Denki Kikai Seizōgyō ni okeru Nenshō Rōdōsha no Rōdō Jittai Chōsa Kekka.* Tokyo: Rōdō Shō Fujin Shōnen Kyoku, 1963.

Rosenberg, Nathan. *Perspectives on Technology.* Cambridge: Cambridge University Press, 1976.

———. *Inside the Black Box: Technology and Economics.* Cambridge: Cambridge University Press, 1982.

Said, Edward. *Beginnings: Intention and Method.* New York: Basic Books, 1975.

Saitō Takenori. "Americanization and Postwar Japanese Management: A Bibliographical Approach." *Japanese Yearbook on Business History* 12 (1995), 5–23.

Samuels, Richard J. *"Rich Nation, Strong Army": National Security and the Technological Transformation of Japan.* Ithaca: Cornell University Press, 1994.

Sand, Jordan. "House and Home in Modern Japan, 1880s–1920s." Dissertation: Columbia University, 1996.

Sandee Asahi. Various issues.

Sano Shinichi. *Kyokaiden: Shōriki Matsutarō to Kagemushatachi no Isseiki.* Tokyo: Bungei Shunju, 1994.

Sansom, Sir George B. *Japan in World History.* New York: International Secretariat, Institute of Pacific Relations, 1951.

Sanyō Denki KK. *Sanyō Denki 30-nen no ayumi.* Osaka: Sanyō Denki KK, 1980.

Sasaki Satoshi. "The Emergence of the Productivity Improvement Movement in Postwar Japan and Japanese Productivity Missions Overseas." *Japanese Yearbook on Business History* 12 (1995), 39–72.

Sasaki Takeshi et al., eds. *Sengoshi dai jiten.* Tokyo: Sanseido, 1991.

Satō, Kimiyori. *Kaden shukoku wo kizuita jū nin.* Tokyo: Sōsō Shuppan Sentaa, 1980.

Schama, Simon. *Citizens: A Chronicle of the French Revolution.* New York: Alfred Knopf, 1989.

Schudson, Michael. *Advertising, the Uneasy Persuasion: Its Dubious Impact on American Society.* London: Routledge, 1990 (1984).

Schumpeter, Joseph A. *The Theory of Economic Development.* Oxford: Oxford University Press, 1934.

———. *Business Cycles: A Theoretical, Historical and Statistical Analysis of the Capitalist Process.* Abridged. Philadelphia: Porcupine Press, 1989 (1939).

———. *Capitalism, Socialism and Democracy.* Third edition. New York: Harper and Row, 1950.

———. *History of Economic Analysis.* New York: Oxford University Press, 1954.

Sciberras, E. "Technical Innovation and International Competitiveness in the Television Industry." *OMEGA: The International Journal of Management Science* 10:6 (1982), 585–92.

Scranton, Philip. "Manufacturing Diversity: Production Systems, Markets, and an American Consumer Society, 1870–1930." *Technology and Culture* 35:3 (July 1994), 476–505.

Sekiguchi Sueo. "Gijutsu yunyūsha to shite no Nihon." *Chokusetsu tōshi to gijutsu iten.* Ed. Sekiguchi Sueo and Tran Van Tho. Tokyo: Nihon Keizai Kenkyūjo, 1986.

Seligman, Edwin Robert Anderson. *The Economic Interpretation of History.* New York: Columbia University Press, 1917.

Shakai kyōkiku. Various issues.

Shibata Hidetoshi. *Sengo masu komi kayūki.* Tokyo: Chūō Kōron Sha, 1985.

Shils, Edward. "The Concept and Function of Ideology." *International Encyclopedia of the Social Sciences.* New York: Crowell, Collier and MacMillan, 1968.

Shimotani Masahiro. "The Formation of Distribution *Keiretsu*: The Case of Matsushita Electric." *The Origins of Japanese Industrial Power.* Ed. Etsuo Abe and Robert Fitzgerald. Ilford, Essex: F. Cass, 1995.

Shin Seikatsu Undō Kyōkai. *Moriagaru shinseikatsu undō: shin seikatsu undō zenkoku kyōgikai kara.* Tokyo: Shin Seikatsu Undō Kyōkai, 1955.

———. *Shin Seikatsu Undō Kyōkai kiyaku oyobi yakuin meibō: Showa 31.* Tokyo: Shin Seikatsu Undō Kyōkai, 1956.

———. *Shin seikatsu undō yoron chōsa, dai isshū.* Tokyo: Shin Seikatsu Undō Kyōkai, 1956.

Shirane Uyayoshi and Wakui Kōtarō. *Nihon no gijutsu 100-nen.* 5 vols. Tokyo: Chikuma Shobō, 1987.

Shisō. Various issues.

Shizuoka Daigaku Terebijon Gijutsushi Henshū Iinkai. *Shizuoka daigaku terebijon gijutsu shi*. Hamamatsu: Hamamatsu Denshi Kōgaku Shōrei Kai, 1987.

Shōfū. Various issues.

Shomin seikatsushi kenkyūkai, ed. *Dō jidaijin no seikatsu shi*. Tokyo: Misotsu Sha, 1989.

Shōriki, Matsutarō. *Watakushi no higan*. Tokyo: Orion Sha, 1965.

Shūkan asahi. Various issues.

Shūkan josei jishin. Various issues.

Slater, Don. *Consumer Culture and Modernity*. Cambridge: Polity Press, 1997.

Smith, Adam. *The Wealth of Nations*. 1776. Chicago: University of Chicago Press, 1976.

Smith, Robert J. *Kurusu: The Price of Progress in a Japanese Village, 1951–1975*. Stanford: Stanford University Press, 1978.

Smits, F. M., ed. *A History of Engineering and Science in the Bell System. Electronics Technology (1925–1975)*. Indianapolis: AT&T Bell Laboratories, 1976.

Society, Science, and Technology in Japan. Complete issue. *Cahiers d'Histoire Mondiale*, IX:2 (1965).

Solow, Robert. "Technical Change and the Aggregate Production Function." *Review of Economics and Statistics* 39 (1957).

Sōmu chō tōkei kyoku. *Nihon chōki tōkei sōran*. 5 vols. Tokyo: Nihon Tōkei Kyōkai, 1988.

Son Il Sun. "Kōdo seichōki ni okeru kaden ryūtsū kōzō no henka." *Keizaigaku kenkyū* 35 (1992).

Sony Corporation. *Genryū: Sony Challenge 1946–1968*. Tokyo: Sony Corporation, 1986.

Sōrifu Tōkei Kyoku. *Kokusai Tōkei Yōran*. Tokyo: Ōkurashō Insatsu Kyoku, 1962.

Stanfield, James Ronald. *Economics, Power and Culture*. Basingstoke: MacMillan, 1995.

Statistics Department of the Bank of Japan. *Economic Statistics of Japan*. Tokyo: Bank of Japan. Various years.

Stauth, G., and B. S. Turner. "Nostalgia, Postmodernism and the Critique of Mass Culture." *Theory, Culture and Society* 5 (1988), 2–30.

Sunaga Kinsaburō. "American Technical Assistance Programs and the Productivity Movement in Japan." *Japanese Yearbook on Business History* 12 (1995), 23–38.

Supreme Commander Allied Powers. Records, various.

Swedberg, Richard. *Joseph A. Schumpeter: The Economics and Sociology of Capitalism*. Princeton: Princeton University Press, 1991.

Tabb, William K. *The Postwar Japanese System: Cultural Economy and Economic Transformation*. Oxford: Oxford University Press, 1995.

Tada, Michitaro. "The Glory and Misery of 'My Home.'" *Authority & the Individual: Citizen Protest in Historical Perspective*. Ed. J. Victor Koschmann. Tokyo: University of Tokyo Press, 1978.

Takayanagi Kenjiro. *Terebi kotohajime.* Tokyo: Yūhikaku, 1986.

Tatsuno, Sheridan. *Created in Japan: From Imitators to World Class Innovators.* New York: Harper and Row, 1990.

Tedlow, Richard S., and Richard R. John, Jr., eds. *Managing Big Business: Essays from the Business History Review.* Boston: Harvard Business School, 1986.

Teich, Mikules. "Electrical Research, Standardization and the Beginnings of the Corporate Economy." *Historical Studies in International Corporate Business.* Ed. Helga Nussbaum, Alice Teichova, and Maurice Levy-Leboyer. Cambridge: Cambridge University Press, 1989.

Teishinshō. *Teishinshō jigyōshi.* Tokyo: Teishinshō, 1940–41.

Teranishi, Jurō, and Kosai Yutaka, eds. *The Japanese Experience of Economic Reforms.* Basingstoke: MacMillan, 1993.

Terebijon Gijutsu Shi Henshū Iinkai. *Terebijon gijutsu shi.* Tokyo: Terebijon Gijutsu Shi Henshū Iinkai, 1971.

Thomas, J. E. *Learning Democracy in Japan.* London: Sage Publications, 1985.

Thompson, John B. *Ideology and Modern Culture: Critical Social Theory in the Era of Mass Communication.* Cambridge: Polity Press, 1990.

Tilton, John E. *International Diffusion of Technology: The Case of Semiconductors.* Washington: Brookings Institution, 1971.

Time: The International News Magazine. Various issues.

Tobin, Joseph J., ed. *Re-Made in Japan: Everyday Life and Consumer Taste in a Changing Society.* New Haven: Yale University Press, 1992.

Tokunaga Shigeyoshi, Nomura Masami, and Hiramoto Atsushi. *Nihon kigyō: sekai senryaku to jissen—Denshi sangyō no gurōbaruka to "Nihonteki keiei."* Tokyo: Dōbunkan, 1991.

Tokyo Shibaura Denki KK. *Tokyo Denki kabushiki kaisha 50-nen shi.* Tokyo: Tokyo Shibaura Denki KK, 1940.

———. *Tokyo Shibaura Denki Kabushiki Kaisha 85-nen shi.* Tokyo: Tokyo Shibaura Denki KK, 1964.

———. *Toshiba hyaku-nen shi.* Tokyo: Tokyo Shibaura Denki KK, 1977.

Tokyo-to Denki Kenkyūjo: *Denki Kenkyūjo yon-jūnen shi.* Tokyo: Tokyo Denki Kenkyūjo, 1974.

Tōshiba Eizō Kan Jigyōbu. *Tōshiba buraun kan jigyō 40-nen shi.* Tokyo: Tōshiba Eizō Kan Jigyōbu, 1992.

Toshiba rebyū. Various issues.

Tsurumi Shunsuke. *Sengo Nihon no taishū bunka shi.* Tokyo: Iwanami, 1984.

Tsūshō Sangyō Daijin Kanbō Chōsa Tōkei Kyoku. *Kikai tōkei nenpō.* Tokyo: Nihon Kikai Kōgyō Rengō Kai. Various years.

Tsūshō Sangyō Daijin Kanbō Chōsa Tōkeibu. *Kōgyō Tōkeihyō, Sangyō hen, Shōwa 35-nen.* Tokyo: Tsūshō Sangyō Daijin Kanbō Chōsa Tōkeibu, 1963.

Tsūshō Sangyō Shō. *Kikai tōkei nenpō.* Tokyo: Tsūshō Sangyō Shō. Various years.

———. *Tsūshō sangyō shō nenpō.* Tokyo: Tsūshō Sangyō Shō, 1950.

———. *Gaishi dōnyū.* Tokyo: Tsūshō Sangyō Shō, 1953.

———. *Denshi kōgyō nenkan: 1959 nendo.* Tokyo: Denpa Shinbun Sha, 1960.

———. *Gaikoku gijutsu dōnyū no genjō to mondaiten.* Tokyo: Tsūshō Sangyō Shō Kigyōkyoku, 1962.

———. *Tsūshō sangyō shō nijūnenshi.* Tokyo: Tsūshō Sangyō Shō, 1969.

———. *Shōkō seisaku shi.* Tokyo: Shōkō Seisaku Shi Kankō Kai, 1972.

———. *Shōkō seisaku shi.* Tokyo: Tsūshō Sangyō Shō, 1985.

Tsūshō Sangyō Shō Denki Tsūshin Ka. *Nihon no toranjisuta rajio kōgyō.* Tokyo: Kōgyō Shuppan Sha, 1959.

Tsūshō Sangyō Shō Kigyō Kyoku. *Gaishi dōnyū: sono seido to jittai.* Tokyo: Tsūshō Sangyō Chōsa Kai, 1960.

Tsūshō Sangyō Shō Kōgyō Gijutsu Chō. *Gijutsu hakusho.* Tokyo: Kōgyō Shinbun Sha, 1949.

Tsūshō Sangyō Shō Sangyō Kōzō Chōsa Kai. *Nihon no sangyō kōzō.* Tokyo: Tsūshō Sangyō Kenkyū Kai, 1964.

Tsutsui, William M. "W. Edwards Deming and the Origins of Quality Control in Japan." *Journal of Japanese Studies* 22:2 (1996), 295–325.

Uchida Hoshimi. "Big Business and the Adoption of New Technology in Japan: The Electrical Equipment and Chemical Industries, 1890–1920." *Development and Diffusion of Technology.* Ed. Akio Ōkōchi and Hoshimi Uchida. Tokyo: Tokyo University Press, 1980.

———. *Kōgyō shakai e no henbō to gijutsu.* Vol. 5. *Gijutsu no shakai shi.* Tokyo: Yūhaisha, 1983.

United Nations. *Yearbook of National Accounts Statistics.* Various years.

United States Congress. *Congressional Record.* Various issues.

United States Department of Commerce. *Annual Survey of Manufactures, 1960.* Washington: U.S. Government Printing Office, 1960.

Uyehara, Cecil H. *U.S.-Japan Science and Technology Exchange: Patterns of Interdependence.* Boulder: Westview Press, 1988.

Veblen, Thorstein. *The Theory of the Leisure Class.* New York: Mentor Books, 1953 (reprint of 1899).

Vogel, Ezra F. *Japan's New Middle Class.* Berkeley: University of California Press, 1965.

Wakabayashi Naoki. *Kaden sangyō seichō no kiseki.* Tokyo: Denpa Shinbun Sha, 1992.

Wakasugi Ryūhei. "A Consideration of Innovative Organization: Joint R&D of Japanese Firms." *Evolving Technology and Market Structure.* Ed. Arnold Heertje and Mark Perlman. Ann Arbor: University of Michigan, 1990, 209–26.

Wallerstein, Immanuel. *The Modern World-System III: The Second Era of Great Expansion of the Capitalist World Economy, 1730s–1840s.* San Diego: Academic Press, 1974.

Watanabe Susumu. "The Diffusion of New Technology, Management Styles and Work Organization in Japan: A Survey of Empirical Studies." *Technical Change as a Social Process.* Paris: Organization for Economic Cooperation and Development, 1991.

Weber, Max. *The Theory of Social and Economic Organization.* Trans. A. M. Henderson and Talcott Parsons. Ed. Talcott Parsons. Glencoe: The Free Press, 1947.

———. *Economy and Society: An Outline of Interpretive Sociology.* Berkeley: University of California Press, 1978.

Welch, David. *The Third Reich: Politics and Propaganda.* London: Routledge, 1993.

Wray, William D. *Mitsubishi and the N.Y.K., 1870–1914.* Cambridge: Harvard University Press, 1984.

Yamada Shōgo. *Kaden Konjaku Monogatari.* Tokyo: Sanseido, 1983.

Yamamoto Kiyoshi. *Tōshiba sōgi (1949-nen).* Tokyo: Ochanomizu Shobō, 1983.

Yamamoto Taketoshi and Tsuganezawa Toshihiro. *Nihon no Kōkoku.* Tokyo: Nihon Keizai Shinbun Sha, 1986.

Yamashita Toshihiko. *The Panasonic Way.* Tokyo: Kodansha International, 1989.

Yamazaki Hiroaki, Yonekawa Shinichi, and Shimokawa Kōichi, eds. *Sengo Nihon keiei shi.* 3 vols. Tokyo: Tōyō Keizai Shinpō Sha, 1990–91.

Yasuba Yasukichi and Inoki Takenori, eds. *Nihon keizai shi 8: kōdo seichō.* Tokyo: Iwanami Shoten, 1989.

Yomiuri shinbun. Various years.

Yoshida Tōmei. "Tsūshinki kigyō no musen heiki bumon shinshutsu." *Senji keizai to Nihon kigyō.* Ed. Shimotani Hiroshi. Tokyo: Shōwadō, 1990.

Yoshikawa Hideo and Joanne Kauffman. *Science Has No National Borders.* Cambridge: MIT Press, 1994.

Yuasa Mitsutomo. *Nihon no kagaku gijutsu 100-nen shi.* Tokyo: Chūō Kōron Sha, 1980.

Yūka shōken hōkoku sho. Various companies.

Yūsei Shō. *Zoku teishin jigyōshi.* Tokyo: Yūsei Sho, 1960–63.

———. *Denpa shōshi.* Tokyo: Yūsei Sho, 1971.

"Zadankai: Shin seikatsu undō wa nani wo mezashi, dō susumetara yoi ka." *Shakai Kyōiku,* 10:4 (April 1955).

Zen Koku Chiiki Fujin Dantai Renraku Kyōgikai. *Shin seikatsu undō jisseki hōkokusho.* Zen Koku Chiiki Fujin Dantai Renraku Kyōgikai, 1957.

Index

Adachi Kenzō, 26–27
Adas, Michael, 9
add-on products, as means to increase
 production and sales, 131
Admiral Radio, 220
Adorno, Theodor, 28, 172
advertising, American: mass marketing
 techniques, 18, 28, 128, 136; as radio
 stations' income source, 26
advertising, Japanese, 190; aimed at children, 150, 165, 167, 190, 237; early
 proposals for financing television, 86; by
 electrical goods companies, 153–56,
 171–73; slanting toward housewives, 20
Affluent Society, The (Galbraith), 131,
 236
Aida Yutaka, 202
Akahata (newspaper), 80
Akanabe Sukemi, 198
akarui seikatsu. See "bright life," the
Akihabara district, Tokyo, as postwar
 electronics market, 48–49, 68
Akihito, Prince, 173–75
Alps Denki (electronics firm), 119
Althusser, Louis, 144
Amishima Tsuyoshi, 25, 92–93, 94–95,
 96, 97
Anderson, Andy, 114, 120

Anglo-American Council of Productivity,
 124
appliances, electric, 20; fans, 140; rice
 cookers, 154, 161, 178. *See also* refrigerators; television sets; washing machines
Araya Seizō, 100
Arlie, James, 120
Arrighi, Giovanni, 222
Asahi (newspaper), 84, 176, 187
assembly techniques: and dexterity of
 young women, 207–8, 213, 218–19,
 229; postwar Japanese, 99–100,
 102–3, 122
austerity program (Dodge Line), 59, 64,
 66, 186
*Autobiography of an Electronics Leader,
 Japan* (TV documentary), 110
automation, attempts in transistor production, 207
automobiles: Japanese worker-hour productivity, 122; sales of Fords to American workers, 17–18
autonomy, ideology of: *kokusanka* movement, 34–35, 60, 226, 229; in 1930s
 Japan, 27
awards, for productive workers, 215
Ayukawa Gisuke, 73–74

223–24; role in working-couples scenarios, 175–77; traditional family attitudes toward, 181–82; as transistor girls, 3, 5, 110, 134, 207–19; working hours in factories, 209, 211. *See also* housewives, Japanese
Women's Own Weekly *(Shūkan josei jishin)*, 170–71
Woolworth, 220
workers: influence of middle-class publications, 21; and productivity, 122; in textiles compared to electric goods, 209–10; wages and consumer marketing, 17
working couples *(tomo kasegi)*, as consumers, 175–77
World War II, Japan: Battle of Solomon Islands, 39; infrastructure damage in

Tokyo, 44–45, 46, 139; military's control of electronics industry, 35–41; radar developments, 34, 36–40; shortages of electronic materials, 39, 48
Würtzburg radar, development in wartime Germany, 38–39

Yamada Shōgo, 179–80
Yamaguchi Ryōchū, 46–47
Yao (television set company), 102
Yasuda Shōji, 85
Yomiuri (Tokyo newspaper), 75–76, 80, 84–85
Yoshida cabinet, on role of RRC, 91–92
Yoshida Shigeru, 86, 88, 89, 96, 105, 106

Zworykin, Vladimir D., 33

Text: 10/13 Sabon
Display: Rotis Semi Sans
Composition: Impressions
Printing and binding: Edwards Brothers